INDIAN WILLS

RECORDS OF THE BUREAU OF INDIAN AFFAIRS

1911 - 1921
BOOK TWO

TRANSCRIBED BY

JEFF BOWEN

NATIVE STUDY
Gallipolis, Ohio
USA

Originally published:
Baltimore, Maryland
2006

Reprinted by:

Native Study LLC
Gallipolis, OH
www.nativestudy.com

Library of Congress Control Number: 2020915163

ISBN: 978-1-64968-027-3

Book cover photograph taken by Jeff Bowen, October, 1998, titled *Early Morning at Fort Toulouse*, where the Coosa and Tallapoosa Rivers meet, Wetumpka, Alabama.

Made in the United States of America.

INTRODUCTION

These documents were found in the *Guide to Records in the National Archives of the United States Relating to AMERICAN INDIANS* on page 98, "eight volumes of copies of Indian wills, 1911-21, that, pursuant to the act of 1910 and an act of February 13, 1913 (37 Stat. 678), were referred to the Bureau and the Office of the Secretary of the Interior for Approval."

The Native American wills and probate records were listed under, "RECORDS OF THE LAW AND PROBATE DIVISIONS." The Law and Probate Divisions evolved from the Land Division that handled legal matters until a separate law office was established in 1907. By 1911, this office was mostly called the Law Division. An act of June 25, 1910 (36 Stat. 855), authorized by the Secretary of the Interior, was to determine the heirs of deceased Indian trust allottees; both the Land Division and the Law Division handled work resulting from this legislation. In 1913, an Heirship Section was established in the land Division that later was mostly concerned with probate work. By 1917, the Division was usually called the Probate Division.

The wills themselves were never filmed until they were discovered by the author and filmed in 1996. The wills and probate records consisted of 2568 pages.

The wills are not numbered in any certain order; there are 181 pages of wills without index in this volume, consisting of approximately 101 different wills. The majority of the wills are of western origin and a few eastern ones that will be reproduced as more volumes are completed.

In *Book Two* there is one will that was actually taken to the highest office in the land, the President of the United States. Also one woman bequeathed to her husband her fishing location and two canoes.

Some of the tribes included among the wills are Sioux, Arickara, Apache, Comanche, Chippewa, Ukie and Wylackie, Omaha, Blackfoot, Squaxin band, Yuma, Cheyenne-Arapahoe, Siletz, Sac and Fox, Quinaielt, Crow, Iowa, Otoe and Missouria, Umatilla, Piegan, Klamath, and many more.

Jeff Bowen
Gallipolis, Ohio
NativeStudy.com

FROWEN CROW FEATHER

Last Will and Testament of Frowen Crow Feather
of Kind County of Carson, South Dak   June 17, 1918

In the name of God, Amen.

I Frowen Crow Feather of the Standing Rock Res. S.D. being of failing health but of sound mind and memory Do make and declare this to be my last will and testement[sic] in manner as follows to wit:

First   I give, decree and bequeath to Frances Crow Feather, one issue wagon, 1 set issue harness, one stable plow, harrow, one gray saddle horse branded 1093 right thigh, H.H. on left thigh, and the north quarter of the 32 twp, 23 N of Range 28 east of the Black Hills Meridian, South Dak, containing 160 acres.

Second to Martina Stack (or Stock) and Mrs. Iron Horn to be divided equally[sic] the South East quarter of Sec 32 twp 23 N of Range 28 east of the Black Hills Meridian, South Dak containing 160 acres.

All other property belonging to me not mentioned above is to be sold and money to be spent in settlement of my estate.

Third   That Eugene Bear King be Administrator for the estate.

Frowen Crowfeather

My commission expires April 27th 1922
Eugene Bear King
Not. Public

Signed, Sealed, published and declared by said Frowen Crow Feather in our presence, as and for his last will and testament, and at his request and in our presence and in the presence of each other. We have hereunto subscribed our names as attesting witness there to.

Mrs Francis Crowfeather
George (Last Name Illegible)
Henry A Stewart

Indian Wills, 1911 – 1921 Book Two
Records of The Bureau of Indian Affairs

Department of The Interior,
Office of Indian Affairs, Washington,
DEC 29 1920

It is respectfully recommended that the within will be approved under the Act of June 25, 1910 (36 Stats. L., 855-6) as amended by Act of February 14, 1913 (37 Stats. L., 678).

C G Haake
Assistant Commissioner

Department of The Interior
Office of The Secretary JAN -5 1921

The within will is approved under the Act of June 25, 1910 (36 Stats. L., 855-6) as amended by Act of February 14, 1913 (37 Stats. L., 678).

S G Hopkins
Assistant Secretary

▲▼▲▼▲▼▲▼▲▼▲▼▲▼

TATOHEYA or ISAAC KITTO

LAST WILL AND TESTAMENT OF TATOHEYA OR ISAAC KITTO.

I Tatoheya or Issac[sic] Kitto, of the County of Knox State of Nebraska, being of sound mind and memory do make and declare this to be my last will and testament, hereby revoking any and all wills heretofore made by me.

FIRST: I will and bequeath all of my original allotment to my step son Thomas Kitto subject to the condition that my wife Martha Kitto shall have the use, occupancy and benefits of my said allotment during her lifetime for her support. The description of my allotment is the North half of the North-east quarter Section three Township thirty-two North of range four West of the 6th P.M. Nebraska.

In witness whereof I have hereunto set my hand and seal this 2nd, day of October, 1918.   *his*
                    Tatoheya or Isaac Kitto   [thumb print]
                                                  mark

SIGNED SEALED PUBLISHED AND DECLARED this 2nd day of October as and for my last will and testament, and at his request and in

2

his presence, and in the presence of each other we have hereunto set our names as attesting witnesses,

B J Young   Santee, Nebraska
John (Illegible last name)   Santee, Nebraska

Department of The Interior,
Office of Indian Affairs, Washington,
                          Dec 16 - 1920
It is recommended that the within will be approved pursuant to the provisions of the Act of June 25, 1910 (36 Stats. L., 855-6) as amended by Act of February 14, 1913 (37 Stats. L., 678).

> Respectfully,
> *E B Meritt*
> Assistant Commissioner

Department of The Interior
Office of The Secretary Dec. 30- 1920

The within will is approved pursuant to the provisions of the Act of June 25, 1910 (36 Stats. L., 855-6) as amended by Act of February 14, 1913 (37 Stats. L., 678).

> *S G Hopkins*
> Assistant Secretary

State of Nebraska   )
) SS
County of Knox   ))

   I Tatoheya or Isaac Kitto hereby declare on oath that I am sixty eight years old and that my reasons for making the will which I have this day executed are as follows: I have no children or grand-children living; that my step son Thomas Kitto has helped my[sic] and taken care of me for more than twenty years; that my wife is very old and when she is done with my property I want it to go to the said Thomas Kitto as a reward for what he has done for me.   *his*
                          Isaac Kitto   [thumb print]
Witness to mark.   *mark*
G J Frazier

3

Subscribed and sworn to before me this 2nd day of October, 1918

Wm J Young

Notary Public

▲▼▲▼▲▼▲▼▲▼▲▼▲▼

OFFICE OF INDIAN AFFAIRS
RECEIVED
DEC 18 1920
102416

JOHN YOUNG

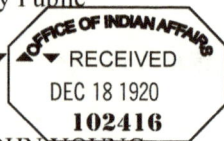

LAST WILL AND TESTAMENT OF JOHN YOUNG

I, John Young, ages[sic] 54, a member of the Arickara Tribe of Indians, residing on the Fort Berthold Indian Reservation, North Dakota, being of sound mind and disposing memory, do hereby make, declard[sic] and publish this as my last will and testament, hereby revoking and annulling any and all other wills heretofore made by me. I wish all my just debts be paid.

1st. I do hereby will and bequeath and devise to my wife, Etta L. Young, an undivided one-half interest in and to the following described real estate: (Etta L. Young is 36 years of age:)

The North-west quarter of the South-east quarter, (NW1/4SE1/4), Section Four, (4), Township One Hundred Forth-six[sic] (146), North Range Eighty-eight, (88),; and the North-east quarter of the North-west Quarter, (NE1/4NW1/4), Section Thirty-one, (31), Township One Hundred Forth-seven[sic], (147) North of Range Eighty-seven, (87), and the South One-half of the South-east Quarter, (S1/2SE1/4), Section Thirty, (30), Township One Hundred Forth-seven[sic], (147), North Range Eighty-seven, (87), and the North One-half of the North-east Quarter, (N1/2NE1/4), Section Thirty-one, (31), Township One Hundred Forty-seven, (147), all West of the 5th P.M., in North Dakota, containing a total of Two Hundred Forty (240) acres, more or less according to the U.S. Govt. Survey thereof;

and 2nd. I do hereby will and bequeath unto the said Etta L. Young, the following: an undivided one-half interest in and to 3 gray mares, three black mares, 1 brown mare, 1 bay mare, 1 gelding, black, 2 yrs old, 3 bay geldings 2 yrs. old, 1 sorrell horse 3 yrs. old, 1 yearling colt, (horse), 2 gray horses, all branded JJ left hip.

and 3rd, I do hereby will and bequeath unto the said Etta L. Young, an undivided one-half interest in and to the following machinery; 2 wagons, (new), 1 spring wagon, 2 sets work heavy harness, 1 set light harness, 1 bob-sled, 1 light sled, 1 moving machine, 1 horse rake, 1 disc harrow, 1 sulky plow, 1 walking plow, 1 farming mill, 1 new wind mill, 1 walking cultivator and 1 10 ft. harrow, and all other miscellaneous small tools.

and 4th. I do hereby will and bequeath unto the said Etta L. Young, all the furniture now being in my house which is situated in the NE1/4NW1/4 Sec. 31, T. 147 N.R. 87 W.

and 5th. I do hereby will and bequeath unto Francis Young, ages[sic] three, my adopted son, an Arickara, rising on the Fort Berthold Reservation, North Dakota, an undivided one half interest in and to the real estate above described.

and 6th. I do hereby will and bequeath unto the said Francis Young, an undivided one-half interest in and to all of the above described personal property with the exception of the household furniture, as above described as being willed to my wife, Etta L. Young.

IN WITNESS WHEREOF I have hereunto published and declared the foregoing instrument to be my last will and testament, at Elbowoods, N.D., on this Twenty-fourth day of September, A.D., 1917, and have hereunto affixed my name as evidence thereof.

(signed) John Young.

On the Twenty-fourth day of September, A.D., 1917, at Elbowoods, N.D. we, the undersigned, were requested to sign the foregoing instrument, as witnesses to the will of John Young, by the said John Young making such request, and he at the same time declaring it to be his last will and testament, and publishing it as such, he signing his name in our presence, and we subscribing thereto, each for himself, in his presence, and in the presence of each other.

(signed)   James Eagle
Elbowoods, N.D.

(signed)   Byron H Wilde
Elbowoods, N.D.

5

CERTIFICATE

I hereby certify that I have compared the paper hereto attached with the last will and testament of John Young, as the same appears on file at the Office of the Fort Berthold Agency, North Dakota, and that I find the said attached paper to be a true copy of said will and of the whole thereof.
Elbowoods, N.D.
December 13, 1920

B. O. Angell
Examiner of Inheritance.

Probate
102416-20
 M H W
Approval of will
John P. Young
Fort Berthold Agency,
North Dakota

Department of The Interior,
Office of Indian Affairs, Washington,
JAN 13 1921

It is hereby recommended that the within will of John P. Young, deceased Arickara Indian, of the Fort Berthold Agency, North Dakota, be approved in accordance with the provisions of the Act of June 25, 1910 (36 Stats. L., 855-6) as amended by Act of February 14, 1913 (37 Stats. L., 678).

Respectfully,
C F Hawke
Acting Assistant Commissioner

Department of The Interior
Office of The Secretary JAN 14 1921

The within will of John P. Young, deceased Arickara Indian, of the Fort Berthold Agency, North Dakota, is hereby approved in accordance with the Act of June 25, 1910 (36 Stats. L., 855-6) as amended by Act of February 14, 1913 (37 Stats. L., 678).

S G Hopkins
Assistant Secretary

▲▼▲▼▲▼▲▼▲▼▲▼▲▼▲▼

CLARA WHITE BULL

WILL

CLARA WHITE BULL, BEING OF SOUND MIND AND OVER THE AGE OF TWENTY ONE YEARS, DOES HEREBY DECLARE THIS TO BE HER LAST WILL AND TESTAMENT;

FIRST: AFTER MY DEATH SHALL FIRST BE PAID ALL BURIAL EXPENSES AND ALL LEGITIMATE DEBTS ON CLAIMS AGAINST MY ESTATE.

SECOND: TO MY GRAND DAUGHTER, MARY NIGHT PIPE, OF ROSEBUD AGENCY, SOUTH DAKOTA, I BEQUEATH THE SUM OF $1.00.

THIRD: TO MY STEP-GRANDSON, JOHN WHITESELL, OF MAHTO, S. D., I BEQUEATH ALL THE RESIDUE OF MY ESTATE , BOTH REAL AND PERSONAL, INCLUDING THE FOLLOWING DESCRIBED LANDS: THE WEST HAVE A SECTION EIGHT; TMP. 21 N., RANGE 28 E., 5TH P.M., CONTAINING 320 ACRES. ALSO MY INTEREST IN THE ESTATE OF WHITE BULL, RECEIVED STANDING ROCK ALLOTTEE NO. 1649 SAID LANDS BEING DESCRIBED AS THE E. SECTION 25, S 1/2 SECTION 24, TWP. 30 N., RANGE 80 W., 5TH P.M.. CONTAINING 640 ACRES.

FOURTH: LASTLY, I DO HEREBY NOMINATE, CONSTITUTE AND APPOINT THE OFFICER IN CHARGE OF THE STANDING ROCK INDIAN RESERVATION, EXECUTOR OF THIS MY LAST WILL AND TESTAMENT.

ALL WILLS ISSUED PRIOR TO THIS TIME ARE HEREBY ANNULLED AND MADE VOID, BEING SUPERCEDED BY THIS WILL.

IN TESTIMONY WHEREOF I HAVE HEREUNTO SET MY HAND THIS 31ST DAY OF MAY, 1915.

WITNESSES: *her*
EG Means   *Clara White Bull* [thumb print]
James B Kitch   *mark*

STATE OF NORTH DAKOTA)
                       :
    COUNTY OF SIOUX   )

7

Indian Wills, 1911 – 1921 Book Two
Records of The Bureau of Indian Affairs

WE THE UNDERSIGNED CERTIFY THAT ON THE 31ST DAY OF MAY, 1915, CLARA WHITE BULL, TO US PERSONALLY KNOWN, SUBSCRIBED THE ABOVE AND FOREGOING INSTRUMENT, DECLARING IT TO BE HER LAST WILL AND TESTAMENT; THAT AT HER REQUEST AND IN HER PRESENCE AND IN THE PRESENCE OF EACH OTHER WE SUBSCRIBED OUR NAMES AS ATTESTING WITNESSES.

> *EG Means*
> P.O.   *Ft Yates, N.D.*
> *James B Kitch*
> P.O.   *Ft Yates, N.D.*

Department of the Interior,
Office of Indian Affairs, Washington,
DEC 17 1920

It is respectfully recommended that the within will of Mrs. Clara Whitebull, deceased Standing Rock Sioux Allottee No. 3677, be approved according to the Act of June 25, 1910 (36 Stats. L. 855-6) as amended by Act of February 14, 1913 (37 Stats. L. 678).

> *EB Merritt*
> Assistant Commissioner

Department of The Interior
Office of The Secretary, Washington

The within last will and testament of Mrs. Clara Whitebull, deceased Standing Rock Sioux Allottee No. 3677, is hereby approved according to the Act of June 25, 1910 (36 Stats. L. 855-6) as amended by Act of February 14, 1913 (37 Stats. L. 678).

> *S G Hopkins*
> Assistant Secretary

▲▼▲▼▲▼▲▼▲▼▲▼▲▼

ALICE TWO SHIELDS

LAST WILL AND TESTAMENT

OF

Alice Two Shields #2510   *Died Sept 12 - 1917*

IN THE NAME OF GOD, AMEN.

Indian Wills, 1911 – 1921 Book Two
Records of The Bureau of Indian Affairs

I, **Alice Two Shields nee Red Fox** OF **Fort Yates, N.D.** BEING OF SOUND MIND, MEMORY AND UNDERSTANDING, DO HEREBY MAKE AND PUBLISH THIS MY LAST WILL AND TESTAMENT, HEREBY REVOKING AND ANNULLING ALL WILLS BY ME HERETOFORE MADE, IN MANNER AND FORM FOLLOWING. THAT IS TO SAY.

FIRST; I DIRECT THAT ALL MY JUST DEBTS AND FUNNERAL[sic] EXPENSES, AND EXPENSES OF MY LAST ILLNESS SHALL BE PAID BY MY EXECUTOR HEREINAFTER NAMED AS SOON AFTER MY DECEASE AS CONVENIENT;

SECOND; I GIVE, DEVISE AND BEQUEATH TO

My daughters Philomine and Melda Redfox to take equal shares in the following described lands: W/2 of Sec. 17 Twp. 129 N., R. 83 W. 5th, P.M. in North Dakota, containing 320 acres, said land being my original allotment.

To my husband Joseph Redfox, the following described land #3550-SE/4 of Sec. 18 Twp. 129 N., R. 83 W. 5th, P.M. in N.D. containing 160 acres; said land being inherited land of which I was sole Heir. To my husband Joseph Redfox and two children- Philomine and Melda, in equal shares the following described land W/2 of Sec. 25 Twp. 131 N., of R. 82 W. 5th, P.M. in North Dakota containg[sic] 320 acres.

THIRD; ALL THE REST AND RESIDUE OF MY ESTATE, BOTH REAL, AND PERSONAL AND MIXED, I GIVE, DEVISE AND BEQUEATH TO MY LAWFUL HEIRS AS DETERMINED AFTER MY DECEASE.

AND, I DO HEREBY NOMINATE, CONSTITUTE AND APPOINT _____ EXECUTOR OF THIS MY LAST WILL AND TESTAMENT.

IN TESTIMONY WHEREOF, I HAVE SET MY HAND AND SEAL TO THIS, MY LAST WILL AND TESTAMENT, AT **Fort Yates, North Dakota**; THIS **2nd** DAY OF **August**, IN THE YEAR OF OUR LORD ONE THOUSAND, NINE HUNDRED AND **seventeen**

AND LASTLY, I HEREBY REQUEST **Francis B. Zahn** TO SIGN MY NAME TO THIS MY LAST WILL AND TESTAMENT AND WITNESS THE SAME.

Alice Two Shield[sic]
TESTATOR OR TESTATRIX

SIGNED, SEAL, PUBLISH AND DECLARED BY SAID **Alice Two Shields nee Red Fox** IN OUR PRESENCE, AS AND FOR **her** LAST WILL AND TESTAMENT, AND AT **her** REQUEST AND IN OUR PRESENCE AND IN THE PRESENCE OF EACH OTHER, WE HAVE HEREUNTO SUBSCRIBED OUR NAMES AS ATTESTING WITNESSES THERETO.

Frances B. Zahn	OF **Fort Yates, N. D.**
Louis M Eichhorn	OF **Fort Yates, N. D.**
Jesse Graybears	OF ***Fort Yates, N. D.***

9

Indian Wills, 1911 – 1921 Book Two
Records of The Bureau of Indian Affairs

Department of the Interior,
Office of Indian Affairs, Washington,
DEC 17 1920
It is respectfully recommended that the within will be approved according to the Act of June 25, 1910 (36 Stats. L. 855-6) as amended by Act of February 14, 1913 (37 Stats. L. 678).

EB Merritt
Assistant Commissioner

Department of The Interior
Office of The Secretary, Washington

The within will of Alice Twoshield{sic}, deceased Standing Rock Sioux Allottee No. 2510 is hereby approved under the Act of June 25, 1910 (36 Stats. L. 855-6) as amended by Act of February 14, 1913 (37 Stats. L. 678).

S G Hopkins
Assistant Secretary

▲▼▲▼▲▼▲▼▲▼▲▼▲▼▲▼

SKAKIN or SKAWIN

LAST WILL AND TESTAMENT
-------------OF-------------
SKAKIN.

IN THE NAME OF GOD, AMEN.

I **Skawin** of **Bullhead, S. Dak** being of sound mind, memory and understanding, do hereby make and publish this my last will and testament, hereby revoking and annulling all wills by me heretofore made, in matter and forth following, that is to say.

First: I direct that all my just debts and funeral expenses, and expenses of one last illness shall be paid by my executor hereinafter named as soon after my decease as convenient.

Second: I give, devise and bequeath to
Annie Rosebud, my daughter, the E. 1/2 of the N. 1/2 of the N. 1/2 of the Sec 20, Tp. N. of Range 25. E.B.H.M.

To my grandson, James Rosebud, I give the W. 1/2 of the N. 1/2 of Sec 20. Tp 21, N. of Range 25. E.B.H.M. also 2 mares and a colt Branded J.K. left hip. I do this for his kindness to me, also for his support.

Third: All the rest and residue of my estate, both real and personal and mixed, I give, devise and bequeath to my lawful heirs as determined after my decease.

And, I do hereby nominate, constitute and appoint, _____ executor of this my last will and testament.

In Testimony Whereof, I have set my hand and seal to this, my last will and testament at *Bullhead S.Dak.* this *1st* day of *Dec.* in the year of our Lord one thousand, nine hundred and *Nineteen*

And lastly, I hereby request _____ to sign my name to this my last will and testament and witness the same.

her

S Kawin　　[thumb print]

(Testator or Testratrix) *mark*

Signed, sealed, published and declared by said *SKawin* in our presence, as and for *her* last will and testament, and at *her* request and in our presence, and in the presence of each other, we have hereunto subscribed our names as attesting witnesses thereto.

MG Hatch	of *Bullhead, S. D.*
Martin Yellow Earring	of *Bull Head, S.D.*
John Shave Bear	of *Bullhead, S.D.*

Department of the Interior,
Office of Indian Affairs, Washington, DEC 20 1920

It is respectfully recommended that the within will of Skawin, deceased Standing Rock Sioux Allottee No. 1238, be approved according to the Act of June 25, 1910 (36 Stats. L. 855-6) as amended by Act of February 14, 1913 (37 Stats. L. 678).

EB Merritt
Assistant Commissioner

Indian Wills, 1911 – 1921 Book Two
Records of The Bureau of Indian Affairs

Department of The Interior
Office of The Secretary, Washington

The within will of Skawin, deceased Standing Rock Sioux Allottee No. 1238 is hereby approved according to the Act of June 25, 1910 (36 Stats. L. 855-6) as amended by Act of February 14, 1913 (37 Stats. L. 678).

S G Hopkins
Assistant Secretary

▲▼▲▼▲▼▲▼▲▼▲▼▲▼▲▼

JULIA DESANTEL
DEPARTMENT OF THE INTERIOR

UNITED STATES INDIAN SERVICE
Omak, Wash.
Jan. 8, 1917

I Julia Desantel being of sound mind do hereby bequeath to Maxim Desantel, Johnne Desantel, Adolph Desantel, Rose Roderford and Olive Pearson and Francis Desantel, Felix Desantel, Duncan Desantel, Victor Desantel & Elmer Desantel and Philomine Lynn each ($1.00) one dollar and all the balance of my property both personal and real including my allotment held in trust for me by the Government. I bequeath to my daughter, Mary Gengro.

My reason for giving the bulk of my property to Mary Gengro is that she has had all the care of me in my old age. I having lived with her for the last seven years and none of the other children have contributed to my support in that time.

If it be necessary to have an executor for this estate I hereby appoint Mary Gengro my executor.

her
Witnesses: *Julia Desantel* [thumb print]
   W A Talbert   *mark*
      Omak, Wash.
   C E Weastersking
      Omak, Wash.

               Stephen Bunner
               Interpreter

Probate
74819-17

Department of The Interior,
Office of Indian Affairs,

The within will of Julia Desantel, deceased allottee No. 219, of the Colville tribe is respectfully recommended for approval, pursuant to the provisions of the Act of June 25, 1910 (36 Stats. L., 855-6) as amended by Act of February 14, 1913 (37 Stats. L., 678).

Respectfully,
E B Merritt
Assistant Commissioner

Department of The Interior
Office of The Secretary

The within will of Julia Desantel, deceased allottee No. 219, of the Colville tribe is hereby approved in pursuant to the provisions of the Act of June 25, 1910 (36 Stats. L., 855-6) as amended by Act of February 14, 1913 (37 Stats. L., 678). By the terms of the will $1.00 each is left to eleven children and grandchildren named and all the residue of her property to the daughter, Mary Gengro. The designation of an executor is not recognized.

S G Hopkins
Assistant Secretary

▲▼▲▼▲▼▲▼▲▼▲▼▲▼

FRANK NO HORSE

Kind So. Dak Aug 2, 1918

I Frank No Horse of the Standing Rock Reservation, S D. being of failing health but of sound mind and memory do make and declare this to be my last will and testament in manner as follows to wit:

First

I give, device[sic] and bequeth[sic] to Sidney Bear Heart one 4 yr old gelding color black branded 71 right thigh one bay gelding 4 yrs old

13

branded 70 right thigh two 2 year old steers with white faces branded 70 right side 1 cow and calf red.

Second

> *I give device and bequeth[sic] to Pretty Bull all other stock and property belonging to me with the exception of one roan mare branded 70 right thigh 3 yrs old which I desire shall be sold to pay for my coffin and funeral expenses.*

Frank No Horse

Signed sealed and published and declared by said Frank No Horse as his last will and testament at his request and in our presence and in the presence of each other. We have hereunto subscribed our names, as attesting witnesses thereto. Witness to signiture[sic] and will

> *John Sack Interpreter*
> *William End of Horn*
> *Henry A. Stewart*

Department of the Interior,
Office of Indian Affairs, Washington,

DEC 23 1920

It is respectfully recommended that the within last will and testament of Frank No Horse, deceased Standing Rock Sioux Allottee No. 565, be approved according to the Act of June 25, 1910 (36 Stats. L. 855-6) as amended by Act of February 14, 1913 (37 Stats. L. 678).

> *C F Hawke*
> *Acting* Assistant Commissioner

Department of The Interior
Office of The Secretary, Washington

The within will of Frank No Horse, deceased Standing Rock Sioux Allottee No. 565, is hereby approved according to the Act of June 25, 1910 (36 Stats. L. 855-6) as amended by Act of February 14, 1913 (37 Stats. L. 678).

> *S G Hopkins*
> Assistant Secretary

▲▼▲▼▲▼▲▼▲▼▲▼▲▼▲▼

SHELL or PANKESKAWIN

LAST WILL AND TESTAMENT

IN, THE NAME OF GOD, AMEN.

I, **Shell or Pankeskawin** of **Kenel, S.D.** being of sound mind, memory and understanding, do hereby make and publish this my last will and testament, hereby revoking and annulling all wills by me heretofore made, in manner and form following, that is to say

First; I direct that all my just debts and funeral expenses, and expenses of my last illness shall be paid by my executor hereinafter named as soon after my decease as convenient;

Second; I give and bequeath to my daughter, Mrs. Joseph Takes the Shield, five hundred dollars ($500.00). To my grandson, Sam Red Pheasant, I also give and bequeath five hundred dollars ($500.00). To Mrs. Charles Iron Horn, my grand-daughter, I give fifteen dollars ($15.00). To her son, Mark Iron Horn, I give fifteen dollars ($15.00). To my greatgrandson, Frank Jewett, I give fifteen dollars ($15.00). And to my greatgranddaughter, Maggie Jewett, I give fifteen dollars ($15.00). This money to be paid from the proceeds from my land recently sold. Each beneficiary to receive an amount from each payment proportionate to the entire sum willed to them. To Mrs. Joseph Takes the Shield, I give my Issue Wagon and harness also one black mare. To Sam Red Pheasant one iron grey gelding, also an Issue Plow and Harrow.

Third; All the rest and residue of my estate, both real, and personal and mixed, I give and bequeath to my lawful heirs as determined after my decease.

And, I do hereby nominate, constitute and appoint the Superintendent of Standing Rock Reservation executor of this my last will and testament.

In testimony whereof, I have set my hand and seal to this my last will and testament, at **Kenel, S. D.** this twenty-sixth day of October, in the year of our Lord one thousand, nine hundred and sixteen.

And lastly, I hereby request W.F. Mullally to sign my name to this my last will and testament and witness the same.

	W.F. Mullally, Principal	
	Kenel, S.D.	*her*
Witness to thumb mark	*Otto R Kopplin*	*Shell or Pankeskawin* [thumb print]
	Farmer	Testatrix *mark*

15

Signed, sealed, published and declared by said Shell, or Pankeskawin in our presence, as and for her last will and testament and at her request and in our presence and in the presence of each other, we have hereunto subscribed our names as attesting witnesses thereto.

Otto R Kopplin	of	*Kenel S.D*
D S Hatch	of	" " "
W.F. Mullally	of	*Kenel, S.D.*

Probate
85070-20
  V L L

Department of The Interior,
Office of Indian Affairs, Washington,
                    NOV 30 1920
It is recommended that the within will of Pankeskawin or Shell be under the Act of June 25, 1910 (36 Stats. L., 855-6) as amended by Act of February 14, 1913 (37 Stats. L., 678).

Respectfully,
E B Meritt
Assistant Commissioner

Department of The Interior
Office of The Secretary

The within will of Pankeskawin or Shell is approved under the Act of June 25, 1910 (36 Stats. L., 855-6) as amended by Act of February 14, 1913 (37 Stats. L., 678).

S G Hopkins
Assistant Secretary

▲▼▲▼▲▼▲▼▲▼▲▼▲▼

PHILIP EATING WALKING

Rosebud Reservation,
Wood, So. Dak.,
October 13, 1916

TO WHOM IT MAY CONCERN:

I, Philip Eating Walking, a member of the Sioux Tribe and now a resident of the Rosebud reservation at this time being of sound mind, do this day will and wish that all my monies deposited to my credit in agency office from sale of lands, etc. be equally divided between my brother, Had Watch and my wife, Ida Eating

Walking, and all personal belongings other than monies deposited, such as live stock, farming implements, household goods, to my wife, Ida Eating Walking, after my death.

his
Philip Eating Walking [thumb print]
mark

Witnesses to mark:
    Henry Stranger Horse
    (Signature illegible)

Department of the Interior,
Office of Indian Affairs, Washington,
        JAN 18 1921

The within will is recommended to be approved in so far as it relates to live stock, farming implements and household goods under the provisions of the Act of June 25, 1910 (36 Stats. L. 855-6) as amended by Act of February 14, 1913 (37 Stats. L. 678).

EB Merritt
Assistant Commissioner

Department of The Interior
Office of The Secretary, Washington

The within will of is hereby approved in so far as it relates to live stock, farming implements and household goods under the provisions of the Act of June 25, 1910 (36 Stats. L. 855-6) as amended by Act of February 14, 1913 (37 Stats. L. 678).

S G Hopkins
Assistant Secretary

▲▼▲▼▲▼▲▼▲▼▲▼▲▼

QUAV-A-YETCHY
LAST WILL AND TESTAMENT.

OFFICE OF INDIAN AFFAIRS
RECEIVED
JUN 21 1918
84704

Apache, Oklahoma,
Oct. 2, 1918

I, Quav-a-yetchy, Comanche Indian allottee No. 811, 80 years of age, residing near Apache, Caddo County, Oklahoma, being now in good health, strength of body and mind, but sensible of the uncertainty of life, and desiring to make disposition of my property and affairs while in health and strength do hereby make, publish and declare the following to be my last will and testament, hereby revoking and cancelling all other or former wills by me at any time made.

1. I direct the payment of all my just debts and funeral expenses.

2. I give and devise to my beloved cousin, nearest relative, who has taken care of me for the last eleven years while I was blind, all of my property, real and personal of which I may did[sic] possessed. This is to include my interest in and to the South East Quarter (SE1/4) of Section Thirty-two (32) Township Four (4) North, Range Eleven (11) West of the Indian Meridian, being Comanche allotment No. 850, allotted to Po-po-a-cut, deceased allottee. In L H 60337-15, F E, I was declared the sole heir of said estate. This beneficiary is my sole heir at law so far as I am able to determine, and I direct that she take all of my property.

This will is made subject to the approval of the Secretary of the Interior.

IN WITNESS WHEREOF, I, Quav-a-yet-chy[sic], have to this my last will and testament, consisting of two sheets of paper, subscribe my name this *2* day of *Oct*, 1918.   *Her*

Quavayetchy [thumb print]

Witnesses: *mark*

Nathan Kah rah rah
Apache, Okla

Jack Mahseet
Apache, Okla

Subscribed by Quav-a-yetchy, in the presence of each of us, the undersigned, and at the same time declared by here to us to be her last will and testament, and we, thereupon, at the request of Quav-a-yetchy, in her presence, and in the presence of each other sign our names hereto as witnesses this *2* day of *Oct,* 1918.

Nathan Kah rah rah
Apache, Okla
Jack Mahseet
Apache, Okla.

Indian Wills, 1911 – 1921 Book Two
Records of The Bureau of Indian Affairs

INTERPRETER'S CERTIFICATE.

I hereby certify on honor that I acted as interpreter during the execution of the foregoing last will and testament of Qua-v-a-yetchy; that I interpreted fully and completely all of the terms of said instrument to her before I was executed by Quav-a-yetchy, and that every devise and condition therein contained meets with her full approval and consent, and that said will was drawn strictly in accordance with her desires and directions. I further certify that I have no interest in this matter whatsoever, and that I speak both the Comanche Indian, as well as the English language fluently.

Signed this *2* day of *Oct.* 1918

Jack Mahseet

Interpreter.

Department of the Interior,
Office of Indian Affairs, Washington,

JAN 21 1921

It is hereby recommended that the within last will and testament of Quav-a-yetchy, Comanche Indian allottee No. 811, be approved in accordance with the provisions of the Act of June 25, 1910 (36 Stats. L. 855-6) as amended by Act of February 14, 1913 (37 Stats. L. 678).

E B Meritt

Assistant Commissioner

Department of The Interior
Office of The Secretary, Washington

The within will of Quav-a-yetchy, Comanche Indian allottee No. 811, is hereby approved in accordance with the provisions of the Act of June 25, 1910 (36 Stats. L. 855-6) as amended by Act of February 14, 1913 (37 Stats. L. 678).

S G Hopkins

Assistant Secretary

▲▼▲▼▲▼▲▼▲▼▲▼▲▼▲▼

WILLIAM JUDAH JIM

Know all men by these presents:

Indian Wills, 1911 – 1921 Book Two
Records of The Bureau of Indian Affairs

That I, William Judah Jim, of the City of Chiloquin, County of Klamath, State of Oregon, being of sound mind and realizing that I am abut to die, do hereby make, publish and declare this to be my last will and testament, hereby revoking all former wills and codicils heretofore made by me.

I direct my executrix hereinafter names, to pay all my just debts and funeral expenses out of my estate as soon after my decease as possible.

I give and bequeath to my wife Mary Cowan Judah Jim, that portion and interest in my estate that is allowed her under existing laws, and no more.

I give and bequeath all the residue, rest and remainder of my property, wherever situated, both real and personal to my nephew Leslie Bryant, of Chiloquin, Or. and to his heirs, executors, administrators and assigns forever.

I hereby nominate and appoint my sister – Lillian Bryant of Chiloquin, Or. to be executrix hereof. I desire that my said executrix shall not be required to furnish any bond to carry out the terms of this my last will and testament.

I desire that after my death, my body be returned to Chiloquin, Or. for interment and a suitable but inexpensive tombstone be placed over my grave.

Given under my hand and seal at Leavenworth, Kansas, this January 26th.1918.

William Judah Jim

Signed, published and declared by the above named William Judah Jim to be his last will and testament, in our presence who, at his request and in his presence, and in the presence of each other, do hereby set our hands as witnesses at Leavenworth, Kansas, our place of residence, this January 26th.1918.

A H Leonard
Thos. W. Morgan

Department of The Interior,
Office of Indian Affairs, Washington,
JAN 18 1921

Indian Wills, 1911 – 1921 Book Two
Records of The Bureau of Indian Affairs

It is recommended that the within will be approved under the Act of June 25, 1910 (36 Stats. L., 855-6) as amended by Act of February 14, 1913 (37 Stats. L., 678).

E B Meritt
Assistant Commissioner

Department of The Interior
Office of The Secretary JAN 25 1921

The within will is approved under the Act of June 25, 1910 (36 Stats. L., 855-6) as amended by Act of February 14, 1913 (37 Stats. L., 678).

S G Hopkins
Assistant Secretary

▲▼▲▼▲▼▲▼▲▼▲▼▲▼

VIRGINIA (DUCEPT) BOUCHER

LAST WILL AND TESTAMENT
of
VIRGINIA (DUCEPT) BOUCHER

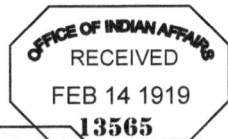

OFFICE OF INDIAN AFFAIRS
RECEIVED
FEB 14 1919
13565

OFFICE OF INDIAN AFFAIRS
RECEIVED
DEC 21 1920
103227

IN THE NAME OF GOD, AMEN.

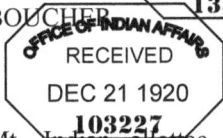

I, Virginia (Ducept) Boucher, Turtle Mt. Indian allottee No. G-036592, residing at Belcourt, N.D., being of lawful age, sound mind, memory and understanding, do hereby make and publish this my last Will and Testament, hereby revoking and annulling all Wills by me heretofore made, in the manner and form following, that is to say:

FIRST: I direct that all my just debts and funeral expenses and the expenses of my last illness, shall be paid as soon after my decease as shall be convenient.

SECOND: I give devise and bequeath to my 3 minor children, Robert Ducept, William Francois Decept and Della Ducept, my undivided one-third interest in the NE/4 of Sec. 31, T 162, R 70, which interest I inherited per Law-Heirship 20266-14, from the estate of Henry Ducept, deceased Turtle Mt. Indian allottee No. R-308.

THIRD: To the following names persons I give, devise and bequeath nothing, viz: Alphonse Ducept. Veronica (Ducept) Renault, and Jean Ducept.

IN TESTIMONEY[sic] WHEREOF?[sic] I have placed upon this paper in lieu of my signature, since I cannot write my name, an impression of my right thumb, and have with typewriter, before my thumb mark, in signature of this my last Will and Testament, at Belcourt, N.D., on this 5th day of February, in the year of our Lord One Thousand Nine Hundred and nineteen.   Her

Virginia (Ducept) Boucher[thumb print]

Mark

SIGNED, SEALED, Published and Declared.

By the said Virginia (Ducept) Boucher, in our presence, as and for her last Will and Testament, at her request and in her presence, and in the presence of each other, we have hereunto subscribed our names as attesting witnesses thereto, and the signature of Virginia (Ducept) Boucher was written of front of her thumb mark with typewriter as her signature to this Will and Testament by Everett Euneau, at her request and in her presence and in our presence.

> *Alphonse Ducept*
> P.O. Belcourt, N.D.
> *Petercia Ascellaes*
> P.O. Belcourt, N.D.
> *Everett Euneau*
> Belcourt, N.D.

Pro
103227-20
 R T B
Department of The Interior,
Office of Indian Affairs, Washington,
                    JAN 22 1921

It is recommended that the within will of Virginia (Ducept) Boucher, Turtle Mountain Chippewa allottee #G-036592 be approved under the Act of June 25, 1910 (36 Stats. L., 855-6) as amended by Act of February 14, 1913 (37 Stats. L., 678).

> Respectfully,
> *E B Meritt*
> Assistant Commissioner

Indian Wills, 1911 – 1921 Book Two
Records of The Bureau of Indian Affairs

Department of The Interior
Office of The Secretary   JAN 22 1921

The within will of Virginia (Ducept) Boucher, Turtle Mountain Chippewa allottee #G-036592 is approved in accordance with the Act of June 25, 1910 (36 Stats. L., 855-6) as amended by Act of February 14, 1913 (37 Stats. L., 678).

S G Hopkins
Assistant Secretary

▲▼▲▼▲▼▲▼▲▼▲▼▲▼▲▼

WILLIAM CADOTTE

LAST WILL AND TESTAMENT
OF
William Cadotte #83

IN THE NAME OF GOD, AMEN.

I, *William Cadotte* OF *Wakpala, S. Dakota* BEING OF SOUND MIND, MEMORY AND UNDERSTANDING, DO HEREBY MAKE AND PUBLISH THIS MY LAST WILL AND TESTAMENT, HEREBY REVOKING AND ANNULLING ALL WILLS BY ME HERETOFORE MADE, IN MANNER AND FORM FOLLOWING. THAT IS TO SAY:

FIRST; I DIRECT THAT ALL MY JUST DEBTS AND FUNNERAL[sic] RXPENSES AND EXPENSES OF MY LAST ILLNESS SHALL BE PAID BY MY EXECUTOR HEREINAFTER NAMED AS SOON AFTER MY DECEASE AS CONVENIENT;

SECOND; I GIVE, DEVISE AND BEQUEATH TO

Samuel Cadotte, Sr., the residue after selling one-half of the north half of Section 27, Twp. 23, Range 25, and paying my reimbursable debts.

THIRD; ALL THE REST AND RESIDUE OF MY ESTATE BOTH REAL AND PERSONAL AND MIXED, I GIVE, DEVISE AND BEQUEATH TO MY LAWFUL HEIRS AS DETERMINED AFTER MY DECEASE.

AND, I DO HEREBY NOMINATE, CONSTITUTE AND APPOINT _____ EXECUTOR OF THIS MY LAST WILL AND TESTAMENT.

IN TESTIMONY WHEREOF, I HAVE SET MY HAND AND SEAL TO THIS, MY LAST WILL AND TESTAMENT, AT *Fort Yates, North Dakota*, THIS

23

twenty-eighth DAY OF *October*, IN THE YEAR OF OUR LORD, ONE
THOUSAND NINE HUNDRED AND *eighteen*.

AND LASTLY I HEREBY REQUEST _____ TO SIGN MY NAME
TO THIS MY LAST WILL AND TESTAMENT AND WITNESS THE SAME.

William Cadotte
TESTATOR OR TESTATRIX

SIGNED, SEAL, PUBLISH AND DECLARED BY SAID *William Cadotte* IN
OUR PRESENCE AS AND FOR *his* LAST WILL AND TESTAMENT, AND AT *his*
REQUEST AND IN OUR PRESENCE AND IN THE PRESENCE OF EACH OTHER,
WE HAVE HEREUNTO SUBSCRIBED OUR NAMES AS ATTESTING WITNESSES
THERETO.

Ethil M Cunningham OF *Fort Yates, N. Dak.*
Ferdinand J Charcoal OF *Fort Yates N.Dak.*

Department of the Interior,
Office of Indian Affairs, Washington,

JAN 18 1921

It is respectfully recommended that the within will of William Cadotte,
deceased Standing Rock Sioux Allottee No. 83, be approved under the
Act of June 25, 1910 (36 Stats. L. 855-6) as amended by Act of February
14, 1913 (37 Stats. L. 678).

EB Merritt
Assistant Commissioner

Department of The Interior
Office of The Secretary, Washington

JAN 18 1921

The within will of William Cadotte, deceased Standing Rock Sioux
Allottee No. 83, is hereby approved under the Act of June 25, 1910 (36
Stats. L. 855-6) as amended by Act of February 14, 1913 (37 Stats. L.
678).

S G Hopkins
Assistant Secretary

▲▼▲▼▲▼▲▼▲▼▲▼▲▼▲▼

WYLACKIE CHARLIE

Last Will and Testament of Wylackie Charlie

Indian Wills, 1911 – 1921 Book Two
Records of The Bureau of Indian Affairs

I, Wylackie Charlie, about sixty eight years of age, an Indian residing on the Round Valley Indian Reservation, Mendocino County, California, and a member of the Ukie and Wylackie tribe of Indians, being of sound mind and memory and of a disposing disposition, do hereby devise and bequeath to Lizzie Lawley (formerly Lizzie Wright) and Sallie Duncan, In equal shares, the former named being my second cousin and the last named my nearest friend, and both Indian women of the Round Valley Indian Reservation, in Mendocino County, all of my estate, both real and personal which I now hold or which I may hereafterbecome entitled to, such reality being my trust allotments held under restrictions and more particularly described as follows:

Allotment No. 368, being Lot No. 17, section 30, Township 23, Range 12 W West[sic] of M.D.M. containing 10 (ten) acres;
and
S1/2 of S1/2 of NE1/4 of SE1/4 of SE1/4, section 17, Township 23, Range 13 West of M.D.M. containing fifty (50) acres;

In the event of my demise I am found to be the heir of any other property, either personal or real, located on the Round Valley Indian Reservation or elsewhere, I bequeath and give to the aforesaid Lizzie Lawley and Sallie Duncan, all my interests in such estates, to be divided equally between them, share and share alike.

Further: In the event that I am possessed of any cattle of whatsoever description, cows, steers, calves, etc., that the same be sold immediately and the proceeds turned over to my estate, to be divided equally between the aforesaid devisses[sic], at the time of the settlement of my estate.

Further: That before any division of my estate is made, I desire that all my just and honest debts be paid and that in the event that one or both of them pay the expenses inciden[sic] to my death and burial, that such sum be deducted from any moneys to the credit of my estate and reimbursed the party or parties assuming the payment of such expenses:

I know of no other person or persons who are nearer related to me that Lizzie Lawley and in the event that such may be found after my demise, I wish the bequests herein made to be I force for the reason that Lizzie Lawley and Sallie Duncan, each and both have taken care of me during my last sickness and I take this method of showing my appreciation and gratitude for all both have done for me.

Witnesses   Wylackie Charlie   his
Fred Major   thumb mark
Albert M Brown   both of Covelo, Calif.

Subscribed and sworn to before me this *4* day of September 1919.

W.W. McCombe
Supt

Department of The Interior,
Office of Indian Affairs, Washington,

JAN 15 1921

It is hereby recommended that the within will of Wylackie Charlie, deceased Indian of the Wylackie Tribe, be approved pursuant to the provisions of the Act of June 25, 1910 (36 Stats. L., 855-6) as amended by Act of February 14, 1913 (37 Stats. L., 678).

E B Meritt
Assistant Commissioner

Department of The Interior
Office of The Secretary JAN 18 1921

The within will of Wylackie Charlie, deceased Indian of the Wylackie Tribe, is hereby approved pursuant to the provisions of the Act of June 25, 1910 (36 Stats. L., 855-6) as amended by Act of February 14, 1913 (37 Stats. L., 678).

S G Hopkins
Assistant Secretary

▲▼▲▼▲▼▲▼▲▼▲▼▲▼

NARCISE PRETTY FACE
Original
WILL

I, **Narcise Pretty Face** of Pine Ridge Agency, South Dakota, Allottee number .... Do hereby make and declare this to be my last will and testament, in accordance with Section 2 of the Act of June 25, 1910, (36 stat. 855-858) and Act of February 14, 1913, (Public No. 381), hereby revoking all former wills made by us:

1. I hereby direct that as soon as possible after my decease, that all my debts, funeral and testamentary expenses be paid out of my personal estate.

Indian Wills, 1911 – 1921 Book Two
Records of The Bureau of Indian Affairs

2. I give and devise my allotment on the Pine Ridge Reservation, South Dakota, described as follows:

S/2 of NE/4 of Sec 22, Twp 109, R 72 W

in the following manner:

to my wife, Antonia Pretty Face:

The land inherited by me from my sister, Nancy Pretty Face (containing 160 acres) to my three children, Josephine, Peter and Joseph.

The property inherited from the estate of my grandfather I give to Joseph Sierro and Hillaria Sierro, the brother and sister of my wife.

The land inherited by me from my step-father, Charging Hawk, (160 acres), half to my wife and half to my three children.

3. I give and bequeath all of my personal property of whatsoever nature and wheresoever situated unto

4. All the rest of my property, real or personal, now possessed or hereafter acquired, of whatsoever nature and wheresoever situated, I hereby give, devise and bequeath unto

my wife, Antonia Pretty Face. (The property now consists of three horses and three wagons)

In witness whereof I have hereunto set my hand this **8**th day of **February** 1917

Narcise Pretty face

The above statement was, this **8th** day of **February** 1917 signed and published by **Narcise Pretty Face** as **his** last will and testament, in the joint presence of the undersigned, the said **Narcise Pretty Face** then being of sound and vigorous mid and free from any constraint or compulsion; whereupon we, being without any interest in the matter other than friendship, and being well acquainted with **him** but not members of **his** family, immediately subscribed our names hereto in the presence of each other and of the said testator, for the purpose of attesting the said will, as requested us to do. And that I, ... at the

testa.....'s request have written .... name in ink, and that .... affixed ....
thumb-marks. *(Note: "........" are areas left blank on the original.)*

		Post Office Address
H E Wright	**Farmer**	**Pine Ridge, S. D.**
Roland R. Cross	**Agency Physician**	**Pine Ridge, S. D.**

Pine Ridge, South Dakota.
Feb 17 1917

    I hereby certify that I have fully inquired into the mental competency of the Indian signing the above will; the circumstances attending the execution of the will; the influence that may have induced its execution, and the names of those entitled to share in the estate under the law of descent in South Dakota: reasons for the disposition of the property proposed by the will differing from disposition had the property descended by operation of law.

    I respectfully forward this will with the recommendation that it be .....approved.

John R Brennan
Supt. & Spl. Disb. Agent.

Probate 2C366-1917
Department of The Interior,
Office of Indian Affairs, Washington,
JAN 17 1921

The within will of Narcise Pretty Face is hereby recommended for approval in accordance with the provisions of the Act of June 25, 1910 (36 Stats. L., 855-6) as amended by Act of February 14, 1913 (37 Stats. L., 678).

Respectfully,
E B Meritt
Acting Assistant Commissioner

Department of The Interior
Office of The Secretary JAN 18 1921

The within will is hereby approved in accordance with the Act of June 25, 1910 (36 Stats. L., 855-6) as amended by Act of February 14, 1913 (37 Stats. L., 678).

S G Hopkins
Assistant Secretary

▲▼▲▼▲▼▲▼▲▼▲▼▲▼▲▼

MRS. STRIKES THE KETTLE

Indian Wills, 1911 – 1921 Book Two
Records of The Bureau of Indian Affairs

LAST WILL AND TESTAMENT
OF
Mrs. Strikes The Kettle.

IN THE NAME OF GOD, AMEN.

I, **Mrs. Strikes The Kettle** OF **Fort Yates, N. D.** BEING OF SOUND MIND, MEMORY AND UNDERSTANDING, DO HEREBY MAKE AND PUBLISH THIS MY LAST WILL AND TESTAMENT, HEREBY REVOKING AND ANNULLING ALL WILLS BY ME HERETOFORE MADE, IN MANNER AND FORM FOLLOWING, THAT IS TO SAY:

FIRST; I DIRECT THAT ALL MY JUST DEBTS AND FUNNERAL[sic] EXPENSES AND EXPENSES OF MY LAST ILLNESS SHALL BE PAID BY MY EXECUTOR HEREINAFTER NAMED AS SOON AFTER MY DECEASE AS CONVENIENT;

SECOND; I GIVE, DEVISE AND BEQUEATH TO

My childern[sic] John, Joseph and George Pleets, Rose Tiokasin, and Mrs. Annie Dubray, taking equal shares in the following described lands: SE/4 of Sec. 26, Twp. 20 N. R. 22 and SW/4 of Sec. 11 Twp. 22 N of R. 22 containing 320 acres. Also equal shares in my undivided interest of one-half, in the estate of my deceased husband Strike-the-kettle, allottee No. 1344, or sell the land soon after my decease and the money derived therefrom be divided equally among the above named childern[sic]. Also to the above named childern my undivided interest in personal property of which I have a half interest, derived from the estate of my husband Strike The kettle[sic].

THIRD; ALL THE REST AND RESIDUE OF MY ESTATE, BOTH REAL, PERSONAL AND MIXED, I GIVE, DEVISE AND BEQUEATH TO MY LAWFUL HEIRS AS DETERMINED AFTER MY DECEASE.

AND, I DO HEREBY NOMINATE, CONSTITUTE AND APPOINT _____ EXECUTOR OF THIS MY LAST WILL AND TESTAMENT.

IN TESTIMONY WHEREOF, I HAVE SET MY HANDS AND SEAL TO THIS MY LAST WILL AND TESTAMENT, AT **Fort Yates, North Dakota** THIS **15th** DAY OF **August** IN THE YEAR OF OUR LORD ONE THOUSAND, ONE HUNDRED AND **Seventeen**.

AND LASTLY, I HEREBY REQUEST **Francis B. Zahn** TO SIGN MY NAME TO THIS MY LAST WILL AND TESTAMENT AND WITNESS THEREOF. *her*

Mrs. Strikes the Kettle [thumb print]
(TESTATOR OR TESTATRIX)   *mark*

SIGNED, SEALED, PUBLISHED AND DECLARED BY SAID **Mrs. Strike[sic] The Kettle** IN OUR PRESENCE AS AND FOR **her** LAST WILL AND TESTAMENT AND AT

29

Indian Wills, 1911 – 1921 Book Two
Records of The Bureau of Indian Affairs

her REQUEST AND IN OUR PRESENCE AND IN THE PRESENCE OF EACH OTHER, WE
HAVE HEREUNTO SUBSCRIBED OUR NAMES AS ATTESTING WITNESSES THERETO.

Frances B Zahn   OF   **Fort Yates, N. D.**
Louis W Eichhorn, MD OF   **Fort Yates, N. D.**

Department of the Interior,
Office of Indian Affairs, Washington,
                DEC 30 1920

It is respectfully recommended that the within will of Mrs. Strike The
Kettle be approved under the Act of June 25, 1910 (36 Stats. L. 855-6) as
amended by Act of February 14, 1913 (37 Stats. L. 678).

CF Hawke
Acting Assistant Commissioner

Department of The Interior
Office of The Secretary, Washington
            JAN -3 1921

The accompanying will of Mrs. Strike The Kettle is hereby approved
under the Act of June 25, 1910 (36 Stats. L. 855-6) as amended by Act of
February 14, 1913 (37 Stats. L. 678).

S G Hopkins
Assistant Secretary

▲ ▼ ▲ ▼ ▲ ▼ ▲ ▼ ▲ ▼

OFFICE OF INDIAN AFFAIRS
RECEIVED
OCT 14 1920
84496

OFFICE OF INDIAN AFFAIRS
RECEIVED
DEC 14 1920
101370

PAUL BEAVER or BALD HEAD

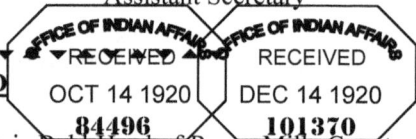

I, Paul Beaver, whose Indian name is Bald Head of Roger Mills County,
State of Oklahoma, being in poor health, but of sound and disposing mind
and sensible of the uncertainty of life and desiring to make disposition of
my property and affairs while in strength of mind do hereby make publish
and declare the following to be my last will and testament, hereby
revoking and cancelling all other or former wills by me at any time made.
(1) I direct the payment of all my just debts and funeral expenses.
(2) I give and devise to my daughter, Bertha Beaver, all the real property
which I may own or be entitled to at the time of my death including the
one-half interest I acquired in my wife's allotment at her death and the
quarter that was allotted to me and for which patent has been issued.

(3) I give and bequeath to my daughter Bertha Beaver all the personal property of which I may die possessed be the same of whatever kind or description.

4. I hereby appoint and designate Frank H. Roby, Sole executor of this, my last will and testament.

In witness whereof, I, Paul Beaver (Indian name Baldhead) have to this my last will and testament consisting of one sheet of paper, subscribed my name this 17th day of October, 1918.

Paul Beaver.

Bald Head.

Subscribed by Paul Beaver, whose Indian name is Baldhead, in the presence of each of us, the undersigned and at the same time declared by him to us to be his last will and testament, and we, thereupon at the request of Paul Beaver, in his presence and in the presence of each other, sign our names hereto as witnesses this 17th day of October, 1918.

Lee Dorroh, Hammon, Okla.

Homer P. Hirt, Hammon, Okla.

A.A. Brown, Hammon, Okla.

State of Oklahoma,
Roger Mills County, ss.

I, Judson Cunningham, Court Clerk in and for said County and State, do hereby certify the above and foregoing instrument a true and correct copy of the last will and Testament as the same appears of record in my office.

In witness whereof, I have hereunto set my hand and affixed the seal of said Court, this 12th day of September, 1919.

Judson Cunningham

Court clerk

By, *M. Prestridge*, Deputy.

Department of the Interior,
Office of Indian Affairs, Washington FEB -4 1921

In accordance with the Act of June 25, 1910, 36 Stat., L. 855 as amended by the act of February 14, 1913, the within will of Bald Head or Paul Beaver is hereby recommended for approval insofar as it covers trust property now under the jurisdiction of the Secretary of the Interior. No executor or administrator will be recognized.

E B Meritt

Assistant Commissioner

Department of the Interior,
Office of the Secretary.

FEB 19 1921

Pursuant to the Act of June 25, 1910, 36 Stat., L. 855 as amended by the act of February 14, 1913, the above will of Bald Head or Paul Beaver is hereby recommended for approval insofar as it covers trust property now under the jurisdiction of the Secretary of the Interior. No executor or administrator will be recognized.

S G Hopkins
Assistant Secretary.

▲▼▲▼▲▼▲▼▲▼▲▼▲▼▲▼

PON-SHE-HA SHERIDAN

LAST WILL AND TESTAMENT
of
PON-SHE-HA SHERIDAN,
An Omaha Indian.

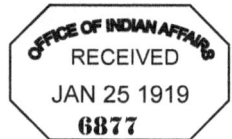

OFFICE OF INDIAN AFFAIRS
RECEIVED
JAN 25 1919
6877

I, Pon-she-ha Sheridan, a resident of Thurston County, Nebraska, and a member of the Omaha Tribe of Indians, being of sound and disposing mind and memory, do make, publish and declare this my Last Will & Testament:

1st. I direct that the sum of One Hundred Dollars ($100.00) be paid to the grandchildren of my deceased daughter, Ma-she-ha-the Kemp, living at the time of my decease, said sum to be paid from any trust funds or other moneys belonging to me.

2nd. I give, bequeath and devise to my son, Henry Sheridan

The West Half (W1/2) of the Northeast Quarter (NE1/4) of Section Fifteen (15), in Township Twenty-five (25), North, of Range Eight (8), in Thurston County, Nebraska, being my own allotment, TO HAVE AND TO HOLD during the full term of his natural life, and should he survive my daughter, Minnie Sheridan Woodhull and my granddaughter, Mabel Gilpin, I give, devise and bequeath my said allotment to him, his heirs and assigns. But in the event of the death of my son Henry Sheridan, leaving my daughter, Minnie Sheridan Woodhull and my granddaughter Mabel Gilpin, or either of them, him surviving, I give, devise and bequeath my said allotment to my said daughter and granddaughter aforesaid, or the survivor of them, in equal shares.

3rd. All the rest, residue, and remainder of my said estate, real, personal, or mixed, I give, devise and bequeath to my son Henry Sheridan.

4th. This has been executed by me under and by virtue of the authority of the Act of Congress of June 25, 1910, and any amendments thereto, providing for the disposal of Indian trust allotments by will.

In testimony whereof I, Pon-she-ha Sheridan, hereunto subscribe my name this 6th day of December, 1918.   *her*

Pon-she-ha-Sheridan[thumb print]
In the presence of   *mark*
(No names given)

The above and foregoing instrument was subscribed, published and declared by Pon-she-ha Sheridan to be her last will and testament in our presence, and in the presence of each of us, and we at the same time at her request, in her presence and in the presence of each other hereto subscribed our names and residences as attesting witnesses, this 6th day of December, 1918.

Rachel Sheridan   *Walthill Nebraska*
Lazrus Woodhull   *Walthill Nebraska*

Department of The Interior,
Office of Indian Affairs, Washington,
JAN 22 1921
The within will of Ponsheha Sheridan, deceased Omaha allottee #298-N is hereby recommended for approval under the Act of June 25, 1910 (36 Stats. L., 855-6) as amended by Act of February 14, 1913 (37 Stats. L., 678).

Respectfully,
E B Meritt
Assistant Commissioner

Indian Wills, 1911 – 1921 Book Two
Records of The Bureau of Indian Affairs

Department of The Interior
Office of The Secretary FEB 17 1921

The within will of Ponsheha Sheridan is hereby approved under the Act of June 25, 1910 (36 Stats. L., 855-6) as amended by Act of February 14, 1913 (37 Stats. L., 678).

S G Hopkins
Assistant Secretary

▲▼▲▼▲▼▲▼▲▼▲▼▲▼▲▼

JANE HIGHBEAR

LAST WILL AND TESTAMENT
of
Jane Highbear allottee No. 3686

OFFICE OF INDIAN AFFAIRS
RECEIVED
JUL 27 1916

IN THE NAME OF GOD, AMEN.

I, **Jane Highbear** OF **Cannon Ball, N. D.** BEING OF SOUND MIND, MEMORY AND UNDERSTANDING, DO HEREBY MAKE AND PUBLISH THIS MY LAST WILL AND TESTAMENT, HEREBY REVOKING AND ANNULLING ALL WILLS BY ME HERETOFORE MADE, IN MANNER AND FORM FOLLOWING, THAT IS TO SAY:

FIRST; I DIRECT THAT ALL MY JUST DEBTS AND FUNNERAL[sic] EXPENSES AND EXPENSES OF MY LAST ILLNESS SHALL BE PAID BY MY EXECUTOR HEREINAFTER NAMED AS SOON AFTER MY DECEASE AS CONVENIENT;

SECOND; I GIVE, DEVISE AND BEQUEATH TO

Jane Has Tricks one-half of my undivided one-third interest in the estate of my deceased husband, Joseph Highbear, Standing Rock Allottee No. 1690, consisting of his allotment described as the W/2 SE/4, SE/4 SE/4, W/2 NE/4 SE/4, Sec. 35, Twp. 134 N., . 79 W., 5th P.M., and E/2, Sec. 10, Twp. 132 N., R. 81 W. 5th P.M., E/2 SW/4 and lots 1, 5 and 6, Sec. 19, Twp. 23 N., R. 26 E., B.H.M., containing 640.33 acres; for the reasons that the said Mrs. Has Tricks has taken care of me off and on prior to my husband's death, and has taken exclusive care of me since the 4th of July, 1916, and I want to live with her until my death and she has promised to care for me until then. (My original allotment is described as No. 3686, the E/2, Sec. 26, Twp. 23 N., R. 21 E., B.H.M., containing 320 acres.)

THIRD; ALL THE REST AND RESIDUE OF MY ESTATE, BOTH REAL, PERSONAL AND MIXED, I GIVE, DEVISE AND BEQUEATH TO MY LAWFUL HEIRS AS DETERMINED AFTER MY DECEASE.

AND, I DO HEREBY NOMINATE, CONSTITUTE AND APPOINT ###########
EXECUTOR OF THIS MY LAST WILL AND TESTAMENT.

IN TESTIMONY WHEREOF, I HAVE SET MY HANDS AND SEAL TO THIS MY LAST
WILL AND TESTAMENT, AT **Fort Yates, North Dakota** THIS **eleventh** DAY OF
July IN THE YEAR OF OUR LORD ONE THOUSAND, ONE HUNDRED AND **sixteen**.

AND LASTLY, I HEREBY REQUEST **Asa Littlecrow** TO SIGN MY NAME TO
THIS MY LAST WILL AND TESTAMENT AND WITNESS THEREOF.   *her*

Jane Highbear   [thumb print]
(TESTATOR OR TESTATRIX)   *mark*

SIGNED, SEALED, PUBLISHED AND DECLARED BY SAID **Jane Highbear** IN
OUR PRESENCE AS AND FOR **her** LAST WILL AND TESTAMENT AND AT **her** REQUEST
AND IN OUR PRESENCE AND IN THE PRESENCE OF EACH OTHER, WE HAVE HEREUNTO
SUBSCRIBED OUR NAMES AS ATTESTING WITNESSES THERETO.

Interpreter

Asa Littlecrow	OF	*Fort Yates, N.D.*
S.J. Beueke	OF	*Fort Yates, N.D.*
L. McLowdy	OF	*Fort Yates, N.D.*

Department of the Interior,
Office of Indian Affairs, Washington,
JAN 22 1921

It is respectfully recommended that the within will of Jane Highbear, or
Mrs. Jane Highbear, deceased Standing Rock Sioux Allottee No. 3683, be
approved according to the Act of June 25, 1910 (36 Stats. L. 855-6) as
amended by Act of February 14, 1913 (37 Stats. L. 678).

CF Hawke
Acting Assistant Commissioner

Department of The Interior
Office of The Secretary, Washington

The accompanying will of Jane Highbear, or Mrs. Jane Highbear,
deceased Standing Rock Sioux Allottee No. 3683, is hereby approved
according to Act of June 25, 1910 (36 Stats. L. 855-6) as amended by Act
of February 14, 1913 (37 Stats. L. 678).

S G Hopkins
Assistant Secretary

▲▼▲▼▲▼▲▼▲▼▲▼▲▼▲▼

Indian Wills, 1911 – 1921 Book Two
Records of The Bureau of Indian Affairs

DEPARTMENT OF THE INTERIOR

UNITED STATES INDIAN SERVICE

State of Montana ⎤
        ⎬ *s.s.*
County of Glacier ⎦

       I, Boy, being of sound mind but realizing that the end of my earthly career is near do make this my last will and testament:
First: To my son, Oscar Boy, I give, will and bequeath the forty acres remaining unsold of my original allotment from the U.S. Government and also two thirds of all other property real or personal of which I may die seized.
Second: To my son, Raymond Boy, I give, will and bequeath the residue of my estate.
Dated this 21ˢᵗ day of February.   *his*
A.D. 1920   *Boy* [thumb print]
                                        mark

          ⎡ *John Old Chief*
Witnesses⎨   *Chief Polise*[sic]
          ⎣ *ErnestCutfinger*

Department of The Interior,
Office of Indian Affairs, Washington,
            FEB -2 1921
It is hereby recommended that the within will of Boy, deceased Piegan allottee No. 507, Blackfeet Agency in the State of Montana, be approved in accordance with the provisions of the Act of June 25, 1910 (36 Stats. L., 855-6) as amended by Act of February 14, 1913 (37 Stats. L., 678), and the regulations of the Department.

                        Respectfully,
                        EB Meritt
                        Assistant Commissioner
Department of The Interior
Office of The Secretary

The within will of Boy, deceased Piegan allottee No. 507, Blackfeet Agency in the State of Montana, is hereby approved in accordance with the provisions of the Act of June 25, 1910 (36 Stats. L., 855-6) as amended by Act of February 14, 1913 (37 Stats. L., 678), and the regulations of the Department.

Indian Wills, 1911 – 1921 Book Two
Records of The Bureau of Indian Affairs

S G Hopkins
Assistant Secretary

▲▼▲▼▲▼▲▼▲▼▲▼▲▼▲▼

DAVID PRESTON or WHITE WEASEL

I, David Preston or White Weasel being of sound mind and memory, having in mind clearly and full understanding of how I wish to dispose of my property, in view of my advanced age and in certainty of life do make this my last will and testament, here by revoking and annulling any other wills by me made, and I do here by publish the same: to the effect, that is to say:

First. To my beloved daughter, Hattie Preston Porter, I give, grant and devise the north half of the Southwest quarter of Section Twenty one (21) Township Twenty-four (24) north, Range Eight (8) East of 6th P.M. in Nebraska which said land is my allotment. Said Hattie Preston Porter being my only living child who has lived with my wife and I and cared for us and for whom we have great affection & gratitude.

Second: To my beloved wife and steadfast companion, Da-ah-be Preston, for her life, the use of all my remaining land and estate of what so ever kind and character, and after death as here in provided. All my personal estate I give to my beloved wife, Da-ah-be Preston.

Third: To my dear grandchild, Mabel Porter, the child of my only daughter Hattie Preston Porter, This child has been like our own child to my wife and I. I give, grant and devise the South half of the South west quarter of Section twenty-one (21) Township twenty-four (24) north and of Range Eight east of the 6th P.M. in Nebraska, subject first to the life use of my wife Da ah be Preston; Second, to the use of my daughter Hattie Preston Porter, after the death of her mother, until my grandchild shall be twenty two years of age. Should said Mabel Preston die under 22 yrs of age without issue to her mother, Hattie Preston Porter.

Fourth, I give, devise & grant to the children of my grandson, The-ka-bazhe or Dave Walker, the west half of the Northwest quarter of Section Thirty Six (36) Township Twenty five (25) north and of Range (9) nine east of the 6th P.M. in Nebraska subject first to the use of my beloved wife Da ah be Preston, and second to the use of Dave Walker or The ka bazhe until his youngest child shall be twenty five years of age.

Fifth, To my beloved daughter, Hattie Preston Porter, The Northeast quarter of North east quarter[sic] of Section Thirty Six (36) Township Twenty-five (25) north and of Range (9) Nine east of the 6th P.M. in Nebraska subject to the life use of my beloved wife Da ah be Preston. In view of the intention of my wife to give by will to Mary McNeil forty acres and as she has had forty acres from us and some money, I do not desire to give or grant any thing from my estate to her. Also as to Jim Wood, a grandson, my wife is to will to him a part of her land so I do not desire that any part of my land or estate shall go to him. Written on three pages.

Witness my hand, at my home near Macy, Nebraska, this 10th day of January 1917.

	his thumb
David Preston	[thumb print]
White Weasel	*mark*

We the undersigned witnesses signed this will as witnesses to the thumb mark of David Preston or White Weasel at his request, that it was written in our presence and as he requested & directed and he signed it in our presence and we signed it in the presence of each other at the place and on the date written to said Will. Residence Walthill, Neb.

''	''	*Gary P Meyers*
''	''	*William F Springer*
#3459 Macomb St, N.W. Washington DC		*Thomas L Sloan*

Probate 41488-18
Department of The Interior,
Office of Indian Affairs, Washington,

The within will of David Preston, Omaha allottee No. 411-0 is hereby recommended for disapproval in accordance with the Act of June 25, 1910 (36 Stats. L., 855-6) as amended by Act of February 14, 1913 (37 Stats. L., 678).

C F Hawke
Acting Assistant Commissioner

Department of The Interior
Office of The Secretary SEP 24 1920

The within will of David Preston, Omaha allottee No. 411-0 is hereby disapproved in accordance with the Act of June 25, 1910 (36 Stats. L., 855-6) as amended by Act of February 14, 1913 (37 Stats. L., 678).

S G Hopkins
Assistant Secretary

▲▼▲▼▲▼▲▼▲▼▲▼▲▼▲▼

JOE PETERS

MY LAST WILL AND TESTAMENT.

Know All Men by these Presents, that I, Joe Peters, an Indian, residing in Thurston County, Washington, being of sound mind and memory do make, publish, and declare this my last Will and Testament.

I

After the payment of my just debts and funeral; expenses, I devise my property as follows:

To my wife, Mollie Peters, one third of my property, both real and personal, and to each of my children, Jameson Murphy Peters, and Earl Robert Peters, one third of my property, both real and personal

II

I hereby appoint my beloved wife, Mollie Peters, as executrix for this my Law[sic] Will and Testament, and request that she be permitted to serve without bonds, and she shall not be required to take out Letters of Administration, or make any report to the court, or to do anything further than the administration of this Will to probate as required by the law of the State of Washington as in the case of non-intervention Wills.

III

I hereby revoke any former will be[sic] me made.

IV

I hereby request the Indian Department to approve this will, and that it apply to any land on any Indian Reservation.

Dated Jan. 3, 1919.

(Signed) Joe Peters.

The undersigned hereby certify that in our presence and in the presence of each other Joe Peters signed this instrument and declared it to be his last will and testament.

Witnessed at the request of Joe Peters.

(Signed) Wayne L. Bridgford
(Signed) E. N. Steele

VERIFICATION

I HEREBY CERTIFY, That the above is a true and correct copy of the original will of Joe Peters, and that I know the signature of the said Joe Peters, and that his signature appears on the original will. That the original will cannot be submitted to the Department at this time for the reason that the same will have to be probated in the State court at an early date.

(Illegible Signature)

February 25, 1919.   Examiner of Inheritance

Probate
18920--19
 J W H

Department of The Interior,
Office of Indian Affairs, Washington,

JAN 21 1921

The within will of Joe Peters, unallotted Indian of the Squaxin band, is respectfully recommended for approval pursuant to the provisions of the Act of June 25, 1910 (36 Stats. L., 855-6) as amended by Act of February 14, 1913 (37 Stats. L., 678), so far as it applies to his trust property.

Respectfully,
EB Meritt
~~Acting~~ Assistant Commissioner

Department of The Interior
Office of The Secretary SEP 24 1920

The within will of Joe Peters, unallotted Indian of the Squaxin band, is hereby approved pursuant to the provisions of the Act of June 25, 1910 (36 Stats. L., 855-6) as amended by Act of February 14, 1913 (37 Stats. L., 678), so far as it applies to his trust property.

S G Hopkins
Assistant Secretary

OFFICE OF INDIAN AFFAIRS
RECEIVED
AUG 12 1918
67386

▲▼▲▼▲▼▲▼▲▼▲▼▲▼▲▼

JERRY GREGORY   RECEIVED
JUN 21 1918   *Redding, Calif*
GREENVILLE INDIAN SCHOOL, CALIF   *June 5, 1918*

I, Jerry Gregory, being of sound mind and disposing memory, and being aware of the uncertainty of this life, do hereby make this my last will and testament disposing of all my property as follows:--

Indian Wills, 1911 – 1921 Book Two
Records of The Bureau of Indian Affairs

First.- I give and bequeath to Mary Montgomery Fifty ($50.00) Dollars, because she took care of me when I was sick last winter.

Second:- I give and bequeath to my step-mother, Tilda Gregory One Hundred Fifty ($150.00) Dollars, because she cared for me.

Third:- I give and bequeath all the rest of my property both real & personal to my sister, Lena Gromas.

signed Jerry Gregory

We the undersigned witnesses hereby sign as witnesses to the signature of the testator, at his request & in his presence.

signed: H. F. Roller

signed: Sadie Mae Farlane

Probate
67386-18
 J W H

Department of The Interior,
Office of Indian Affairs, Washington,

FEB 19 1921

The within will of Jerry Gregory, is hereby recommended for approval in accordance with the Act of June 25, 1910 (36 Stats. L., 855-6) as amended by Act of February 14, 1913 (37 Stats. L., 678).

Respectfully,
EB Meritt
Assistant Commissioner

Department of The Interior
Office of The Secretary FEB 24 1921

The within will of Jerry Gregory, is hereby approved in accordance with the Act of June 25, 1910 (36 Stats. L., 855-6) as amended by Act of February 14, 1913 (37 Stats. L., 678).

S G Hopkins
Assistant Secretary

▲▼▲▼▲▼▲▼▲▼▲▼▲▼

ROBERT WALKING CLOUD
DEPARTMENT OF THE INTERIOR
UNITED STATES INDIAN SERVICE
Shields   North   Dakota

Sept 10, 1917

TO WHOM IT MAY CONCERN,

    I, Robert Walking Cloud, do depose and bequeath the following personal property are as follows: first I give my two head of cattle, and the other head of cattle one cow and calf I give to my Neice[sic], Frances Murphy, and one yearling heifer, I give to my Sister Nancy Walking Cloud, and one dry cow I give to my Father, these cattle are all branded I730 right side and Diamond S, right hip, and two head of horses one mare black and one golden bay, both branded I730, these two head of horses I give to my Father, and one issue wagon and harness I give to my Father, and my land or allottment, of the south west quarter of Sec. 26, TWP 132, Range 83, this land I give to my Youngest Sister, Nancy Walking Cloud, this completes what I have to say in disposing of my Personal property and also my Real Estate, before the following persons to wit: William Payton, Farmer, and John Holy Elkface, Policeman, the above two men are witnesses to my Testament, that I have on this 10th day of Sept. 1917.

Witnesses,   *Robert Walking Cloud*

William Payton

John Holy Elk Face

Department of the Interior,
Office of Indian Affairs, Washington,
FEB 8 1921

IT IS RESPECTFULLY RECOMMENDED THAT the within will of Robert Maurice Walking Cloud, deceased Standing Rock Sioux Allottee No. 2405, under the Act of June 25, 1910 (36 Stats. L. 855-6) as amended by Act of February 14, 1913 (37 Stats. L. 678).

EB Meritt
~~Acting~~ Assistant Commissioner

Department of The Interior
Office of The Secretary, Washington
FEB 17 1921

The accompanying will of Robert Maurice Walking Cloud, deceased Standing Rock Sioux Allottee No. 2405, is hereby approved according to the Act of June 25, 1910 (36 Stats. L. 855-6) as amended by Act of February 14, 1913 (37 Stats. L. 678).

S G Hopkins
Assistant Secretary

▲▼▲▼▲▼▲▼▲▼▲▼▲▼▲

JAMES IRON MOCCASIN

OFFICE OF INDIAN AFFAIRS
RECEIVED
AUG 12 1918
67386

State of South Dakota)
)
County of Lewey)

IN THE NAME OF GOD, AMEN.

BE IT REMEMBERED THAT I, James Iron Moccasin, Cheyenne River Sioux, Allottee NO. 350, aged *73* years, being of sound and disposing mind and memory, do hereby publish, make and dclare[sic] this as and for my last Will and Testament, hereby revoking all other Wills or Codicils.

First, I hereby give, devise and bequeath to Agnes Iron Moccasin, my wife, that portion of my allotment NO. 350 described as the E1/2 of SW1/4 of Section 26 and the E1/2 of the NW1/4 of Section 35 Twp. 14 Range 28 E of E.H.M. containing 160 acres more or less.

Second, I hereby give, devise and bequeath to my three living sons, Leon Iron Moccasin, Truby Iron Moccasin, and Moses Iron Moccasin, the remainder portion of my allotment, also my interest in all inherited equally among them.

IN WITNESS WHEREOF, I have hereunto put my hand (or thumb Mark) and seal this 13th day of December 191, at La Plant, S.D. in the presence of two attesting witnesses.

his

Witnesses (To thumb mark sig.) *Robert Iron Moccasin*[thumb print]
Testator *mark*
John J Backus Who subscribed testators[sic] name.
Paul Kills Trio John J Backus subscribed the name of testator

Signed, SEALED, PUBLISHED, AND DECLARED AS AND for his last Will and TESTAMENT by the said James Iron Moccasin and at his request and in his presence and in the presence of each other we have hereunto subscribed our names as attesting witnesses the day and year first above mentioned.

John J Backus   *Paul Kills Trio*
La Point, S.D.   *La Plant, S.D.*

43

Indian Wills, 1911 – 1921 Book Two
Records of The Bureau of Indian Affairs

Department of The Interior,
Office of Indian Affairs, Washington,
FEB 23 1921
It is hereby recommended that the within will of James Iron Moccasin, deceased Cheyenne River Sioux allottee No. 350, be approved in accordance with the provisions of the Act of June 25, 1910 (36 Stats. L., 855-6) as amended by Act of February 14, 1913 (37 Stats. L., 678), and the regulations of the Department.

Respectfully,
EB Meritt
Assistant Commissioner

Department of The Interior
Office of The Secretary   FEB 24 1921

The within will of James Iron Moccasin, deceased Cheyenne River Sioux allottee No. 350, is hereby approved in accordance with the provisions of the Act of June 25, 1910 (36 Stats. L., 855-6) as amended by Act of February 14, 1913 (37 Stats. L., 678), and the regulations of the Department.

S G Hopkins
Assistant Secretary

▲▼▲▼▲▼▲▼▲▼▲▼▲▼▲▼

WOLF BELLY
LAST WILL AND TESTAMENT OF WOLF BELLY
IN THE NAME OF GOD Amen

I, WOLF BELLY, of Geary, Blaine County, State of Oklahoma, being now in fair heath[sic], strength and clear in mind, but sensible of the uncertainity[sic] of life, and certainity[sic] of death, and desiring to make disposition of my property and affairs while in hea/th[sic] and strength do hereby make, publish, and declare the following to be my last WILL AND TESTAMENT.

1. I give, devise and bequeath to my only daughter Meat now about 34 years of age residing with me, all of my Real Estate known and described as allotment No. 343 of Government land allotted to me being described as the Southwest quarter of section seventeen (17) in Township fourteen (14) North of Range eleven (11) W.I.M., containing one hundred sixty (160) acres of land.

2. I also bequeth[sic] to said daughter Meat any and all personal property of which I may be possessed at my death and direct the payment of all just debts and funeral expenses.

3. I hereby appoint my said daughter Meat as sole Executrix without bond of this my last WILL AND TESTAMENT.

IN WITNESS whereof, I Wolf Belly, have to this my last WILL AND TESTAMENT CONSISTING ONE SHEET of paper, subscribed this the 10th day of June 1913.

his

Wolf Belly [thumb print]

mark

Robert Burns

Dewitt C Hayes

Subscribed by Wolf Belly in the presence of us the undersigned and declared by him to be his last WILL AND TESTAMENT, and at the request of Wolf Belly, in his presence and in the presence of each other sign our names hereto as witnesses this the 10th day of June 1913.

Interpreter.

Robert Burns

John White

W. H Hall

F.E. Farrell

Department of The Interior,
Office of Indian Affairs, Washington,
FEB 16 1921

It is recommended that the within will be approved pursuant to the provisions of the Act of June 25, 1910 (36 Stats. L., 855-6) as amended by Act of February 14, 1913 (37 Stats. L., 678).

Respectfully,

EB Meritt

Assistant Commissioner

Department of The Interior
Office of The Secretary   FEB 23 1921

The within will is hereby approved pursuant to the provisions of the Act of June 25, 1910 (36 Stats. L., 855-6) as amended by Act of February 14, 1913 (37 Stats. L., 678), except the provision appointing an executrix, which can not be recognized.

S G Hopkins

Assistant Secretary

▲▼▲▼▲▼▲▼▲▼▲▼▲▼▲▼

ELLEN STA-SHIN-I-MA

WILL

Wellpinit, Washington,
December 3, 1915.

KNOW ALL MEN BY THESE PRESENTS, that I, the undersigned Ellen Sta-shin-i-ma being of sound mind but infirm body, realizing the uncertainty of life, and the care and expense which I cause to my niece, Alice Wynne, with whom I make my home I hereby will and bequeath to said Alice Wynne in the event of my death, all of my property both real and personal.

(Sgd) *Ellen Sta-shin-i-ma* [thumb print]

Witnesses:

Joe Sherwood
(Illegible signature)

Probate
4719-21
J W H

Department of The Interior,
Office of Indian Affairs, Washington,
FEB -4 1921

The within will of Ellen Staw-shin-i-ma[sic], deceased Spokane allottee #130, is hereby recommended for approval under the Act of June 25, 1910 (36 Stats. L., 855-6) as amended by Act of February 14, 1913 (37 Stats. L., 678).

Respectfully,
EB Meritt
Assistant Commissioner

Department of The Interior
Office of The Secretary FEB 25 1921

The within will of Ellen Staw-shin-i-ma[sic], deceased Spokane allottee #130, is hereby approved under the Act of June 25, 1910 (36 Stats. L., 855-6) as amended by Act of February 14, 1913 (37 Stats. L., 678).

S G Hopkins
Assistant Secretary

▲▼▲▼▲▼▲▼▲▼▲▼▲▼▲▼

STEVEN CHANDLER
Last Will and Testament

I, Steven Chandler, allottee No. 121 of the Yuma Indian Reservation, in the County of Imperial, State of California, do hereby make, publish and declare this my last Will and Testament, in manner and form following:

First: I direct that all my just debts be paid as soon after my death as conviently[sic] can be done.

Second: I give and bequeath to my wife, Marie Chandler, should she survive me, the NW/4 of SE/4 of NE/4 of Sec. 12, Twp. 165, Range 22E, S.B. Mer., to me being an allotment to me from the U.S. Government in the Yuma Indian Reservation, in Imperial County, State of California, also giving and bequeathing to my said wife, Marie Chandler, all of my personal property of which I might be possessed at the time of my death, and also any and all other real estate not herein mentioned or described of which I might be the owner at the time of my death and all interest which I might have in such real estate at the time of my death I give and bequeath to my said wife, Marie Chandler.

Third: I nominate, constitute and appoint my said wife, Marie Chandler, executrix of this my last Will and Testament, and direct that she not be required to furnish any bond or other security in the execution of her trust.

In Witness Thereof, I have hereunto subscribed my name by mark this 30th day of November, 1920.

his

Steven Chandler [thumb print]

mark

The foregoing instrument was subscribed by thumb mark and published and declared by Steven Chandler, by and for his last Will and Testament in our presence and in the presence of each other, and we, at the same time, whereunto subscribe our names and residence as attesting witnesses this 30th day of November, 1920. We furthermore attest that the Testator, Steven Chandler, was in his right mind at the time he signed this instrument.

Norman W Justus   Residing in Imperial County, California.

Wilford H. Wimms   Residing in Imperial County, California.

Department of The Interior,
Office of Indian Affairs, Washington,
FEB 16 1921

The within will of Steven Chandler, is hereby recommended for approval under the Act of June 25, 1910 (36 Stats. L., 855-6) as amended by Act of February 14, 1913 (37 Stats. L., 678).

> Respectfully,
> *EB Meritt*
> Assistant Commissioner

Department of The Interior
Office of The Secretary FEB 25 1921

The within will of Steven Chandler, is hereby approved under the Act of June 25, 1910 (36 Stats. L., 855-6) as amended by Act of February 14, 1913 (37 Stats. L., 678). The designation of executrix is not recognized.

> *S G Hopkins*
> Assistant Secretary

▲▼▲▼▲▼▲▼▲▼▲▼▲▼▲▼

DAH-TAH-HAY

LAST WILL AND TESTAMENT
of
DAH-TAH-HAY, Apache Allottee No. 582.

OFFICE OF INDIAN AFFAIRS
RECEIVED
JUN 17 1919
52483

I, DAH-TAH-HAY, Apache Indian Allottee No. 582, of Apache, Caddo County, Oklahoma, being of sound and disposing mind and memory and sensible of the uncertainty of life, desiring to make provision for the disposition of any and all property, rights, interests and estates of which I may die seized and possessed, do hereby make, publish, and declare this, my last will and testament, in manner and form a follows, that is to say:

First. I direct the payment of all my just debts and funeral expenses.

Second. I give and devise to my step-son, Howard Soontay, also called Allen Soontay, Apache Indian allottee No. 934, his heirs or devisees, The West Half of my Allotment, the same being a tract of land situated in Caddo County, Oklahoma, described as follows, to-wit, The North west quarter (NW/4) of Section Fourteen (14) in Township Five (5) North of Range Twelve (12) west of the Indian Meridian in Oklahoma;

Third. I give and devise to Isabel Tsatahsisco, Apache Indian Allottee No. 3280, her heirs or devisees, The East Half of the above described land (my allotment); said Isabel Tsatahsisco, being the daughter of Freddie Tsa-tah-sis-co and Rachel Ese-tah-lo, Apaches.

Fourth. I give, devise and bequeath all other property, rights, interests and estates, of whatsoever kind or nature and wheresoever situated, of which I may die possessed or seized, or to which I may be entitled, to the said Howard Soontay and Isabel Tsatahsisco, their heirs or devisees, in equal shares, and to the exclusion of all other persons whomsoever.

Fifth. I hereby revoke and cancel any and other and former will by me at any time made, and direct, that on the approval hereof by The Secretary of the Interior, all and singular the provisions hereof shall be of full force and effect.

IN WITNESS WHEREOF, I have executed the within and foregoing instrument (one page only) by causing my name to be subscribed hereto by an attesting witness, and the impression by me of my right thumb mark, this Fifth day of November, 1913.   *her*
                    Dah tah hay [thumb print]
                                mark

The foregoing instrument of one page only, was, on this Fifth day of November, 1913, executed by Dah-tah-hay by herself causing her name to be subscribed thereto by Spencer Hilton, and by the impression of the thumb mark of Dah-tah-hay by herself thereon set, in the presence of each of us, and said instrument was by her declared to be her last will and testament, and at her request and in her presence and in the presence of each other, we subscribe our names as witnesses, with our respective place of residence, the day and year above written.

WITNESSES:)   *Spencer Hilton* residing at *Anadacko, OK*
)   *Alonzo Chalepah* residing at *Apache, Okla.*

Alonzo Chalepah, being duly sworn, on his oath declares that he acted as Interpreter and fully and correctly interpreted all the above and foregoing to Dah-tah-hay, and am satisfied that she understood and was fully qualified to execute the same.

                    Alonzo Chalepah

Subscribed and sworn to before me this 5th day of November, 1913.

                    E L Ellis Special Indian Agent

Indian Wills, 1911 – 1921 Book Two
Records of The Bureau of Indian Affairs

Department of The Interior,
Office of Indian Affairs, Washington,
FEB -9 1914
It is recommended that the within will be approved pursuant to the provisions of the Act of June 25, 1910 (36 Stats. L., 855-6) as amended by Act of February 14, 1913 (37 Stats. L., 678).

Respectfully,
EB Meritt
Assistant Commissioner

Department of The Interior
Office of The Secretary FEB -9 1914

The within will is hereby approved pursuant to the provisions of the Act of June 25, 1910 (36 Stats. L., 855-6) as amended by Act of February 14, 1913 (37 Stats. L., 678).

S G Hopkins
Assistant Secretary

▲▼▲▼▲▼▲▼▲▼▲▼▲▼▲▼

CHIEF EAGLE
WILL

I, **Chief Eagle**, of Pine Ridge Agency, South Dakota, Allottee number **6853** do hereby make and declare this to be my last will and testament, in accordance with Section 2, of the Act of June 25, 1910, (36 Stat. 855-858), and Act of February 14, 1913, (Public No. 381), hereby revoking all former wills made by me;

1. I hereby direct that, as soon as possible after my decease that all my debts and funeral and testamentary expenses be paid out of my personal estate.

2. I give and devise my allotment on the Pine Ridge Reservation, South Dakota, described as follows:
The N/2 of Sec. 20 in Twp. 39 N. of Range 41 west of the 6th P.M., South Dakota, containing 320 acres.

in the following manner:
To my wife, Angelina Chief Eagle: the N/2 of the NE/4 of Sec. 20 in Twp 39 N. of Range 41 west of the 6th P.M.

To my son, Otto Chief Eagle: the S/2 of NE/4 of Sec. 20 in Twp. 39 N. of Range 41 west of the 6th P.M.
To my son, Peter Chief Eagle: the NW/4 of Sec. 20 in Twp. 39 N. of Range 41 west of the 6th P.M.

3. I give and bequeath all of my personal property of whatsoever nature and wheresoever situated unto
To my wife, Angelina Chief Eagle and my sons, Otto and Peter Chief Eagle, in equal shares.

4. All the rest of my property, real now possessed or hereafter acquired, of whatsoever nature and wheresoever situated, I hereby give, devise and bequeath unto
my wife, Angelina Chief Eagle and my sons, Otto and Peter Chief Eagle, in equal shares.

In witness whereof I have hereunto set my hand this **23rd** day of **November** 1914. 					*his mark*
						Chief Eagle [thumb print]

The above statement was, this **23rd** day of **November** 1914, signed and published by **Chief Eagle** as **his** last will and testament, in the joint presence of the undersigned, the said **Chief Eagle** then being of sound and vigorous mind and free from any constraint or compulsion; whereupon we, being without any interest in the matter other than friendship, and being well acquainted with **him** but not members of **his** family, immediately subscribed our names hereto in the presence of each other and of the said testator, for the purpose of witnessing the said will, as **he** requested us to do, **his name being signed by George A. Trotter, one of the witnesses, at his request.**

Post Office Address.

George A Trotter			**Kyle, South Dakota.**
Peter Bull Bear			**Kyle, South Dakota.**

						Pine Ridge, South Dakota
						NOV 30 1914
I hereby certify that I have fully inquired as to the mental competency of the Indian, signing the above will; the circumstances attending the execution of the will; the influence that may have induced its execution, and the names of the entitled to share in the estate under the

law of decent in South Dakota; reasons for the disposition of the property proposed by the will, differing from disposition had the property descended by operation of law.

I respectfully forward this will with the recommendation that it be ___approved.

John R. Brennan
Supt. & Spl. Disb. Agent.

Department of The Interior,
Office of Indian Affairs, Washington,

The within will of Chief Eagle is recommended for approval in accordance with the provisions of the Act of June 25, 1910 (36 Stats. L., 855-6) as amended by Act of February 14, 1913 (37 Stats. L., 678).

Respectfully,
EB Meritt
Assistant Commissioner

Department of The Interior
Office of The Secretary DEC 22 1914

The within will of Chief Eagle is hereby approved in accordance with the provisions of the Act of June 25, 1910 (36 Stats. L., 855-6) as amended by Act of February 14, 1913 (37 Stats. L., 678).

Bo Sweeney
Assistant Secretary

▲ ▼ ▲ ▼ ▲ ▼ ▲ ▼ ▲ ▼ ▲ ▼ ▲ ▼

GA-THU-BAE or WILLIAM THOMAS

In the Name of God, Amen.

I, Ga-thu-bae or William Thomas of (Blank) in the County of **Thurston**, State of **Nebraska** , being of sound mind and memory, and considering the uncertainty of this frail and transitory life, do therefore make, ordain, publish and declare this to be my last **WILL AND TESTAMENT**:

FIRST, I order and direct that my Execut...... hereinafter named, pay all my just debts and funeral expenses as soon after my decease as conveniently may be.

SECOND, After the payment of such funeral expenses and debts, I give, devise and bequeath

To my beloved wife Me-grae-to-in Thomas I give the use during her life all of the south-west quarter of section eight (8) township twenty four (24) north of range ten (10) east of 6th P.M. containing 160 acres of land in Thurston County, in the state of Nebraska.

THIRD. At the death of my said wife I divide my said allotment of land as follows,

To my son Theodore Thomas the north-west 40 acres of said quarter sec.

To my son Charles Thomas the south-west 40 acres of said quarter sec.

To my daughter Lottie Lasley the nort-east[sic] 40 acres of said quarter sec.

To my daughter Fanny Baxter the south-east 40 acres of said quarter sec, together with all of the improvements thereon.

LASTLY, I make, constitute and appoint **Thomas R. Ashley of Decatur, Nebraska** to be Executor of this my last Will and Testament, hereby revoking all former Wills by me made.

IN WITNESS WHEREOF, I have hereunto subscribed my name and affixed my seal, this **7th** day of **January** in the year of our Lord, one thousand nine hundred **fourteen.** [thumb print] *his mark*
Ga-Thu-bae William Thomas

This instrument was on the day of the date thereof, signed, published and declared by the said testator **Ga-thu-bae or William Thomas**, to be his last Will and Testament, in the presence of us who at his request have subscribed our names thereto as witnesses in his presence and in the presence of each other.

James M Lambert
Peter (Last name illegible)
Mary Tyndall Mitchell

State of Nebraska   ()
                  () ss,
Burt County   ()

Indian Wills, 1911 – 1921 Book Two
Records of The Bureau of Indian Affairs

Mary T. Mitchell being first duly sworn says that she is a member of the Omaha Tribe of Indians and speaks and understands both the english[sic] and Omaha Indian language and that she interpreted the contents of this will to the testator William Thomas before he affixed his thumb mark to the same.

Witness my hand this 22nd day of August 1917.

Mary Tyndall Mitchell

Subscribed to in my presence and sworn to before me this 22nd day of August 1917.

William B Barnard
Notary Public

Probate
30149-19

Department of The Interior,
Office of Indian Affairs, Washington,

MAY 19 1919

The within will of Ga-thu-bae or William Thomas, Omaha allottee No. 778, is respectfully recommended for approval in accordance with the provisions of the Act of June 25, 1910 (36 Stats. L., 855-6) as amended by Act of February 14, 1913 (37 Stats. L., 678).

Respectfully,
EB Meritt
Assistant Commissioner

Department of The Interior
Office of The Secretary MAY 20 1919

The within will of Ga-thu-bae or William Thomas, Omaha allottee No. 778 is hereby approved in accordance with the provisions of the Act of June 25, 1910 (36 Stats. L., 855-6) as amended by Act of February 14, 1913 (37 Stats. L., 678). By the terms of the will the SW/4 of Sec. 8, T. 24 N., R. 10 E., 6th P.M., Nebraska, passes for life to testator's widow, Megraetoin (Megraetae) Thomas, and after her death the NW/4 thereof to his son Theodore Thomas, the SW/4 to his son, Charles Thomas, the NE/4 to his daughter, Lottie Lasley, the SE/4 to his daughter, Fannie Baxter.

SG Hopkins
Assistant Secretary

▲▼▲▼▲▼▲▼▲▼▲▼▲▼▲▼

<u>MARY TYNER nee VESSER</u>

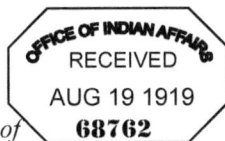

Codicil No. 1 to
Last Will and Testament of
Mary Tyner

OFFICE OF INDIAN AFFAIRS
RECEIVED
AUG 19 1919
68762

Know all men by these presents:

That I, Mary Tyner, nee Vesser, being of sound mind and disposing will but conscious of the uncertainty of life and desiring to make final disposition of my property, hereby publish and declare this to be a codicil to my last will and testament heretofore made, which will is in the hands of the Shawnee Indian Agency, as follows, to wit:-

1. That in case of the death of the said Elijah A Tyner, without issue, I hereby will and bequeath unto my beloved daughter, Mary Manyow, all my property, real and personal, by me owned, and wherever located.

2. In all other respects, I hereby ratify and confirm my said last will and testament.

Witness my hand to this my last will and testament, consisting of one (1) sheet of paper this April 20, 1918.

Mary Tyner

Witnesses to the signature of Mary Tyner, nee Vesser, to this her last will and testament who subscribed the same in our presence and at the same time declared to us the same to be her last will and testament, and unto which we subscribe our names as witnesses at her request and in her presence and in the presence of each other.

Witness our hands this April 30ᵗʰ 1918.   *Post Office*

    Harry Vandecar   *Tecumseh, Okla R#5*
    Joseph (Illegible)   *Maud, Okla R#2*
    S.F Bailey   *Maud, Okla*

Department of The Interior,
Office of Indian Affairs, Washington, APR -4 1919

The within codicil to the will of Mary Tyner, is submitted for approval under the Act of June 25, 1910 (36 Stats. L., 855-6) as modified by Act of February 14, 1913, 37 Stats. L., 678), and the Regulations of the Department.

Respectfully,
EB Meritt
Assistant Commissioner

55

Indian Wills, 1911 – 1921 Book Two
Records of The Bureau of Indian Affairs

Department of The Interior
Office of The Secretary APR 10 1919

The within codicil to the will of Mary Tyner is hereby approved under the Act of June 25, 1910 (36 Stats. L., 855-6) as modified by Act of February 14, 1913 (37 Stats. L., 678), and the Regulations of the Department.

SG Hopkins
Assistant Secretary

▲▼▲▼▲▼▲▼▲▼▲▼▲▼▲▼

JOSEPHINE BOYNTON BLACKMAN

LAST WILL AND TESTAMENT OF JOSEPHINE BOYNTON BLACKMAN

I, Jospehine[sic] Boynton Blackman, of Canadian County, Oklahoma, being at this time of sound and disposing mind, and desiring to make disposition of my property and business affairs, do hereby make, publish and declare the following to be my last WILL AND TESTAMENT, hereby revoking any and all wills by me heretofore made.

First: I hereby give and bequeath to my husband, John Blackman, my "New Ear*d*" automobile, and hereby direct that there be paid to him from moneys now to my credit in the Agency Office at Concho, Oklahoma, the sum of One thousand Dollars. I further direct that the contract now existing between myself and John Keller, for the building and construction of a dwelling house, at a cost of Seven Hundred dollars, be carried into effect, and the building constructed accordingly: Further that said building, when complete, as well as the ten acres of ground on which said building is to be located, and which was heretofore deeded to my by said John Blackman, is hereby given and bequeathed to my husband, John Blackman. The description of the above mentioned ten acres is as follows:

Second: I hereby give and bequeath to my Uncle, American Horse any and all interest I may have in any and all of the horses, wagons, mules, harness and agricultural implements purchased by my mother, Medicine Sack sometime ago for the use of said American Horse.

Third: I further give and bequeath to my Uncle, American Horse the sum of Five hundred dollars; the same to be paid to him direct from any moneys now to my credit or that my hereafter be placed to the credit of my estate. This bequest is made as a small recognition of his many kindnesses to me and to my mother and brothers.

I further give an[sic] bequeath to my brother Richard Boynton, all my interest, as shown by the records at the Agency as follows:

A one-third interest in the allotment of Arapahoe Woman, No. 539, being the NW1/4 Sec. 33, T. 15, T. 13, 160 acres.

A one-third interest in the allotment of Medicine Sack, No. 252, being the S1/2 of SE1/4 Sec. 7, T. 12, R. 7, 80 acres.

A one-sixth interest in the allotment of Mrs. American Horse, No. 251, being the SE1/4, Sec. 6, T. 13, R. 12, 160 acres.

A 2/52 interest in the allotment of Red Woman, No. 509, being the E1/2 of SW1/4 and lots 3 & 4, Sec. 7, T. 12, R. 7, 155.58a.

A 1/6 interest in the allotment of Mrs. Chester Arthur, No. 973 being the E1/2 of Sw1/4 and lots 3 & 4, in Sec. 18, T. 16, R. 11, containing 152.57 acres.

A one-third interest in the allotment of Northern, or Sadie Alfrey, No. 166, being the N1/2 of SW1/4 of Sec. 8, T. 15, R. 8, 80a.

A one-third interest in the allotment of Lame, No. 557, being the SW1/4 of Sec. 22, T. 15, R. 13, 160 acres.

A one-third interest in the Waldo Reed allotment, No. 1894, being the NW1/4 of Sec. 27, T. 17, R. 12, containing 160 acres.

I further direct that in case of my death any and all just debts, including funeral expenses &c., shall be paid from any moneys to the credit of my estate, and that all the remainder and residue of my estate, of whatsoever kind or character shall become the property of my brother Richard Boynton.

In witness whereof I, Josephine Boynton Blackman have to this my last will and testament, subscribed my name on this the Seventh day of April, 1917.

Witnesses   *Josephine Boynton Blackman*

   E. M Goss

   (*Illegible*) *Scott*

PROBATE
51862-17
 W H G

Department of The Interior,
Office of Indian Affairs, Washington,
              APR -3 1919

Indian Wills, 1911 – 1921 Book Two
Records of The Bureau of Indian Affairs

It is recommended that the within will of Josephine Boynton (Blackman), deceased allottee No. 1484-B of the Cheyenne-Arapahoe Tribe, dated April 7, 1917, be approved in accordance with the Act of June 25, 1910 (36 Stats. L., 855-6) as amended by Act of February 14, 1913 (37 Stats. L., 678).

Respectfully,
EB Meritt
Assistant Commissioner

Department of The Interior
Office of The Secretary APR 14 1919

The within will of Josephine Boynton (Blackman), deceased allottee No. 1484-B of the Cheyenne-Arapahoe Tribe, dated April 7, 1917 is approved in accordance with the Act of June 25, 1910 (36 Stats. L., 855-6) as amended by Act of February 14, 1913 (37 Stats. L., 678).

S G Hopkins
Assistant Secretary

▲▼▲▼▲▼▲▼▲▼▲▼▲▼

ANDREW SMITH
WILL OF ANDREW SMITH.
Siletz Allottee No. 401.
--o--

I, Andrew Smith, an Indian man, residing on the Siletz Reservation, Oregon, being of legal age, (Records show 66 years), of sound mind and acting under no duress or undue influence, do hereby voluntarily declare this to be my last will and testament.

I give, devise and bequeath unto my step-son, Fred Freeman, all my own allotment, No. 401, that I own at this time, described as Lot No. 9, Section 2, and Lots No. 14, 15 and 16, Section 3, T. 7 S. R. 11 W of Williamette Meridian, containing 58.01 acres.

I give, devise and bequeath unto my wife, Annie Smith, all of my interest in the Foster Smith Allotment, No. 403, described as the S1/2 of SW1/4, Section 8, T. 10 S. R. 9 W of Williamette Meridian, containing 81.50 acres. (Law-Heir. 111099-15, T D M).

I give, devise and bequeath unto my wife, Annie Smith, any and all personal property that I may possess at the time of my death.

Witness My hand and seal, this 23d day of November, 1917, at Siletz, Oregon.

His right

Andrew Smith [thumb print]

WITNESSES TO SIGNATURE:

Thumb mark

    R D Burgess
        Siletz, Ore.
    Arthur Bensell
        Siletz, Ore.

Signed, sealed, published and declared by Andrew Smith, as and for his last will and testament, in our presence and in the presence of each of us, on this 23d day of November, 1917.

        R D Burgess
            Siletz, Oregon
        Arthur Bensell
            Siletz, Oregon

Codicil to be attached to and become a part of the Will executed by Andrew Smith, Siletz Allottee No. 401, on Novemver[sic] 23, 1917.

---o---

I, Andrew Smith, Siletz Allottee No. 401, being of legal age, of sound mind and acting under no duress or undue influence, do hereby voluntarily declare that it is my wish and intention and d hereby modify and change my last will and testament, dated and executed on November 23d, 1917, to include my cousin, Jane Bensell, as one of the beneficiaries under said will, be hereinafter provided.

I give, devise and bequeath unto my cousin, Jane Bensell, wife of Ed. Bensell, twenty acres of the Foster Smith allotment No. 403, which I inherited, (Law-Heir. 111099-15), the said twenty acres being a strip of even width extending across the west and of the S1/2 of the SW1/4 of Section 8, T. 10 S. R. W. of Williamette Meridian.

It is my wish that this codicil be considered in connection with and become a part of my Will dated November 23, 1917, and I hereby reaffirm and declare said instrument as modified by this codicil to be my last will and testament.

Witness my hand and seal, this *25th* day of May, 1918, at Siletz, Oregon.   His Right

Andrew Smith [Thumb print]

WITNESSES TO SIGNATURE: Thumb Mark.

F M Carter
        Siletz, Oregon
Arthur Bensell
        Siletz, Oregon.

Signed, sealed published and declared by Andrew Smith, as and for his last will and testament or codicil modifying his Will dated November 23d, 1917, in our presence and in the presence of each of us, this *25th* day May, 1918.

F M Carter
Siletz, Oregon
Arthur Bensell
Siletz, Oregon.

Probate 86827-18

Department of The Interior,
Office of Indian Affairs, Washington, MAR 25 1919

The within will and codicil thereto of Andrew Smith, Siletz allottee No. 401, is hereby recommended for approval in accordance with the Act of June 25, 1910 (36 Stats. L., 855-6) as modified by Act of February 14, 1913, 37 Stats. L., 678).

Respectfully,
EB Meritt
Assistant Commissioner

Department of The Interior
Office of The Secretary

The within will and codicil thereto of Andrew Smith, Siletz allottee No. 401, is hereby approved in accordance with the Act of June 25, 1910 (36 Stats. L., 855-6) as modified by Act of February 14, 1913 (37 Stats. L., 678).

SG Hopkins
Assistant Secretary

▲▼▲▼▲▼▲▼▲▼▲▼▲▼▲▼

Indian Wills, 1911 – 1921 Book Two
Records of The Bureau of Indian Affairs

<u>BESSIE RINGING SHIELD</u>

WILL

I, **Bessie Ringing Shield,** of Pine Ridge Agency, South Dakota, Allottee number **2420** do hereby make and declare this to be my last will and testament, in accordance with Section 2 of the Act of June 25, 1910, (36 Stat. 855-858), and Act of February 14, 1913, (Public No. 381), hereby revoking all former wills made by me:

1. I hereby direct that, as soon as possible after my decease, that all my debts and funeral and testamentary expenses be paid out of my personal estate.

2. I give and devise my allotment on the Pine Ridge Reservation, South Dakota, described as follows:
    The east half of Section eighteen in Township thirty-eight north of Range thirty-three west of the Sixth Principal Meridian, S. Dak. Containing three hundred twenty acres:
    And all the inherited land I am entitle to or interested.

In the following manner:

    To be equally divided to my four children, Moses Ringing-shield, Lucy Ringing-shield, William Ringing-shield and John Ringing-shield.

    " I desire to include this statement, I desire to have Bear-run-in-woods and wife to be my children's guardian: "

3. I give and bequeath all of my personal property of whatsoever nature and wheresoever situated unto **my four children, Moses, Lucy, William and John Ringing-shield. (to be equally divided)**

4. All the rest of my property, real or personal, now possessed or hereafter acquired, of whatsoever nature and wheresoever situated, I hereby give, devise and bequeath unto **my four children, Moses, Lucy, William and John Ringing-shield. Robert Crazy-thunder, my husband who has deserted me, while I am sick in bed, left and join the show, no desire to support me. I do no desire to share of my property both in real and personally.**

In witness whereof I have hereunto set my hand this **25th** day of **April,** 1916.   her mark.
Bessie Ringing-shield   [thumb print]

The above statement was this **25th** day of **April,** 1916, signed and published by **Bessie Ringing Shield** as **her** last will and testament, in the joint-process of the undersigned, the said **Bessie Ringing Shield** then being of sound and vigorous mind and free from any constraint or compulsion; whereupon we, being without any interest in the matter other than friendship, and being well acquainted with **her,** but not members of **her** family, immediately subscribed our names hereto in the presence of each other and of the said testator, for the purpose of attesting the said will, as **she** requested us to do.

	Post Office
Chas D Parkhurst	Porcupine, S. Dak.
Oliver J Eagle	Porcupine, S. Dak.

Pine Ridge, South Dakota,

Sept. 26 - 1918

I hereby certify that I have fully inquired into the mental competency of the Indian, signing the above will; the circumstances attending the execution of the will; the influence that may have induced its execution, and the names of those entitled to share in the estate under the law of descent in South Dakota; reasons for the disposition of the property proposed by the will, differing from disposition had the property descended by operation of law.

I respectfully forward this will with the recommendation that it be *dis*approved.

Henry M Tidwell
Supt. & Spl. Disb. Agent.

P R O B A T E .

80755-18

Department of The Interior,
Office of Indian Affairs, Washington,

APR 1 1919

Indian Wills, 1911 – 1921 Book Two
Records of The Bureau of Indian Affairs

The within will of BESSIE RINGING SHIELD is hereby recommended for *dis*approval in accordance with the provisions of the Act of June 25, 1910 (36 Stats. L., 855-6) as amended by Act of February 14, 1913 (37 Stats. L., 678).

Respectfully,
EB Meritt
Assistant Commissioner

Department of The Interior
Office of The Secretary APR 10 1919

The within will is hereby approved in accordance with the provisions of the Act of June 25, 1910 (36 Stats. L., 855-6) as amended by Act of February 14, 1913 (37 Stats. L., 678).

SG Hopkins
Assistant Secretary

▲▼▲▼▲▼▲▼▲▼▲▼▲▼

LUCY WANATU

I *Lucy Wanatu* being of full age and of sound and disposing mind and memory do declare this to be my last will and testament.

First:- I direct that all my just debts be paid.

Second:- I will and bequeath all my property of which I may die seized as follows: Funds on deposit to my credit as Individual Indian Money under the supervision of the Superintendent of the Sac & Fox Sanatorium, Toledo, Iowa, and any other property which I may have at the time of my death.
To my brother George Young Bean one half (1/2); to my father Young Bean one-half (1/2)

I hereby nominate the Superintendent of the Sac & Fox Reservation, to be my executor, without bond, of this my last will and testament.

In witness whereof I have hereunto set my hand and seal to this my last will and testament, this 30th day of May 1918. *her*

Lucy Wanatu [thumb print]
thumb

Witness:
> *Robert Lyon*
> *Earl Lyon*

We hereby certify that on this 30th day of May, 1918 in Toledo Township, Tama County Iowa, _____ to us personally known did in our presence make the foregoing instrument and declare same to be her last will and testament: and we at her request and in her presence and in the presence of each other do subscribe our names as witnesses thereto.

> *Robert Lyon*
> *Earl Lyon*

Certificate of Interpreter.

I, *John Papake, Jr.*, do solemnly swear that I have interpreted the attched[sic] will and testament from the English into the Indian language and that to the best of my knowledge and belief *Lucy Wanatu* understands the contents of same.

> *John Papake, Jr.*

Subscribed and sworn to before me this 30th day of May 1918.

> *Robert Lyon*
> Notary Public.

My commission expires July 4, 1918.

95041-18

Department of The Interior,
Office of Indian Affairs, Washington,
> APR -8 1919

The within will is hereby recommended for approval in accordance with the provisions of the Act of June 25, 1910 (36 Stats. L., 855-6) as amended by Act of February 14, 1913 (37 Stats. L., 678).

> Respectfully,
> *EB Meritt*
> Assistant Commissioner

Department of The Interior
Office of The Secretary APR -9 1919

The within will is hereby approved in accordance with the provisions of the Act of June 25, 1910 (36 Stats. L., 855-6) as amended by Act of February 14, 1913 (37 Stats. L., 678).

SG Hopkins
Assistant Secretary

▲ ▼ ▲ ▼ ▲ ▼ ▲ ▼ ▲ ▼ ▲ ▼ ▲ ▼

ELLEN CHOW CHOW DIXON

W I L L.

IN THE NAME OF GOD, AMEN:

I, Ellen Chow Chow Dixon, allottee No. 13, of the Quinaielt Indian Reservation, Grays Harbor County, State of Washington, at the age of about 56 years, wife of John Dixon, allottee No. 19, being of sound and disposing mind and memory, and not acting under duress, menace, fraud, or undue influence of any person or persons whatsoever, do make, publish and declare this my Last Will and Testament in manner following, hereby revoking any and all wills heretofore made by me.

I direct that all my just debts and obligations be paid, first and to that end I nominate and appoint, John Dixon, my husband, as Executor of this my last will and testament, and I direct that he be and is hereby empowered to take hold, and be seized and possessed of and vested with the title of my estate for the purpose of carrying into effect this will and without the intervention of any Court or of the issuance of any letters Testamentary or of Administration, except to admit this will to probate and to cause a true inventory of the property of the estate to be filed and notice be published to creditors, all subject to the will of the Indian Department of the United States Government.

I hereby expressly provide, that no bond be given for securing and so far as in any case may be the said Executor be and he is hereby relieved from the supervision of all courts.

I hereby direct in order to secure the payment of my debts, and settlement of said estate that the said Executor be, and he is empowered to make any and all contracts, sales or other instruments necessary to carry out the provisions of my will.

I further give and devise, and bequeath my allottment, No. 13, as follows: To John Dixon, my husband, one-half, the balance to be devided equally among the following relatives: William Mason, one eight,

65

Maggie Cultee, one eight, Rosa Garfield, one eight, Johnson Waukenas, one-eight.

I further give and devise, and bequeath my fishing location, and two canoes to John Dixon, my husband.

I further direct that the said John Dixon, handle my estate until such time as he thinks best to close the same with the approval of the proper authority of the United States Government.

In witness whereof, I have hereunto set my hand and seal this 24th day of December A.D., 1915.

Her right
[thumb print]
thumb mark
Ellen Chow Chow Dixon

The foregoing instrument consisting of one page and a half, or 47 lines, is the last will and testament of Ellen Chow Chow Dixon, and was on the day and year above-named, signed, sealed, published and declared to be her last will and testament by the said Ellen Chow Chow Dixon, in the presence of us, who, at her request and in her presence, and in the presence of each other, have subscribed our names as witnesses thereto, and we do hereby solembly[sic] certify that the said Ellen Chow Chow Dixon was not acting under duress or restraint, and was of sound and disposing mind and memory.

Lell Hardy
Financial Clerk
Taholah, Washington.

J. H. Hulett
Day School Teacher
Taholah, Washington.

E E. Ogden, Jr.

77893-1918

Department of The Interior,
Office of Indian Affairs, Washington,

APR 18 1919

The within will is hereby recommended for approval in accordance with the provisions of the Act of June 25, 1910 (36 Stats. L., 855-6) as amended by Act of February 14, 1913 (37 Stats. L., 678), with the exception of an executor is recognized in connection therewith.

Respectfully,
EB Meritt
Assistant Commissioner

Department of The Interior
Office of The Secretary APR 19 1919

The within will is hereby approved in accordance with the provisions of the Act of June 25, 1910 (36 Stats. L., 855-6) as amended by Act of February 14, 1913 (37 Stats. L., 678), with the exception of an executor is recognized in connection therewith.

SG Hopkins
Assistant Secretary

▲▼▲▼▲▼▲▼▲▼▲▼▲▼

PAHAMANIWIN

W I L L.

OFFICE OF INDIAN AFFAIRS
RECEIVED
DEC 11 1911
106173

I, **PAHAMANIWIN**, #2597, at this time a resident of Norton County, North Dakota, and being of sound and disposing mind and memory, do make, publish and declare this to be my last will, hereby revoking all former wills by me made.

Item 1. I give and devise to **MRS. BLACK TIGER**, my **NEICE**, in lieu of her rights by descent or otherwise in my real property, the following described lands: **E/2 W/2 and Lots 1, 2, 3, & 4 of Sec. 31, T. 132, N., R. 82 W., 5th P.M., in North Dakota, containing 306.52 acres.**

Witness my hand and seal this **Sixth** day of **December, 1911**, in the County of **Norton**, State of North Dakota.   Her
Witnesses: PAHAMANIWIN [thumb print]
Wm Heinull   mark
Clark Yates

The foregoing instrument, signed, sealed and acknowledged by said testatrix, as and for her last will, in our presence, who, at her request, in her presence, and in the presence of each other, have subscribed our names as witnesses thereto this Sixth day of December, 1911.

Witness: *Albert Noheart*
Wm Heinull   *Fort Yates, N.D.*
Clark Yates

Indian Wills, 1911 – 1921 Book Two
Records of The Bureau of Indian Affairs

Subscribed and sworn to before me this 6th day of December, 1911.

J Y Hamilton
Superintendent.

Probate 106173-11

Department of The Interior,
Office of Indian Affairs, Washington,
APR 18 1919

The within will of Pa ha man I win is hereby recommended for approval in accordance with the provisions of the Act of June 25, 1910 (36 Stats. L., 855-6) as amended by Act of February 14, 1913 (37 Stats. L., 678).

EB Meritt
Assistant Commissioner

Department of The Interior
Office of The Secretary APR 21 1919

The within will is hereby approved in accordance with the provisions of the Act of June 25, 1910 (36 Stats. L., 855-6) as amended by Act of February 14, 1913 (37 Stats. L., 678).

SG Hopkins
Assistant Secretary

▲▼▲▼▲▼▲▼▲▼▲▼▲▼▲▼

SARRAH LONG DOG nee BIRD HEAD

Original
WILL

Died 3-20-17

OFFICE OF INDIAN AFFAIRS
RECEIVED
MAY 21 1917
19930

I, **Sarrah Long Dog (nee Bird Head)** of Pine Ridge Agency, South Dakota, Allottee number **491** do hereby make and declare this to be my last will and testament, in accordance with Section 2 of the Act of June 25, 1910, (36 stat. 855-858) and Act of February 14, 1913, (Public No. 381), hereby revoking all former wills made by us:

1. I hereby direct that as soon as possible after my decease, that all my debts, funeral and testamentary expenses be paid out of my personal estate.

2. I give and devise my allotment on the Pine Ridge Reservation, South Dakota, described as follows:

NE/4 of Section 32, Twnp-38, North Ranged 42, W. of the 6th P.M. in South Dakota. containing 160 acres.
in the following manner:
I desire to will to My father John Bird Head and to my son Neville Long Dog, to be even devided between them.

3. I give and bequeath all of my personal property of whatsoever nature and wheresoever situated unto **My father John Bird Head and my son Neville Long Dog.**

4. All the rest of my property, real or personal, now possessed or hereafter acquired, of whatsoever nature and wheresoever situated, I hereby give, devise and bequeath unto **my father John Bird Head and to my son Neville Long Bull**[sic]

In witness whereof I have hereunto set my hand this **19th** day of **M A R C H** 1917

her

Sarah Long Dog	[thumb print]
(nee Bird Head)	*mark*

The above statement was, this **19th** day of **M a r c h** 1917 signed and published by **Sarah Long Dog (nee Bird Head)** as **her** last will and testament, in the joint presence of the undersigned, the said **Sarah Long Dog** then being of sound and vigorous mid and free from any constraint or compulsion; whereupon we, being without any interest in the matter other than friendship, and being well acquainted with **her** but not members of **her** family, immediately subscribed our names hereto in the presence of each other and of the said testator, for the purpose of attesting the said will, as requested us to do. And that I, **Chas. D. Parkhurst** at the testa.....'s request have written **her** name in ink, and that **I** affixed **her** thumb-marks. *(Note: "........" are areas left blank on the original.)*

Post Office Address

Chas D Parkhurst	**PORCUPINE, S. D.**
Oliver J Eagle	**PORCUPINE, S. D.**

Pine Ridge, South Dakota.

I hereby certify that I have fully inquired into the mental competency of the Indian signing the above will; the circumstances attending the execution of the will; the influence that may have induced its execution, and the names of those entitled to share in the estate under the law of descent in South Dakota: reasons for the disposition of the property proposed by the will differing from disposition had the property descended by operation of law.

I respectfully forward this will with the recommendation that it be *dis* approved.

AM Landman

Acting Supt. & Spl. Disb. Agent.

Probate
49930-17
V L D

Department of The Interior,
Office of Indian Affairs, Washington,

APR 19 1919

The within will of Sarah Long Dog, nee Bird Head, is hereby recommended for approval in accordance with the provisions of the Act of June 25, 1910 (36 Stats. L., 855-6) as amended by Act of February 14, 1913 (37 Stats. L., 678).

EB Meritt
Assistant Commissioner

Department of The Interior
Office of The Secretary APR 25 1919

The within will of Sarah Long Dog is hereby approved in accordance with the provisions of the Act of June 25, 1910 (36 Stats. L., 855-6) as amended by Act of February 14, 1913 (37 Stats. L., 678).

SG Hopkins
Assistant Secretary

▲▼▲▼▲▼▲▼▲▼▲▼▲▼▲▼

BIN DI GI I ASH

RESERVE WIS.
Lac Courte Oreilles Reservation.

The last will and testament of Bin di gi i ash a Lac Courte Oreilles Indian of the Chippewa Tribe.

I Bin di gi i ash. Being of sound mind, do of my own free will without persuasion or influence, bequeath to my grand daughter Jennie Martin, the daughter of my son Joseph Martin, my allotment #369 comprising the following described lands,
SW1/4 of the SE1/4, and SE1/4 of the SW1/4, Sec. one T. 39 R.. 8,

situated on the Lac Courte Orielles Reservation in Sawyer County
Wisconsin.

Signed Bin di gi i ash.

his
thumb
mark

Witnesses to signature.

A.E. Whiteis   Govt. Farmer

Willis Isham   Indian Police

Reserve Wis.

Dated this 17th day of February 1914.

STATE OF WISCONSIN

COUNTY OF SAWYER   } ss

> **OFFICE OF INDIAN AFFAIRS**
> **RECEIVED**
> **JAN -3 1919**
> **1143**

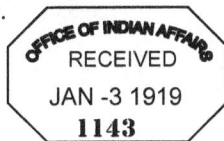

I, *John K Swenson* County Judge for Sawyer County, Wisconsin,
the same being a court of record, do hereby certify, that I have carefully
compared the annexed and foregoing *will and certificate of probate* with
the original now on file in my office, and, that *it is a* correct and true cop*y*
thereof.

In witness whereof, I have hereunto set my hand,
and affixed the seal of said court this *23d* day of *Dec 1918*

John K Swenson
COUNTY JUDGE

State of Wisconsin   )

Sawyer County   ) ss   Be it remembered that on the 6th day of
February, A.D. 1917, at the City of Hayward in said County, lursuant[sic]
to Notice duly given, as required by law, at a regular term of the County
Court of said County of Sawyer, Willis Isham one of the subscribing
witnesses to the last will and testament of Bin di gi i ash, late, of the
Town of Reserve, in said County, deceased hereunto annexed was
produced and duly sworn and examined, and the proofs having been
heard before said Court, and the Court having therupon[sic] found that
said instrument was in all things duly executed as his last will and
testament by the said Bin di gi i ash, thereupon said instrument was by
the order and decree of said Court duly allowed and admitted to probate,
as and for the last will and testament of Bin di gi I ash, deceased.

Seal

In Testimony Whereof, I have hereunto set my hand
and affixed the seal of the County Court of said
County, at the city of Hayward, this 6th day of
February A. D. 1917.

Sgd. John K. Swenson, County Judge.

Probate
13826-17

Department of The Interior,
Office of Indian Affairs, Washington,

I have the honor to recommend that the certified copy of the will of Bindigiiash, or Bindigeiash, be laid before the President of the United States for his approval in accordance with the Treaty of September 30, 1854 (10 Stats. L. 1109).

Cate Sells
Commissioner

Department of The Interior
Office of The Secretary APR -3 1919

I have the honor to recommend that the certified copy of the will of Bindigiiash, or Bindigeiash, be approved in accordance with the Treaty of September 30, 1854 (10 Stats. L. 1109).

Franklin K Payne
Secretary

The White House,
    16 April 1919
Approved:
    Woodrow Wilson

▲▼▲▼▲▼▲▼▲▼▲▼▲▼▲▼

COMES BACK NIGHT

WILL

___

    I, **Comes Back Night** of Pine Ridge Agency, South Dakota, Allottee number ...... do hereby make and declare this to be my last will and testament, in accordance with Section 2 of the Act of June 25, 1910, (36 stat. 855-858) and Act of February 14, 1913, (Public No. 381), hereby revoking all former wills made by us:

1. I hereby direct that as soon as possible after my decease, that all my debts, funeral and testamentary expenses be paid out of my personal estate.

2. I give and devise my allotment on the Pine Ridge Reservation, South Dakota, described as follows:
    S/2 Section 14, Twnp-36, N. Range 43 West of the 6th P.M. in

South Dakota. Containing 320 acres.

in the following manner:

    I desire to will SW/4 to Iron Cloud, and the SE/4 to be devided to the following; Red Necklace, Runs For Hills and Holy Bear, James Fools-Crow.

3. I give and bequeath all of my personal property of whatsoever nature and wheresoever situated unto **Iron Cloud**

4. All the rest of my property, real or personal, now possessed or hereafter acquired, of whatsoever nature and wheresoever situated, I hereby give, devise and bequeath unto **Iron Cloud**

In witness whereof I have hereunto set my hand this **12th** day of **March,** 1917

her

Comes Back Night   [thumb print]

Comes Back Night   *mark*

    The above statement was, this **12th** day of **March,** 1917 signed and published by **Comes Back Night** as **her** last will and testament, in the joint presence of the undersigned, the said **Comes Back Night** then being of sound and vigorous mid and free from any constraint or compulsion; whereupon we, being without any interest in the matter other than friendship, and being well acquainted with **her** but not members of **her** family, immediately subscribed our names hereto in the presence of each other and of the said testator, for the purpose of attesting the said will, as requested us to do. And that I, **have** at the testa.....'s request have written **her** name in ink, and that **I** affixed **her** thumb-marks. *(Note: "........" are area left blank on the original.)*

Post Office Address

Chas D Parkhurst	**Porcupine, S. D.**
John Rock	**Porcupine, S. D.**

Pine Ridge, South Dakota.

October 10, 1918

    I hereby certify that I have fully inquired into the mental competency of the Indian signing the above will; the circumstances attending the execution of the will; the influence that may have induced its execution, and the names of those entitled to share in the estate under the law of descent in South Dakota: reasons for the disposition of the property proposed by the will differing from disposition had the property descended by operation of law.

Indian Wills, 1911 – 1921 Book Two
Records of The Bureau of Indian Affairs

I respectfully forward this will with the recommendation that it be approved.

(Signature Illegible)
Supt. & Spl. Disb. Agent.

Probate
83058-18
V L D

Department of The Interior,
Office of Indian Affairs, Washington,

MAY 8 1919

The within will of Comes Back Night, is hereby recommended for approval in accordance with the provisions of the Act of June 25, 1910 (36 Stats. L., 855-6) as amended by Act of February 14, 1913 (37 Stats. L., 678).

EB Meritt
Assistant Commissioner

Department of The Interior
Office of The Secretary MAY 17 1919

The within will of Comes Back Night is hereby approved in accordance with the provisions of the Act of June 25, 1910 (36 Stats. L., 855-6) as amended by Act of February 14, 1913 (37 Stats. L., 678).

SG Hopkins
Assistant Secretary

▲▼▲▼▲▼▲▼▲▼▲▼▲▼▲▼

BYRON RED EAGLE

Busby, Mont., Aug 2nd 1917

To Whom it May Concern:-

Greetings, In the presence of Peter Twobirds and Ira Blackbird I make this my last will and testament:-

The land which I have been occupying together with all there is on the same I give to my son Willis who is to occupy in my stead when I have passed away.

I also bequeath to him all my stock both cattle and horses, with the exception of a heifer of the Pine Ridge stock which I give to Mrs. Bessie Sioux.

I do not want Strangeowl to take anything from the place, nor is he to make any hay on the place, I do not want him to have any share in any of my property

Byron Red Eagle [thumb print]

74

Indian Wills, 1911 – 1921 Book Two
Records of The Bureau of Indian Affairs

                                                          his
                                    Peter Two Birds [thumb print]
                    Witnessed by   mark
                                    Issac Blackbird [thumb print]
Written by *G.A. Lissocheld*
        Missionary   *Died Aug 21, 1919*

Probate
27638-18
MHW

Approved will,
Byron Red Eagle,
Tongue River, Mont.

Department of The Interior,
Office of Indian Affairs, Washington,
                                   APR 28 1919
The within will of Byron Red Eagle, is hereby recommended for approval
in accordance with the provisions of the Act of June 25, 1910 (36 Stats.
L., 855-6) as amended by Act of February 14, 1913 (37 Stats. L., 678).
                                   EB Meritt
                                   Assistant Commissioner

Department of The Interior
Office of The Secretary   MAY -6 1919

Pursuant to the provisions of the Act of June 25, 1910 (36 Stats. L., 855-
6) as amended by Act of February 14, 1913 (37 Stats. L., 678), and the
regulations of the Department, I hereby approve the within will of Byron
Red Eagle, deceased unallotted northern Cheyenne Indian of the Tongue
River Reservation in Montana.
                                   SG Hopkins
                                   Assistant Secretary

▲▼▲▼▲▼▲▼▲▼▲▼▲▼▲▼
BEANS or OMNICA
                        Lakeview S.D. Nov 19th 16
        This is what Beans desires me to say in regards to his will, he is
yet in good sound mind, he want[sic] to have his son <u>Noisy</u> <u>Owl</u> *have*
where he leaves[sic] that is his land, and whatever money will be left
after his debts are paid

75

Done before me this day Nov 19th 16

Witness --

> *Mary C Scovel, Housekeeper*
> *Henry Iron Star*
> *Fannie White Hawk*

Beans
[thumb print] *His mark*

Probate
44190-18
2794-16
 MHW

Approved will Beans or
Omnica, Rosebud, S.Dak.

Department of The Interior,
Office of Indian Affairs, Washington,

APR 29 1919

The within will of Beans or Omnica, deceased Rosebud Sioux allottee No. 1747 is hereby recommended for approval in accordance with the provisions of the Act of June 25, 1910 (36 Stats. L., 855-6) as amended by Act of February 14, 1913 (37 Stats. L., 678), and the regulations of the Department.

> *EB Meritt*
> Assistant Commissioner

Department of The Interior
Office of The Secretary MAY -6 1919

Pursuant to the provisions of the Act of June 25, 1910 (36 Stats. L., 855-6) as amended by Act of February 14, 1913 (37 Stats. L., 678), and the regulations of the Department, I hereby approve the will of Beans or Omnica, deceased Rosebud Sioux allottee No. 1747.

> *SG Hopkins*
> Assistant Secretary

▲▼▲▼▲▼▲▼▲▼▲▼▲▼▲▼

HIGH CHIEF

<u>LAST WILL AND TESTAMENT OF HIGH CHIEF</u>

IN THE NAME OF GOD, AMEN:

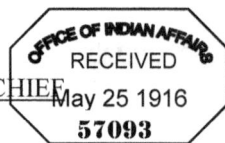

OFFICE OF INDIAN AFFAIRS
RECEIVED
May 25 1916
57093

Indian Wills, 1911 – 1921 Book Two
Records of The Bureau of Indian Affairs

Know all men by these presents, that I, High Chief, a Cheyenne Indian, of Canadian County, Oklahoma, being of lawful age and of sound and disposing mind, and being senisble[sic] of the uncertainty of life and the certainty of death, and desiring to make disposition of all property of which I may die possessed, do hereby make, publish and declare the following to be my last Will and Testament:

I direct the payment of all my just debts and obligations and the expenses of a decent burial, together with a suitable monument and an iron fence around my grave, from such moneys as may be to my credit: The auditing and payment of above to be under the direction of the Superintendent of the Cheyenne and Arapahoe Agency.

I give and bequeath to my adult children, Lillard High Chief, Lela High Chief, Magpie and Flying-Around, one dollar each, to be paid from any money remaining to my credit on the books of the Agency.

I give and bequeath to my minor son, Charlie and my minor daughter Eudora, and to my sister Elk Feathers, all moneys remaining to my credit after payment made as above, share and share alike.

I give and bequeath to my two minor children, Charlie and Eudora, in equal shares, the remainder and residue of all remaining personal property, including two gray horses, one farm wagon, one buggy, one spring wagon, household furniture & I give and bequeath to my son Charlie High Chief, my war bonnet, and to my daughter Eudora a beaded buckskin dress.

I give and bequeath to my daughter Eudora and to my son Charlie, in equal shares all the real estate of which I may die possessed, including two lots in the town of Calumet, with all improvements thereon, also all lands allotted to me at the Pine Ridge Agency, South Dakota and recorded as allotment No. 4728, and including also any other lands or interests in lands of which I may die possessed.

I direct that any and all personal property, stock &c., of any and all kinds now under the jurisdiction of the Pine Ridge Agency be sold for cash, and the proceeds thereof to be placed to the credit of my son Charlie and my daughter Eudora, in equal shares, with the Superintendent at the Cheyenne and Arapahoe Agency, to be expended for their benefit as their necessities mat[sic] require.

In witness whereof I, High Chief, have to this my last WILL and TESTAMENT, subscribed my name this Sixteenth day of May, 1916, clearly understanding all of its provisions, as interpreted to me by Robert Burns, an Indian of my own tribe, and hereby revoking any and all will or wills heretofore made by me.

Witness,   *High Chief*

    W.W. Scott

    JS Bonnim

Subscribed by High Chief in the presence of us, the undersigned, and declared by him to be his last will and testament, and at the request of High Chief, in her[sic] presence and in the presence of each other, sign our names hereto as witnesses, this 16th day of May, 1916.

                                       JS Bonnim

                                       A.H Spears

                                       W.W. Scott

Probate

57093-16

V L D

Department of The Interior,

Office of Indian Affairs, Washington,

                    MAY 6 1919

The within will of High Chief, is hereby recommended for approval in accordance with the provisions of the Act of June 25, 1910 (36 Stats. L., 855-6) as amended by Act of February 14, 1913 (37 Stats. L., 678), so far as trust property is concerned.

                    EB Meritt

                    Assistant Commissioner

Department of The Interior

Office of The Secretary   APR 25 1919

The within will is hereby approved in accordance with the provisions of the Act of June 25, 1910 (36 Stats. L., 855-6) as amended by Act of February 14, 1913 (37 Stats. L., 678), so far as trust property is concerned.

                    SG Hopkins

                    Assistant Secretary

▲▼▲▼▲▼▲▼▲▼▲▼▲▼▲▼

Probate
46314-18
W H G

Department of The Interior,
Office of Indian Affairs, Washington,
MAY 12 1919
It is recommended that the within will of Olive Hairy Wolf or The Eagle, deceased allottee No. 1014, of the Crow Agency, be approved in accordance with the Act of June 25, 1910 (36 Stats. L., 855-6) as amended by Act of February 14, 1913 (37 Stats. L., 678).

Respectfully,
E B Meritt
Assistant Commissioner

Department of The Interior
Office of The Secretary MAY 15 1919

The within will of Olive Hairy Wolf or The Eagle, deceased allottee No. 1014, of the Crow Agency, is hereby approved in accordance with the Act of June 25, 1910 (36 Stats. L., 855-6) as amended by Act of February 14, 1913 (37 Stats. L., 678).

S G Hopkins
Assistant Secretary

▲▼▲▼▲▼▲▼▲▼▲▼▲▼

FRANKLIN DUPUIS

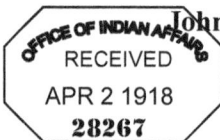

The
John H. Lynds Mill and Elevator Co.
DEALERS IN
GRAIN, COAL AND LIVE STOCK
WHITE CLOUD, KAS.

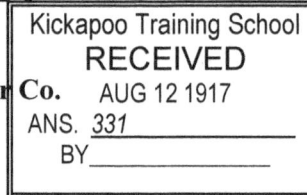

OFFICE OF INDIAN AFFAIRS
RECEIVED
APR 2 1918
28267

Kickapoo Training School
RECEIVED
AUG 12 1917
ANS. *331*
BY_____

Franklin Dupuis "Will made in Triplicate ,

I, Franklin Dupuis, of lawful age, of Brown Co, Kansas, being of sound mind and memory, make and publish this my last will and testament as follows,

First, I will and desire that my funeral expenses and all my debts be paid.

Second, I will, devise and bequeath to my grandson Levi Dupuis, One Dollar.

Third, I will, devise and bequeath to my grandson Louis Dupuis, One Dollar.

Fourth, I will, devise and bequeath to my grandson O.C. Edwards Dupuis, One Dollar.

Fifth, I will, devise and bequeath to my Son Charles Dupuis, all of the balance of my estate, wether[sic] real, mixed or personal of which I may die seased[sic].

Sixth, I here by appoint George Nuzum, my Executor, of this my last will and testament and require that the Probate Court or other authorities shall grant him letters without requiring him to give bond.

Franklin Dupuis His Thumb
[thumb print]
Mark

Witnesseth[sic] my thumb mark this *30* day of *May* 1916.

Franklin Dupuis

We, the undersigned signed our names here to as witnesses at the request of the testator and in his presence and in the presence of each other, who made his thumb mark there to in our presence and declared the same to be his last will and testament.

Ida Ogden
James Whitecloud

Probate
28267-18
W H G
Department of The Interior,
Office of Indian Affairs, Washington,
MAY 13 1919

It is recommended that the within will of Franklin Dupuis (Frank Dupuis), deceased allottee No. 76 of the Iowa tribe, be approved under the Act of June 25, 1910 (36 Stats. L., 855-6) as amended by Act of February 14, 1913 (37 Stats. L., 678).

Respectfully,
E B Meritt
Assistant Commissioner

Department of The Interior
Office of The Secretary MAY 15 1919

The within will of Franklin Dupuis (Frank Dupuis), deceased allottee No. 76 of the Iowa tribe, is hereby approved in accordance with the Act of June 25, 1910 (36 Stats. L., 855-6) as amended by Act of February 14, 1913 (37 Stats. L., 678).

S G Hopkins
Assistant Secretary

▲▼▲▼▲▼▲▼▲▼▲▼▲▼▲▼

DAY

Original
WILL

I, **Day** of Pine Ridge Agency, South Dakota, Allottee number **2027**. Do hereby make and declare this to be my last will and testament, in accordance with Section 2 of the Act of June 25, 1910, (36 stat. 855-858) and Act of February 14, 1913, (Public No. 381), hereby revoking all former wills made by us:

1. I hereby direct that as soon as possible after my decease, that all my debts, funeral and testamentary expenses be paid out of my personal estate.

2. I give and devise my allotment on the Pine Ridge Reservation, South Dakota, described as follows:
 S/2 of Sec. 25, T 40, R 39. 320 acres

 Also inherited land, allotment No. 2026, described as follows:
 All of Sec. 16, T 40, R 38. 640 acres

 Also, inherited land, allotment No. 2028, described as the SW/4 of Sec. 36, T 40, R 39. 160 acres.

in the following manner:
 SE/4 of Sec. 25, T 40, R. 39, to my daughter, Annie R.C.T. Lodge.
 SW/4 of Sec. 25, T 40, R. 39, to my son, Edward Brown.
 N/2 of Sec. 16, T 40, R. 38, to my daughter, Mrs. Black Feather.
 S/2 of Sec. 16, T 40, R. 38, to my son, William Brown.

SW/4 of Sec. 36, T 40, R 39, to my daughter, Jennie Red Feather.

3. I give and bequeath all of my personal property of whatsoever nature and wheresoever situated unto

One ID mare, set of double harness, and issue wagon, to granddaughter Angelina Brown. One ID mare to daughter, Jennie Red Feather.

4. All the rest of my property, real or personal, now possessed or hereafter acquired, of whatsoever nature and wheresoever situated, I hereby give, devise and bequeath unto

my six children, share and share alike.

In witness whereof I have hereunto set my hand this **15th** day of **January** 1916.

her

Day [thumb print]

mark

The above statement was, this **15th** day of **January** 1916 signed and published by **Day** as **her** last will and testament, in the joint presence of the undersigned, the said **Day** then being of sound and vigorous mid and free from any constraint or compulsion; whereupon we, being without any interest in the matter other than friendship, and being well acquainted with **her** but not members of **her** family, immediately subscribed our names hereto in the presence of each other and of the said testator, for the purpose of attesting the said will, as **she** requested us to do. And that I **H.E. Wright** at the testa**trix**'s request have written **her** name in ink, and that **I** affixed **her** thumb-marks.

Post Office Address

H E Wright	**Pine Ridge, S. D.**
J Miller	**Pine Ridge, S. D.**

Pine Ridge, South Dakota.

Jan -3 1916

I hereby certify that I have fully inquired into the mental competency of the Indian signing the above will; the circumstances attending the execution of the will; the influence that may have induced its execution, and the names of those entitled to share in the estate under the law of descent in South Dakota: reasons for the disposition of the property proposed by the will differing from disposition had the property descended by operation of law.

    I respectfully forward this will with the recommendation that it be ___approved.

Henry M Tidwell

Supt. & Spl. Disb. Agent.

Indian Wills, 1911 – 1921 Book Two
Records of The Bureau of Indian Affairs

Probate
5095-16
Department of The Interior,
Office of Indian Affairs, Washington, APR -5 1919

The within will of Day or My Little Cloud, is hereby recommended for approval in accordance with the provisions of the Act of June 25, 1910 (36 Stats. L., 855-6) as amended by Act of February 14, 1913 (37 Stats. L., 678).

EB Meritt
Assistant Commissioner

Department of The Interior
Office of The Secretary APR -8 1919

The within will is hereby approved in accordance with the provisions of the Act of June 25, 1910 (36 Stats. L., 855-6) as amended by Act of February 14, 1913 (37 Stats. L., 678).

SG Hopkins
Assistant Secretary

▲▼▲▼▲▼▲▼▲▼▲▼▲▼▲▼

JENNIE MARTIN

Spokane, Wash
Dec. 2 =1911

My will is that all my just debts and funeral expenses shall by my excutors[sic] *hereinafter named be paid out of my estate.*

I give and bequeath to my niece, Mary Louise Abraham 20 acres of my land which I own on the Spokane Reservation as an allottment, in witness whereof I the said Jennie Martin, have to this my last will and testament consisting of land subscribed my name and affixed my seal this Dec. 2, 1911 in the year of our lord[sic] *nineteen hundred Eleven.*

Signed sealed published and declared be the said Jennie Martin as and for her last will and testament in the presence of us who at her request and in her presence and in the presence of each other have subscribed our name as witness thereunto.

Witness   *Jennie Martin*
W. Baulne   *her* [thumb print] *thumb*
Addie Baulne   *print*

Indian Wills, 1911 – 1921 Book Two
Records of The Bureau of Indian Affairs

91962-17
27983-19

Department of The Interior,
Office of Indian Affairs, Washington,
The within will is hereby recommended for approval according to the provisions of the Act of June 25, 1910 (36 Stats. L., 855-6) as amended by Act of February 14, 1913 (37 Stats. L., 678).

EB Meritt
Assistant Commissioner

Department of The Interior
Office of The Secretary APR -9 1919

The within will is hereby approved according to the provisions of the Act of June 25, 1910 (36 Stats. L., 855-6) as amended by Act of February 14, 1913 (37 Stats. L., 678).

SG Hopkins
Assistant Secretary

▲▼▲▼▲▼▲▼▲▼▲▼▲▼

GEORGE BROWN
THE LAST WILL AND TESTAMENT
of
GEORGE BROWN NO. 2.

I, George Brown, No. 2, being of sound mind, and disposing memory, and of good health, but realizing the uncertainties of life, do hereby make, declare, and publish this MY LAST WILL AND TESTAMENT as follows:

1st.   I desire all my debts that are right and just, including my burial and funeral expenses to be paid.

2nd.   To my wife, Louisa Johnson Brown, I give that part of my allotment described as the NE1/4 of the SW1/4 of Sec. 24, Twp. 26 N. R. 8 E of the 6th P.M. and the NW1/4 of the SE1/4 of Sec. 14, Twp. (?) N. R. 9 E. of the 6th P.M. to be used during her lifetime and at her death to go to my son, George Brown, Jr. and to his heirs forever. In case my wife dies before I do, I wish this part of my allotment to go my son, George Brown, Jr.

3rd.   To my son, George Brown, Jr. I give devise, bequeath that portion of my allotment described as the E1/4 of the SW1/4 of Sec. 27 Twp. 26 N. of R. 8 E. of the 6th P.M. Nebraska and to his heirs forever.

Signed George Brown, No. 2 [thumb print]

The said testator at this time signed his name to the above and foregoing instrument in the presence of the undersigned and at the same time declared it to be his last Will and Testament, and we at his request and in his presence and in the presence of each other do hereby sign our names hereto as attesting witnesses.

Interpreter   *Frank Beaner*

Frank Beaner   *Joseph Grayhair*

Winnebago Agency, Nebraska,
January 12, 1914.

Probate
100422-16
63147-17
 T D M

Department of The Interior,
Office of Indian Affairs, Washington, APR -3 1919

The within will is hereby recommended for approval in accordance with the provisions of the Act of June 25, 1910 (36 Stats. L., 855-6) as amended by Act of February 14, 1913 (37 Stats. L., 678).

EB Meritt
3-FBM-29   Assistant Commissioner

Department of The Interior
Office of The Secretary APR -9 1919

The within will is hereby approved in accordance with the provisions of the Act of June 25, 1910 (36 Stats. L., 855-6) as amended by Act of February 14, 1913 (37 Stats. L., 678).

SG Hopkins
Assistant Secretary

▲▼▲▼▲▼▲▼▲▼▲▼▲▼▲▼

HENRY JONES

Indian Wills, 1911 – 1921 Book Two
Records of The Bureau of Indian Affairs

Will

I, Henry Jones, Otoe and Missouria Indian allottee No. 358 of the State of Oklahoma being of sound mind, but sensible of the uncertainty of life, and desiring to make disposition of my property and affairs while in health and strength, do hereby make and publish and declare the following to be my last will and testament, hereby revoking and cancelling all other or former wills by me at any time made:

First: I direct the payment of all my just debts and funeral expenses.

Second: I give and devise to John Childs Jones the sum of Five dollars (5.00); Vena Barnes the sum of One dollar ($1.00) and Grant C. Barnes the sum of One dollar ($1.00) and all other heirs not mentioned the sum of One dollar each.

Third: I give and devise to my wife Rachel Jones, Ada Pettit and Mary Saunders, my sisters, my entire allotment and my inherited allotment of Sally Jones, deceased, situated on the Otoe Reservation, Oklahoma, divided equally.

Fourth: I give and bequeath to Rachel Jones my wife, one black horse and one gray horse; rack, harness and the remainder of my personal property.

Fifth: I hereby appoint and designate the Superintendent of the Otoe Indian School, sole executor with out bond of this my last will and testament.

In witness whereof, I, Henry Jones, have to this my last will and testament, consisting of three (3) sheets of paper, attested my right thumb mark in the presence of two witnesses.   his
                              Henry Jones [thumb print]
Witnesses   right thumb mark
    Peter C Little
    Norman H. Calvin

Subscribed by Henry Jones, in the presence of us, the undersigned, and at the same time declared by him to be his last will and testament, and we thereupon at the request of Henry Jones, in his presence and in *the presence of each other, sign our names hereto as witnesses this twenty-first day of September, 1918.*

    Horton (Illegible)
    Madge P Dent

Probate
830-19
W H G

Department of The Interior,
Office of Indian Affairs, Washington,

The within will, dated Sept. 1, 1918, of Henry Jones, deceased allottee No. 358-358a of the Otoe and Missouria tribe, is hereby recommended for approval in accordance with the provisions of the Act of June 25, 1910 (36 Stats. L., 855-6) as amended by Act of February 14, 1913 (37 Stats. L., 678).

                    Respectfully,
                    EB Meritt
                    Assistant Commissioner

Department of The Interior
Office of The Secretary APR -2 1919

The within will, dated Sept. 1, 1918, of Henry Jones, deceased allottee No. 358-358a of the Otoe and Missouria tribe, is hereby approved in accordance with the provisions of the Act of June 25, 1910 (36 Stats. L., 855-6) as amended by Act of February 14, 1913 (37 Stats. L., 678).

                    SG Hopkins
                    Assistant Secretary

▲▼▲▼▲▼▲▼▲▼▲▼▲▼▲▼

ANTOINE BOYER
                Original
                WILL

    I, *Antoine Boyer* of Pine Ridge Agency, South Dakota, Allottee number *1814*. Do hereby make and declare this to be my last will and testament, in accordance with Section 2 of the Act of June 25, 1910, (36 stat. 855-858) and Act of February 14, 1913, (Public No. 381), hereby revoking all former wills made by us:

Indian Wills, 1911 – 1921 Book Two
Records of The Bureau of Indian Affairs

1. I hereby direct that as soon as possible after my decease, that all my debts, funeral and testamentary expenses be paid out of my personal estate.

2. I give and devise my allotment on the Pine Ridge Reservation, South Dakota, described as follows: *The SW1/4 of Sec. 2, in Twp. 41, N of Range 38 W of the 6th P.M. of South Dakota, containing 160 acres.*

in the following manner: *To my daughter Rosa Roulliard, all excepting she is to pay each of my other four children, Mitchel, Ida, Samuel, and Vitel Boyer, the sum of $5.00 each, $20 in all before she receives a deed for the land.*

3. I give and bequeath all of my personal property of whatsoever nature and wheresoever situated unto *my four children, Mitchel, Ida, Samuel, and Vitel, to be divided equally between them.*

4. All the rest of my property, real or personal, now possessed or hereafter acquired, of whatsoever nature and wheresoever situated, I hereby give, devise and bequeath unto *my five children named above to be divided equally between them.*

In witness whereof I have hereunto set my hand this *Thirteenth* day of *February* 191*7*.

Antoine Boyer

The above statement was, this *13th* day of *February* 1916 signed and published by *Antoine Boyer* as *his* last will and testament, in the joint presence of the undersigned, the said *Antoine Boyer* then being of sound and vigorous mid and free from any constraint or compulsion; whereupon we, being without any interest in the matter other than friendship, and being well acquainted with *him* but not members of *his* family, immediately subscribed our names hereto in the presence of each other and of the said testator, for the purpose of attesting the said will, as *he* requested us to do. And that I …….. at the testa…..'s request have written ….. name in ink, and that … affixed …. thumb-marks.

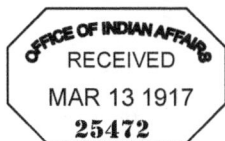

<table>
<tr>
<td>

OFFICE OF INDIAN AFFAIRS
RECEIVED
MAR 13 1917
25472

</td>
<td>

Elmer B Pomeroy   *Wanblee, S. D.*
W A Toisk   *Eastman, S. D.*

</td>
</tr>
</table>

Post Office Address

Pine Ridge, South Dakota.

I hereby certify that I have fully inquired into the mental competency of the Indian signing the above will; the circumstances attending the execution of the will; the influence that may have induced its execution, and the names of those entitled to share in the estate under the law of descent in South Dakota: reasons for the disposition of the property proposed by the will differing from disposition had the property descended by operation of law.

I respectfully forward this will with the recommendation that it be *dis*approved.

John R Brennan
Supt. & Spl. Disb. Agent.

Probate
56366-17

Department of The Interior,
Office of Indian Affairs, Washington,

The within will of Antoine Boyer, is hereby recommended for approval in accordance with the provisions of the Act of June 25, 1910 (36 Stats. L., 855-6) as amended by Act of February 14, 1913 (37 Stats. L., 678).

Respectfully,
EB Meritt
Assistant Commissioner

Department of The Interior
Office of The Secretary SEP 24 1917

The within will is hereby approved in accordance with the provisions of the Act of June 25, 1910 (36 Stats. L., 855-6) as amended by Act of February 14, 1913 (37 Stats. L., 678).

SG Hopkins
Assistant Secretary

SEMKAWETLA

LAST WILL AND TESTAMENT
OF
Semkawetla.

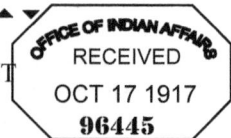

OFFICE OF INDIAN AFFAIRS
RECEIVED
OCT 17 1917
96445

IN THE NAME OF GOD, AMEN.

I, Semkawetla, of Umatilla Indian Reservation, Oregon being of sound mind, memory and understanding, do hereby make and publish this my last will and testament, hereby revoking and annulling all wills by me heretofore made, in manner and form following, that is to say:

Indian Wills, 1911 – 1921 Book Two
Records of The Bureau of Indian Affairs

Department of The Interior
Office of The Secretary MAR 12 1919

The within will is approved pursuant to the provisions of the Act of June 25, 1910 (36 Stats. L., 855-6) as amended by Act of February 14, 1913 (37 Stats. L., 678).

S G Hopkins
Assistant Secretary

▲▼▲▼▲▼▲▼▲▼▲▼▲▼

JOSEPH WALL

Deposited 1/17-1917 by Mrs. E. Munday - C.L. Ellis

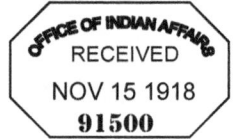

OFFICE OF INDIAN AFFAIRS
RECEIVED
NOV 15 1918
91500

Browning, Mont 1/14 1917
I want to give to my children ----
To Mrs. Maggie Chongnette one sorrel mare and one bay mare

The Gray mare to Mrs. Thresa Black Boy
The Buckskin to Christen Bruno
and the house the stable and al[sic] *bloning*[sic] *to it*
The land to Dora Black Boy 40 acres be side her mother Mrs. Thresa Black Boy
To Mrs. Eva Pabalo 280 acres
To Alex Bruno the wagon
To Maggie Chongnette and Thresa Blackboy I have $125 one hundred twenty five dollars - I want that to go [sic] *burial expencs*[sic] *and the balance to the to*[sic] *above mention*[sic]

Joe Wall

Witness
Mary Wells
Mrs. E Munday
Fish Wolf Robe X

Probate
91500-18
5409-19
 J M T

Department of The Interior,
Office of Indian Affairs, Washington,
FEB 20 1919
92

Indian Wills, 1911 – 1921 Book Two
Records of The Bureau of Indian Affairs

It is recommended that the within will of Joseph Wall, deceased Piegan allottee No. 216, dated January 14, 1917 be approved in accordance with the Act of June 25, 1910 (36 Stats. L., 855-6) as amended by Act of February 14, 1913 (37 Stats. L., 678).

Respectfully,

E B Meritt

Assistant Commissioner

Department of The Interior

Office of The Secretary MAR 12 1919

The within will of Joseph Wall, deceased Piegan allottee No. 216, dated January 14, 1917 is approved in accordance with the Act of June 25, 1910 (36 Stats. L., 855-6) as amended by Act of February 14, 1913 (37 Stats. L., 678).

S G Hopkins

Assistant Secretary

▲▼▲▼▲▼▲▼▲▼▲▼▲▼▲▼

BEAT THEM

DEPARTMENT OF THE INTERIOR

UNITED STATES INDIAN SERVICE

Know all men by these presents; That I, Beat Them, being of sound mind, do hereby make my last will and testament:----

    I have four children living to wit:-- Going Out First, daughter, Never Miss A Shot, son, Bear in The Woods, son, and Good Elk, son.. My Grand daughter, Mabel Two Eagle, has taken good care of me for the past five years and at my death I wish my Estate divided equally among my four children and the said Grand daughter, Mabel Two Eagle.

her mark

Witnesses. --- *W. L. Gardner*   *Beat Them* [thumb print]

           Flora A Gardner   *(Seal)*

53420-1918.

Department of The Interior,

Office of Indian Affairs, Washington,

APR -5 1919

It is recommended that the within will be approved in accordance with the Act of June 25, 1910 (36 Stats. L., 855-6) as amended by Act of February 14, 1913 (37 Stats. L., 678).

Respectfully,

E B Meritt

Assistant Commissioner

Department of The Interior
Office of The Secretary APR -8 1919

The within will is hereby approved in accordance with the Act of June 25, 1910 (36 Stats. L., 855-6) as amended by Act of February 14, 1913 (37 Stats. L., 678).

S G Hopkins

Assistant Secretary

▲▼▲▼▲▼▲▼▲▼▲▼▲▼▲▼

THUNDER HAWK

Original
WILL

OFFICE OF INDIAN AFFAIRS
RECEIVED
NOV 30 1917
100958

I, **Thunder Hawk** of Pine Ridge Agency, South Dakota, Allottee number **1942**. Do hereby make and declare this to be my last will and testament, in accordance with Section 2 of the Act of June 25, 1910, (36 stat. 855-858) and Act of February 14, 1913, (Public No. 381), hereby revoking all former wills made by us:

1. I hereby direct that as soon as possible after my decease, that all my debts, funeral and testamentary expenses be paid out of my personal estate.

2. I give and devise my allotment on the Pine Ridge Reservation, South Dakota, described as follows:

All of section 28 in Twp. 41 north of Range 37 west of the Sixth Principal Meridian, South Dakota, containing six hundred forty acres,

in the following manner:

To my son, Left Hand: the NW/4 of Section 28 in Twp. 41 In of Range 37

To my son, Martin Thunder Hawk: the SW/4 of Section 28 in Twp. 41 north of Range 37.

To my daughter, Sallie Hollow Head: the NE/4 of Section 38 in Twp. 41 north of Range 37.

To my daughter, Mary White Belly: the SE/4 of Section 28 in Twp. 41 north of Range 37.

3. I give and bequeath all of my personal property of whatsoever nature and wheresoever situated unto

my daughter, Mary White Belly

4. All the rest of my property, real ~~or personal~~, now possessed or hereafter acquired, of whatsoever nature and wheresoever situated, I hereby give, devise and bequeath unto

my wife, Red Dog.

In witness whereof I have hereunto set my hand this **2nd** day of **March** 1915.

his mark [thumb print]
Thunder Hawk

The above statement was, this **2nd** day of **March** 1915 signed and published by **Thunder Hawk** as **his** last will and testament, in the joint presence of the undersigned, the said **Thunder Hawk** then being of sound and vigorous mid and free from any constraint or compulsion; whereupon we, being without any interest in the matter other than friendship, and being well acquainted with **him** but not members of **his** family, immediately subscribed our names hereto in the presence of each other and of the said testator, for the purpose of attesting the said will, as **he** requested us to do**, his name being signed by George A Trotter, one of the witnesses, at his request.**

Post Office Address

George A Trotter **Kyle, South Dakota**.
Jacob White Eyes **Kyle, South Dakota.**

Pine Ridge, South Dakota.
Oct. 26, 1917

I hereby certify that I have fully inquired into the mental competency of the Indian signing the above will; the circumstances attending the execution of the will; the influence that may have induced its execution, and the names of those entitled to share in the estate under the law of descent in South Dakota: reasons for the disposition of the property proposed by the will differing from disposition had the property descended by operation of law.

I respectfully forward this will with the recommendation that it be *dis*approved.

C L Ellis
~~Supt. &~~ Spl. ~~Disb. Agent~~
Agent in Charge

Probate
100958-17

Department of The Interior,   MAR -6 1919
Office of Indian Affairs, Washington,

The within will of Thunder Hawk, is hereby recommended for approval in accordance with the provisions of the Act of June 25, 1910 (36 Stats. L., 855-6) as amended by Act of February 14, 1913 (37 Stats. L., 678).

Respectfully,
EB Meritt
Assistant Commissioner

-RSF-13

Department of The Interior
Office of The Secretary   MAR 11 1919

The within will is hereby approved in accordance with the provisions of the Act of June 25, 1910 (36 Stats. L., 855-6) as amended by Act of February 14, 1913 (37 Stats. L., 678).

SG Hopkins
Assistant Secretary

12-RSF-13

▲▼▲▼▲▼▲▼▲▼▲▼▲▼

JOHN WHITE

LAST WILL AND TESTAMENT OF JOHN WHITE
KLAMATH ALLOTTEE, NO. 1317.
Klamath Agency, Oregon

Died
3-21-1917

> OFFICE OF INDIAN AFFAIRS
> RECEIVED
> FEB 23 1917
> **18507**

    I, John White, a Klamath Indian Allottee, No. 1317, aged about 54 years, of the Klamath Reservation in the County of Klamath and State of Oregon, do hereby make, publish and declare this, my last will and testament, as follows:-

    1st. I direct that the expenses of my last illness and funeral expenses be paid.

    2ndly. I give, devise and bequeath unto Jennie White, my wife, Klamath Allottee, No. 1318, Aged 56 years, residing on the Klamath Reservation, near the post office of Yainax, Oregon, all my property, both real and personal, which I may own at the time of my death, or in which I may have any interest, of whatsoever the kind the same may be, or wheresoever situated, to have and to hold unto the said Jennie White, my wife, her heirs and assigns forever.

Indian Wills, 1911 – 1921 Book Two
Records of The Bureau of Indian Affairs

My real property consists of my allotment on the Klamath Reservation, in the County of Klamath, State of Oregon, now held in trust by the Government of the United States, and particularly described as follows:- Allotment No. 1174-1317 -- The south half of the north-east quarter and the north half of the south-east quarter of section seventeen in township thirty-five south of range ten east of the Wilamette Meridian, Oregon, containing one hundred sixty acres.

3rdly. I hereby revoke all former wills by me made.

4thly. I nominate and appoint the Superintendent of the Klamath Reservation, whoever he may be at the time of my death, Executor of this my last will and testament.

In witness whereof, I have hereunto set my hand and seal this 27th day of July, 1916, at Yainax, County of Klamath and State of Oregon.

His

JOHN WHITE [thumb print]

Mark.

The foregoing instrument, consisting of 1 page, was this 27th day of July, 1916 by the said John White, declared to be his last will and testament and was signed and sealed by him in our presence, and in the presence of each other, subscribed our names hereto this 27th day of July, 1916, at Yainax, Oregon.

Sargent Brown	residing at	Chiloquin, Oregon
Chaples S Minor	residing at	Klamath Agency, Oregon.
Fred A Baker	residing at	Klamath Agency, Oregon.

Probate
34353-17
J G McG

Department of The Interior,
Office of Indian Affairs, Washington,

AUG -4 1917

It is recommended that the within will of John White, Klamath allottee No. 1317 be approved in accordance with the Act of June 25, 1910 (36 Stats. L., 855-6) as amended by Act of February 14, 1913 (37 Stats. L., 678).

Respectfully,

E B Meritt

Assistant Commissioner

7-SK-30

Department of The Interior
Office of The Secretary AUG -6 1917

The within will of John White, Klamath allottee No. 1317, is hereby approved in accordance with the Act of June 25, 1910 (36 Stats. L., 855-6) as amended by Act of February 14, 1913 (37 Stats. L., 678).

Alexander Stogelsburg
First Assistant Secretary

▲▼▲▼▲▼▲▼▲▼▲▼▲▼

<u>PHILIP RED ELK</u>

Original
WILL

OFFICE OF INDIAN AFFAIRS
RECEIVED
JUL 12 1917
68745

I, **Philip Red Elk** of Pine Ridge Agency, South Dakota, Allottee number **5618**. Do hereby make and declare this to be my last will and testament, in accordance with Section 2 of the Act of June 25, 1910, (36 stat. 855-858) and Act of February 14, 1913, (Public No. 381), hereby revoking all former wills made by us:

1. I hereby direct that as soon as possible after my decease, that all my debts, funeral and testamentary expenses be paid out of my personal estate.

2. I give and devise my allotment on the Pine Ridge Reservation, South Dakota, described as follows:
The E/3 of section 35, in Twp 42 N. of Range 37 W. of the sixth P.M. of South Dakota, containing 320 acres

in the following manner: **To William Red Elk, my nephew, the SE/4 of section 35, in Twp 42 N. of R37 W of _th[sic] P.M. of So. Dak. 160 A.**
To:- Red Elk, my cousin, The NE/4 of section 35, in Twp 42 N. of Range 37 W of the 6th. P.M. of So. Dak, 160 acres.

3. I give and bequeath all of my personal property of whatsoever nature and wheresoever situated unto **Red Elk, my cousin, all that is left after all my debts and funeral expenses are paid.**
I own 2 mares, 1 gray horse, 2 cows, 1 wagon, set harness, farm implements, and a small amount of other personal property, all to be bequeathed as stated above.

4. All the rest of my property, real or personal, now possessed or hereafter acquired, of whatsoever nature and wheresoever situated, I hereby give, devise and bequeath unto **Red Elk, my cousin.**

98

In witness whereof I have hereunto set my hand this **seventh** day of **February 1916**.

Philip Red Elk

The above statement was, this **7th** day of **February** 1916 signed and published by **Philip Red Elk** as **his** last will and testament, in the joint presence of the undersigned, the said **Philip Red Elk** then being of sound and vigorous mid and free from any constraint or compulsion; whereupon we, being without any interest in the matter other than friendship, and being well acquainted with **him** but not members of **his** family, immediately subscribed our names hereto in the presence of each other and of the said testator, for the purpose of attesting the said will, as **he** requested us to do.

```
OFFICE OF INDIAN AFFAIRS
RECEIVED
JUL 18 1917
68745
```

Post Office Address

Elmer B Pomeroy **Wanblee, So. Dak.**
Noah Bad Wound **Wanblee, So. Dak.**

Pine Ridge, South Dakota.
Jul 13 1917

I hereby certify that I have fully inquired into the mental competency of the Indian signing the above will; the circumstances attending the execution of the will; the influence that may have induced its execution, and the names of those entitled to share in the estate under the law of descent in South Dakota: reasons for the disposition of the property proposed by the will differing from disposition had the property descended by operation of law.

I respectfully forward this will with the recommendation that it be *dis*approved.

C L Ellis
~~Supt. & Spl. Disb. Agent~~
Special *Agent in Charge*

Probate
68745-17
V L D

Department of The Interior,
Office of Indian Affairs, Washington, JAN 30 1919

The within will of Philip Red Elk, is hereby recommended for approval in accordance with the provisions of the Act of June 25, 1910 (36 Stats. L., 855-6) as amended by Act of February 14, 1913 (37 Stats. L., 678).

Respectfully,
EB Meritt
Assistant Commissioner

Indian Wills, 1911 – 1921 Book Two
Records of The Bureau of Indian Affairs

Department of The Interior
Office of The Secretary   JAN 30 1919

The within will is hereby approved in accordance with the provisions of the Act of June 25, 1910 (36 Stats. L., 855-6) as amended by Act of February 14, 1913 (37 Stats. L., 678).

SG Hopkins
Assistant Secretary

▲▼▲▼▲▼▲▼▲▼▲▼▲▼

ANPETUKICAGAPIWIN or MAKE HER DAY
A WILL.

OFFICE OF INDIAN AFFAIRS
RECEIVED
OCT 17 1913
122800

I, Anpetukicagupiwin, of Greenwood, Yankton Indian Agency, State of South Dakota, being of sound mind and memory, and considering the uncertainty of this frail and transitory life, do therefore make, publish and declare this to be my last Will and Testament, that is to say:

First.--After all my lawful debts are paid and discharged, I give and beque*a*th unto my grand-daughter Mrs. Mary Packard Spider The South half of the Southwest quarter of the Northwest quarter of Section nine, in Township ninety-six, North of Range Sixty-five, --Twenty acres.

Second.--I give and bequeth[sic] unto my grand-daughter, Mrs. Elizabeth Redbird Gullikson the North half of the Southwest quarter of the Northwest quarter of Section Nine, in Township Ninety-six, North of Range Sixty-five, being Twenty acres.

Third.--I give to my grand-daughter Mrs. Lucy Traversie Rouse all of my personal property of whatever nature includ[sic]-- my dwelling house or houses on any of the above described land.

Fourth.--I give and beque*a*th unto my grand-daughters, after all my lawful debts are paid, and funeral expenses are paid, the residue of any money may then be held in trust for me by the Superintendant[sic] in charge of Yankton Indian Agency, S.D., and also any personal account of money so held for me by the said Superintendant[sic], be divided equally, share and share alike between: Mrs. Mary Packard Spider, Mrs. Lucy Traversie Rouse, Euphrasia Deloria Bubuna, Mrs. Anna Bruguier, and Mrs. Mary Mato Young.

Fifth.--I hereby appoint Rev. John Flockhart, Greenwood, South Dakota, to be executor of this my last WILL and TESTAMENT, hereby revoking all former Wills by me made.

In Witness Whereof, I have hereunto subscribe my name and affixed my thumb mark the Seventeenth day of June, in the year of our Lord One thousand nine hundred and twelve.   *Her thumb*

Subscribed & sworn to before   *Anpetukicagupiwin* [thumb print]
me this 17th of June, 1912   *mark*
          J. Foster, Notary

The above written instrument was subscribed and thumb mark affixed by the said Anpetukicagapiwin in our presence, and acknowledged by her to each of us; and she at the same time declared the above instrument, so subscribed and thumb marked, to be her last Will and Testament; and we at her request, have signed our names as witnesses hereto, in her presence, and in the presence of each other, and written opposite our names our respective places of residence.

John Flockhart	*Greenwood, S. Dak*
Robert Obeshaw	*Greenwood, S. Dak*
Simon Spider	*Greenwood, S. Dak*

Probate
11029-18
MHW

Department of The Interior,
Office of Indian Affairs, Washington,   JAN 30 1919

The within will of Anpetukicagapiwin or Make Her Day, Yankton Sioux Allottee No. 635, is hereby recommended for approval in accordance with the provisions of the Act of June 25, 1910 (36 Stats. L., 855-6) as amended by Act of February 14, 1913 (37 Stats. L., 678), insofar as it relates to her original allotment.

Respectfully,
EB Meritt
Assistant Commissioner

Department of The Interior
Office of The Secretary   FEB 15 1919

Pursuant to the provisions of the Act of June 25, 1910 (36 Stats. L., 855-6) as amended by Act of February 14, 1913 (37 Stats. L., 678) and the regulations of the Department I hereby approve the within will of

Indian Wills, 1911 – 1921 Book Two
Records of The Bureau of Indian Affairs

Anpetukicagapiwin or Make Her Day, Yankton Sioux Allottee No. 635, executed the 17th day of June 1912, insofar as it relates to her original allotment.

SG Hopkins
Assistant Secretary

▲▼▲▼▲▼▲▼▲▼▲▼▲▼▲▼

SAMPSON SURROUNDED

Original
WILL

OFFICE OF INDIAN AFFAIRS
RECEIVED
JUL 9 - 1917
60051

I, **Sampson Surrounded** of Pine Ridge Agency, South Dakota, Allottee number ____. Do hereby make and declare this to be my last will and testament, in accordance with Section 2 of the Act of June 25, 1910, (36 stat. 855-858) and Act of February 14, 1913, (Public No. 381), hereby revoking all former wills made by us:

1. I hereby direct that as soon as possible after my decease, that all my debts, funeral and testamentary expenses be paid out of my personal estate.

2. I give and devise my allotment on the Pine Ridge Reservation, South Dakota, described as follows:

(I have not received my trust patent yet)

in the following manner:

To my sister, Lucy Surrounded.

3. ~~I give and bequeath all of my personal pro~~perty of whatsoever nature and ~~wheresoever situated unto~~ *(Above marked out on original.)*

4. All the rest of my property, real or personal, now possessed or hereafter acquired, of whatsoever nature and wheresoever situated, I hereby give, devise and bequeath unto **my sister, Lucy Surrounded. Property consists of three head of cattle, a wagon, house, etc.; also my interest in the estate of Kettle Coat, deceased.**

In witness whereof I have hereunto set my hand this **25th** day of **August** 1915.
Sampson Surrounded

The above statement was, this **25th** day of **August** 1915 signed and published by **Sampson Surrounded** as **his** last will and testament, in the joint presence of the undersigned, the said **Sampson Surrounded** then being of

GUIDE WOMAN

LAST WILL AND TESTAMENT OF *Guide Woman*

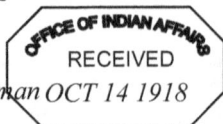

> OFFICE OF INDIAN AFFAIRS
> RECEIVED
> OCT 14 1918

Manderson, South Dakota,
March 29/1917.

Know ye all men by these presents, that I *Guide Woman* a Sioux Indian, age seventy five years, do of my own free will and accord without any undue influence being asserted upon me by any persons whatsoever, and being in my right mind at the present time, make this as my own will and testament, bequeathing all my earthly affects as follows:

Section 1.

It is my will that my lands be equally divided between my two heirs, the same being, Mrs. Kate Blind Man, and one whose name is Rough Feather both my own lawful children. The following described land to become the property of the aforesaid Mrs. Kate Blindman, in the event of my death, to wit; *SE1/4 of Section 1, in Twp. 38 North of Range 45 west.*

It is my will that the following described land shall become the property of the heir referred to as Rough Feather on the event of my death, to wit: *The Lots 6 and 7 and the east 1/2 of SW1/4 of Sec 6, Twp. 38 North, and the NW1/4 of NW1/4 of Sec 33 in Twp. 39 north all in R. 44 west of sixth P.M.*

Section 2.

All of my money which is about $500.00 shall be used in defraying all legitimate expenses incident to *life and* my death, and the remainder being bequeath as follows:

> *One half of what remains to each of the two heirs heretofore mentioned.*

Section 3.

All of my personal effects and any other property not included in sections 1 and 2 shall at my death become the property of, *Mrs. Kate Blind Man.*

This will is executed by me in the presence of the witnesses whose signatures or marks are hereunto affixed, after the various provisions of the same have been interpreted and fully explained to me, by D.A.Lincoln, through one *Polly Holy Rock* who acts as the interpreter, and all being done in the presence of the witnesses

her
[thumb print]   *Guide Woman Testator*
thumb impression

Robert Plume	Witness	*Smokes*
Smoke	Witness	[thumb print]
Polly Holy Rock	Acting Interpreter	*thumb impression*

Probate
83053-18
V L D

Department of The Interior,
Office of Indian Affairs, Washington, FEB 19 1919

The within will of Guide Woman, is hereby approved in accordance with the provisions of the Act of June 25, 1910 (36 Stats. L., 855-6) as amended by Act of February 14, 1913 (37 Stats. L., 678).

EB Meritt
Assistant Commissioner

Department of The Interior
Office of The Secretary   FEB 20 1919

The within will is hereby approved in accordance with the provisions of the Act of June 25, 1910 (36 Stats. L., 855-6) as amended by Act of February 14, 1913 (37 Stats. L., 678).

SG Hopkins
Assistant Secretary

▲▼▲▼▲▼▲▼▲▼▲▼▲▼

GEORGE COMES FLYING

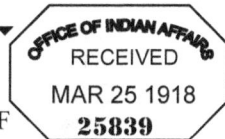

OFFICE OF INDIAN AFFAIRS
RECEIVED
MAR 25 1918
25839

LAST WILL AND TESTAMENT OF
GEORGE COMES FLYING, CROW CREEK
ALLOTTEE No. 1005.
----O----

I, George Comes Flying, 27 years of age, in Indian of the Crow Creek Indian agency, in the state of South Dakota, being of sound mind, memory, and understanding, do hereby make and publish this my last will and testament, hereby revoking and annulling all wills by me heretofore made, that is to say:

FIRST: I direct that all my just debts and funeral expenses and expenses of my last illness shall be paid as son after my decease as shall be convenient.

SECOND: I am posessed[sic] of an allotment of land within the Crow Creek Reservation, in the State of South Dakota, which is described as the South East quarter (SE1/4) Section twenty-five (25) Township One hundred and eight north (108) Range Seventy-two west (72) of the 5th P.M. South Dakota, containing 160 acres, the same having been allotted to me under the Act of March 2, 1889, on the 8th day of January 1913, I give, devise, and bequeath my said allotment of land, to the following named persons, to wit:

To my aunt Mrs. Thomas Tuttle, 50 years of age, the whole of my above described allotment, and also my share in all of the inherited lands located on this and other reservations in which I may at this time or hereafter be declared heir to, this as a part compensation for her support and care for me during my last illness.

I also give, devise and bequeath to my above named aunt, all horses and cattle of which I may be posessed[sic] at the time of my decease, and all other personal property to which I may be be[sic] posessed[sic] and not herein otherwise mentioned.

AND LASTLY: I am satisfied that the officers of the Department of the Interior of the United States will make proper provision for carrying into effect of this my last will and testament, therefore, I have not appointed an executor to administer my estate.

IN TESTIMONY WHEREOF, I have set my hand and seal to this my last will and testament at the home of my above named aunt which is located on the Crow Creek reservation, in the State of South Dakota, this 21st day of March, 1918.

George Comes Flying

Signed, sealed, published and declared by the said George Comes Flying, in out[sic] presence, as and for his last will will[sic] and testament, and at his request and in his presence and in the presence of each other we have hereto subscribed our names as attesting witnesses thereto.

Indian Wills, 1911 – 1921 Book Two
Records of The Bureau of Indian Affairs

> *Peter W. Lightfoot*
> Ft. Thompson, S. Dak.
> *Harriet E. Burt*
> Ft. Thompson, S. Dak.
> *Maurice Head*
> Ft. Thompson, S. Dak.

Probate
74823-18

Department of The Interior,
Office of Indian Affairs, Washington,   FEB 24 1919

The within will of George Comes Flying, Lower Yanktonai Sioux allottee No. 1005, is respectfully recommended for approval in accordance with the provisions of the Act of June 25, 1910 (36 Stats. L., 855-6) as amended by Act of February 14, 1913 (37 Stats. L., 678).

> *EB Meritt*
> Assistant Commissioner

Department of The Interior
Office of The Secretary   FEB 26 1919

The within will of George Comes Flying, Lower Yanktonai Sioux allottee No. 1005, is hereby approved in accordance with the provisions of the Act of June 25, 1910 (36 Stats. L., 855-6) as amended by Act of February 14, 1913 (37 Stats. L., 678).

> *SG Hopkins*
> Assistant Secretary

▲▼▲▼▲▼▲▼▲▼▲▼▲▼

SPOTTED BEAR

WILL

Dead ▬▬▬▬▬▬

I, **Spotted Bear** of Pine Ridge Agency, South Dakota, Allottee number **5055**. Do hereby make and declare this to be my last will and testament, in accordance with Section 2 of the Act of June 25, 1910, (36 stat. 855-858) and Act of February 14, 1913, (Public No. 381), hereby revoking all former wills made by us:

1. I hereby direct that as soon as possible after my decease, that all my debts, funeral and testamentary expenses be paid out of my personal estate.

Indian Wills, 1911 – 1921 Book Two
Records of The Bureau of Indian Affairs

2. I give and devise my allotment on the Pine Ridge Reservation, South Dakota, described as follows: **NE1/4 of sec 33, Range 37 w 6th prin. Merid in Bennet County, South Dakota; to my sister, Scabby legs, and to her three children, Ellis Cut, Raymond Cut, and Lucinda Cut, to be divided equally among them**

in the following manner:

Scabby Legs to recieve[sic] 40 acres, Ellis Cut to recieve[sic], Raymond Cut to receive[sic] 40 acres, and Lucinda Cut to recieve[sic] 40 acres. The whole to be divided as nearly equal as may be.

3. I give and bequeath all of my personal property of whatsoever nature and wheresoever situated unto **my sister, Scabby Legs. It consists of one roan horse branded C on the left hip, one set of harness, and one lumber wagon. All money due me to be divided equally between Scabby Legs and Ellis Cut, Raymond Cut, and Lucinda Cut.**

4. All the rest of my property, real or personal, now possessed or hereafter acquired, of whatsoever nature and wheresoever situated, I hereby give, devise and bequeath unto

his
Spotted Bear [thumb print]
mark

In witness whereof I have hereunto set my hand this....... day of .... 191....

The above statement was, this **15** day of **November** 191.... signed and published by **Spotted Bear (5055)** as **his** last will and testament, in the joint presence of the undersigned, the said **Spotted Bear** then being of sound and vigorous mind and free from any constraint or compulsion; whereupon we, being without any interest in the matter other than friendship, and being well acquainted with **him** but not members of **his** family, immediately subscribed our names hereto in the presence of each other and of the said testator, for the purpose of attesting the said will, as **he** requested us to do. And that I **Robert Two Elk**. at the testa **or**.'s request have written **his** name in ink, and that **he** affixed **his** thumb-marks.

Post Office Address
Robert Two Elk   Wanblee, S. D.
Thomas Thunder Hawk Wanblee, S.D.

Indian Wills, 1911 – 1921 Book Two
Records of The Bureau of Indian Affairs

Pine Ridge, South Dakota.
October 9, 1918

I hereby certify that I have fully inquired into the mental competency of the Indian signing the above will; the circumstances attending the execution of the will; the influence that may have induced its execution, and the names of those entitled to share in the estate under the law of descent in South Dakota: reasons for the disposition of the property proposed by the will differing from disposition had the property descended by operation of law.

I respectfully forward this will with the recommendation that it be **dis**approved.

Henry M Tidwell
Supt. & Spl. Disb. Agent.

Probate
83055-18

Department of The Interior,
Office of Indian Affairs, Washington,

The within will of Spotted Bear, is hereby recommended for approval in accordance with the provisions of the Act of June 25, 1910 (36 Stats. L., 855-6) as amended by Act of February 14, 1913 (37 Stats. L., 678).

Respectfully,
EB Meritt
Assistant Commissioner

Department of The Interior
Office of The Secretary MAR -1 1919

The within will is hereby approved in accordance with the provisions of the Act of June 25, 1910 (36 Stats. L., 855-6) as amended by Act of February 14, 1913 (37 Stats. L., 678).

SG Hopkins
Assistant Secretary

▲▼▲▼▲▼▲▼▲▼▲▼▲▼▲▼

SE-NO-YA

LAST WILL AND TESTAMENT

Anadarko, Oklahoma,
February 13, 1917

I, Se-no-ya, Comanche Indian allottee 516, 65 years of age, of disposing mind, but sensible of the uncertainty of life, and desiring to make disposition of my property and affairs while in health and strength do hereby make, publish, and declare the following to be my last will and testament, thereby revoking and cancelling all other or former wills by me at any time made.

FIRST: I direct the payment of all my just debts and funeral expenses.

SECOND: I give and devise to my beloved wife, Louise Matilda Se-no-ya, Comanche Indian allottee 517, the sum of $10.00 to be paid to her out of any funds which may be to my credit at my death, payment to be made by the officer of the Kiowa Indian Agency, Anadarko, Okla.

THIRD: I give and devise all of my trust allotment of land, comprising the S.E. of 33 - 7 North - 9 in Caddo County, Oklahoma, being Comanche Indian allotment 516, to my beloved daughter, Margaret Se-no-ya, an unallotted Comanche Indian on the Kiowa Indian Reservation in Oklahoma. This beneficiary has received no allotment of land upon any Indian Reservation in the United States. All the rest of my children have been allotted, and their allotments are held in trust by the United States, and my wife and I have agreed that in order to bring the benefit of trust allotment of land to my said daughter that I devise all of my interest in and to my said allotment to said unallotted child. I give and bequeath all of the rest and residue and remainder of all my property of which I ma die possessed, real and personal; to my beloved wife, Louise Matilda Se-no-ya.

I declare the following persons would my sole heirs at law were I to die intestate:

FIRST: My wife, Louise Matilda Se-no-ya.
SECOND: Alice Se-no-ya, daughter.
THIRD: Lucas Se-no-ya, son.
FOURTH: Philomena Se-no-ya, daughter.
FIFTH: Margaret Se-no-ya, daughter.
SIXTH: Heirs of Thomas Se-no-ya, deceased.   Thomas Se-no-ya was my son, and he was killed during last month at Chickasha, Okla., and his heirs have not yet been determined by the Interior Department.
SEVENTH: James Se-no-ya, son.

This will is made subject to the approval of the Secretary of the Interior.

In witness whereof I, Se-no-ya, have to this, my last will and testament, consisting of four sheets of paper, subscribed my name this *13* day of *February* 1917.

his thumb
Senoya   [thumb print]
mark

Witnesses:
(Signature Illegible)
(Signature Illegible)

Subscribed by Se-no-ya in the presence of each of us, the undersigned, and at the same time declared by him to us to be his last will and testament, and we thereupon at the request of Se-no-ya, in his presence and in the presence of each other sign our names hereto as witnesses this thirteenth day of February, 1917.

(Signature Illegible)
Anadarko, Okla.
(Signature Illegible)
Anadarko, Okla.

I, *Calliy Jarvey*, hereby certify on honor that I acted as interpreter during the execution of the foregoing will and testament and that I have truly interpreted all the content thereof to the testator before his execution of said instrument and that said will was drawn strictly in accordance with his desires and directions. I further certify that I have no interest in this matter whatsoever.

Calliy Jarvey

Probate
W H G

Department of The Interior,
Office of Indian Affairs, Washington,
JAN 21 1919
It is recommended that the within will of Se-no-ya be approved under the Act of June 25, 1910 (36 Stats. L., 855-6) as amended by Act of February 14, 1913 (37 Stats. L., 678), and the Regulations of the Department.

E B Meritt
Assistant Commissioner

Indian Wills, 1911 – 1921 Book Two
Records of The Bureau of Indian Affairs

Department of The Interior
Office of The Secretary FEB 26 1919

The within will of Se-no-ya, is hereby approved under the Act of June 25, 1910 (36 Stats. L., 855-6) as amended by Act of February 14, 1913 (37 Stats. L., 678), and the Regulations of the Department.

SG Hopkins
Assistant Secretary

▲▼▲▼▲▼▲▼▲▼▲▼▲▼▲▼

SADIE SHE-MA-MY

Binger, Okla Aug 15 – 1917

I, Sadie She-ma-my, about 28 years of age, of sound and disposing mind, but desirous o making disposition of my property and affaris wile in sound mind, do hereby make, publish and declare the following to be my last will and testament, hereby revoking and cancelling all other or former wills by me at any time made.

First:
I direct the payment of all my just debts and funeral expenses.

Second:
I give and devise all of my property of which I may die possessed which is to include my trust allotment of land comprising the S.E1/4, 32, Township 10 north of Range 10 West of the Indian Meridian known upon the rolls of the Interior Department as Caddo Indian allotment No. 724, to my five children in equal shares to wit:

(a) To my son Charlie Shemamy, unallotted
(b) To my son Edward Shemamy, unallotted
(c) To my daughter Clara Shemamy, unallotted
(d) To my daughter Alice Shemamy, unallotted
(e) To my son Edgar Shemamy, unallotted

All of the above mentioned children are to share equally in and to all of my property, so that they will each take one-fifth interest in and to my estate.

I more specifically direct that my husband, Joshua Longhat, Caddo allottee #608, shall not share in my estate and I hereby disinherit said husband entirely. My reasons for this disinheritance are set forth in an affidavit made by me the date which affidavit I desire considered in connection with this my last will and testament.

112

Un testimony whereof, I, Sadie Shemamy, have to this my last will and testament consisting of three sheets of paper, affixed my hand and seal this 15th day of August, 1917, near Binger, Caddo County, Oklahoma.

Witnesses	*Sadie Shemamy* [thumb print]
Jas Prickett	*her thumb*
Anadarko, Okla.	*Mark*
R.R. Hickox	
Binger, Okla.	

Subscribed by Sadie Shemamy in the presence of each of us the undersigned witnesses at the same time declaring to us that the above instrument was and is her last will and testament, and we thereupon, at the request of Sadie Shemamy, in her presence and in the presence of each other, sign our names hereto as witnesses this 15th day of August, 1917, near Binger, Caddo County, Oklahoma.

Jas Prickett
Anadarko, Okla.
R. R. Hickox
Binger, Okla.

Department of The Interior,
Office of Indian Affairs, Washington,
JAN 29 1919

It is recommended that the within will of Sadie She-ma-my, deceased Caddo allottee No. 724, be approved pursuant to the provisions of the Act of June 25, 1910 (36 Stats. L., 855-6) as amended by Act of February 14, 1913 (37 Stats. L., 678).

E B Meritt
Assistant Commissioner

Department of The Interior
Office of The Secretary FEB 28 1919

The within will of Sadie She-ma-my, deceased Caddo allottee No. 724, is approved pursuant to the provisions of the Act of June 25, 1910 (36 Stats. L., 855-6) as amended by Act of February 14, 1913 (37 Stats. L., 678).

S G Hopkins
Assistant Secretary

▲▼▲▼▲▼▲▼▲▼▲▼▲▼▲▼

WHITE GIRL or TOUCHING GROUND

LAST WILL AND TESTAMENT OF WHITE GIRL OR TOUCHING GROUND

I, White Girl (Touching Ground), of Clinton, State of Oklahoma, being of sound and disposing mind and memory and understanding, do make and publish this my last will and testament, hereby revoking and annulling all wills and codicils by me made.

FIRST: I direct the payment of all my just debts and funeral expenses.

SECOND: I give, devise, and bequeath to my beloved husband, Black Wolf, and to my beloved granddaughter, Big Pipe Woman, each to have an undivided one-half interest therein to the following real estate, to-wit: the North 1/2 of the South Last 1/4 of Section Eleven (11), Township Sixteen (16), Range Twelve (12), East of Indian Meridian in Blaine Co, Okla, containing 80 acres and being a part of my original allotment; and my undivided one-third interest in and to the North West 1/4 of Section Eleven (11), Township Sixteen (16), Range Twelve (12), West of Indian Meridian in Blaine Co, Okla, same being the original allotment of Touching Ground, and my undivided one-sixth interest in and to the South East 1/4 of Section Eleven (11), Township Sixteen (16), Range Twelve (12) West of Indian Meridian in Blaine Co, Okla., same being the allotment of Small Back (Wolf Floating Down River).

THIRD: I give, devise, and bequeath to my esteemed friend, Woman Owns Spotted Horses, the sum of Fifty Dollars ($50.00), to be paid to her from such moneys as I may have at the time of my death;

FOURTH: I give, devise, and bequeath, all of my property, both real and personal, of which I may die posessed[sic], excepting such as herein before set forth, to be equally divided between my beloved husband, Black Wolf, and my beloved grand-daughter, Big Pipe Woman.

IN TESTIMONY WHEREOF, I have hereunto set my hand and seal at Clinton, Oklahoma, this *22nd* day of March, Nineteen Hundred and Seventeen.

WITNESSES: *her*[thumb print] *mark*
J.B. Ediger   *White Girl Touching Ground*
Brinton Packer
ENTERPRETER:
Alfrid Heal of Bird

OLIVE HARRY WOLF or THE EAGLE

Last Will and Testament
Of
Olive Harry Wolf or The Eagle

IN THE NAME OF GOD, AMEN,

I, **Olive Harry Wolf or The Eagle** of **Crow Agency, Mont.** being of sound mind, memory, and understanding, do hereby make and publish this, my last will and testament, hereby revoking and annulling all wills by me heretofore made, in manner and form following, that is to say:

First: I direct that all my just debts and funeral expenses, and expenses of my last illness shall be paid by my executor hereinafter named as soon after my decease as convenient:

Second: I give, devise and bequeath to

Paul Harry Wolf, my husband, the Two cream colored mares bought last year, and all the harness;

To Pretty Back of the Neck, my aunt, the old black mare without the colt, which belongs to my husband.

To Takes Quick, who has been good to me, the little buckskin mare.

Third: All the rest and residue of my estate, both real and personal and mixed, I give devise and bequeath to my lawful heirs as determined after my decease.

And lastly: I do hereby nominate, constitute and appoint **The Superintendent of the Crow Reservation** executor of this my last will and testament.

In testimony whereof, I have set my hand and seal to this, my last will and testament, at **Crow Agency**, Montana, this **25th** day of **May** in the year of our Lord one thousand nine hundred and **Eighteen**. *her*

Olive Harry Wolf [thumb print]
mark

Signed, sealed, published, and declared by said **Olive Harrywolf or The Eagle** in our presence, as and for **her** last will and testament, and at **her** request and in our presence, and in the presence of each other, we have hereunto subscribed our names as attesting witnesses thereto.

C Hasbury of **Crow Agency, Mont.**
N.J. Perkins of **Crow Agency, Mont.**

Indian Wills, 1911 – 1921 Book Two
Records of The Bureau of Indian Affairs

FIRST, I direct that all my just debts and funeral expenses and expenses of my last illness shall be paid by my executor, hereinafter named as soon after my decease as shall be convenient;

SECOND, I give, devise and bequeath to ANNIE GEORGE of Umatilla reservation, Oregon, my allotment on said reservation, described as the SE/4 of NE/4 Sec. 1, T. 2 N., R.34, and the SW/4 of NW/4 Sec. 29, T. 3 N., R. 35 E., P.M. Oregon, 80 acres.

THIRD, All the rest and residue of my estate, both real, personal and mixed I give, devise and bequeath to said Annie George.

AND LASTLY, I do hereby nominate, constitute and appoint

IN TESTIMONY WHEREOF, I have set my hand and seal to this my last will and testament, at Umatilla *Agency, Oreg.* this *1st* day of October in the year of our Lord One Thousand Nine Hundred Seventeen.

her

Semkawetla {thumb print]

mark

SIGNED, SEALED, PUBLISHED and declared by the said Semkawetla in our presence as and for her last will and testament and at her request and in her presence, and in the presence of each other we have hereunto subscribed our names as attesting witnesses thereto.

Amy M. Hazen

Leo Sampson

James A Linnaden

Probate

96445-17

T D M

Department of The Interior,

Office of Indian Affairs, Washington,

MAR -6 1919

It is recommended that the within will be approved pursuant to the provisions of the Act of June 25, 1910 (36 Stats. L., 855-6) as amended by Act of February 14, 1913 (37 Stats. L., 678).

Respectfully,

E B Meritt

Assistant Commissioner

sound and vigorous mid and free from any constraint or compulsion; whereupon we, being without any interest in the matter other than friendship, and being well acquainted with **him** but not members of **his** family, immediately subscribed our names hereto in the presence of each other and of the said testator, for the purpose of attesting the said will, as **he** requested us to do.

	Post Office Address
OL Post	**Pine Ridge, S. D.**
RM Stelzner	**Pine Ridge, S. D.**

Pine Ridge, South Dakota.
Jun 28 1917

I hereby certify that I have fully inquired into the mental competency of the Indian signing the above will; the circumstances attending the execution of the will; the influence that may have induced its execution, and the names of those entitled to share in the estate under the law of descent in South Dakota: reasons for the disposition of the property proposed by the will differing from disposition had the property descended by operation of law.

I respectfully forward this will with the recommendation that it be ___approved.

(No Signature)
Supt. & Spl. Disb. Agent.

Probate
66051-18

Department of The Interior,
Office of Indian Affairs, Washington,   **FEB 10 1919**

The within will of Sampson Surrounded, is hereby approved in accordance with the provisions of the Act of June 25, 1910 (36 Stats. L., 855-6) as amended by Act of February 14, 1913 (37 Stats. L., 678).

EB Meritt
Assistant Commissioner

Department of The Interior
Office of The Secretary   **FEB 21 1919**

The within will is hereby approved in accordance with the provisions of the Act of June 25, 1910 (36 Stats. L., 855-6) as amended by Act of February 14, 1913 (37 Stats. L., 678).

SG Hopkins
Assistant Secretary

▲▼▲▼▲▼▲▼▲▼▲▼▲▼▲▼

Indian Wills, 1911 – 1921 Book Two
Records of The Bureau of Indian Affairs

Signed, published and declared by White Girl (Touching Ground) the above named testator, as for her last will and testament, in our presence, who, at her request and in her presence, and in the presence of each other, have hereunto subscribed our names as attesting witnesses.

J.B. Ediger
Brinton Packer

PROBATE
106845-17
32360-17
M H W

Department of The Interior,
Office of Indian Affairs, Washington,
MAR -6 1919

The within will of White Girl (Touching Ground), Cheyenne allottee No. 777, is hereby approved pursuant to the provisions of the Act of June 25, 1910 (36 Stats. L., 855-6) as amended by Act of February 14, 1913 (37 Stats. L., 678).

Respectfully,
EB Meritt
Assistant Commissioner

Department of The Interior
Office of The Secretary

The within will of White Girl (Touching Ground), Cheyenne allottee No. 777, is hereby approved pursuant to the provisions of the Act of June 25, 1910 (36 Stats. L., 855-6) as amended by Act of February 14, 1913 (37 Stats. L., 678).

SG Hopkins
Assistant Secretary

▲▼▲▼▲▼▲▼▲▼▲▼▲▼▲▼

SAMMON WYKALAS

OFFICE OF INDIAN AFFAIRS
RECEIVED
FEB 25 1919
17136

LAST WILL AND TESTAMENT OF SAMMON WYKALAS

IN THE NAME OF GOD, AMEN,

I, Shannon Wykalas, allottee No. 743, of the Yakima Indian Reservation, Washington, and a resident of Yakima County, Washington, being of sound and disposing mind, memory and understanding, considering the certainty of death and the uncertainty of the time thereof, and being desirous to settle my worldly affairs, and thereby be the better prepared to leave this world when it shall please the Almighty to call me hence, do therefore make and publish this my last Will and Testament, hereby revoking and annulling all wills by the heretofore made, in manner and form following, that is to say:

FIRST, I give and bequeath to my beloved niece, Matelia Pims, who is Yakima allottee No. 2794, all my property, both real and personal, that I may die possessed of, also any property, both real and personal, that I may hereafter acquire.

SECOND, I have a wife now living, named Mollie Wykalas, who is Yakima allottee No. 744, but have no children, or issue of dead children, no brothers or sisters, father or mother now living; and to my beloved wife, Mollie Wykalas, I devise and bequeath the sum of Five Dollars, as she has an allotment of her own, and also an allotment inherited from a deceased daughter; and is old and feeble and would have no use for my land at my death.

The devise of all my property, both real and personal, to my beloved niece, Matelia Pims, is made in recognition of the faithful services she has performed in keeping me and my wife for a number of years, and the fact that she has promised to keep my wife and me until we die. I understand and know that I have other nieces and nephews, but this is the only one that has taken care of me, and I wish her to have my entire estate.

All the rest and residue of my estate, both real and personal and mixed, I bequeath and devise to my niece, as aforesaid, and to her heirs and assigns forever.

IN TESTIMONY WHEREOF, I have set my hand and seal to this, my last Will and Testament, at Fort Simcoe, Washington, Yakima County. This 10th day of April, 1910.

His [thumb print] mark

Witnesses to Mark: Sammon Wykalas
        Stuart H Elliott Examiner of Inheritance,
                        Ft. Simcoe, Wash.

John M Williams Stenographer,
Ft. Simcoe, Wash.

SIGNED, SEALED, PUBLISHED, AND DECLARED, by Sammon Wykalas, the above-named testator, as and for his last Will and Testament, in our presence and at his request and in his presence, and in the presence of each other, we have hereunto subscribed our names as attesting witnesses.

> *Stuart H Elliott*
> Residence *Ft. Simcoe Wash.*
> *Abraham Lincoln*
> Residence *Ft Simcoe Wash.*

This will was made in the presence of the following-named persons:

> Stuart H. Elliott
> John M. McClelland
> Abraham Lincoln
> William Charley
> Ida Tweyuth
> Sophine Stahy
> Sammon Wykalas

and consists of three sheets.

> *Stuart H Elliott*
> Examiner of Inheritance.

Probate
86157-17
17136-18
   TDM

Department of The Interior,
Office of Indian Affairs, Washington,
FEB 23 1919
The within will of is hereby recommended for approval in accordance with the provisions of the Act of June 25, 1910 (36 Stats. L., 855-6) as amended by Act of February 14, 1913 (37 Stats. L., 678).

> Respectfully,
> E B Meritt
> Assistant Commissioner

Department of The Interior
Office of The Secretary

The within will of is hereby approved in accordance with the Act of June 25, 1910 (36 Stats. L., 855-6) as amended by Act of February 14, 1913 (37 Stats. L., 678).

S G Hopkins
Assistant Secretary

▲▼▲▼▲▼▲▼▲▼▲▼▲▼

OFFICE OF INDIAN AFFAIRS
RECEIVED
APR 27 1918
36083

FLAGG (OCOBO)

In the Name of God, Amen. *I,* **Flagg (Ocobo)** *of Crow Creek* **Indian Reservation** *in the County of* **Buffalo***, and the State of South Dakota, being of sound mind and memory, and considering the* uncertainity[sic] *of this frail and transitory life, do therefore make, ordain, publish and declare this to be my Last Will and Testament:*

First, I order and direct that my **Execut***ors* *hereinafter named, pay all my just debts and funeral expenses as soon after my decease as conveniently may be.*

Second, After the payment of such funeral expenses and debts, I give, devise and bequeath: **all my right, title and interest in my allotment described as the South half of section 11, Township 106 North, Range 70 West if the 5th principal meridian, South Dakota, as follows:**

To my wife, Blue Hen, the South half of the South half of section 11, Twp. 106 N, R. 70 W.,

To my son Howard Ocobo, the North half of the South West quarter of section 11, Twp. 106 N, R. 70 W.,

To my daughter Annie Ocobo, the North half of the South East quarter of Section 11, Twp. 106 N. R. 70 W.,

THIRD, I give, devise and bequeath all my right, title and interest in the allotment of my son, Albert Ocobo, Jr. (deceased) whose land is described as the South East quarter of Section 34, Township 109,

North, Range 71 West of the 5th principal meridian, South Dakota, to my wife Blue Hen.

FOURTH, I give, devise and bequeath all my right title and interest in the allotment of my son Isaac Ocobo, (deceased) whose land is described as the South West quarter of Section 35, Township 109 North, Range 71 West of the 5th principal meridian, South Dakota, to my daughter Annie Ocobo.

FIFTH, I give, devise and bequeath all my right title and interest in the allotment of my daughter Grace Ocobo (deceased) whose land is described as the South East quarter of section 35, Township 109 North Range 71 West of the 5th principal meridian, South Dakota, to my son Howard Ocobo.

Lastly, I make, constitute and appoint **The Officers of the Interior Department of the United States of America** *to be the Executor of this, my Last Will and Testament, hereby revoking all former Wills by me made.*

IN TESTIMONY WHEREOF, I have hereunto subscribed my name and affixed my seal the **twelfth** *day of* **March** *in the year of our Lord One Thousand Nine Hundred* **nineteen.**   *his*

Flagg (Ocobo) [thumb print] *(SEAL)*

mark

THIS INSTRUMENT was, on the day of the date thereof, signed, published and declared by said testator **Flagg (Ocobo)** *to be his Last Will and Testament, in our presence, who at his request, have subscribed our names hereto as witnesses, in his presence and in the presence of each other.*

> ***Theron H Stein*** *residing at* **Fort Thompson, So. Dak.**
> ***Joe Irving***   *residing at* **Fort Thompson, So. Dak.**

Probate
36083-18
R T B

Department of The Interior,
Office of Indian Affairs, Washington,
                    MAR -6 1919
It is recommended that the within will of Flagg or Ocobo, Lower Yanktonai Sioux allottee No. 128, executed March 12, 1917, be approved

pursuant to the provisions of the Act of June 25, 1910 (36 Stats. L., 855-6) as amended by Act of February 14, 1913 (37 Stats. L., 678).

Respectfully,
EB Meritt
Assistant Commissioner

Department of The Interior
Office of The Secretary MAR -7 1919

The within will of Flagg or Ocobo, Lower Yanktonai Sioux allottee No. 128, executed March 12, 1917, is approved pursuant to the provisions of the Act of June 25, 1910 (36 Stats. L., 855-6) as amended by Act of February 14, 1913 (37 Stats. L., 678). No executors to be recognized.

S G Hopkins
Assistant Secretary

▲▼▲▼▲▼▲▼▲▼▲▼▲▼▲▼

SANTEE WOMAN
L A S T W I L L A N D T E S T A M E N T

OFFICE OF INDIAN AFFAIRS
RECEIVED
DEC 10 1917

I, Santee Woman, of Mellette County in the State of South Dakota being of sound mind and memory, and without children f my own to enjoy my property after my death, and considering the uncertainty of life, do therefore make, ordain, publish and declare this to be my last will and testament.

FIRST: It is my desire and I order and direct that all of my debts be paid after my death, if there are any.

Second: I give, devise and bequeath all of my property, both real and personal, consisting of the South One-half (S 1/2) of Section Twenty-three (23) in Township Forth-three (43) North of Range Twenty-eight (28) West of the Sixth (6th) Principal Meridian in Mellette County South Dakota, and certain cattle, same being all of the cattle of which I shall die seized, to my nephew, Samuel Black Wolf, the son of my beloved sister.

IN TESTIMONY WHEREOF, I have hereunto subscribed my name this thirtieth day of November, A.D., 1915.   *her*
Santee Woman [thumb print]
mark

Indian Wills, 1911 – 1921 Book Two
Records of The Bureau of Indian Affairs

Witnesses to mark
    CE Kell
    Hugh Mullin

THIS INSTRUMENT was, on the day of the date thereof, signed published and declared by said testatrix, Santee Woman, to be her last will and testament, in our presence, who at her request have subscribed our names hereto as witnesses, in her presence, and in the presence of each other.

    C E Kell   residing at *White River* So. Dak.
    Hugh Mullin residing at *White River* So. Dak.

Probate
112261-17
  L L

Department of The Interior,
Office of Indian Affairs, Washington,
                    JAN 22 1919
Pursuant to the Act of June 25, 1910, 36 Stat., L. 855 as amended by the act of February 14, 1913, the within will of Santee Woman (Wife No. 1), deceased Rosebud Sioux allottee, is hereby recommended for approval.

                        Respectfully,
                        EB Meritt
                        Assistant Commissioner
Department of The Interior
Office of The Secretary JAN 28 1919

The within will of Santee Woman (Wife No. 1), deceased Rosebud Sioux allottee, is approved pursuant to the Act of June 25, 1910 (36 Stats. L., 855-6) as amended by Act of February 14, 1913 (37 Stats. L., 678).

                        S G Hopkins
                        Assistant Secretary

▲▼▲▼▲▼▲▼▲▼▲▼▲▼▲▼
COYOTE LOOKS UP or BOOHAH-BAH-COSHE-KASH

IN THE NAME OF GOD AMEN,

I, Coyote Looks Up, (English Name) or Boohah-bah-coshe-kash (Indian Name) of Crow Agency, in the County of Big Horn, State of Montana, eighty-six years of age and being of sound and disposing mind and memory and not acting under duress, menace, fraud or undue influence or any person whatsoever, do make and publish and declare this to be my last will and testament in the manner following, that is to say:

I hereby give and bequeath to my good friend "No Name", all my property, both real and personal, of which I may die possessed. And particularly my allotment number 482 being the Lot one, section nineteen, north half of the Northwest quarter, Section twenty, Township five south, Range thirty-two east, and the north-east quarter and east half of the northwest quarter, Section twenty-one, Township eight south, Range thirty-two east, containing three hundred-twenty six and twenty-four hundredths acres, to have and to hold and receive possession and all the benefits therefrom and finally to receive full and complete title thereto as fully as I might to.

I hereby direct that this my last Will and Testament shall be executed and carried into effect by the Commissioner of Indian Affairs through his Official Representatives and that no bond shall be required.

IN WITNESS WHEREOF, I have hereunto set my hand and seal this tenth day of December, A.D. 1913. His

Coyote Looks Up [thumb print]

Mark.

The foregoing instrument, consisting of page one, was at the date thereof, by the said Coyote Looks Up, or Boohah-bah-coshe-kash, signed and sealed and published as and declared to be his last Will and Testament, in presence of us, who, at his request and in his presence and in the presence of each other have subscribed our names as witnesses thereto.

James B Kitos of Crow Agency, Montana.
S.J Shick of Crow Agency, Montana.
EJ Boos of Crow Agency, Montana.

Department of The Interior,
Office of Indian Affairs, Washington,
JAN 22 1919

The within will, dated December 10, 1913, of Coyote Looks Up, deceased Crow allottee No. 482, is hereby recommended for approval in accordance with the Act of June 25, 1910 (36 Stats. L., 855-6) as amended by Act of February 14, 1913 (37 Stats. L., 678).

Respectfully,

EB Meritt

Assistant Commissioner

Department of The Interior
Office of The Secretary JAN 23 1919

The within will, dated December 10, 1913, of Coyote Looks Up, deceased Crow allottee No. 482, is hereby approved in accordance with the Act of June 25, 1910 (36 Stats. L., 855-6) as amended by Act of February 14, 1913 (37 Stats. L., 678).

Signed S G Hopkins

Assistant Secretary

▲▼▲▼▲▼▲▼▲▼▲▼▲▼

TAKES THE IRON

To Whom it may concern
I Takes The Iron, widow of Short Bull, being of sound mind, do devise and bequeath all property of whatever nature I am possessed to be divided and and[sic] apportioned as follows, to wit
One half of all I possess to go to my nephew Eagle Turns
The remainder one half to go to my adopted daughter, Trace Long Ear.
Dated this 7th day of December 1915.

	SPCope Farmer				*Her*
Witnesses			*Takes The Iron*		[thumb print]
	Carl Crooked Arm				*mark*
	Interpereter[sic]				

PROBATE
95953-18
J M T
Department of The Interior,
Office of Indian Affairs, Washington,

JAN 23 1919

Indian Wills, 1911 – 1921 Book Two
Records of The Bureau of Indian Affairs

The within will of Takes The Iron, deceased row allottee No. 163, is hereby recommended for approval in accordance with the provisions of the Act of June 25, 1910 (36 Stats. L., 855-6) as amended by Act of February 14, 1913 (37 Stats. L., 678).

Respectfully,

E B Meritt

Assistant Commissioner

Department of The Interior

Office of The Secretary JAN 27 1919

Pursuant to the provisions of the Act of June 25, 1910 (36 Stats. L., 855-6) as amended by the Act of February 14, 1913 (37 Stats. L., 678), the within will of Takes The Iron, executed Dec. 9 1915, is hereby approved.

S G Hopkins

Assistant Secretary

▲▼▲▼▲▼▲▼▲▼▲▼▲▼

ME-TA-GAE-ZE WEBSTER

I, Me-ta-gae-se Webster, Macy, Nebraska, being of sound mind and memory, do make and publish this my last will and testament.

1. My allotment of land which I hold by Trust Patent under the Act of Congress of August 7, 1882 and the amendatory Act thereof of March 3, 1893 to wit: The North one-half of South-east quarter of Section fourteen, Township Twenty-five and Range Seven East of the Sixth Principal Meridian and containing 80 acres.

2. All my rights and title in and to the Frank Webster allotment consisting of the Southwest quarter of Section Twenty-six Township Twenty-five, Range nine.

I devise and bequeath to my four children, Peter Webster, Ta-gra-ha Robinson, Sarah Webster Robinson McCauley, and Anna Webster Reese, all of my rights and title to the Frank Webster allotment, each of the above named children to share equally.

I devise and bequeath to my three grand children and children of my deceased son Samuel Webster, Louis Webster, Jane Webster Stabler and Nellie Webster one-half interest in my own allotment described above. Each of the above named children to share equally in this one-half interest in my allotment.

3. This remaining one-half interest in my allotment I devised[sic] and bequeath to my children and grand-children as follows: 1/5 interest to each of my four children, viz, Peter Webster, Ta-gra-ha Robinson, Sarah Webster Robinson McCauley and Anna Webster Reese; and the remaining one-fifth interest in one half of my allotment in equal shares to Louis Webster, Jane Webster Stabler and Nellie Webster, children of my deceased son Samuel Webster.

I hereby revoke all my former wills made by me.

In witness whereof I have hereunto set my hand this 16th day of March 1915 and do hereby declare the same to be my last will and testament. her

Me-ta-gae-ze Webster [thumb print]
mark

We, whose names are hereunto subscribed do hereby certify that Me-ta-he-ze Webster, the testatrix subscribed her name to this instrument in our presence and in the presence of each of us and declared at the same time in our presence and hearting that this instrument was her last will and testament and we at her request signed our names hereto in her presence as attesting witnesses.

Selas Wood
Allen Peabody

I recommend that the foregoing instrument be approved by the Commissioner of Indian Affairs and the Secretary of the Interior as required by law.

_____

Dated this day of ....

Washington, D.C.

The above will is hereby approved.

_____

Commissioner of Indian Affairs

The above will is hereby approved.

_____

Secretary of Interior

PROBATE
66446-18
J M T

Department of The Interior,
Office of Indian Affairs, Washington,   JAN 18 1919

The within will of Me-ta-ga-e Webster, deceased Omaha allottee No. 802-n, is hereby recommended for disapproval in accordance with the provisions of the Act of June 25, 1910 (36 Stats. L., 855-6) as amended by Act of February 14, 1913 (37 Stats. L., 678).

Respectfully,
E B Meritt
Assistant Commissioner

Department of The Interior
Office of The Secretary JAN 23 1919

Pursuant to the provisions of the Act of June 25, 1910 (36 Stats. L., 855-6) as amended by the Act of February 14, 1913 (37 Stats. L., 678), the within will of Me-ta-ga-e Webster, executed March 16, 1915, is hereby disapproved.

S G Hopkins
Assistant Secretary

▲▼▲▼▲▼▲▼▲▼▲▼▲▼▲▼

METAGAE WEBSTER

THE LAST WILL & TESTAMENT
of
METAGAE WEBSTER

I, Metagae Webster, of the Omaha Reservation in Thurston County, Nebraska, do hereby make and publish this instrument to be my Last Will and Testament.

First.

I am an Omaha Indian and am holding an allotment of land in Thurston County, Nebraska, on the Omaha Reservation under trust patent of allotment issued to me under the At of Congress of August 7, 1882, and its amendatory act which allotment is hereinafter described. And I am including said premises in this my Last Will and Testament under the authority of the Act of Congress of June 25, 1910, providing for the testamentary disposition of allotted Indian lands.

Second.

I direct that all of my just debts and funeral expenses be paid as soon as possible after my decease, and as conveniently as can be paid, but the payment of such debts shall in no wise be a lien upon my real estate herein described.

Third.

I give, devise and bequeath unto my son, Peter Webster, the North Half of the Southeast Quarter of Section 14, in Township 25, North of Range 7, East of the 6th Principal Meridian, in Thurston County, Nebraska, the same being my allotment No. 802, conveying after my death and upon the approval hereof all of the entire estate, right, and title, and interest therein to my said beneficiary forever, and I direct the Secretary of the Interior to issue unto my said son, Peter Webster, a fee simple patent therefore at the proper time.

Fourth.

I hereby revoke any former will or testamentary disposition made by me at any time prior hereto.

IN WITNESS WHEREOF, I have hereunto subscribed my name in Thurston County, Nebraska, on this 15th day of September, 1914, and do hereby declare the above instrument to be my Last Will and Testament.

her
Metagae Webster [thumb print]
mark

In the Presence of
    Henrietta Freemont
    Susan La F. Picotte

The foregoing instrument was subscribed, published, and declared by Metagae Webster to be her Last Will and Testament in our presence, and in the presence of each of us on this 15th day of September, 1914, and we at the same time at her request and in her presence and in the presence of each other hereunto subscribe our names and residence as the attesting witnesses hereto, this 15th day of September 1914.

Henrietta Freemont
Susan La F. Picotte

PROBATE
66446-18
J M T

Department of The Interior,   JAN 18 1919
Office of Indian Affairs, Washington,

The within will of Me-ta-ga-e Webster, deceased Omaha allottee No. 802-n, is hereby recommended for disapproval in accordance with the provisions of the Act of June 25, 1910 (36 Stats. L., 855-6) as amended by Act of February 14, 1913 (37 Stats. L., 678).

Respectfully,
E B Meritt
Assistant Commissioner

Department of The Interior
Office of The Secretary   JAN 23 1919

Pursuant to the provisions of the Act of June 25, 1910 (36 Stats. L., 855-6) as amended by the Act of February 14, 1913 (37 Stats. L., 678), the within will of Me-ta-ga-e Webster, executed September 15, 1914, is hereby disapproved.

S G Hopkins
Assistant Secretary

▲▼▲▼▲▼▲▼▲▼▲▼▲▼▲▼

PHILLIP EAGLE TURNS

Last Will and Testament
of
Phillip Eagle Turns

IN THE NAME OF GOD, AMEN.

I, *Phillip Eagle Turns* of *St. Xavier, Mont.* being of sound mind, memory and understanding, do hereby make and publish this my last will and testament, hereby revoking and annulling all wills by me heretofore made, in manner and form following, that is to say:

First; I direct that all my just debts and funeral expenses; and expenses of my last illness shall be paid by my executor hereinafter named as soo after my decease as convenient;

Second; I give, devise and bequeath to

Richard Wallace one half of my estate, both real and personal and mixed.

Third; All the rest and residue of my estate, both real, and personal and mixed, I give, devise and bequeath to my lawful heirs as determined after my decease.

And lastly; I do hereby nominate, constitute and appoint *the Superintendent of Crow Reservation* executor of this my last will and testament.

In testimony Whereof, I have set my hand and seal to this, my last will and Testament, at *St. Xavier* Montana, this *5th* day of *July* in the year of our Lord one thousand nine hundred and *seventeen.*

Phillip Eagle Turns

Signed, sealed, published and declared by said *Phillip Eagle Turns* in our presence, as and for *his* last Will and Testament, and at *his* request and in our presence, and in the presence of each other, we have hereunto subscribed our names as attesting witnesses thereto.

Barney Old Coyote	of	*St. Xavier, Mont.*
Philip Ironhead	of	*St. Xavier, Mont.*
Thomas Gardner	of	*St. Xavier, Mont.*

Subscribed and sworn to before me this 6th day of July, A.D. 1917

W. T. Foster

Notary Public

My commission expires April 24, 1919.

Probate
58813-18
J M T
Department of The Interior,   JAN 18 1919
Office of Indian Affairs, Washington,

Indian Wills, 1911 – 1921 Book Two
Records of The Bureau of Indian Affairs

The within will dated July 5, 1917, of Philip[sic] Eagleturns, Crow allottee No. 559, is hereby recommended for approval in accordance with the provisions of the Act of June 25, 1910 (36 Stats. L., 855-6) as amended by Act of February 14, 1913 (37 Stats. L., 678).

> Respectfully,
> *EB Meritt*
> Assistant Commissioner

Department of The Interior
Office of The Secretary JAN 23 1919

The within will dated July 5, 1917, of Philip[sic] Eagleturns, Crow allottee No. 559, is hereby approved in accordance with the Act of June 25, 1910 (36 Stats. L., 855-6) as amended by Act of February 14, 1913 (37 Stats. L., 678).

> *S G Hopkins*
> Assistant Secretary

▲▼▲▼▲▼▲▼▲▼▲▼▲▼

WITECAWIN or SOPHIA RENVILLE

WILL

I, Witecawin, of Agency Township, Roberts County, State of South Dakota, being of sound mind and memory, and in consideration of the uncertainty of this frail and transitory life, do therefore, ordain, make, publish, and declare this to be my LAST WILL and TESTAMENT.

First:- I order and direct that the executor, hereinafter named, pay all my just debts and funeral expenses as soon after my decease as conveniently may be.

Second:- After the payment of such funeral expenses and debts, I give, devise, and bequeath unto my grand daughter Vivian Renville, that part of my original allotment, on the Sisseton-Wahpeton, S. Dak. Res. described as the Northwest quarter of the Northeast quarter (MW/4 of NE/4), Section Sixteen (16), Township One hundred and twenty four (124) North, Range Fifty one (51) West, 5th Principal Meridian; To my daughter Emma Renville Blackstone, I give, devise, and bequeath that part of my original allotment, on said reservation, described as the

130

Northeast quarter of the Northeast quarter (NE/4 of NE/4), Section 16, Township One hundred and twenty four (124) North., Range Fifty one (51) West, 5th Principal Meridian, All of which is located in the state of South Dak.

Lastly:- I make. constitute, and appoint Supt. E. D. Massman, or his successor in office, to be executor of this my last will and Testament, hereby revoking all former wills made by me.

IN TESTIMONY WHEREOF, I have hereunto subscribed my name and affixed my seal, this 22nd day of March, 1916.

Witnesses to mark:-   *her mark*
(Signature illegible)   *Witecawin* [thumb print]
(Signature illegible)

THIS INSTRUMENT was on the day of the date thereof, signed, published and declared by the said testator Witecawin, to be her Last Will and Testament, in our presence, who at her request, have subscribed our names thereto as witnesses, in her presence, and in the presence of each other.

J. H. (Last name illegible)
Sisseton, S. D.
Simon (Last name illegible)
Sisseton, S. Dak.

Probate
78428-17

Department of The Interior,
Office of Indian Affairs, Washington,
JAN 23 1919

The within will of Witecawin or Sophia Renville, is hereby recommended for approval in accordance with the provisions of the Act of June 25, 1910 (36 Stats. L., 855-6) as amended by Act of February 14, 1913 (37 Stats. L., 678).

Respectfully,
EB Meritt
Assistant Commissioner

Department of The Interior
Office of The Secretary   JAN 27 1919

The within will of Witecawin or Sophia Renville, is hereby approved in accordance with the Act of June 25, 1910 (36 Stats. L., 855-6) as amended by Act of February 14, 1913 (37 Stats. L., 678).

S G Hopkins
Assistant Secretary

▲▼▲▼▲▼▲▼▲▼▲▼▲

OFFICE OF INDIAN AFFAIRS
RECEIVED
FEB 21 1916
18960

TANINYANWANKEWIN

LAST WILL AND TESTAMENT OF TANINYANWANKEWIN.

IN THE NAME OF GOD, AMEN;

I, Taninyanwankewin, of Charles Mix County, State of South Dakota, being of sound and disposing mind and memory but being uncertain of life and certain of the approach of death, and desiring to dispose of all my worldly possessions while I still have the power to do so, do make and declare this to be my last will and testament hereby revoking and annulling any and all wills heretofore made by me.

First:-I give devise and bequeath unto my niece, Wakicunzana, the sum of $50.00

Second:-I give, devise, and bequeath unto my grand-nephew, Charles Cordier, all of my real estate consisting of my own allotment given to me by the Government, and described as follows, to-wit- The NW/4 of the NW/4 of Section 27, and the E/2 of the NE/4 of Section 28, in Township 97 North of Range 63, West, containing One Hundred Twenty (120) acres according to the Government Survey; and after all my just debts and funeral expenses have been paid and a monument purchased and erected on my grave to cost not less than $100.00, whatever amount of money remains in the hands of the superintendent of Yankton Agency, which now amounts to $612.71, shall go to my grand-nephew, Charles Cordier; also all my inherited interests of every description, both real estate and personal property, including my interests in the estate of my deceased husband, Tatankanajin; my deceased son, Tasunkesapa; and my deceased sister, Hintunkasanwin.

IN TESTIMONY WHEREOF, I have set my hand and seal, this 16th day of June, 1915, at Greenwood, S.D. Charles Nix County, South Dakota.

	her
Witnesses:	Taninyanwankewin [thumb print]
David Zephin	mark
Charlotte Schulz	

Signed, Sealed, Published, and Declared, this 16th day of June, 1915, by the said Taninyanwankewin, in our presence, as and for her last will and testament, and at her request, and in her presence, and in the presence of each other, we have hereunto subscribed our names as attesting witnesses.

David Zephin
David Simmons

Probate
49805-13
 M H W

Department of The Interior,
Office of Indian Affairs, Washington,
NOV -9 1918

The within will of Taninyanwakewin, deceased Yankton Sioux allottee No. 129, is hereby recommended for approval in accordance with the provisions of the Act of June 25, 1910 (36 Stats. L., 855-6) as amended by Act of February 14, 1913 (37 Stats. L., 678).

Respectfully,
EB Meritt
Assistant Commissioner

Department of The Interior
Office of The Secretary NOV 22 1918

The within will of Taninyanwakewin, deceased Yankton Sioux allottee No. 129, is hereby approved in accordance with the Act of June 25, 1910 (36 Stats. L., 855-6) as amended by Act of February 14, 1913 (37 Stats. L., 678).

S G Hopkins
Assistant Secretary

▲▼▲▼▲▼▲▼▲▼▲▼▲▼▲▼

LOUIS BLAINE

Last Will and Testament
of
Louis Blaine

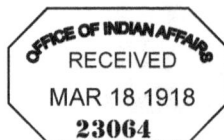

OFFICE OF INDIAN AFFAIRS
RECEIVED
MAR 18 1918
23064

IN THE NAME OF GOD, AMEN.

I, *Louis Blaine* of *Crow Agency, Mont* being of sound mind, memory, and understanding, do hereby make and publish this, my last will and testament, hereby revoking and annulling all wills by me heretofore made, in manner and form following, that is to say:

First: I direct that all my just debts and funeral expenses, and expenses of my last illness shall be paid by my executor hereinafter names as soon after my decease as convenient:

Second: I give, devise and bequeath to

Billie Steel one half of my money after debts and funeral expenses are paid, and request that he care for my daughter Media during her minority; one fourth of my money to my daughter Media Blaine, and one fourth of my money to Buffalo That Shakes who has taken care of me. All the balance of my property, real and personal, to my daughter Media Blaine.

Third: All the rest and residue of my estate, both real and personal and mixed, I give, devise and bequeath to my lawful heirs as determined after my decease.

And lastly: I do hereby nominate, constitute and appoint *Supt Crow Agency* executor of this my last will and testament.

In testimony whereof, I have set my hand and seal to this, my last will and testament, at *Crow Agency*, Montana, this *1st* day of *January* in the year of our Lord, one thousand nine hundred and *seventeen.*

Louis Blaine

Signed sealed, published and declared by said *Louis Blaine* in our presence, as and for *his* last will and testament, and at *his* request and in our presence and in the presence of each other, we have hereunto subscribed our names as attesting witnesses thereto.

Edward Lawrance	of	*Crow Agency, Mont.*
Alfred E Wager	of	*Crow Agency, Mont.*
C D Munro	of	*Crow Agency, Mont.*

Probate
23064-18

Department of The Interior,
Office of Indian Affairs, Washington,
NOV 21 1918
The within will of Louis Blaine, Crow allottee No. 664, is hereby recommended for approval in accordance with the provisions of the Act of June 25, 1910 (36 Stats. L., 855-6) as amended by Act of February 14, 1913 (37 Stats. L., 678).

Respectfully,
EB Meritt
Assistant Commissioner

Department of The Interior
Office of The Secretary NOV 23 1918

The within will of Louis Blaine, Crow allottee No. 664, is hereby approved in accordance with the Act of June 25, 1910 (36 Stats. L., 855-6) as amended by Act of February 14, 1913 (37 Stats. L., 678), and the testator's daughter, Media Blaine is found to be entitled to the real estate, and $365.41, Billie Steel to $730.80, and Buffalo that Shakes to $365.41. A fee of $15 is to be collected by the superintendent under Act of May 18, 1916 (36 Stat. 123-7).

S G Hopkins
Assistant Secretary

RECEIVED
MAY 6- 1918
38215

MRS. BILL THOMAS

DEPARTMENT OF THE INTERIOR

RECEIVED
DEC 16 1915
134165

UNITED STATES INDIAN SERVICE

Kiowa Indian Agency
Anadarko, Oklahoma, Nov. 22, 1915

LAST WILL AND TESTAMENT OF MRS. BILL THOMAS.

I, Mrs. Bill Thomas, of Caddo County, Oklahoma, sound in body and mind, but sensible of the uncertainty of life, and desiring to make disposition of my property and affairs while in health and strength, do hereby make, publish and declare the following to be my last will and testament, hereby revoking and canceling all other and former wills by me at any time made.

First: I hereby direct the payment of all my funeral expenses.

Second:-I give and devise to Josie Thomas Keechi, Wichita Indian allottee No. 587, my daughter, to Willie Thomas, Caddo Indian allottee No. 650, my son, and to Lillie Hoag, unallotted, my granddaughter, being the daughter of my daughter Nellie Thomas, Caddo Indian allottee No. 218, in equal shares, all f my property of which I may die possessed which is to include my trust allotment of land, being the North-East quarter of Section 21, township 10 north, of Range 11 West, of the Indian Meridian, in Caddo County Oklahoma, being known upon the rolls of the Interior Department as Caddo Indian allotment No. 584. By this devise Josie Thomas Keechi, Willie Thomas, and Lillie Hoag will share in my estate to the extent of one-third each.

In the event that I should die intestate my estate would be divided among my three children, Nellie, Josie and Willie, but owing to the fact that I am devising one-third of my estate to Lillie Hoag, daughter or my daughter Nellie Thomas Coffee, Caddo Indian allottee No. 218, I am not remembering her, and am not devising any of my property to my said daughter Nellie. This meets with her full approval.

In witness whereof, I have to this, my last will and testament, consisting of three sheets of paper, subscribed my name this 22nd day of November, 1915, at Kiowa Indian Agency, Anadarko, Oklahoma.

her thumb mark

Witnesses: *Mrs. Bill Thomas* [thumb print]

Chambers T. Prickett
Levi Kemble

Subscribed by Mrs. Bill Thomas, Wichita Indian allottee No. 584, in the presence of each of us, the undersigned, and at the same time declared by her to us to be her last will and testament, and we, thereupon at the request of Mrs. Bill Thomas, Wichita Indian allottee No. 584, in her presence, and in the presence of each other, sign our names hereto as witnesses this 22nd day of November, A.D.1915, at Kiowa Indian

Agency, Anadarko, Oklahoma.

> *Chambers T Prickett*
> P.O. *Anadarko, Okla*
> *Levi Kemble*
> P.O. *Anadarko, Okla*

INTERPRETER'S CERTIFICATE.

I, Oliver Exendine, hereby certify on honor that I acted as interpreter during the execution of the foregoing last will and testament by Mrs. Bill Thomas, Wichita Indian allottee No. 584; that I interpreted correctly all the contents of said will to said testatrix, that she fully understands all the terms thereof, and that this will was drawn in accordance with her wishes and directions. I further certify that I have no interest in this matter.

Signed this 22nd day of November, 1915, at Kiowa Indian Agency, Anadarko, Oklahoma.

> *Oliver W Exendine*
> Interpreter

Department of The Interior,
Office of Indian Affairs, Washington,
JAN 15 1917

The within will dated November 22, 1915, of Mrs. Bill Thomas, Caddo allottee No. 584, is hereby recommended for approval in accordance with the provisions of the Act of June 25, 1910 (36 Stats. L., 855-6) as amended by Act of February 14, 1913 (37 Stats. L., 678).

> Respectfully,
> *EB Meritt*
> Assistant Commissioner

Department of The Interior
Office of The Secretary NOV 23 1918

The within will of Mrs. Bill Thomas, Caddo allottee No. 584, is hereby approved in accordance with the Act of June 25, 1910 (36 Stats. L., 855-6) as amended by Act of February 14, 1913 (37 Stats. L., 678),

> *Bo Sweeney*
> Assistant Secretary

▲▼▲▼▲▼▲▼▲▼▲▼▲▼▲▼

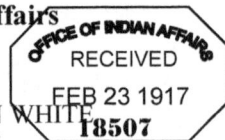

OFFICE OF INDIAN AFFAIRS
RECEIVED
FEB 23 1917
18507

JOHN WHITE

LAST WILL AND TESTAMENT OF JOHN WHITE
KLAMATH ALLOTTEE NO. 1317
Klamath Agency, Oregon.

I, John White, a Klamath Indian Allottee, No. 1317, aged about 54 years, of the Klamath Reservation in the County of Klamath and State of Oregon, do hereby make, publish and declare this my last will and testament, as follows:-

1st. I direct that the expenses of my last illness and funeral expenses be paid.

2ndly. I give, devise and bequeath unto Jennie White, my wife, Klamath Allottee, No. 1318, aged 56 years, residing on the Klamath Reservation, near the post office of Yainax, Oregon, all my property, both real and personal, which I may own at the time of my death, or in which I may have any interest, of whatsoever the kind the same may be, or wheresoever situated, to have and to hold unto the said Jennie White, my wife, her heirs and assigns forever.

My real property consists of my allotment on the Klamath Reservation, in the County of Klamath, State of Oregon, now held in trust by by[sic] the Government of the United States, and particularly described as follows:- Allotment No. 1174-1317 -- The south half of the north-east quarter and the north half of the south-east quarter of section seventeen in township thirty-five south of range ten east of the Wilamette Meridian, Oregon, containing one hundred sixty acres.

3rdly. I hereby revoke all former will by me made.

4thly. I nominate and appoint the Superintendent of the Klamath Reservation, whoever he may be at the time of my death, Executor of this my last will and testament.

In witness whereof, I have hereunto set my hand and seal this 27th day of July, 1916, at Yainax, County of Klamath and State of Oregon.

His
JOHN WHITE [thumb print]
Mark.

The foregoing instrument, consisting of 1 page, was this 27th day of July, 1916 by the said John White, declared to be his last will and testament and was signed and sealed by him in our presence and we, at his request and in his presence, and in the presence of each other, subscribed our names hereto this 27th day of July, 1916, at Yainax, Oregon.

Indian Wills, 1911 – 1921 Book Two
Records of The Bureau of Indian Affairs

Sargent Brown   residing at **Chiloquin, Oregon.**
Charles S Minor   residing at **Klamath Agency, Oregon.**
Fred A Zaker   residing at **Klamath Agency, Oregon.**

Probate
34353-17
J G McG

Department of The Interior,
Office of Indian Affairs, Washington,
AUG -4 1917

It is recommended that the within will of John White, Klamath allottee No. 1317, be approved pursuant to the provisions of the Act of June 25, 1910 (36 Stats. L., 855-6) as amended by Act of February 14, 1913 (37 Stats. L., 678).

Respectfully,
EB Meritt
Assistant Commissioner

Department of The Interior
Office of The Secretary AUG -6 1917

The within will of John White, Klamath allottee No. 1317, is approved pursuant to the provisions of the Act of June 25, 1910 (36 Stats. L., 855-6) as amended by Act of February 14, 1913 (37 Stats. L., 678).

Alexander Stogelshug
First Assistant Secretary

▲▼▲▼▲▼▲▼▲▼▲▼▲▼▲▼

FREDERICK SOUND OF THE GUN

DEPARTMENT OF THE INTERIOR

UNITED STATES INDIAN SERVICE

Pryor, Mont.
May 20, 1916

I, Frederick Sounds of the Gun, being in sound mind at present time give to Plentycoos, one half of all of my property both personal and real estate. Plentycoos has taken care of me since the death of my father Sounds of the Gun and I have lived with her since the death of my mother.

No other person was interested in my welfare.

The other half of my property both personal and real estate I give to my heirs as determined by the Indian Department, but if no heirs are found to exist I give all my property to Plentycoos.

his thumb

Frederick Sounds of the Gun[thumb print]

mark

Witness H.L. Oberlander, Physician, Pryor, Mont.

     John Frost

        Clark

           Pryor, Mont.

Probate

79753-18

J M T

Department of The Interior,

Office of Indian Affairs, Washington,

                   JAN -9 1919

The within will dated May 20, 1916, of Frederick Sounds Gun or Sounds The Gun, deceased Crow minor allottee No. 1865, is hereby recommended for disapproval in accordance with the provisions of the Act of June 25, 1910 (36 Stats. L., 855-6) as amended by Act of February 14, 1913 (37 Stats. L., 678).

Respectfully,

EB Meritt

Assistant Commissioner

Department of The Interior

Office of The Secretary   JAN 16 1919

The within will dated May 20, 1916, of Frederick Sounds Gun or Sounds The Gun, deceased Crow minor allottee No. 1865, is hereby disapproved in accordance with the Act of June 25, 1910 (36 Stats. L., 855-6) as amended by Act of February 14, 1913 (37 Stats. L., 678).

S G Hopkins

Assistant Secretary

▲▼▲▼▲▼▲▼▲▼▲▼▲▼▲▼

STRIKES THE ONE GOES IN THE HOUSE

Pryor, Mont.
Oct 30 - 1916

I Strikes the One Goes In the House, wife of Prettytail, being of sound mind and memory declare this to be my last will and testament, to wit.

I give device[sic] and bequeath a two seated spring wagon to Prettytail my husband.

I desire that all the balance and residue of my property be divided equally between my two nephews Michael Blue Moccasin and Pretty Coyote.

My reason for not giving more of my property to Prettytail my husband is for the reason that he has repeatedly quarreled with me and now has left me and I am in a helpless condition.

My two nephews are providing for me

her
Strikes the One Goes in the House [thumb print]
mark

Witness

    H L Oberlander - Physician
        Pryor, Mont.
    Henry Russell
        Pryor, Mont.

Probate
37087-18
J M T

Department of The Interior,
Office of Indian Affairs, Washington,
JAN -9 1919
The within will, dated October 30, 1916, of Strikes The One In The House (Strikes One Going In The House), deceased Crow allottee No. 1981, is hereby recommended for approval in accordance with the provisions of the Act of June 25, 1910 (36 Stats. L., 855-6) as amended by Act of February 14, 1913 (37 Stats. L., 678).

            Respectfully,
            EB Meritt
            Assistant Commissioner

Department of The Interior
Office of The Secretary JAN 16 1919

The within will, dated October 30, 1916, of Strikes The One In The House (Strikes One Going In The House), deceased Crow allottee No. 1981, is hereby approved in accordance with the Act of June 25, 1910 (36 Stats. L., 855-6) as amended by Act of February 14, 1913 (37 Stats. L., 678).

S G Hopkins
Assistant Secretary

▲▼▲▼▲▼▲▼▲▼▲▼▲▼▲▼

NAH-WATCH

OFFICE OF INDIAN AFFAIRS
RECEIVED
JUN 14 1918

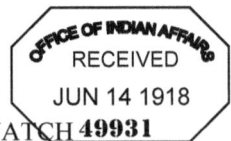

LAST WILL AND TESTAMENT OF NAH-WATCH **49931**

     I, Nah-watch, Comanche Indian allottee No. 757, of Comanche County, State of Oklahoma, being now in good health, strength of body and mind, but sensible of the uncertainty of life, and desiring to make disposition of my property and affairs while in health and strength, do hereby make, publish and declare the following to be my last will and testament, hereby revoking and cancelling all other or former wills by me at any time made.

     1. I hereby direct the payment of all my just debts and funeral expenses.

     2. It is my will, and I, hereby, direct that my farm, comprising lots three and four of the South East Quarter, and the Fr., North West quarter, Section Twenty-nine (29), all in Township Three (3) North, Range Eleven (11) West of the Indian Meridian, in Comanche County, Oklahoma, being known upon the rolls of the Interior Department as Comanche Indian allotment No. 757, be divided into two equal parts, by a line running East and West, and that the South half of said allotment, together with all the improvements and appartenances[sic] thereunto belonging, be given, and I, hereby, will and devise the same to my wife, Chi-woon-ny, a Comanche Indian allottee No. 758; and that the North half of said allotment of land be given, and I hereby will and devise the same to the four children of my deceased sister, Tan-nee, Comanche Indian allottee No. 764; Maude Chaht-in-ne-yack-que, Comanche Indian

allottee No. 765; Son-au-quoot, other wise known as Rachel Chaht-in-ne-yack-que. Comanche Indian allottee No. 766; Ralph Chaht-in-ne-yack-que, Comanche Indian allottee No. 767; and Robert Chaht-in-ne-yack-que Comanche Indian allottee No. 1489, said property to be divided equally among said four children, or those surviving at the time of my death, and I also, hereby, will and devise the South half of said allotment, above described, to the above named four children, or those surviving at the time of my death, to be equally divided among them, in the event that my said wife shall depart this life prior to my decease.

3. I give and bequeath to my wife, Chi-woon-ny, Comanche Indian allottee No. 758, all of the interest accrued or accruing from a certain investment of One Thousand Dollars ($1000.), in notes and mortgages, on real estate in Dallas, Texas, said investment having been made in the year 1903, which became due and payable July 28, 1909, and which was renewed for five years from that date. I further direct that at the death of my wife the whole of this investment of One Thousand Dollars ($1000.) with all the accrued interest thereon, be given to the above named four children, viz., Maude Chaht-in-ne-yack-que, Comanche Indian allottee No. 765; Son-au-quoot, (Rachel Chaht-in-ne-yack-que), Comanche Indian allottee No. 766; Ralph Chaht-in-ne-yack-que, Comanche Indian allottee No. 767; and Robert Chaht-in-ne-yack-que Comanche Indian allottee No. 1489. I further direct that the sum of Fifteen Hundred Dollars ($1500.00), whether the same may be in cash or invested in real estate, shall, at my death, be divided as follows, among the children of my deceased sister, Tan-nee, Comanche Indian allottee No. 764, as follows:

To Maude Chaht-in-ne-yack-que, Comanche Indian allottee No. 765, I bequeath the sum of Five Hundred Dollars ($500.00).

To Son-au-quoot, otherwise known as Rachel Chaht-in-ne-yack-que. Comanche Indian allottee No. 766, I bequeath the sum of Four Hundred Dollars ($400.00).

To Ralph Chaht-in-ne-yack-que, Comanche Indian allottee No. 767, I bequeath the sum of Four Hundred Dollars ($400.00).

To Ralph Chaht-in-ne-yack-que, Comanche Indian allottee No. 767, I bequeath the sum of Two Hundred Dollars ($200.00).

I further direct that each of these said children shall have his or her part of the interest that may have accrued on the said sum of Fifteen Hundred Dollars, ($1500.00) at the time of my death.

5. I further direct that if at my death I am possessed of any horses, that two of the horses be given to Ralph Chaht-in-be-yack-que, Comanche Indian allottee No. 765; and that two of the horses be given to Robert Chaht-in-ne-yack-que Comanche Indian allottee No. 1489; and I also direct that any and all farm implements possessed by me at the time of my death be equally divided between the said Ralph and Robert Chaht-in-ne-yack-que.

6. I further direct that all the rest, residue, and remainder of my estate, whether real or personal, or mixed, of which I may die possessed, shall be divided in equal forces, one-half to go to my said wife, and one-half to be equally divided among the said four children, or those surviving me, share and share alike, and I further will and direct that at the death of my said wife that the property devised to her in this clause shall go to, and be divided among the said four children of my said deceased sister, or those surviving me, share and share alike.

7. I hereby direct said wife, Chi-woon-ny, Comanche Indian allottee No. 758, and the above named children of my deceased sister, Tan-nee, Comanche Indian allottee No. 764, to be my nearest of kin, and only living relation.

8. I hereby designate and appoint, Henry Sluyter, executor, without bond, of this my last will and testament, in so far as it concerns property, over which the United States exercises no control and supervision; and I hereby direct that in the event of my death before the children of my deceased sister, heretofore referred to in this will, or any one of them. shall become of age, that he the said Henry Sluyter, shall act as Guardian of such minors until they shall attain their majority, and shall have full control of their property herein bequeath and devised to them, subject to such control as the United States may legally have over the trust property, referred to herein, and I hereby that he shall invest and manage the same in such manner as may seem best for such minors.

This will, in so far as it concerns my trust allotment of land, is made subject to the approval of the Secretary of the Interior.

In Witness Whereof, I, Nah-watch, Comanche Indian allottee No. 75, have to this my last will and testament, consisting of four sheets of paper, subscribed my name this *4* day of *March* 1916.

	his	
	Nah-watch [thumb print]	
Witnesses:	Testator	*mark*
Abe Ray		
Preston Pohocsacat		

Nah-watch, Comanche Indian allottee No. 757, being unable to sign his name to the foregoing instrument, affixed his right thumb mark hereto, and requested me, the undersigned, *Abe Ray*, to sign his name hereto for him, and in his behalf, which I thereupon did, at the request of Nah-watch, Comanche Indian allottee No. 757, in his presence and in the presence of each other, signed our names hereto as witnesses, this *4* day of *March*, 1916, at *Fort Sill Sub Agency Lawton Comanche* County, Oklahoma.

Abe Ray NS Indian Farmer
Lawton, Okla
P.O. ___

P.O. *Preston Pohocsacat*
P.O. *Lawton, Okla*

INTERPRETER'S CERTIFICATE.

I, *Preston Pohocsacat*, hereby certify on honor that I acted as interpreter during the execution of the foregoing will of Nah-watch, Comanche Indian allottee No. 757, that I fully and interpreter[sic] all the contents thereof, and that he fully and truly understands all the terms thereof.

That this will was drawn strictly in accordance with his directions and desires; and that I speak both the Comanche Indian and the English languages fluently.

Signed this *4* day of *March*, 1916.

Preston Pohocsacat
Interpreter.

Indian Wills, 1911 – 1921 Book Two
Records of The Bureau of Indian Affairs

Department of The Interior,
Office of Indian Affairs, Washington,

APR -4 1917

It is recommended that the within will of Nah-watch, Comanche allottee #757, be approved under the provisions of the Act of June 25, 1910 (36 Stats. L., 855-6) as amended by Act of February 14, 1913 (37 Stats. L., 678), in so far as it applies to trust property.

Respectfully,

EB Meritt

Assistant Commissioner

Department of The Interior
Office of The Secretary, Washington

APR 10 1917

The accompanying will of Nah-watch, Comanche allottee #757, is hereby approved under the Act of June 25, 1910 (36 Stats. L. 855-6) as amended by Act of February 14, 1913 (37 Stats. L. 678), in so far as it applies to trust property.

S G Hopkins

Assistant Secretary

▲ ▼ ▲ ▼ ▲ ▼ ▲ ▼ ▲ ▼ ▲ ▼ ▲ ▼ ▲ ▼

MRS. CLARA GOOD nee CLARA STRONGLEFTHAND

----W I L L----

I, MRS. CLARA GOOD, nee CLARA STRONGLEFTHAND, being of sound mind and in a weak physical condition, sensible of the uncertainty of life and the certainty of death do hereby-

GIVE, DEVISE, and BEQUEATH all of my property of every kind and character, consisting of my interest in the allotment of my deceaed husband, Bigman, and two deceased daughters, both of whom died unmarried and without issue; and all other land interests which I may have on the Crow Reservation or anywhere else. Also two mares, two colts, and all other personal property which may belong to me at the time of my death, to the following:

Good, my husband, One ($1.00) Dollar
Stronglefthand Woman, my mother, 1 (one) mare, branded M9

Fannie Seminole, my daughter, Half (1/2) of the remaining part
Grover Wolfvoice, my son, the other half of the remaining part

My reasons for leaving only $1.00 to my husband are: that since I have been in poor health he and his people not only neglected me but were unkind and in many ways mistreated me. When I desired to visit my mother, Mrs. Stronglefthand Woman, and daughter, Fannie Seminole living at Lame Deer, my husband refused to accompany me on said visit. I had to depend on my son hearing of my condition by chance and coming for me in order to give me an opportunity to see my mother and daughter at a time when my condition of health was such I did not expect to live long. When my son, Grover Wolfvoice came for me to bring me from Crow Agency to Tongue River Agency to visit my mother and daughter, the food which I had purchased was not sent along by my husband and his people but instead thereof, food which was unfit aor any human being to eat was put in for me. There was a can of milk which had been opened and spoiled put in as a part of the food.

At times when I would ask my husband to repair the fence on my place his sister would interfere and not let him go. My former husband's place is an excellent medow[sic] but Good, my husband has neglected it and it is going to ruin.

I have heard that Good, my husband wanted to obtain a divorce from me and that he said as soon as he had sufficient money he would take it through Court.

I have already given my husband a big mare and also a find[sic] saddle animal and at the time we were married I had $30.00 which he took from me for his own use.

SIGNED AND SEALED, on this twenty-sixth day of July, 1917, TONGUE RIVER AGENCY, MONTANA.

Her

CLARA GOOD nee Clara Stronglefthand [thumb print]

Mark

WE CERTIFY ON HONOR, that Clara Good, nee Clara Stronglefthand, signed the foregoing instrument as her free and voluntary act, and that the signing of the instrument was in our presence and that we were all present and witnesses[sic] her signature at the same time.

WE FURTHER CERTIFY that we believe the said Clara Good nee Clara Stronglefthand understood fully what she was doing at the time and that the same is her true will.

> *His*
> *Austin Texas* [thumb print]
> *Eugene J Fisher   Mark*
> *Eugene Standing Elk*
> *Marion M Chapman*

64671-18
Probate
M.H.W.
Approval of will Clara Wolfvoice, Big Man
or Bearwoman, Crow Agency Mont.
Department of The Interior,
Office of Indian Affairs, Washington,

The within will of Clara Wolfvoice, Bigman or Bearwoman, or Stronglefthand, deceased allottee No. 2379, is hereby recommended for approval in accordance with the provisions of the Act of June 25, 1910 (36 Stats. L., 855-6) as amended by Act of February 14, 1913 (37 Stats. L., 678), and the regulations of the Department.

> Respectfully,
> *EB Meritt*
> Assistant Commissioner

Department of the Interior,
Office of the Secretary.   DEC 27 1918

Pursuant to the Act of June 25, 1910, 36 Stat., L. 855 as amended by the act of February 14, 1913, (37 Stat L. 678) and the regulations of the Department I hereby approve the within will of Clara Wolfvoice, Bigman, Bearwoman, or Stronglefthand, deceased allottee No. 2379.

> *S G Hopkins*
> 10-LSC-18   Assistant Secretary.

▲▼▲▼▲▼▲▼▲▼▲▼▲▼▲▼

JUSTINE BLUECLOUD WAKEMAN or JUSTINE BLUECLOUD

LAST WILL AND TESTAMENT

I, Justine Bluecloud Wakeman in the County of Roberts, and State of South Dakota, being of sound mind and memory, and considering the uncertainty of this frail and transitory life, do therefore make, ordain, publish and declare this to be my LAST WILL AND TESTAMENT.

First. I order and direct that the executor, hereinafter named, pay all my just debts and funeral expenses as soon after my decease as conveniently may be.

Second. After the payment of such funeral expenses and debts I give, devise and bequeath: To my cousin, Henry Redearth, the S.E. Quarter of the S.W. Quarter of section 33, Township 124, Range 51 in Roberts County, South Dakota, beng a part of my allotment as a Sisseton Indian. This land is bequeathed to Henry Redearth because he as cared for me for several months and supported my husband and myself while I have been ill, and I desire that he have this land as partial payment for the great amount of care and attention he and his family have given me and are giving me at the present time. To my husband, Soloman Wakeman, I bequeath the remainder of my allotment, being the S.E. Quarter of the S.E Quarter and the S.W. quarter of the S.E. Quarter in section 26, Township 124 Range 51, and the N.W. quarter of the S.E. Quarter in section 33-124-51, and my undivided interests in the estates of John M. Bluecloud, Sis-Wah. Allottee No. 1285, and Nora Bluecloud, Sis-Wah. Allottee No. 226, and any other undivided interests I may have in any estates, the heirs of which are now determined or may be determined.

Lastly, I make, constitute and appoint E.D. Mossman, Supt. & Sp'l. Disb. Agent, or his successor in office, to be Executor of my Last Will and Testament, hereby revoking all former Wills by me made.

In Witness Whereof, I have hereunto subscribed my name and affixed my seal the seventh day of May, in the year of our Lord One Thousand Nine Hundred and Seventeen.

Justine Bluecloud Wakeman

This instrument was on the day of the date thereof signed, published and declared by the said testator, Justine Bluecloud Wakeman, to be her Last Will and Testament in our presence, who at her request have subscribed our names thereto as witnesses in her presence and in the presence of each other.

E.A. Henninger
(Signature Illegible)

Probate
59014-17
66569-18
 MHW

Approval of will of Justine Bluecloud Wakeman,
Sisseton, S. D.

Department of The Interior,
Office of Indian Affairs, Washington, DEC 24 1918

The within will of Justine Bluecloud Wakeman or Justine Bluecloud deceased Sisseton-Wahpeton allottee No. 228, is hereby recommended for approval in accordance with the provisions of the Act of June 25, 1910 (36 Stats. L., 855-6) as amended by Act of February 14, 1913 (37 Stats. L., 678), and the regulations of the Department and that the clerical error in the description of part of said land; viz Section 33, be construed to be Section 26.

Respectfully,
EB Meritt
Assistant Commissioner

Department of the Interior,
Office of the Secretary.   DEC 27 1918

Pursuant to the Act of June 25, 1910, 36 Stat., L. 855 as amended by the act of February 14, 1913, (37 Stat L. 678) and the regulations of the Department I hereby approve the within will of Justine Bluecloud Wakeman or Justine Bluecloud, deceased Sisseton-Wahpeton allottee No. 228 and construe the clerical error in the description of part of said land, viz: Section 33, to be Section 26.

S G Hopkins
Assistant Secretary.

▲▼▲▼▲▼▲▼▲▼▲▼▲▼▲▼

FLAT BACK

Last Will and Testament
of
Flat Back

IN THE NAME OF GOD, AMEN.

Indian Wills, 1911 – 1921 Book Two
Records of The Bureau of Indian Affairs

I, **Flat Back**, of **Crow Agency, Montana** being of sound mind, memory, and understanding, do hereby make and publish this my last will and testament, hereby revoking and annulling all wills by me heretofore made, in manner and form following, that is to say:

First; I direct that all my just debts and funeral expenses, and expenses of my last illness shall be paid by my executor hereinafter names as soon after my decease as convenient;

Second; I give, devise and bequeath to

Edson Firebear one half of all my property both real and personal. This is in consideration of care given me during my old age as I am blind and helpless.
To my wife, Many Talks with Him, the balance of my property, if she survives me. If my wife should die first I desire that her half of my property shall go to Carry Wallace, the wife of Edson Firebear, for her care of myself and wife in our old age.

Third;   All the rest and residue of my estate, both real, and personal and mixed, I give, devise and bequeath to my lawful heirs as determined after my decease.

And lastly; I do hereby nominate, constitute and appoint **Superintendent Crow Agency** executor of this my last will and testament.

In testimony Whereof, I have set my hand and seal to this, my last will and Testament, at **Crow Agency** Montana, this **15th** day of **March** in the year of our Lord one thousand nine hundred and **fifteen**

His
Flat Back [thumb print]
Mark

Signed, sealed, published and declared by said **Flat Back** in our presence, as and for **his** last Will and testament, and at **his** request and in our presence, and in the presence of each other, we have hereunto subscribed our names as attesting witnesses thereto.

Josephine Laforge	of	*Crow Agency Mont.*
CD Munro	of	" " "
P. N. Loukes	of	" " "

Probate
37145-18
J M T

Department of The Interior,
Office of Indian Affairs, Washington,
DEC 24 1918
It is recommended that the within will, dated March 15, 1915, of Flat Back, deceased Crow allottee No. 1468, of the Crow Agency, be approved pursuant to the provisions of the Act of June 25, 1910 (36 Stats. L., 855-6) as amended by Act of February 14, 1913 (37 Stats. L., 678).

Respectfully,
EB Meritt
Assistant Commissioner

Department of The Interior
Office of The Secretary DEC 27 1918

The within will dated March 15, 1915, of Flat Back, deceased Crow allottee No. 1468, of the Crow Agency, is approved pursuant to the provisions of the Act of June 25, 1910 (36 Stats. L., 855-6) as amended by Act of February 14, 1913 (37 Stats. L., 678).

S G Hopkins
Assistant Secretary

▲▼▲▼▲▼▲▼▲▼▲▼▲▼▲▼

BRYAN SHIELD BEAR

Last Will and Testament
of
Bryan Shield Bear

IN THE NAME OF GOD, AMEN.

I, **Bryan Shield Bear**, of **Crow Agency, Montana** being of sound mind, memory, and understanding, do hereby make and publish this my last will and testament, hereby revoking and annulling all wills by me heretofore made, in manner and form following, that is to say:

First; I direct that all my just debts and funeral expenses, and expenses of my last illness shall be paid by my executor hereinafter names as soon after my decease as convenient;

Second; I give, devise and bequeath to

my wife, **Olive Elk**, all of my property, both real and personal, of which I may die possessed. I make this bequest to her for the reason that she, and she alone, has taken care of me in my last illness.

Third;   All the rest and residue of my estate, both real, and personal and mixed, I give, devise and bequeath to my lawful heirs as determined after my decease.

And lastly; I do hereby nominate, constitute and appoint **Superintendent of Crow Agency** executor of this my last will and testament.

In testimony Whereof, I have set my hand and seal to this, my last will and Testament, at **Crow Agency, Montana**[sic] Montana, this 4th day of **December** in the year of our Lord one thousand nine hundred and **sixteen**

Bryan Shield Bear

Signed, sealed, published and declared by said **Bryan Shield Bear** in our presence, as and for **his** last Will and testament, and at **his** request and in our presence, and in the presence of each other, we have hereunto subscribed our names as attesting witnesses thereto

his

Chas Wilson [thumb print]	of	**Crow Agency Montana.**
Norman J Perkins mark	of	**Crow Agency Montana**
CD Munro	of	**Crow Agency Montana**

Witness to Will and to mark of Chas Wilson

Department of The Interior,
Office of Indian Affairs, Washington,
                    DEC 20 1918

The within will, dated December 4, 1916, of Bryan Shield Bear, deceased allottee No. 2307 of the Crow Agency, Montana, is hereby recommended for approval in accordance with the provisions of the Act of June 25, 1910 (36 Stats. L., 855-6) as amended by Act of February 14, 1913 (37 Stats. L., 678).

Respectfully,
EB Meritt
Assistant Commissioner

Department of The Interior
Office of The Secretary

The within will, dated December 4, 1916, of Bryan Shield Bear, deceased allottee No. 2307 of the Crow Agency, Montana, is hereby approved in accordance with the Act of June 25, 1910 (36 Stats. L., 855-6) as amended by Act of February 14, 1913 (37 Stats. L., 678).

S G Hopkins
Assistant Secretary

▲▼▲▼▲▼▲▼▲▼▲▼▲▼▲▼

CORNER OF THE MOUTH

Last Will and Testament
of
Corner Of The Mouth

OFFICE OF INDIAN AFFAIRS
RECEIVED
JUL 30 1918
63567

IN THE NAME OF GOD, AMEN.

I, *Corner Of The Mouth*, of *Lodge Cross Mont* being of sound mind, memory, and understanding, do hereby make and publish this my last will and testament, hereby revoking and annulling all wills by me heretofore made, in manner and form following, that is to say:

First: I direct that all my just debts and funeral expenses, and expenses of my last illness shall be paid by my executor hereinafter names as soon after my decease as convenient;

Second: I give, devise and bequeath to

To my wife, Takes Pretty Sealfs[sic] *one half of all my property both real and personal. Also one half of all monies to my credit in banks or elsewhere*

To my adopted daughter Agnes Old Bull One hald of all my property both real and personal also one half of all monies to my credit in banks or elsewhere. I also select and designate Dan Old Bull as a proper person to care and look after all stock left by me till such stock is divided according to the terms of this will.

Third: All the rest and residue of my estate, both real, and personal and mixed, I give, devise and bequeath to my lawful heirs as determined after my decease.

And lastly: I do hereby nominate, constitute and appoint *Supt C.H. Ashbury or his successor in office* executor of this my last will and testament.

In testimony whereof, I have set my hand and seal to this, my last will and Testament, at *Lodge Grass* Montana, this *Sixth* day of *October*

Indian Wills, 1911 – 1921 Book Two
Records of The Bureau of Indian Affairs

in the year of our Lord one thousand nine hundred and *Seventeen*.

his
Corner of the Mouth [thumb print]
mark

Signed, sealed, published and declared by said **Corner Of The Mouth** in our presence, as and for *his* last Will and testament, and at *his* request and in our presence, and in the presence of each other, we have hereunto subscribed our names as attesting witnesses thereto .

(Signature Illegible)	of	*Lodge Grass Mont*
George E Hill	of	*Lodge Grass*
James Hill	of	*St. Xavier Montana*

Probate
63567-18
 J M T

Department of The Interior,
Office of Indian Affairs, Washington,
DEC 20 1918

It is recommended that the within will, dated October 6, 1917, of Corner of the Mouth, deceased allottee No. 1418, of the Crow Agency, Montana, be approved pursuant to the provisions of the Act of June 25, 1910 (36 Stats. L., 855-6) as amended by Act of February 14, 1913 (37 Stats. L., 678).

Respectfully,
EB Meritt
Assistant Commissioner

Department of The Interior
Office of The Secretary   DEC 21 1918

The within will dated October 6, 1917, of Corner of the Mouth, deceased allottee No. 1418, of the Crow Agency, Montana, is approved pursuant to the provisions of the Act of June 25, 1910 (36 Stats. L., 855-6) as amended by Act of February 14, 1913 (37 Stats. L., 678).

S G Hopkins
Assistant Secretary

▲▼▲▼▲▼▲▼▲▼▲▼▲▼▲▼

KILLS TWICE

Last Will and Testament
of
Kills Twice

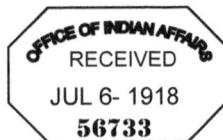

```
OFFICE OF INDIAN AFFAIRS
RECEIVED
JUL 6- 1918
56733
```

IN THE NAME OF GOD, AMEN.

I, *Kills Twice*, of *Crow Agency Mont* being of sound mind, memory, and understanding, do hereby make and publish this my last will and testament, hereby revoking and annulling all wills by me heretofore made, in manner and form following, that is to say:

First: I direct that all my just debts and funeral expenses, and expenses of my last illness shall be paid by my executor hereinafter names as soon after my decease as convenient;

Second: I give, devise and bequeath to *Dominic Old Elk, who has cared for me during my old age. My allotment No. 2350 on Crow Reservation Montana described as Lots 1,2, 3 and 4 of Sec. 3 T[6.S.R.31E. My only known relatives are Olk Elk and Sings the Last Song. Nephews, these I do not wish to inherit in my land for reason that have given me no assistance or care in my old age. Any other persons who may make any clams to above lands I wish cut out from inheritance for same reason.*

Third: All the rest and residue of my estate, both real, and personal and mixed, I give, devise and bequeath to my lawful heirs as determined after my decease.

And lastly: I do hereby nominate, constitute and appoint *The Supt of Crow Reservation Mont* executor of this my last will and testament.

In testimony whereof, I have set my hand and seal to this, my last will and Testament, at *Crow Agency* Montana, this *12th* day of *March* in the year of our Lord one thousand nine hundred and *Fourteen*.

> *his*
> *Kills Twice [thumb print]*
> *mark*

Signed, sealed, published and declared by said *Kills Twice* in our presence, as and for *her* last Will and testament, and at *her* request and in our presence, and in the presence of each other, we have hereunto subscribed our names as attesting witnesses thereto .

> *George E Hill* of   *Crow Agency Montana*
> *James Laforge* of

Indian Wills, 1911 – 1921 Book Two
Records of The Bureau of Indian Affairs

Probate
56733-18
J M T

Department of The Interior,
Office of Indian Affairs, Washington,
                    DEC 14 1918
The within will, dated March 12, 1914, of Kills Twice, deceased Crow allottee No. 2350, is hereby recommended for approval in accordance with the provisions of the Act of June 25, 1910 (36 Stats. L., 855-6) as amended by Act of February 14, 1913 (37 Stats. L., 678).

> Respectfully,
> *EB Meritt*
> Assistant Commissioner

Department of The Interior
Office of The Secretary   DEC 17 1918

The within will, dated March 12, 1914, of Kills Twice, deceased Crow allottee No. 2350, is hereby approved in accordance with the Act of June 25, 1910 (36 Stats. L., 855-6) as amended by Act of February 14, 1913 (37 Stats. L., 678).

> *S G Hopkins*
> Assistant Secretary

▲▼▲▼▲▼▲▼▲▼▲▼▲▼▲▼

MARY BRAIDS HIS FOREHEAD

LAST WILL AND TESTAMENT.

In the Name of God, Amen. *I, Mary Braids His Forehead, a Rosebud Sioux allottee #(blank) age 89 years of White River in the County of Mellette, and State of South Dakota, being of sound mind and memory, and considering the uncertainty of this frail and transitory life, do therefore make, ordain, publish and declare this to be my Last Will and Testament.*

First, I order and direct that my Execut..... hereinafter named, pay all my just debts and funeral expenses as soon after my decease as conveniently may be.

Second, After the payment of such funeral expenses and debts, I give, devise and bequeath:

(1) To my husband, James Braids His Forehead whose age is 78 years

157

Two hundred ($200⁰⁰) Dollars in cash from my trust funds held by the Superintendent of the Rosebud Indian Reservation

(2)   To my grandson, Edward White Buffalo, whose age is twenty (21) years One hundred ($100⁰⁰) Dollars in cash from the above said funds.

(3)   My grandson, Edward Roy Crump, aged thirty eight (38) years shall have One hundred ($100) Dollars in cash from the above said funds. Providing that he comes to see me.

(4)   To my granddaughter, Mary Elizabeth Crump, One hundred ($100) Dollars in cash from the funds described in section (1) hereof. Providing that she come to see me.

(5)   In case the grandson and grandaughter[sic] named in sections 3 and 4 do not come to see me the amounts named in those sections shall go to my son Joseph White Buffalo whose age is forty three (43) years.

(6)   All of the balance of my trust funds and all of any other property belonging to me or due me shall go to my son, Joseph White Buffalo, mentioned in section 5 hereof.

(7)   The above named beneficiaries are the only heirs I have and know.

Endorsement of Will
No. 47041-18

Department of The Interior,
Office of Indian Affairs, Washington,
                              Dec. 20, 1918
The within Will is hereby recommended for approval in accordance with the provisions of the Act of June 25, 1910 (36 Stats. L., 855-6) as amended by Act of February 14, 1913 (37 Stats. L., 678).

Respectfully,
EB Meritt
Assistant Commissioner

Department of The Interior
Office of The Secretary   DEC 17 1918

The within Will is hereby approved in accordance with the Act of June 25, 1910 (36 Stats. L., 855-6) as amended by Act of February 14, 1913 (37 Stats. L., 678).

S G Hopkins
Assistant Secretary

▲▼▲▼▲▼▲▼▲▼▲▼▲▼▲▼

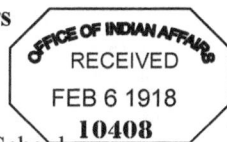

DAISY PADDY

State of Oregon	)	Klamath Indian School
	ss	Klamath Agency, Oregon
County of Klamath	)	June 2, 1915

LAST WILL AND TESTAMENT OF DAISY PADDY
KLAMATH ALLOTTEE, NO. 1229

I, DAISY PADDY, Klamath Allottee No. 1229, of the Klamath Reservation, County of Klamath, and State of Oregon, being of sound mind and memory, do hereby make, publish and declae this, my last will, in manner and form as follows, that is to say:-

First.   I direct the payment of all my just debts and funeral expenses, which may be paid under the laws and regulations of the United States.

Second.   I give and bequeath unto my daughter, Mollie Lalakes John, the sum of Five Dollars, ($5.00).

Third.   I give, devise and bequeath my allotment on he Klamath Reservation, in the County of Klamath, and State of Oregon, consisting of the following described land:- N1/2 of NW1/4; and N1/2 of SE1/4 of NW1/4. of Section 16, Township 33, Range 7; and Lot 21, Section 29, Township 35, Range 7,- 140 acres, and all other real property, wherever situate, or any interest therein, of which I may die possessed, or to which I may be entitled, together with all other personal property, except that bequeathed herein, of whatsoever kind the same may be, which I may own at my death, or in which I may have any interest,- to my nephew, WILLIAM CRAWFORD, to have and to hold the same to the said WILLIAM CRAWFORD, and his heirs, forever.

Fourth.   I hereby revoke any and all former wills by me made.

Fifth.   In witness whereof, I have hereunto set my hand and seal, this 2nd day of June, 1915, at the Williamson Bridge, on the Klamath Reservation in Oregon.
Her

DAISY PADDY [thumb print]
Mark.

The foregoing instrument, consisting of one page, was at the date hereof, by the said Daisy Paddy, signed, sealed and published as, and declared to be, her last will and testament, in the presence of us, who, at her request, and in her presence and in the presence of each other, have subscribed our names as witnesses hereto.

159

Ada Rice	residing at	*Klamath Agency Ore.*
Rose Wright	residing at	*Klamath Agency Ore*
Fred A Jakes	residing at	*Klamath Agency, Ore.*

Probate
10408-18
T D M

Department of The Interior,
Office of Indian Affairs, Washington,
DEC 12 1918

The within will is hereby recommended for approval in accordance with the provisions of the Act of June 25, 1910 (36 Stats. L., 855-6) as amended by Act of February 14, 1913 (37 Stats. L., 678).

Respectfully,
EB Meritt
Assistant Commissioner

Department of The Interior
Office of The Secretary

The within will is hereby approved in accordance with the Act of June 25, 1910 (36 Stats. L., 855-6) as amended by Act of February 14, 1913 (37 Stats. L., 678).

S G Hopkins
Assistant Secretary

▲▼▲▼▲▼▲▼▲▼▲▼▲▼

ELIZABETH DAVE or AD-ZO-LITZA

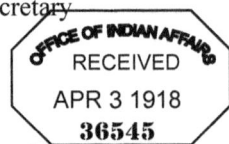

OFFICE OF INDIAN AFFAIRS
RECEIVED
APR 3 1918
36545

I, Elizabeth Dave - Indian name - Ad-zo-litza - being of sound mind, memory and understanding but weak in body and realizing the uncertainty of life do make, publish and declare this my last will and testament, hereby revoking any former will by me at any time heretofore made-

First, I direct the payment of my just debts and funeral expenses and the erection at my grave of a suitable but not expensive monument.-

I give devise and bequeath to Charles Hillaire who has been my best friend and has looked after me for many years, the same as a son, all the property of which I may die seized whether the same be real, personal or mixed and wheresoever situated to have and to hold the same to the said Charles Hillaire, my best friend, his heirs and assigns forever.

In witness to this my last will and testament, I have after the same has been read over and interpreted to me made my mark this 7th day of March 1916.

Elizabeth Dave   her thumb
Ad-zo-litza   [thumb print]
mark

Signed and declared to be the last will of the testator Elizabeth Dave this 7th day of March 1916.
We certify that the said testator made her thumb mark to the will written on two sheets of paper, in our presence, and that we subscribe our names as witnesses to the will (written on two sheets of paper) at the request of the testator, in her presence and in the presence of each other.

Edward Mills
Joseph Hillaire
J. D. Thompson

Probate
56348-18
T D M

Department of The Interior,
Office of Indian Affairs, Washington,
DEC 20 1918

The within will is hereby recommended for approval in accordance with the provisions of the Act of June 25, 1910 (36 Stats. L., 855-6) as amended by Act of February 14, 1913 (37 Stats. L., 678).

Respectfully,
EB Meritt
Assistant Commissioner

Department of The Interior
Office of The Secretary
DEC 26 1918

The within will is hereby approved in accordance with the Act of June 25, 1910 (36 Stats. L., 855-6) as amended by Act of February 14, 1913 (37 Stats. L., 678).

S G Hopkins
Assistant Secretary

▲▼▲▼▲▼▲▼▲▼▲▼▲▼▲▼

MICHAEL BRINGS PLENTY

Mandorson, South Dakota
Jan 8 -- 1918

I Michael Bring[sic] Plenty make my Will to my wif[sic] son father and brother to them on my property what I got

Land description the S1/2 of Sec 26 R44 T39 6th P.M. S.D. containing 320

I will my son Jackob Brings Plenty 1 quarter S.E.1/4 of Sec 26 R44 T39 6th P.M. S.D. containing 160 also personal property

I will my wife Mary Big Boy, 1 quarter S.W.1/4 Sec 26 R44 T39 6th P.M. S.D .containing 160 acres   *his*
                             Michael Brings Plenty [thumb print]
                                          mark
                             James Charges Enemy
                             Strike By Crow

Mary Big Boy
    1 team
    1 wagon
    2 calfs[sic]
    1 yearling heifers
Jackob Bring[sic] Plenty
    1 Bay Horse
    1 Sorrel Horse
    3 cow[sic]
    1 heifer
Joseph White Coyot[sic]
    1 set Harness
John Bring[sic] Plenty
    1 Bay Horse
    1 Log House   *his*
                             Michael Brings Plenty [thumb print]
                                          mark
                             James Charges Enemy
                             Strike By Crow

Indian Wills, 1911 – 1921 Book Two
Records of The Bureau of Indian Affairs

Department of The Interior,
Office of Indian Affairs, Washington,
NOV 26 1918

It is recommended that the within will of Michael Brings Plenty be approved pursuant to the provisions of the Act of June 25, 1910 (36 Stats. L., 855-6) as amended by Act of February 14, 1913 (37 Stats. L., 678).

Respectfully,

E B Meritt

Assistant Commissioner

Department of The Interior
Office of The Secretary

The within will of Michael Brings Plenty is hereby approved pursuant to the provisions of the Act of June 25, 1910 (36 Stats. L., 855-6) as amended by Act of February 14, 1913 (37 Stats. L., 678).

S G Hopkins

Assistant Secretary

▲ ▼ ▲ ▼ ▲ ▼ ▲ ▼ ▲ ▼ ▲ ▼ ▲ ▼ ▲ ▼

ANDREW WALLACE

Last Will and Testament
of
Andrew Wallace

IN THE NAME OF GOD, AMEN.

I, *Andrew Wallace* of *Lodge Grass Mont* being of sound mind, memory, and understanding, hereby revoking and annulling all wills by me heretofore made, in manner and form following, that is to say:

First: I direct that all my just debts and funeral expenses, and expenses of my last illness shall be paid by my executor hereinafter named as soon after my decease as convenient;

Second: I give, devise and bequeath to

My wife Jamie Wallace one half of all my real estate, one half of all my live stock, one half of all my other personal property except household goods of which I bequeath all to her. Also to my wife, above named, I bequeath all cash and money on hand, in banks or elsewhere to my credit.

To my son, Harry Wallace, I bequeath one half of all my real estate, one half of all my live stock also one half of all my other personal property except as before mentioned. *All the above property to be divided under the supervision of the Supt of Crow Agency or his appointee.*

Third: All the rest and residue of my estate, both real, and personal and mixed, I give devise and bequeath to my lawful heirs as determined after my decease.

And lastly I do hereby nominate, constitute and appoint *Supt C.H. Asbury or his successor in office* executor of this my last will and testament.

In testimony whereof, I have set my hand and seal to this, my last will and testament, at *Lodge Grass*, Montana, this *Thirty First* day of *October* in the year of our Lord one thousand nine hundred and *Seventeen*.   *His*

Andrew Wallace [thumb print]
Mark

Signed, sealed, published and declared by said *Andrew Wallace* in our presence, as and for *his* last will and testament, and at *his* request and in our presence, and in the presence of each other, we have hereunto subscribed our names as attesting witnesses thereto.

(Signature Illegible)	of	*Lodge Grass Mont*
George Hill	of	*Lodge Grass Mont*
Flora Deputee	of	*Lodge Grass Mont*

Department of The Interior,
Office of Indian Affairs, Washington,
NOV 15 1918

The within will of Andrew Wallace Crow allottee No. 1598, executed Oct. 31, 1917, is recommended for approval under the Act of June 25, 1910 (36 Stats. L., 855-6) as amended by Act of February 14, 1913 (37 Stats. L., 678), and it is found that his widow and son, Jennie Wallace and Harry Wallace, are entitled to the property both real and personal, in equal shares, except that the household goods go to the widow.

Respectfully,
EB Meritt
Assistant Commissioner

Department of The Interior
Office of The Secretary
NOV 30 1918

The within will of Andrew Wallace Crow allottee No. 1598, executed
Oct. 31, 1917, is recommended for approval under the Act of June 25,
1910 (36 Stats. L., 855-6) as amended by Act of February 14, 1913 (37
Stats. L., 678), and it is found that his widow and son, Jennie Wallace and
Harry Wallace, are entitled to the property both real and personal, in
equal shares, except that the household goods go to the widow.

S G Hopkins
Assistant Secretary

▲▼▲▼▲▼▲▼▲▼▲▼▲▼

SABIN CARLIN

St Ignatius, Montana.
June NINTH 1914

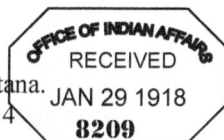

OFFICE OF INDIAN AFFAIRS
RECEIVED
JAN 29 1918
8209

I, Sabin Carlin, being of a sound and disposing mind and memory,
do hereby publish this as my Last Will and Testament as follows:

I hereby bequeath, at the time of my death unto Mrs. T.L.Cope of
St Ignatius, Montana, all real property of which I may die seized or in
which I have any rght, title or interest, and particularly all my right and
title and interest in and to that certain tract of land allotted me by the
US.Government described as follows: The NE1/4 and the NW1/4 of the
NE1/4 of Section 15, Twp 18 N Range 20 West M.P.M.

WITNESS my hand and seal this the 9th day of June 1914.

her thumb

Witnesses: *Sabin Carlin* [thumb print]
    GH Beckwith St Ignatius Mont   *mark*
    Elizabeth Ashley St Ignatius Mont

State of Montana   )
) ss.
County of Missoula)   On this the 9th day of June 1914, before me,
G.H. Beckwith a Notary public for the State of Montana, personally
appeared Sabin Carlin, known to me personally to be the person who
subscribed her name to the above instrument and acknowledged to me,
through Elizabeth Ashley of St Ignatius, acting as interpreter she

executed the same freely and voluntarily for the purposes therein mentioned as her Last Will and Testament.

In Witness whereof, I hereunto affix my name and Official sea the day and date first above written.

George H. Beckwith
NOTARY PUBLC FOR THE STATE OF MONTANA
RESIDING AT ST. IGNATIUS, MISSOULA COUNTY
MY COMMISSION EXPIRES SEPT. 9TH, 1914.

Probate
8209-18

Department of The Interior,
Office of Indian Affairs, Washington,
NOV 27 1918

The within will is hereby recommended for approval according to the provisions of the Act of June 25, 1910 (36 Stats. L., 855-6) as amended by Act of February 14, 1913 (37 Stats. L., 678), in so far as it embraces property held in trust by the Government of the United States.

Respectfully,
EB Meritt
Assistant Commissioner

Department of The Interior
Office of The Secretary
DEC -7 1918

The within will is hereby approved according to the provisions of the Act of June 25, 1910 (36 Stats. L., 855-6) as amended by Act of February 14, 1913 (37 Stats. L., 678), in so far as it embraces property held in trust by the Government of the United States.

S G Hopkins
Assistant Secretary

▲▼▲▼▲▼▲▼▲▼▲▼▲▼▲▼

MARY KANE
WILL

IN THE NAME OF GOD, AMEN: I, **Mary Kane** age 66, and Indian of the Nez Perce Indian Reservation, Idaho, now residing at **Spalding** Idaho, being of sound mind and disposing memory, and not acting under duress, menace, fraud, or undue influence, of any person whatsoever, do hereby make, publish and declare this my LAST WILL AND TESTAMENT, in the manner following, that is to say:

Indian Wills, 1911 – 1921 Book Two
Records of The Bureau of Indian Affairs

First: I direct that my body be decently buried with proper regard to my station in life, and the circumstances of my estate.

Second: I direct that my funeral expenses and expenses of my last illness be paid from any funds belonging to my estate, or in the custody of the Superintendent of the Nez Perce Indian Reservation, Lapwai, Idaho.

Third: I will and bequeath to my grand-nephew, John Kane, my allotment on the Nez Perce reservation, No. 1995, described as follows:

Lots Twenty-three, twenty-four twenty-five and twenty-six, Section twenty-one, township thirty-four, north, range one West, of Boise Meridian, containing eighty acres.

Fourth: I will and bequeath to the said John Kane, any and all inherited interest, of which I may die possessed, and all personal property of which I may be possessed at the time of my death.

This Will is made succeeding and revoking all previous Wills.

Amelia Andrews, my grand-niece, has recently died and I do not wish her children to inherit any part of my estate because of their behavior toward me, and their unsettled habits.

In witness whereof, I have hereunto put my hand and seal this **8th** day of **Oct.** 1917. *her thumb mark*

Mary Kane [thumb print]

The foregoing instrument was on the date hereof signed, sealed, published and declared by said **Mary Kane** to be her LAST WILL AND TESTAMENT, in the presence of us, and at her request and in her presence, and in the presence of each other, we have subscribed our names as witnesses on the **8th** day of **October** 1917.

Joseph Settler, Indian
Lapwai, Ida
Ida Wagner, Clerk
Lapwai, Idaho
(Signature Illegible)
Clerk, Lapwai, Ida

Probate
1658-18

Department of The Interior,
Office of Indian Affairs, Washington,
FEB 26 1919

The within will of Mary Kane, Nez Perce allottee No. 1995, is hereby recommended for approval according to the provisions of the Act of June 25, 1910 (36 Stats. L., 855-6) as amended by Act of February 14, 1913 (37 Stats. L., 678).

Respectfully,
EB Meritt
Assistant Commissioner

Department of The Interior
Office of The Secretary
FEB 26 1919

The within will of Kane, Nez Perce allottee No. 1995, is hereby approved according to the provisions of the Act of June 25, 1910 (36 Stats. L., 855-6) as amended by Act of February 14, 1913 (37 Stats. L., 678).

S G Hopkins
Assistant Secretary

MARY I. D. ELLIS

WILL.

OFFICE OF INDIAN AFFAIRS
RECEIVED
AUG 7 1917
74321

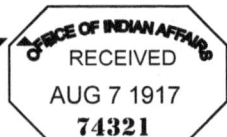

I, Mary I. D. Ellis, Otoe & Missouria Indian allottee No. 172 of the State of Oklahoma, being now in good health, strength of body and mind, but sensible of the uncertainty of life, and desiring to make disposition of my property and affairs while in health and strength, do hereby make and publish and declare the following to be my last will and testament, hereby revoking and cancelling all other or former wills by me at any time made:

FIRST: I direct the payment of all my just debts and funeral expenses.

SECOND: I give and devise to my son, Blaine Faw Faw, my 160 acre allotment on the Otoe & Missouria Indian Reservation, described as follows:

Indian Wills, 1911 – 1921 Book Two
Records of The Bureau of Indian Affairs

Northeast one-fourth (NE/4) of Section 7, Township 23 In Range 2 East of the Indian Meridian, Noble County, Oklahoma.

THIRD: I give and devise to my daughter, Pearl W. Faw Faw Roubidoux, the 160 acre allotment of John Doty, deceased, to which I am the sole heir.

FOURTH: I five and devise to my husband, Samuel Ellis, all of my remaining inherited interests, wherever located.

FIFTH: I give to all my remaining heirs, if there be any, the sum of Five Dollars ($5.00) each.

SIXTH: I give and bequeath all the rest, residue and remainder of my personal property to my husband, Samuel Ellis.

SEVENTH: I hereby appoint and designate the Superintendent of the Otoe Indian Agency, sole executor without bond, of this my last will and testament.

In witness whereof I, Mary . D. Ellis, have to this my last will and testament consisting of one sheet of paper, signed by thumb mark this 2nd day of August 1917.   Her right
Mary I. D. Ellis [thumb print]
thumb mark.

Subscribed by Mary I. D. Ellis in the presence of each of us, the undersigned, and at the same time declared by her to us to be her last will and testament, and we, thereupon at the request of Mary I. D. Ellis, in her presence and in the presence of each other sign our names hereto as witnesses this 2nd day of August 1917.

WITNESSES.	ADDRESS.
Herman Little Crow	*Red Rock Okla*
Thomas Hartico	*Red Rock Okla*
L G Gordon	*Red Rock, Okla*

Probate
74921-17
38792-18
 C F T

Indian Wills, 1911 – 1921 Book Two
Records of The Bureau of Indian Affairs

Department of The Interior,
Office of Indian Affairs, Washington,

JUN 6 1919

The within will of Mary I. D. Ellis, Otoe and Missouria allottee Nos. 172-172-A, is hereby recommended for approval in accordance with the provisions of the Act of June 25, 1910 (36 Stats. L., 855-6) as amended by Act of February 14, 1913 (37 Stats. L., 678).

Respectfully,
EB Meritt
Assistant Commissioner

Department of The Interior
Office of The Secretary

JUN 11 1919

The within will of Mary I. D. Ellis, Otoe and Missouria allottee Nos. 172-172-A, is hereby approved under the provisions of the Act of June 25, 1910 (36 Stats. L., 855-6) as amended by Act of February 14, 1913 (37 Stats. L., 678).

S G Hopkins
Assistant Secretary

▲▼▲▼▲▼▲▼▲▼▲▼▲▼

MRS. GUST THOMAS or NI TAMI GI GI DO KWE

Pahquanhwong, Wisconsin
July 23, 1904.

I, Mrs. Gust Thomas, Ni tamigigidokwe, of the village of Trading Post and in County of Sawyer and State of Wiosconsin being of sound mind, memory and understanding do make my last will and testament in manner and form following: First I give my oldest daughter Kate Hendflyer and my Second Daughter Josephine Thomas and my third daughter Mary B. Thomas and my husband Mr. Gust Thomas, equal shares on my personal property, that is my personal property is now standing or growing on my allottment, that is timber of all kinds that may be sold some time, and the proceeds I desire to my three children and my husband, Mr. Gust Thomas, shall share and share alike and equal shares whatever the same would come to whenever the same is sold. Second I give to my father Pe mo sag jig and also my mother Bim we we gi jig go kew my estate is now in my own name, this estate is my own allotment viz: Lot No. 1 Section 27, Lot No. 2 in section 28, Township No. 40

170

North of Range 6 West, situated in county of Sawyer and in State of Wisconsin the said tract comprising 97.58 acres. I give the above tract to father and mother so they could live thereon and I further desire to have this put on my last will in case my Father and Mother should ever sell the above mentioned tract of of land to remember my three children, and I also wish and desire whenever they should get sick, are apt to die, I respectfully ask them to turn the said tract above mentioned to my three children whose names are given above. I hereby appoint my father Penosejig guardian for my three children. In witness whereof I Nitamigigido Kew Thomas the testator have to this my last will and testament, set my hand and seal this 23 day of Jan. A.D. 1904.

Ni tami gi gi do kew- [Seal]
Thomas, Her mark. *X*

Signed, sealed and declared by the above named Nitami gi gi do kew Thomas as and for her last will and testament in the presence of us, who have hereunto subscribed our names at her request, as witnesses thereto in the presence of the said testator and of each other.

George James, Hayward, Wis.

Antoine Denasha, his *X* mark, Hayward, Wis.

Mrs. Mary James, witness as for his mark, Hayward, Wis.

Certificate of Proof of Will.

State of Wisconsin)
) ss
Sawyer County   )

BE IT REMEMBERED, That on the second day of January A.D. 1917 at Hayward in said county, pursuant to notice duly given, as required by law, at a Regular term of the County Court of said County Aloine[sic] Danasha, one of the subscribing witnesses to the last will and testament of Ni tam i gi gi do kwe Thomas late of the Town of Reserve, in said County, deceased hereunto annexed, was produced and duly sworn and examined.

An the proofs having been heard before said Court, and the Court having thereupon found that said instrument was in all things duly executed as her last will and testament by the said Ni tam i gi gi do kwe Thomas.

Thereupon said instrument was by the order and decree of said Court duly allowed and admitted to probate, as and for the last will and Testament of Ni tam i gi gi do kwe Thomas, deceased.

IN TESTIMONY WHEREOF, I have hereunto set my hand and affixed the seal of the County Court of said County, at the City of Hayward this 2nd day of January A.D. 1917.

John K. Swenson, County Judge.

County
Court
Seal

Probate
7137-17
Department of The Interior,
Office of Indian Affairs, Washington, MAY 18 1919

I have the honor to recommend that the certified copy of the will of Mrs. Gust Thomas or Ni-ta-mi-gi-gi-do-kwe be laid before the President for approval.

Cate Sells
Commissioner

5-FBM-1
Department of The Interior
Office of The Secretary MAY 16 1919

I have the honor to recommend that the certified copy of the will of Mrs. Gust Thomas or Ni-ta-mi-gi-gi-do-kwe be approved.

Franklin K Payne
Secretary

The White House,
Woodrow Wilson
Approved:

▲▼▲▼▲▼▲▼▲▼▲▼▲▼▲▼

CHAUNCEY EAGLE HORN

LAST WILL AND RESTAMENT[sis].

IN THE NAME OF GOD, AMEN. I, Chauncey Eagle Horn, of Fort Meade, in the County of Meade and State of South Dakota, of the age of 41 years, and being of sound and disposing mind and memory, and not acting under duress, menace, fraud or undue influence of any person whatever, do make, publish and declare this my last will and testament, in the manner following, to-wit:

First. I direct that my body be properly buried in the cemetery at Okreek, in the County of Todd, on the Rosebud Indian Reservation, in the State of South Dakota, provided that it be convenient and possible that my body might be so buried, and that such burial be had in keeping with my circumstances, and under the charge and direction of the Episcopal Minister who at the time is in charge of the church parish at Okreek.

Second. It is my will that my just debts, and the charges of my last sickness and burial be paid as soon as conveniently may be after my decease.

Third. I give, devise and bequeath unto my wife Mollie Eagle Horn an undivided one third interest in and to all of my property whatsoever, real, personal and mixed, wheresoever situated.

Fourth. I give, devise and bequeath unto my beloved son, Nicholas Eagle Horn, an undivided one third interest in and to all of my property whatsoever, real, personal and mixed, wheresoever situated.

Fifth. I give, devise and bequeath unto my beloved daughter, Annie Eagle Horn, an undivided one third interest in and to all of my property whatsoever, real, personal and mixed, wheresoever situated.

Sixth. I make no devise or bequest or provision in any manner for any children born unto my wife after the date of this instrument.

Seventh. I do hereby nominate, constitute and appoint Frank Noisy Creek, by brother-in-law, of Rosebud Agency on the Rosebud Reservation in the State of South Dakota, to be my executor of this my last will.

IN WITNESS WHEREOF, I have hereunto subscribed my name at Sturgis, Meade County, South Dakota, this 25th day of August, A.D., 1917.

Chauncey Eagle Horn

The foregoing instrument, consisting of two pages, including the page signed by the testator, was at the date thereof, by Chauncey Eagle Horn, the maker thereof, signed in our presence, and in the presence of each other, and at the time of his subscribing said instrument he declared that it was his will, and at his request and in his presence and in the presence of each other, we have hereunto subscribed our names as witnesses thereto.

M. J. Kerper
Residing at Sturgis, South Dakota.

H. L. Smith
Residing at Sturgis, South Dakota.

Department of The Interior,
Office of Indian Affairs, Washington,

18235-1919   JUN 14 1919

It is recommended that the within will be approved pursuant to the provisions of the Act of June 25, 1910 (36 Stats. L., 855-6) as amended by Act of February 14, 1913 (37 Stats. L., 678).

Respectfully,
EB Meritt
Assistant Commissioner

Department of The Interior
Office of The Secretary   JUL -7 1919

The within will is hereby approved pursuant to the provisions of the Act of June 25, 1910 (36 Stats. L., 855-6) as amended by Act of February 14, 1913 (37 Stats. L., 678).

S G Hopkins
Assistant Secretary

▲▼▲▼▲▼▲▼▲▼▲▼▲▼▲▼

ITSKAKA or SMALL EYES

OFFICE OF INDIAN AFFAIRS
RECEIVED
MAY 15 1918
41160

LAST WILL AND TESTAMENT.

IN THE NAME OF GOD, AMEN:

I, Itasaka, of Umatilla Indian Reservation, Oregon, being of sound mind, memory and understanding, do hereby make and publish this my last will and testament, hereby revoking and annulling all wills by me heretofore made, in manner and form following, that is to say:

FIRST: I direct that all my just debts and funeral expenses, and expenses of my last illness, shall be paid as soon after my decease as shall be convenient.

SECOND: I give, devise and bequeath to Mrs. Allen Patawa, of Umatilla Indian Reservation, Oregon, one-half of my allotment on said reservation, described as the SE/4 of NW/4 Sec. 11, T. 2 N., R. 33. E. W., Oregon, 40 acres; and to Mrs August Alexander, of Umatilla Indian Reservation, Oregon, the remaining half of my allotment described as the SW/4 of the SE/4 Sec. 28, T. 2 N., R. 33, E., W. M., Oregon, 40 acres.

In the event that there is any restricted Individual Indian money to my credit at my death I want it to be divided equally between Mrs. Allen Patawa and Mrs. August Alexander.

IN TESTIMONY WHEREOF, I have set my hand and seal to this, my last will and testament, at Umatilla Agency, this 22d day of April, in the year of our Lord, One Thousand Nine Hundred and Eighteen.

her
Itskaka   [thumb print]
mark.

Signed, sealed, published and declared by the said Itskaka, in our presence, as and for her last will and testament, and at her request and in our presence, and in the presence of each other, we have hereunto subscribed our names as attesting witnesses thereto.

A.M. Hazen, Asst. Clk.
Charles Van Pelt

August Alexander
Umatilla Indian Agency,
Pendleton, Oregon.

Department of The Interior,
Office of Indian Affairs, Washington,
JUL 10 1919

The proposed will of Itskaka or Small Eyes, deceased allottee No. 85 on the Umatilla Reservation in Oregon, which paper is dated April 22, 1918 is hereby recommended for disapproval according to the Acts of June 25, 1910 (36 Stat. L. 855-6), and February 14, 1913, (37 Stat. l., 678).

Respectfully,
EB Meritt
Assistant Commissioner

Department of The Interior
Office of The Secretary JUL 14 1919

The proposed will of Itskaka or Small Eyes, deceased allottee No. 85 on the Umatilla Reservation in Oregon, which paper is dated April 22, 1918 is hereby disapproved according to the Acts of June 25, 1910 (36 Stat. L. 855-6), and February 14, 1913, (37 Stat. l., 678).

S G Hopkins
Assistant Secretary

▲ ▼▲ ▼▲ ▼▲ ▼▲ ▼▲ ▼▲ ▼

MARY PORTIS

I, Mary Portis, of Pine Bluff, Arkansas, being of sound mind and memory, and desiring to make disposition of my earthly goods, chattels and real estate so that they may pass to those whom I would have enjoy them when I am dead, do make, declare and publish this instrument as my Last Will and Testament, hereby revoking all other wills heretofore made by me.

FIRST: I desire that all my just debts shall be paid.

SECOND: It is my desire that a family monument shall be erected by my executor herein named to make the last resting place of myself and my dear ones who have gone before, and the selection, character and price of said monument I leave to my executor.

THIRD: To Misses Bettie Aiken, Eliza Aiken, Rosa Aiken and Jennie Aiken, of Pine Bluff, Arkansas, nieces of my husband, J. M. Portis, I give, devise and bequeath, in fee simple, my farm on Wabbaseka Bayou, in Jefferson County, Arkansas, being the farm at one time occupied and worked by Isaac Hartley; and the sum of Five hundred dollars ($500.00) each, to be paid as soon after my death as may be without damage to my estate. If either of said parties shall die before my death, it is my desire that the share in said farm herein devised to such deceased legatee shall vest in the survivor or survivors, and the money bequests herein provided for such as may die shall be paid pro rata to the survivor or survivors. If all of said persons shall die before me, without children living at the time of their death, then said lands and money bequests shall return to my estate and be vested as hereinafter provided.

FOURTH: To my cousin, Mrs. Agnes Clary, daughter of my uncle, Paul Dereuisseaux, and wife of W. J. Clary of Altheimer, Arkansas, I give, devise and bequeath the sum of Five hundred dollars ($500.00) in cash, and also direct that my executor shall surrender and deliver to her, as a gift from me, the note and deed of trust which I now hold executed by the said Agnes Clary and W. J. Clary; and I also give, devise and bequeath to the said Mrs. Agnes Clary the North half of the Northeast quarter of Section Thirty-three (33), Township Twenty-nine (29) North, Range Twenty-three (23) East of the Indian Meridian, in Ottawa County, Oklahoma.

FIFTH: To the Sisters of Mercy, Little Rock, Arkansas, where I was educated, I give, devise and bequeath the sum of One thousand dollars ($1000.00).

SIXTH: To the Annunciation Academy, located at Pine Bluff, Arkansas, I give, devise and bequeath the sum of Five hundred Dollars ($500.00).

SEVENTH: To the St. Joseph's Hospital, Hot Springs, Arkansas, I give, devise and bequeath the sum of Five hundred dollars ($500.00).

EIGHTH: To the Little Rock Orphanage, a Catholic institution located at Little Rock, Arkansas, I give, devise and bequeath the sum of Five hundred dollars ($500.00).

177

Indian Wills, 1911 – 1921 Book Two
Records of The Bureau of Indian Affairs

NINTH: To St. Peter's Orphanage, of Memphis, Tennessee, I give, devise and bequeath the sum of Five hundred dollars ($500.00).

TENTH: To the Sisters of the Good Shepherd, located at Hot Springs, Arkansas, I give, devise and bequeath the sum of Five hundred dollars ($500.00).

ELEVENTH: To St. Mary's School, Rock Creek, Oklahoma, I give, devise and bequeath the sum of Five hundred dollars ($500.00).

TWELTH: To St. Joseph's Catholic Church, Pine Bluff, Arkansas, I give, devise and bequeath the sum of Five thousand dollars ($5000.00).

THIRTEENTH: To my cousin, John B. Dereuisseaux, son of my uncle, Paul Dereuisseaux, I give, devise and bequeath the sum of Five hundred dollars ($500.00).

FOURTEENTH: It is my desire that a memorial to cost Five hundred dollars ($500.00) shall be erected in St. Joseph's Catholic Church, at Pine Bluff, Arkansas, and I desire that all of my family shall be remembered in the Holy Sacrifice of the Mass that is said daily in said church.

FIFTEENTH: To the St. Joseph's Catholic Cemetery, of Pine Bluff, Arkansas, I give, devise and bequeath the sum of Two hundred dollars ($200.00), which I desire shall be invested in such way that the annual income may be used for the care of my family lot.

SIXTEENTH: For the many services rendered to me at various times, I give, devise and bequeath to Mrs. Minnie Holland, wife of John J. Holland, of Pine Bluff, Arkansas, the sum of One thousand dollars ($1000.00).

SEVENTEENTH: I give, devise and bequeath to Marry Holland, daughter of my friend, Michael Holland, now deceased, the following described lands in Ottawa County, Oklahoma, to-wit: The West half, and the Southeast quarter, and the South half of the Northeast quarter of Section Thirty-three (33), Township Twenty-nine (29) North, Range Twenty-three (23) East of the Indian Meridian; also, my home place located at the corner of Second Avenue and Alabama Street and known as 216 Second Avenue in the City of Pine Bluff, Arkansas; and my two brick storehouses located in the same block as my home on Third Avenue between Alabama and State Streets, in said city of Pine Bluff; also, the farm on the North side of the Arkansas River in Jefferson County, consisting of eighty acres, now occupied by Joe Fogle; also twenty acres, more of less, of land near Pine Bluff on the Warren road, being the same land purchased by me from Mrs. Martha A. Burch; also, all money, bonds, deeds of trust, mortgages, choses[sic] in action, evidences of indebtedness, and also all and every kind of personal and real estate not otherwise herein bequeathed and devised, of which I may die seized and possessed, whether specifically described herein or not. But all of said real and personal estate shall remain under the control, management and possession of my executor herein named, or whoever may be substituted for him, and shall be in his absolute control, and shall not be sold or conveyed, until the said Mary Holland shall reach the age of twenty-five years, and my said executor is hereby directed to collect all rents, royalties and income arising from said real estate and the interest on said government bonds and all other outstanding indebtedness, money in bank, and choses[sic] in action, and shall invest all the income arising from my estate from all sources, and all money of which I may die seized and possessed, in good solvent, interest bearing securities. Out of the income so derived from my said estate bequeathed to the said Mary Holland, my executor is directed to provide for her, the said Mary Holland, a sum ample for her education and maintenance according to her condition in life until she shall reach the age of twenty-five years, and upon her arrival at said age of twenty-five years my said executor is authorized and directed to surrender and deliver to her absolutely all the real estate, personal property, bonds, moneys, the interest and rents accruing in the meantime, and all and every kind of beneficial interest hereby devised, to have and to hold unto her, and unto her heirs, in fee simple forever. If the income herein specified and provided shall for any reason, in the judgment of my executor, be insufficient to provide ample support, education and maintenance for the said Mary Holland, said executor is hereby authorized and directed to use so much of any other money which may come into his hands as such executor as may be required to provide such necessary support, education and maintenance.

EIGHTEENTH: It is my will and desire that the legacies bequeathed to the various persons mentioned herein shall be paid by my executor out of my estate as provided herein as soon after my death as same may be done without injury to my estate.

NINETEENTH: I hereby nominate and appoint my friend and attorney, W. D. Jones, as executor of my said will, and reposing special confidence in him, request that he be permitted to qualify and act as such executor without being required to execute a bond as such executor.

Signed this the 21st day of October, 1918.

Mary Portis

Witness:

Fred T Goode
Jessie H Whyte

PROOF OF WILL

STATE OF AKANSAS

COUNTY OF JEFFERSON

Personally appeared before me, L. T. Sallee, Clerk of the County and Probate Court of Jefferson County, Arkansas, Fred T. Goode and Jessie H. Whyte, to me well known, who being duly sworn, say: That they are the subscribing witnesses to the foregoing instrument of writing purporting to be the Last Will and Testament of Mary Portis, deceased; that said instrument was executed at the time, place and by the person therein named; that the said Mary Portis, the testatrix, was at the time of signing said instrument more than twenty-one years of age and of sound and disposing mind and memory, and that in the presence of both of these affiants she declared it to be her Last Will and Testament, and subscribed her name thereto in the presence of both of these affiants; that at the request of said testatrix affiants wrote their names as witnesses to said Will in her presence and in the presence of each other; that the subscriptions to the foregoing writing are genuine and that said instrument, which is attached hereto, is the identical one that affiants so witnessed and saw the said Mary Portis sign.

Fred T. Goode
Jessie H Whyte

Subscribed and sworn to before me this *13* day of January, 1919.

L.T. Sallee   Clerk.

We, the undersigned, witnesses to the above and foregoing Last Will and Testament of Mary Portis, do hereby certify that the said Mary Portis signed said instrument in our presence and at the same time declared it to be her Last Will and Testament, and we, at her request, and in her presence and in the presence of each other, have signed our names thereto as subscribing witnesses on this the 21st day of October, 1918.

Fred T. Goode
Jessie H. Whyte

Department of The Interior,
Office of Indian Affairs, Washington,
JUN 11 1919

The will of Mary Portis, deceased Quapaw allottee No. 68-69, dated Oct. 21, 1918, is hereby recommended for approval according to the Act of June 25, 1910 (36 Stats. L., 855-6) as amended by Act of February 14, 1913 (37 Stats. L., 678), so far as it affects trust property under the supervision of the Government.

Respectfully,
EB Meritt
Assistant Commissioner

Department of The Interior
Office of The Secretary
JUL 3- 1919

The within will of Mary Portis, deceased Quapaw allottee No. 68-69, dated Oct. 21, 1918, is hereby approved in accordance with the Act of June 25, 1910 (36 Stats. L., 855-6) as amended by Act of February 14, 1913 (37 Stats. L., 678), so far as it affects trust property under the supervision of the Government.

S G Hopkins
Assistant Secretary

▲▼▲▼▲▼▲▼▲▼▲▼▲▼▲▼

www.ingramcontent.com/pod-product-compliance
Lightning Source LLC
Chambersburg PA
CBHW030244030426
42336CB00009B/250

Other Books and Series by Jeff Bowen

1901-1907 Native American Census Seneca, Eastern Shawnee, Miami, Modoc, Ottawa, Peoria, Quapaw, and Wyandotte Indians (Under Seneca School, Indian Territory)

1932 Census of The Standing Rock Sioux Reservation with Births And Deaths 1924-1932

Census of The Blackfeet, Montana, 1897- 1901 Expanded Edition

Eastern Cherokee by Blood, 1906-1910, Volumes I thru XIII

Choctaw of Mississippi Indian Census 1929-1932 with Births and Deaths 1924-1931 Volume I

Choctaw of Mississippi Indian Census 1933, 1934 & 1937, Supplemental Rolls to 1934 & 1935 with Births and Deaths 1932-1938, and Marriages 1936-1938 Volume II

Eastern Cherokee Census Cherokee, North Carolina 1930-1939 Census 1930-1931 with Births And Deaths 1924-1931 Taken By Agent L. W. Page Volume I

Eastern Cherokee Census Cherokee, North Carolina 1930-1939 Census 1932-1933 with Births And Deaths 1930-1932 Taken By Agent R. L. Spalsbury Volume II

Eastern Cherokee Census Cherokee, North Carolina 1930-1939 Census 1934-1937 with Births and Deaths 1925-1938 and Marriages 1936 & 1938 Taken by Agents R. L. Spalsbury And Harold W. Foght Volume III

Seminole of Florida Indian Census, 1930-1940 with Birth and Death Records, 1930-1938

Texas Cherokees 1820-1839 A Document For Litigation 1921

Choctaw By Blood Enrollment Cards 1898-1914 Volumes I thru XVII

Starr Roll 1894 (Cherokee Payment Rolls) Districts: Canadian, Cooweescoowee, and Delaware Volume One

Starr Roll 1894 (Cherokee Payment Rolls) Districts: Flint, Going Snake, and Illinois Volume Two

Starr Roll 1894 (Cherokee Payment Rolls) Districts: Saline, Sequoyah, and Tahlequah; Including Orphan Roll Volume Three

Other Books and Series by Jeff Bowen

Cherokee Intruder Cases Dockets of Hearings 1901-1909 Volumes I & II

Indian Wills, 1911-1921 Records of the Bureau of Indian Affairs Book One

Visit our website at **www.nativestudy.com** to learn more about these
and other books and series by Jeff Bowen

VIRTUAL ACTIVISM

Sexuality, the Internet, and a Social
Movement in Singapore

In *Virtual Activism*, cultural anthropologist Robert Phillips explores the
changes in LGBT activism in Singapore during the period 1993 to 2019.
Based on extensive fieldwork conducted with activist organizations
and individuals, Phillips illustrates key theoretical ideas – including
illiberal pragmatics and neoliberal homonormativity – that, in combination with the introduction of the Internet, have shaped the manner
by which LGBT Singaporeans are framing and subsequently claiming
rights.

Phillips argues that the activism engaged in by LGBT Singaporeans
for governmental and societal recognition is in many respects virtual.
His analysis documents how the actions of activists have resulted in
some noteworthy changes in the lives of LGBT Singaporeans, but nothing as grand as some would have hoped, thus indexing the "not quite"
aspect of the virtual. Yet, *Virtual Activism* also demonstrates how these
actions have encouraged LGBT Singaporeans to fight even harder for
their rights, signalling the possibilities that the virtual holds.

(Anthropological Horizons)

ROBERT PHILLIPS is an assistant professor of anthropology at Ball State
University.

ANTHROPOLOGICAL HORIZONS

Editor: Michael Lambek, University of Toronto

This series, begun in 1991, focuses on theoretically informed ethnographic works that address issues of mind and body, knowledge and power, equality and inequality, the individual and the collective. Interdisciplinary in its perspective, the series makes a unique contribution in several other academic disciplines: women's studies, history, philosophy, psychology, political science, and sociology.

For a list of the books published in this series see page 165.

Virtual Activism

Sexuality, the Internet, and a Social Movement in Singapore

ROBERT PHILLIPS

UNIVERSITY OF TORONTO PRESS
Toronto Buffalo London

ISBN 978-1-4875-0745-9 (cloth)   ISBN 978-1-4875-3628-2 (EPUB)
ISBN 978-1-4875-2513-2 (paper)   ISBN 978-1-4875-3627-5 (PDF)

Anthropological Horizons

Library and Archives Canada Cataloguing in Publication

Title: Virtual activism : sexuality, the Internet, and a social movement in
    Singapore / Robert Phillips.
Names: Phillips, Robert (Professor of anthropology), author.
Series: Anthropological horizons.
Description: Series statement: Anthropological horizons | Includes
    bibliographical references and index.
Identifiers: Canadiana (print) 20200190687 | Canadiana (ebook) 2020019075X |
    ISBN 9781487507459 (cloth) | ISBN 9781487525132 (paper) |
    ISBN 9781487536282 (EPUB) | ISBN 9781487536275 (PDF)
Subjects: LCSH: Gay rights – Singapore – Case studies. | LCSH: Gay
    activists – Singapore – Case studies. | LCSH: Sexual minorities –
    Singapore – Case studies. | LCSH: Gay liberation movement –
    Singapore – Case studies. | LCSH: Internet – Social aspects –
    Singapore – Case studies. | LCSH: Homophobia – Singapore –
    Case studies. | LCGFT: Case studies.
Classification: LCC HQ76.8.S56 P55 2020 | DDC 323.3/264095957—dc23

University of Toronto Press acknowledges the financial assistance to its
publishing program of the Canada Council for the Arts and the Ontario Arts
Council, an agency of the Government of Ontario.

Canada Council   Conseil des Arts
for the Arts   du Canada

ONTARIO ARTS COUNCIL
CONSEIL DES ARTS DE L'ONTARIO
an Ontario government agency
un organisme du gouvernement de l'Ontario

Funded by the   Financé par le
Government   gouvernement
of Canada   du Canada

Canada

Contents

Figures

Acknowledgments

My biggest debt of gratitude goes to the members of Singapore's LGBT communities – past and present – who let me into their lives. It was a privilege to hear their stories. The members of the SiGNeL and Red-QuEEn forums as well as the members of PLU (People Like Us), the Pelangi Pride Centre, and IndigNation deserve special thanks for their kindness in allowing me to be an observant participant both online and in the physical world. During fieldwork, I forged very special friendships with Vikram Chauhan and Sheila Rajamanikam; my time in Singapore would not have been the same without either of you. I am grateful that our lives intersected.

My time at the University of California, Irvine, was especially important to me. I would like to thank my adviser, Tom Boellstorff, one of the most generous and engaging scholars I know. His unwavering encouragement and support over the years have meant a great deal. Victoria Bernal and Mei Zhan deserve thanks as well for their steady academic guidance.

Also at Irvine, many individuals graciously commented on this work in whole or in part over the years including Michael Burton, Ariane Dalla Dea, Karen Leonard, Sylvia Martin, Caroline Melly, Bonnie Nardi, Bill Maurer, Amanda Moore, Keith Murphy, Kavita Philip, Jennifer Terry, and Neha Vora. I was fortunate to have been part of a diverse and engaged cohort of young scholars, including Nanao Akanuma, Janet Alexanian, Rebecca Andersson, Allison Fish, Guillermo Narvaez, Joanna Ortiz, and Cortney Rinker.

My colleagues at Ball State University, in the department of anthropology and beyond, have been especially supportive of this work. Thank you to Homes Hogue, who hired me to my current position, and later department chairs, Jennifer Wies and Jill Coleman. All three continue to offer encouragement and challenge me to be a better scholar. I would also like to thank Yaron Ayalon, Dave Concepción, Jennifer Erickson, Obed Frausto, Francine Freidman, Galit Gertsenzon, Mark Groover, Mark Hill, Melinda Messineo, Kevin Nolan, Kelly Boyer Ontl, Lucas Pint, Jean Marie Place, Caity Placek, Jonathan Spodek, Heidi Stigall, Chris Thompson, Juli Thorson, and Sarah Vitale. Finally, Cailín Murray has been an incredible mentor during my time at Ball State. I am grateful for her friendship and wisdom.

Over the past decade, my work has also benefited greatly from the intellectual engagement provided by the participants at the annual Lavender Languages & Linguistics Conference. Brian Adams-Thies, Ricky Martin, David Peterson, and Denis Provencher read chapters of the manuscript in its later stages and provided helpful feedback. William Leap has been a steadfast supporter of my work since we first met, and I greatly appreciate his support and friendship.

The research presented in this book would not have been possible without a National Science Foundation Dissertation Improvement Grant and funding through the Intel Research Digital Home Group. At the University of California, Irvine research support was provided by the School of Social Sciences, the Department of Anthropology, and the Center for Asian Studies. My final year of writing at Irvine was funded by the University of California Regents dissertation fellowship and a James J. Harvey dissertation fellowship. Early work on this project took place during a postdoctoral fellowship at the Centre for Asia Pacific Transformation Studies (CAPSTRANS) at the University of Wollongong. Funding for the final stages of this project was supplied by the Publications and Intellectual Properties Committee through the Provosts Office and the College of Sciences and Humanities at Ball State University.

Portions of this manuscript have appeared in the following journals: *Anthropologica* (chapter 4) and the *Journal of Language and Sexuality* (chapter 6). Finally, the arguments and opinions outlined in the pages that follow are mine alone and do not necessarily reflect those of my interlocutors.

Note on Terminology

During my time in Singapore, I found that for the most part, the individuals with whom I interacted used the terms "LGBT," "lesbian," "bisexual," or "trans" when referring to themselves and to those in their social and activist circles. Some informants did speak in local terms such as *ah quah* (a derogatory Singlish term for gay men) or *pondan* (Malay for effeminate male or transvestite) at different times and in different contexts. Other Singaporean individuals, many of whom had spent long periods of time out of the country, often used "queer." For the sake of consistency, simplicity, and inclusivity, I primarily utilize LGBT. My research in Singapore suggests that the logic of enumeration, in which a potentially endless number of initialisms beyond LGBT (LGBTQ, and LGBTQI etc.) is insufficient to capture the "unstable identity process" (Phelan 1997, 60) demonstrated by many of my Singaporean interlocutors. Additionally, apart from public figures, most names and many identifying details have been changed to protect the anonymity of informants.

VIRTUAL ACTIVISM

Sexuality, the Internet, and a Social
Movement in Singapore

Chapter One

Little Earthquakes

"I thought you might be interested in this," the email began. "Someone has made a tele-film of *The Morning After* – the play that we saw being read last August." Embedded at the end of the email was a link to a YouTube webpage onto which a long-time Singaporean activist had uploaded a digital copy of the film. The email, received in January 2008, was from Violet, a Malay Singaporean[1] lesbian whom I had befriended in the summer of 2005 while attending a poetry reading organized as part of a recently inaugurated series of events celebrating Singapore's LGBT culture. When the email arrived, I had been back home in Alabama for four months, trying to make sense of the hundreds of pages of field notes, interview transcripts, and archival materials I had collected during my nineteen months in the city-state.

Violet was referring to the short story *The Morning After* by Singaporean writer Suchen Christine Lim (2007). Singapore's Arts Central channel, an entity of the government-owned MediaCorp Group, had produced the film, which was based on the story that had originally been commissioned in 2005 by Singapore's Free Community Church for reading at their Christmas day service. The plot of the story was quite simple.[2] One evening after dinner, David, a teenaged Chinese Singaporean student, sits down with his older brother and recently divorced mother and tells them that he is gay. They reassure him, each in their own way, that they still love him, and everyone moves forward with their lives.

A made-for-television film dealing with LGBT issues, broadcast at 9:00 p.m. on a Sunday evening, would seem unremarkable in many settings. After all, films of this nature have been airing in the West since at least the mid-1980s. But in the Singapore of 2007, it was quite remarkable. Singapore was, and remains, a nation in which official policy dictates "no promotion" of homosexuality, especially within the mass media.[3] As such, many LGBT Singaporeans saw the airing of this program as a ground-breaking event. Additionally, in the decade leading up to 2007, Singapore's LGBT communities had experienced dozens of incidents that indicated their government, and fellow citizens, would never be completely welcoming. Most significantly, the film was broadcast just a few months after Singapore's Parliament had taken the decision to maintain Section 377A of the penal code – the section that criminalizes sexual acts between consenting adult males. While the law was not repealed, the debates surrounding the repeal had a profound effect on the nation.

Several elements within Lim's story are noteworthy. First, the gay son, David, is depicted in a positive light; he is not portrayed as sick or effeminate, as had been the case with so many other gay characters that had appeared on Singaporean television over the years.[4] Second, his mother is accepting of David's homosexuality. There is a moment in which she questions her role in the formation of her son's sexual orientation, yet it is short-lived and drama-free. There is no beating of the chest and wailing, "Why me?" or any of the melodrama sometimes associated with parents who resign themselves to their child "coming out." There is simple acceptance. Third, the story has a happy ending; at the close of the film, David, home on break from his studies at MIT, shares a Christmas dinner with his family. As the meal gets underway, David's boyfriend arrives and is introduced. The camera then pans away from the dinner table as the extended household warmly welcomes David's boyfriend into the family.

I begin with Lim's story (and the story surrounding her story) primarily because, while the positive portrayal of homosexuality in the media was forbidden, the story was nonetheless made into a television movie by a government-subsidized film company and subsequently aired on a Singaporean government-owned television station. This is significant because, as I argue throughout this book, LGBT Singaporeans have embraced the Internet, access to which has encouraged an oftentimes effective online activism. This activism, enacted over the past two decades, had mainstreamed the non-normative sexual subjectivity depicted in the telefilm, thus making it acceptable fare for a Sunday evening broadcast.

Further, it speaks to several threads that run throughout this book. It tells of the difficulties experienced growing up and living in a nation in which male homosexual sex (and by extension a male homosexual subjectivity) is unlawful but ostensibly tolerated by citizens and government alike. In the moments after her son comes out to her, the mother thinks, "From the outside we're a tolerant, multi-religious, multi-cultural, multi-lingual, multi-everything society. But inside there's a hard kernel. Like an apricot's. We can be most unforgiving" (13). Her son, fully aware of the marginalization of sexual minorities within Singaporean society, later tells his mother, "I prayed, mum. I asked God, 'Why?' 'Why me?' I asked him to take it away. I knew God wouldn't take it away when I went to secondary school" (15). The film speaks to the changing nature of the family in Singapore: the mother is divorced, her brother is marrying a divorced woman who already has two children, and her youngest son, David, is getting ready to leave for university in the United States. It speaks to Chinese opportunity within Singaporean society in that David was able to get a scholarship to MIT, a privilege afforded to Singapore's majority Chinese population but not commonly seen within Singapore's minority Malay and Indian communities. It speaks to a cultural recognition of the ongoing presence of homosexuality within Singaporean society; on the evening that David tells his mother that he is gay, he adds, "I want you to know about me before I go to the States, so you won't blame the US or the West for corrupting me" (14). Lastly, the fact that this story was made into a television movie is significant. The positive portrayal of homosexuality in the media was forbidden, yet this telefilm was created and promoted by a government-subsidized film company and was aired on a government-owned television station, thus highlighting the illiberal and often-contradictory nature of many Singaporean policies, especially as they apply to LGBT citizens.

The telefilm ends with the camera lingering on the exterior of the family's apartment block under the moonlit evening sky. The mother, who also serves as the narrator of the story, reflects on the evening's events, "There had been a seismic shift in Singapore that night. No one noticed anything. Nothing seemed to have changed and in fact, nothing really did." The very public, government-endorsed television presentation of Suchen Christine Lim's story also represents one such small seismic shift in which, for the first time, an LGBT character was presented to the public in a positive light. As with Lim's story, this book is one of change; not large, observable seismic shifts, but rather little earthquakes, much like the tremor that occurred in the living room of a Singaporean flat on the evening that a son told his mother that he was gay.

The events and the subsequent transformation described in the pages that follow did not happen overnight – they evolved over decades, sometimes quickly, but more often slowly. It primarily concerns the period between 1993 and 2008 and the changes that occurred allowing LGBT Singaporeans, in the relatively short period of fifteen years, to

move from the secretive shadows in which the main form of communication was an anonymous newsletter to a low-key but very public
celebration of LGBT life and love in Singapore. This book is a historical analysis of how LGBT groups took advantage of new and emerging technologies to empower, and create better lives for, themselves.
It has been written, in part, to assure that new generations of LGBT
individuals – both activists and non-activists – recognize that the new
activism of the Internet and the movements that it has produced are
based on earlier attempts at using the Web to effect change. This Internet-based social movement was only able to take place as it did because
it occurred within a unique framework of illiberal pragmatics paired
with neoliberal homonormativity.

Illiberal Pragmatics

In October 2007, Prime Minister Lee Hsien gave his final speech to Parliament regarding Section 377A. He framed his administration's hesi-
tation to overturn the law around the notion that maintaining it was
in tune with current social mores and attitudes. In the same speech,
however, he highlighted the fact that his government was listening to
and acting in response to public debates surrounding the issue. He acknowledged that his own government recognized that the lives of its
LGBT citizens are often difficult, "They too must have a place in this
society and they too are entitled to their private lives. We shouldn't
make it harder than it already is for them to grow up and to live in a
society where they are different from most Singaporeans" (Lee 2007).
Prime Minister Lee concurred with the widely held public opinion that
Singapore is, by and large, a conservative society and that an outright
repeal of Section 377A could lead to an irreparable division within the
nation. As such, Section 377A was maintained. Yet, in recognition of
the contribution of LGBT Singaporeans to the nation, he pledged that
the law would not be actively enforced. By preserving the law while
simultaneously pledging not to enforce it, Lee was perpetuating the
long-standing strategy of "pragmatism" that has come to inform Singaporean policy since the founding of the nation in 1965. Chua Beng
Huat, a leading Singaporean sociologist, views this pragmatism as
"practical rather than philosophical ... always contextual and never
based on principles of political philosophy ... (and consisting of) dis-
crete and discontinuous acts" (Chua 1995, 69). Simultaneously, the
ideology of pragmatism allows for the incorporation of a neoliberal
"political rationality" (Liow 2011, 243) that naturalizes these types of
policy implementations as necessary and legitimate. Chua notes the

nonsensical and incongruous nature of these policies when he observes that "a particular intervention in a particular region of social life may radically alter the trajectory that an early intervention may have put in place" (Chua 1995, 69).

Building upon Chua's ideas, cultural theorist Audrey Yue took the notion of pragmatism further with her formulation of what she terms "illiberal pragmatics" (2007), a more specific framework within which to view Lee's statement. Yue argues that central to the pragmatism practised by Singapore's government is "the logic of illiberalism where interventions and implementations are potentially always neo-liberal and non-liberal, rational and irrational" (150–1). At the heart of her argument is an underlying notion of "ambivalence," which can be clearly seen in both Lee's decision to maintain but not enforce Section 377A and the decision by a government-owned studio to produce a film that portrays LGBT Singaporeans in a positive light, even though such a portrayal is prohibited. It is in the face of such illogical and ambivalent situations that many LGBT Singaporeans conduct their everyday lives and their activism.

Yue recognizes a collapse of binaries (rational/irrational, neoliberal/non-liberal) in her theory of illiberal pragmatics, and, as she argues, much of the LGBT activism that has emerged in recent years in Singapore is not "based on the Western post-Stonewall emancipation discourse of rights, but through the illiberal pragmatics of survival" (151). For many of my interlocutors, Western LGBT subjectivity and, by extension, Western LGBT rights are based on individual autonomy and a specific language of rights; they prioritize the individual and call for a radical form of assimilation that requires overt social acceptance. Within Singapore, activism that openly challenges the authority of the state is impractical; collective action and civil disobedience are strongly discouraged by strict policy. As such, many with whom I interacted embrace an LGBT activism that relies heavily upon cultural references, focuses on maintaining social balance, and looks beyond the homosexual/heterosexual binary. This form of activism has produced an LGBT liberation movement that is highly conservative, normalizing, and assimilationist. As contradictory as this may sound, I argue throughout this book that it is the only tangible form of activism possible within the framework of Singaporean illiberal pragmatics.

In March 2007, I experienced the logic of illiberal pragmatism when I attended a public talk by a local woman in which she rebuked what she referred to as the "culture of shame" that surrounds trans individuals in Singapore. I was quite interested to hear what she had to say in that while homosexual practices are illegal and culturally stigmatized,

Singaporean surgeons perform sex reassignment surgery and the state allows trans individuals to marry and change gender categories on their national identity cards. After the talk, I approached her, explained my research on LGBT activism in Singapore, and asked her if I could contact her later for an interview. Her reply took me by surprise. "I was born with a medical problem and that problem has been corrected with surgery and drug therapy," she told me. "I am now a heterosexual woman. I am neither L, G, B, nor T – so what exactly does your project have to do with me?" The brashness of her response was tempered by a realization that illiberal pragmatism, the framework within which her transition was performed, is not concerned with assisting non-normative individuals to legally marry spouses; it is not interested in responding to calls for the bureaucratic or legal acceptance of sexual minorities, nor does it recognize and acknowledge indigenous gender traditions.[5] Rather, in this instance, it pathologizes and psychologizes the subjectivities of trans individuals; it converts trans subjectivity into a medical problem with a medical solution, ultimately heteronormalizing and effectively erasing a non-conforming sexual subjectivity. This illiberal formation of trans subjectivity, which could be classified as a "hetero-gender" normative ideology, stands in opposition to a self-determined "gender transgressive" ideology (Edelman 2009, 170) in which the individual recognizes the radical alternative possibilities of self, including living a life outside of the male–female gender binary.

Yue argues that Singapore's illiberal pragmatics of sexuality "involves an active engagement with cultural politics and criticism" and that "this engagement with pragmatism, coupled with the contradictory logic of the illiberal, has enabled [LGBT Singaporeans] to actively use, fit in, and twist the governmental framing of culture" (Yue 2011, 252–3). As outlined in the chapters that follow, LGBT individuals in contemporary Singapore are living out this critical hermeneutical concept through an embrace of a value system that rejects them and their non-normative sexuality.

Neoliberal Homonormativity

Many LGBT Singaporeans, through their interactions on the Internet, have been exposed to Western (or international) and regional LGBT rights discourse and, through local appropriation or, what Merry terms "vernacularization" (2006, 219), have created their own social movement from this transnational bricolage. The resulting Singaporean-specific discourse is a product of the collapse of a set of already tenuous binary categories including east/west, in/out of the "closet," and global/local.

During my time in the city-state, most of the social activists with whom I interacted rejected a conventional antagonistic binary of "us versus them" and replaced it with a more harmonious, culturally relevant, and, most importantly, neoliberal, discourse of "us *and* them." The refusal of most activists to even discuss "rights" in the Western sense, is a reflection of and reaction to several factors, including the incremental increase in tolerance of LGBT Singaporeans by the government. As Chris Tan (2009) reminds us, Singapore is ambitious to stake its claim as a global city and to do so has marketed an embrace of its minority citizens to emphasize notions of open-mindedness. This has taken the form of governmental policy such as declarations that openly gay Singaporeans would be considered for positions in the civil service (Tan 2009), but it has also included sporadic approval of public events of interest to LGBT and other minority communities. In turn, many LGBT Singaporeans have engaged in a form of activism that demonstrates what theorists (Duggan 2002; Oswin 2007; Peterson 2011; Weeks 2007) argue has produced "homonormative" bodies that are complicit within modes of consumption, depoliticization, and desexualization. This evolving LGBT identity, which mirrors the ongoing shift among many Western gay men from seeking liberation *from* to assimilation *into* the cultural mainstream, has led to dramatic changes to LGBT life, especially as same-sex marriage has become the norm. Among gay-identified men for instance, the new homonormativity of neoliberalism has demanded that uninhibited sex, once a hallmark of gay life, take a secondary role to a mainstream gay identity that doesn't challenge heteronormative institutions, including monogamous marriage and consumerism, but rather embraces and celebrates them. As Chang (2015) points out in his discussion of gay men, this incrementalism encourages sexual normativity and eventually divides members of the gay communities into those who conform and deserve equal protection and those who do not and who are subsequently marginalized (see also Brown 2012). Through these processes, social forms that erase the rich sexual and political histories of LGBT communities have become more common in Singapore and elsewhere.

Homonormativity is intrinsically linked with neoliberalism, the dominant worldwide economic model since the 1980s, which stresses a market-driven economy and a minimal role for government. Critical here is the fact that neoliberalism goes beyond simple economic tenets. As an ideology, it stresses the importance of individual freedom as an all-encompassing value and, yet, especially in the instance of Singapore, demands that individual behaviour be altered and controlled. The paradox of neoliberalism informs LGBT subjectivity in Singapore on multiple levels, particularly as a form of governmentality, which Foucault (2002) describes as the "conduct of conduct." This aspect of governmentality involves "technologies of the self," in which individuals police their thoughts, their bodies, and their conduct to conform to a given discourse. By attempting to align their bodily actions with Singaporean discourses of power, LGBT individuals perform what Boellstorff (2008, 120) refers to as "forms of techne turned inward to shape selfhood."

It is not simply individual and group subjectivity that is affected, but as Duggan notes, the culture of neoliberalism has also restructured notions of citizenship so that it is now composed of "consumption, rights, and family values" (Duggan cited in Weiss 2008, 89). Family values, as described in subsequent chapters, forms the framework for the LGBT movement in Singapore, which has become heavily invested in the cultivation of what Oswin (2014, 415) refers to as the "proper family." Significantly, the success of Pink Dot, the large public gathering of LGBT Singaporeans and their supporters, detailed in chapter 6, has relied on a series of annual thematic frameworks built upon ideas of love, kinship, and family. The overarching theme has been "freedom to love." Organizers have maintained this theme but have added additional yearly themes including "focusing on our families" (2010), "home" (2013), and "for family, for friends, for love" (2014). While this may appear to be a straightforward case of LGBT Singaporeans being interpellated into identifying with a homogeneous, international rhetoric of neoliberal assimilation, it is not that simple. The unevenness of 1990s neoliberalism and the resulting lack of ideological homogeneity produced neither ideal citizens nor a monolithic neoliberal subject. This allowed for a localized interpretation and implementation of neoliberal ideology within a distinctly Singaporean framework. I argue that this focus on the "proper family" and "freedom to love" when creating the Singaporean LGBT movement has resulted not only from exposure to contemporary neoliberal forms of homonormativity, but also through the ideology of illiberal pragmatics – all of which became part and parcel of LGBT Singaporean consciousness via interactions on the Internet.

Tongzhi and LGBT Identity in Singapore

As noted in the opening vignette, and discussed in the chapters that follow, many Singaporeans – even those exposed to transnational rights discourse – view sexual identity and the idea of "coming out" differently than most in the West. For our purposes, a brief discussion of the term *tongzhi* (同志) should be helpful. This term was first appropriated contexts in which one's life is situated. The idea of recognizing and sub-sequently integrating oneself into the existing social order is thus key to understanding the concept of *tongzhi*.

Those LGBT Singaporeans exposed to *tongzhi* have certainly not ac-cepted the tenets of this discourse wholesale, and just as *tongzhi* has spread from its origins in Hong Kong and Taiwan unevenly across the globe, so too is its spread across Singapore. There is an unevenness in exposure to *tongzhi* discourse across racial, ethnic, and class lines within the city-state. First, although most Singaporean citizens come from a Chinese background (in which *tongzhi* discourse would make the most sense based on its origins), there are nonetheless sizeable populations of Indian and Malay Singaporeans who do not necessarily share the same sociocultural world views as their Chinese-acculturated counter-parts. Second, few of my Singaporean Chinese interlocutors ever spoke directly of *tongzhi* thought and only a handful were even familiar with the term. Nonetheless, all LGBT Singaporeans that I interviewed, with-out exception, spoke of a world view that was clearly influenced by and resonated with *tongzhi* thought.

For instance, I had met Clarence, an Indian Singaporean at a book launch organized by his partner Vikram. Clarence and I used to spend Tuesday evening having dinner followed by some shopping at a night market. During one of our outings, I asked him if his family knew about his sexual orientation. He answered, "I'm out to my family, but being Indian nobody discusses it because (sounding exasperated) I'm 37 years old and they think it's still a phase. I'm not out to my partner's family because he's not out to them, so ... as far as his family is concerned, we are just best friends." I was intrigued by the fact that he had never cor-rected his partner's family's assumptions regarding the true nature of their relationship. This tacit subjectivity, which assumes that the family already knows one's sexual orientation (see Decena 2011, Leap 2012, Tan 2011) however, is a major component of *tongzhi*. It also resonates strongly with illiberal pragmatics and neoliberal homonormativity. Clarence told me that if he and his partner kept quiet, things would be fine. But, "if you contest it they will take a stand and be against you ... so for the benefit of the family relationships ... at the end of the day it is no big deal because they accept me as a person, and I think that is of more value to me than for them to treat me as a *gay* person."

For Clarence "family relationships" take priority over his individual subjectivity, and like David, the gay Singaporean student in the opening vignette, maintaining harmony within the family is paramount. Clar-ence's comments also make clear that not all LGBT Singaporeans nec-essarily want their sexual subjectivity to be visible and that the Western notion of the "closet" or even being "out" are inadequate for thinking about the life experiences of LGBT Singaporeans. Contributing to the spread of both *tongzhi* thought and neoliberal homonormativity was the Internet.

Internet in Singapore

In the early 1990s Singapore's government began building an information technology infrastructure to facilitate a knowledge-based economy. These efforts intensified in the aftermath of the economic crisis that hit the Asian region in 1997–8. This undertaking boosted the nation's economy and provided low-cost Internet access for average Singaporeans, who were expected to use it primarily for commercial and educational purposes (Ho, Baber, and Khondker 2002, 131).

One unintended consequence of the ubiquitous nature of the Internet in Singapore is that it led to new types of local and global engagements for citizens. This is relevant in that Singapore is a nation in which all forms of mainstream media are tightly controlled by the government and strict codes ensure that few print publications or television programs reach out to LGBT communities. The Internet thus serves as a vital source of alternative information. Many of my interviewees told stories of how they grew up in the pre-Internet era in which the only available forms of information came from government sources. One activist recounted:

> The Internet as you know is encouraged by the government but I don't think they actually calculated that people could go out and find information for themselves, I don't think they knew how big the whole education thing could be, people picking the information that they want, and the discerning part of it, the way that I was brought up, information was just given to me, and the kind of information I had about gay people was negative all the way, but then when I found the Internet, oh my god! (*laughs*) wow!

Another activist, who wrote a regular column for a government-owned newspaper, spoke about how the Internet served as an alternative medium for acquiring information:

> It gives you the impression that you are not alone. It gives you the perspective that you are not some isolated person who thinks completely differently from everyone else. You have people who are like you and you find people who think like you about your current situation. If you are thinking about why the government acts the way it does, and you look for validation to support your point of view in the newspapers, you are never

going to find it, but if you go online you are at least going to find people who have considered things like this.

High-speed broadband access became available in Singapore in late 1998 and intensified the creation and utilization of various online sites that serve the needs of diverse LGBT communities. During the period of research, these included interactive forums such as RedQuEEn and Sayoni, aimed at lesbians, SiGNeL, used primarily by gay men, blogs such as *Yawning Bread* and *PLURAL*, and lifestyle sites such as Herstory, Fridae, and Trevvy. In subsequent years, Singaporean cyberspace became inundated with independently produced digital content such as personal and community blogs, websites, and interactive groups on social networking sites such as Facebook. Individuals and groups have also created video archives on YouTube to document the history of LGBT Singapore, use Twitter to convey vital up-to-the minute information in situations where mainstream media is absent or slow, and write informational entries related to LGBT Singapore within dedicated pages on Wikipedia.[6] Interactions within these discursive sites have allowed many Singaporeans to network with one another as well as with those outside of their home communities. This includes Singaporeans abroad and non-Singaporeans, some of whom at one time lived or worked in the city-state. Most significantly, it allowed for anonymous participation within a virtual public sphere. This was a crucial step for those who, like many of the LGBT Singaporeans with whom I interacted, were not comfortable interacting in the physical world. For many, the transnational nature of these multi-sited interactions was the spark that ignited a renewed interest in participation in the public sphere.

There can be no doubt that the Internet has had profound effects on LGBT communities worldwide (Berry, Martin, and Yue 2003; Campbell 2004; Dhoest, Szulc, and Eeckhout 2017; McGlotten 2013; McLelland 2003), including Singapore. It has been crucial in allowing LGBT Singaporeans to communicate with one another (Ng 1999) and to organize their communities (Chua 2014; Offord 2003; Weiss 2014). Social media platforms have also made a lasting impact on social and political mobilization across the globe (Howard and Parks 2012; Juris 2012) – for example, the "Twitter revolution" that aided in the dismantling of the Tunisian government in 2010–11 and the "Facebook revolution" that accompanied the Romanian presidential election in 2014. Recently, media theorists such as John Postill and Meredith Weiss have written about such activism. In his wide-ranging work covering movements such as the Arab Spring, Spain's indignados, and the global Occupy movement, Postill gives us "freedom technologists" whom he describes as "political actors – both individual and collective – who combine technological know-how with political acumen to pursue greater digital and democratic freedoms" (2016, 149). Similarly, Weiss contributes the idea of "media activism," which she defines as "those tactics that use media as part of social mobilisation" (2014, 91).

While both of these ideas could be used to frame the activities detailed in this book, I want to make clear that online interactions are not the sole manner by which activist spaces were opened. I consider myself neither a techno-optimist (Juris 2012, 260) nor a sceptic; I view the Internet as a tool – nothing more, nothing less. As I outline in chapter 5, the Internet and new media, including social media, complement rather than replace "old media." And, as I argue in chapter 6, the online activism being pursued by Singapore's LGBT communities is most effective when combined with physical world activism. Make no mistake, the Internet has had a profound effect on the lives of many LGBT individuals in Singapore. Yet, it must be remembered that a multitude of factors have been at play in the reconfiguration of the Singaporean public sphere in recent decades – including policy changes related to economics and foreign relations, as well as demographics – and it would be a disservice to simply ascribe these changes to a reductionist technological determinism.

The Online and the Virtual

Writers (including myself) often refer to interactions taking place on the Internet as happening "online" or "in cyberspace." Interactions taking place offline will often be termed "in the real world" or "in real life." In this book, I want to be clear about indicating where events are occurring. As such, I refer to actions taking place offline as happening in the "physical world" in opposition to such phrases as the "real world" in that I do not want to privilege offline interactions over those that take place online; to do so would suggest that online experiences are not as valid as those that take place offline. Rather, I take the position that online interaction is embedded within everyday space in the physical world, not separate from it (Miller and Slater 2000, 7).

A related term, and one that is important to the current volume, is "virtual." This term is often used to denote something digital, as in a "virtual desktop" that is created when one can switch between several different screens on a single display. Virtual is also used to describe something that is artificial or an imitation, as in an online "virtual museum" where one can peruse digital recreations of objects. In many cases, the virtual is used to denote something as a "game," as in virtual gaming via the use of specially designed headsets. This term is also often popularly seen placed in a binary relationship with the "real" or the "actual." Theorists including Deleuze (2002) and Stivale (1998) have used this line of argument when situating the "virtual and the actual" and the "real and the possible" as opposites. Yet, as Shields (1999; 2003) convincingly demonstrates, the virtual exists in an interstitial or liminal state somewhere between the material and the abstract. This is an important idea in that liminal zones, famously described in the context of ritual by Victor Turner (1967) as being "betwixt and between," are places of possibility, potentiality, and change. Shields furthers this notion when he frames rituals as "liminoid virtualities" (Shields 2003, 11); it is in these in-between spaces that pedestrian activities are replaced and transformed by a separate reality – one in which change and possibility predominate. Finally, in McGlotten's work regarding the virtual (2013), he points out that from the dominant cultural point of view, virtual intimacies – those relationships mediated by the digital – are seen to approach, but never quite reach, the real. "[T]hey might index some forms of connection or belonging, but not the ones that really count; they are fantastic or simulated, imaginative, incorporeal, unreal" (McGlotten 2013, 7). In this instance, McGlotten is signalling the "not quite-ness" of the virtual, an almost corrupted and spurious copy of the original. As the title of this book suggests, I claim that the activism engaged in by LGBT Singaporeans for governmental and societal recognition is in many respects virtual. As described in the pages that follow, the movements have resulted in some noteworthy changes in the lives of LGBT Singaporeans, but nothing as grand as some would have hoped, thus indexing the "not quite" aspect of the virtual.

Why Singapore?

To look at how interactions on the Internet impacted the LGBT movement in Singapore, I spent a total of nineteen months in the city-state. The first of these were short three-month visits in the summers of 2004 and 2005 to collect preliminary data. In 2006–7, I spent thirteen consecutive months in Singapore carrying out fieldwork. During this period, I conducted research at several sites, including LGBT organizations that were actively involved in contesting these policies. Significantly, the organizations with which I was interacting were conducting meetings that were against the law and in many instances were also held despite police harassment. Other sites of research included online gathering places, such as LGBT websites, chat rooms, and discussion forums, and LGBT-owned pubs and coffeehouses that served as physical gathering places.

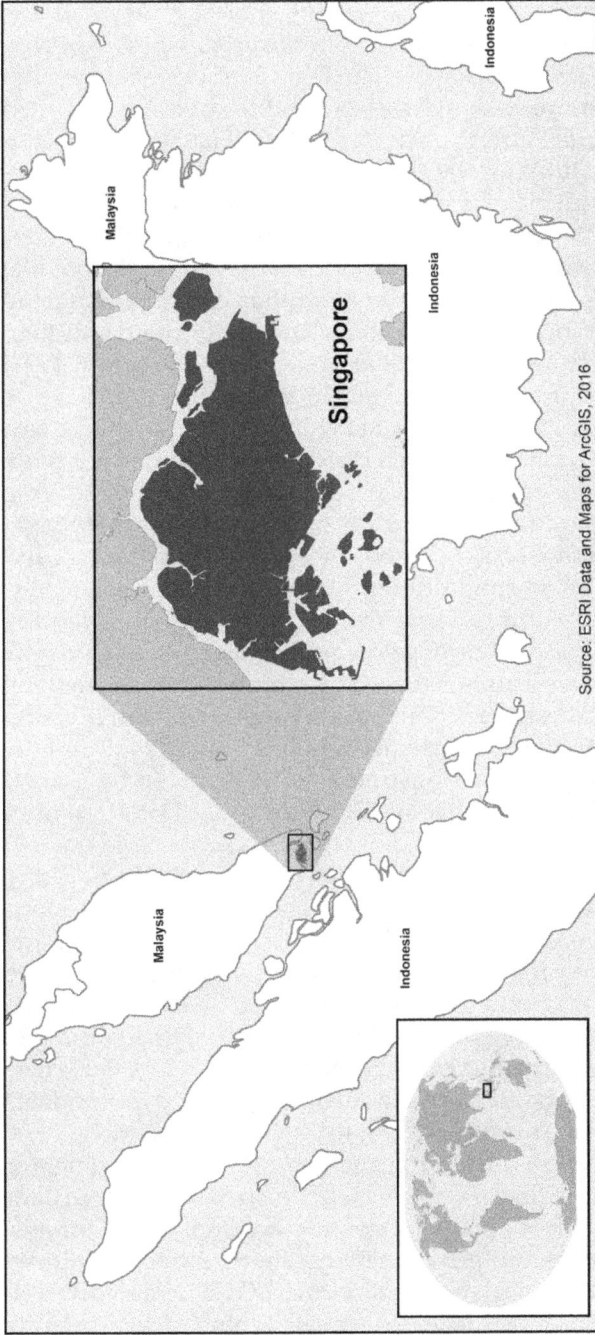

Figure 1. Map of Singapore

At the end of each interview, I would ask the subject if they had any questions for me. On several occasions, interlocutors would ask why I had chosen Singapore for my research. They could not believe that given all the other "more exciting" places I had to choose from, I had settled on their "sterile" and "boring" city-state. Further, while conducting a feasibility study for the project, I met with several Singaporean academics who all asked variations of the same question, "What is so interesting about Singapore?" Besides the illiberal contradictions that shape the life worlds of everyday Singaporeans noted in the opening vignette, Singapore is of interest in that it can be imagined in a variety of ways including as "Disneyland[7] with the death penalty" because of its perceived authoritarian leadership (Gibson 1993) or due to its lack of physical space and relatively recent history as an independent nation, what Marc Augé (2009) might categorize as a "non-place." Singapore has also been described as "important node in international circuits of capital" (Chang, Huang, and Savage 2004, 413), a description that I find particularly apt considering that Singapore has been at the intersection of global flows of people, capital, and information since its founding, through a long British colonial presence, a Japanese occupation, a short merger with neighbouring Malaysia, and finally in its current position as an independent city-state since 1965. Singapore measures fourteen by twenty-six miles, making it one of a few city-states in the contemporary world system. It has an ethnically diverse population, currently totalling 5.4 million; Chinese are the largest ethnic group in Singapore (~74%) followed by Malays (~13%), Indians (~9%), and Others (~3%) (Singapore Department of Statistics 2010).

I attended numerous events staged by LGBT organizations in places ranging from art galleries and pubs to the National Library and sporting venues. I spent long afternoons in well-established gay cruising areas such as shopping malls and public plazas, where I was able to garner valuable information regarding the everyday lives of gay Singaporean men. On most evenings, I would return to the city and drop into any number of clubs catering to LGBT Singaporeans such as Backstage Bar, Cows & Coolies Pub, or Tantric to catch up with my respondents and to scout around for anybody willing to give an interview.

On most days, I also conducted research online. Every morning, for instance, I would scan a dozen or so local online news sources including government-owned newspapers and the accompanying forums, as well as socio-political and personal blogs. I would look for stories in any way related to issues surrounding the LGBT communities in Singapore. In addition, I also made it a point to find stories relating to such allied issues as censorship, gender, nationalism, language, the role of foreigners in Singaporean society, and HIV/AIDS; all of these topics have a direct or indirect bearing on Singapore's LGBT citizens. I created Google search agents that scanned both local and international news outlets and blogs using key phrases such as "Trans Singapore" and "Lesbian Singapore," and "LGBT Southeast Asia." This proved particularly useful in that I assembled information from a diverse set of sources.

Other sources that I scanned daily included blogs and news outlets aimed at or created by members of the LGBT communities. Sources included local blogs that at the time were frequently updated such as *Live today as if there's no tomorrow* and *Salt*Wet*Fish*. I garnered information from non-LGBT sites such as the online version of the nation's highest-selling newspaper, the *Straits Times*, and socio-political blogs such as *Yawning Bread, Mr. Wang Says So, Talking Cock, Singapore Donkey*, and *Mr. Brown*.[8] When I began research in 2004, the *Straits Times* had just incorporated technology that allowed users to comment on articles as well as debate issues within its forums. I was thus able to see a larger picture of how everyday Singaporeans view issues of LGBT equality and related issues. While the *Straits Times* is under direct control of the government, it appeared that there was little interference or censorship in either the comments or forum sections of the online version of the newspaper.

As outlined in subsequent chapters, many of these socio-political blogs utilized varying degrees of satire in their critique of the government and its policies while covering everything from housing policies to rising food prices to the many quirks of Singaporean culture. None focused exclusively on issues dealing with the LGBT communities, but the bloggers and webmasters nonetheless weighed in on these issues when they saw fit. Most importantly, rather than treating LGBT issues as a separate topic, they situated them within the larger context of Singaporean civil society along with such issues as nepotism, press freedoms, and human rights abuses. Through a close reading of these sites, I could better understand what was happening in terms of the shifting perspectives of and on LGBT Singaporeans. Most significantly, these sites allowed Singaporeans of all backgrounds to actively participate, for the first time, in semi-public debates surrounding issues of importance to the nation.

I created several online profiles and logged onto gay portals including local "lifestyle" sites Fridae and Trevvy, and international sites Gay. com and Gaydar that had Singapore chat rooms. Apart from Gaydar, these sites offered a wide variety of online news and entertainment content such as updates on rights movements, both regionally as well as internationally, movie reviews, fashion tips, and city guides aimed at LGBT travellers. While some of these sites will be examined in greater detail later in this book, what I should point out here is that they were all quite interactive. Sites such as Gay.com and Gaydar allowed users to communicate in real time with one another, either through text-based chat clients or via video web cameras. Fridae and Trevvy utilized time-delayed messaging systems, including the ability to send email messages to other users or to send "hearts," "kisses," or "spanks" as an indication of various types of interest. On these sites, I interacted with Singaporean men in a variety of contexts. Sometimes I was online looking to kill some time by chatting with a stranger. Most the time I logged on in my professional role as "ethnographer" and actively sought out individuals to interview for the project, either in the online chat environment or later at a local café. When online as a researcher, I set the bio line on my profile to read, "American researcher looking to interview men for project on LGBT Singapore ... not interested in hook-ups or dates." Many men must not have read my bio because time and again I received messages requesting sexual encounters. Yet, on most occasions that I logged on, I chatted with gay, bisexual, or trans Singaporean men and conducted rich interviews while online. Due to the relative anonymity that comes with this type of communication, it was impossible to definitively determine if the persons with whom I was interacting were truly gay, bisexual, trans, or even Singaporean men. However, most of the men whom I encountered online agreed to continue interviews offline. This way, I could verify most aspects of their identity.

The Structure of the Book

Ultimately, *Virtual Activism* is a book about change. It explores the impact of neoliberal, homonormative, and assimilationist LGBT discourses produced through transnational capitalism and global capital flows that have arrived in Singapore via the Internet. It draws attention to the intense efforts on the part of LGBT Singaporeans to organize their communities and fight for recognition from their government and fellow citizens. In recent decades, government attitudes towards LGBT Singaporeans *appear* to have changed, as evidenced in the chapters that follow. Yet, Parliament has rejected the adoption of the ubiquitous, Western-style LGBT rights framework, endorsed by many activists, and kept laws in place that criminalize homosexual behaviour. This work is not meant to be prescriptive and my goal is not to criticize how LGBT

Singaporeans have gone about creating a social movement. Rather, it is to demonstrate how this movement, which has found limited success, has been produced through a logic of strategic engagement – the only logic possible when operating under illiberal pragmatism.

Chapter 2 looks at how LGBT Singaporeans were depicted by state-controlled media during the period of 1993–2008. Relying on interviews as well as archival data collected from both online and traditional print sources, I position mainstream media as a lens through which to view the conflicted nature of the relationship between LGBT Singaporeans and the nation. I argue that through selective negative portrayal in the press, an overall damaging image of LGBT Singaporeans was continuously being created and re-created. This had a significant influence not only on public opinion about LGBT-related issues, but also on how LGBT Singaporeans came to see themselves and their role as members of the greater nation.

Chapter 3 discusses how and why many LGBT Singaporeans have turned to the Internet to create more satisfying lives for themselves. Primary analysis focuses on the discourse present on three Singaporean sites, SiGNeL and Fridae, aimed primarily at gay and bisexual men, and RedQuEEn, aimed at gender non-conforming women. The groundwork is then laid for the next two chapters, which deal with the often unintended consequences of such online interaction.

Chapter 4 explores how and why the use of technology has been so crucial in the process of opening discussions on topics that had not previously been spoken of in the public sphere. Here, I argue that through blogs, forums, and other interactive online sites, Singaporeans of all persuasions could express opinions, sometimes anonymously and sometimes not, that ultimately led to productive debates regarding issues surrounding citizenship, leading to the development of counterpublics specific to Singapore's LGBT communities.

Chapter 5 returns the focus to the physical world with an analysis of how some LGBT Singaporeans, influenced by online discourse described in previous chapters, had begun the quest for a Western-influenced gay rights movement – one that would be out of place within the confines of illiberal pragmatics. This is followed by an examination of the question of who can frame rights within Singapore. I suggest that, consciously or not, all parties discussed in this chapter were pushing the boundaries of acceptable political discourse, thus further widening the opening of the public sphere that was discussed in chapters 3 and 4. The chapter also highlights how this widening of the public sphere led to a concomitant shift from online activism to activism in the physical world.

Chapter 6 focuses on Pink Dot, a public gathering of LGBT Singaporeans and their supporters first staged in 2009. This annual event exemplifies how many individuals and organizations moved from the physical world to the virtual world and back to the physical world once again. More significantly, it illustrates a local form of activism enacted within the framework of illiberal pragmatics. I also provide an overview of a series of noteworthy events that have taken place since 2008.

In Chapter 7, the Epilogue, I review the main arguments of the book.

in 1989 by a Hong Kong gay activist for the inaugural Lesbian and Gay Film Festival in Hong Kong in an attempt to emphasize the cultural authenticity of same-sex desire in Chinese society (Chou 2000, 1). *Tongzhi* discourse surrounding LGBT rights is a recent invention and the term literally means "comrade." It was appropriated from what were reportedly the "national father" of modern China, Sun Yat-sen's last words, "The revolution has not succeeded, *tongzhi* still need to fight" (1). Appropriated from the political vernacular of the PRC, *tongzhi* is a creatively ironic usage deemed necessary for a repressed group. Many activists in China, Taiwan, Hong Kong and, to a much lesser degree, Singapore reject such terms as "homosexual" due to a perception that it is a Western medical term that brings with it ideas of, among other things, sickness. Other terms such as "gay" and "lesbian" are also seen as being Western, in that central to these terms is not only a "positive, self-claimed identity stressing the right to one's body and homoeroticism, but the modern western discourse of romantic love and individualism" (86). *Tongzhi* is in some respects the Eastern version of a Western LGBT rights discourse and the terms are commensurable on many levels, yet there are differences. The Western LGBT rights model, to which many Singaporeans have been exposed, is based on ideas of autonomy and a language of rights. *Tongzhi*, on the other hand, embraces cultural references, a politics that goes beyond the homo–hetero binary, and focuses primarily on maintaining social harmony. As Chou points out, *tongzhi* is "accepted by many in East Asia and Singapore for its use as an indigenous cultural identity for integrating the sexual into the social" (2). Wei (2007, 582) posits that the internet plays a large role in the promulgation of *tongzhi* discourse in China, and my research confirms that this is also the case in Singapore.

There are recent Chinese equivalents for "coming out," the Western term used to designate when one publicly discloses one's sexual orientation. These include such phrases as *chugui* (出柜 out of the closet) and *chulai* (出來 to go out there). Yet, the phrase that I heard from some Chinese-acculturated Singaporean respondents that mapped most closely onto an indigenous version of "coming out" was quite different. While a phrase such as "coming out" implies a public pronouncement of one's sexual orientation, *hui jia* (回家, homeward or return home) has a much different connotation. Rather than "coming out," which in some cases leads to a rejection by and possible separation from the family, "returning home" implies returning to a safe place where one ultimately belongs. There is no equivalent term in English that corresponds to *jia*, but loosely translated it means home or family. This is not the same as the physical home or family but rather the larger social

Chapter Two

The "Spectral Homosexual" and the Singaporean Media

In August 2006, shortly after arriving in Singapore for extended field-work, I joined Planet Fitness, a popular gym located at Raffles Place in Singapore's financial district. Late on a Sunday afternoon, after my workout, I showered, returned to my locker, and sat down on the bench to start changing back into my street clothes. A young Chinese Singapo-rean man who appeared to be in his late teens was changing his clothes at a locker across the room. At one point, I looked over and noticed that he was staring at me; feeling a bit awkward, I smiled, nodded, and said hello. A few moments later, he walked over and sat down on the bench right next to me, looked me in the eye and quietly asked, "Are you a gay?" Caught off guard, I did not answer him directly. Instead I asked, "Are you?" He replied, "I don't know, but I don't want to become one." When I asked him why he thought that he could "become" gay, he answered, "There was that article on *Wanbao*."[1] The young man was referring to *Lianhe Wanbao* (literally *United Evening Paper*), the Singapore-based Man-darin broadsheet and accompanying website published by Singapore Press Holdings. Before I had the chance to ask him what he had read or why it gave him the idea that he might "become" gay, other men began entering the locker room. The young man jumped up and returned to his locker, finished getting dressed, and quickly exited the room. While I had hoped to see this young man at the gym in the future to continue our conversation, I never encountered him again.

This vignette speaks to two major themes addressed in this chapter. The first, and most significant, theme revolves around the authoritarian state's attempts to regulate society, accomplished through the extensive control of all forms of media (Rodan 1998, 2004), a feat made easier by the fact that Singapore Press Holdings, which publishes nineteen newspapers (including *Lianhe Wanbao*) in four languages, has close ties with the Singaporean government (Asia Sentinel 2013). This control applies to a wide range of topics – not simply those related to LGBT issues or to publications based in Singapore. The degree to which the state suppresses the media, especially foreign publications, is significant. For instance, in October 2006, the Hong Kong-based *Far Eastern Economic Review* (*FEER*) published an interview with opposition leader Chee Soon Juan in which he allegedly suggested that Prime Minister Lee Hsien Loong and his father, Minister Mentor Lee Kuan Yew,[2] were corrupt (*Far Eastern Economic Review* 2006). Both Lees filed libel lawsuits against *FEER* and Chee; this is a widely used and very successful way to silence dissenting voices (Chan 2003; Chronicle.com 2007).[3] Their attorneys demanded apologies, the removal of the article from *FEER*'s website, and the payment of damages and legal fees. The editors of *FEER* offered to print a clarification explaining that it did not mean to imply the defamation claimed by the Lees' lawyers. Several weeks of back and forth between the attorneys representing the Lees and *FEER* resulted in a stalemate. Neither side would respond to the other's communications. Eventually, Singapore's Ministry of Information, Communications and the Arts (MICA) announced new conditions if *FEER* wanted to continue publishing in Singapore. *FEER* was required to appoint a legal representative who could accept lawsuits and post a S$200,000 (US$126,000 in 2006) bond to cover damages from such lawsuits – even those relating to articles already published – if they wished to continue publishing in Singapore (*Far Eastern Economic Review* 2006). In September 2008, after almost two years of litigation, Singapore's High Court ruled in favour of the Lees. The *Far East Economic Review* appealed but the summary judgment was upheld by the Court of Appeal. The *Far Eastern Economic Review* ceased publication in late 2009; there has been speculation that this was due, in large part, to the Singapore lawsuit (Reuters 2009).

The second, yet no less important, theme addressed in this chapter is the state's use of selective strategies and tactics to sway public opinion on contentious issues including homosexuality. This is accomplished, in part, via the media, through the promotion of heterosexuality and the demonization of homosexuality. The marginalization of homosexuality within Singaporean society, and the subsequent construction of the abject figure of the "homosexual," is similar in many respects to the production of the "spectral homosexual" described by David Murray in his work on gay men in Barbados. Murray suggests that discussions presented on talk radio add to an already existing Barbadian "hegemonic discourse in which the ... male homosexual serves a particular semiotic strategy, acting as the key indicator of downward movement of the social respectability of the nation" (Murray 2012, 25). I read

Murray's "spectral homosexual" as an ambivalent figure – a feminized male whose subjectivity is the product of interactions with and influences from a decadent, distinctly non-Barbadian West. This maps well on to the figure of the "homosexual" produced within Singaporean media. In both cases the homosexual comes to index a failed hetero-masculinity, a characteristic seen as a necessary component of a strong and prosperous post-colonial nation-state. This type of discourse can and does have an influence on those who are exposed to it. In the case of the young man described in the opening vignette, a state-affiliated newspaper published an article that purported that somehow one can "become" gay and subsequently revert to the "normal path," suggesting that sexual orientation is a choice. Judging by the young man's reaction to the story, there is the possibility that this propagation of state ideology was, at least in this case, effective. Murray also cautions (2012, 28) that it is highly problematic to assume a uniform national or societal position on homosexuality based on media discourse, and I certainly agree. At the same time, as I demonstrate, the media have played a significant role in public perceptions of LGBT Singaporeans.

To illustrate the impact of these two strategies, I begin by looking at examples of media produced by LGBT Singaporeans in response to strategies deployed by the state designed to suppress LGBT organizing. I examine portions of print newsletters initially published in 1993 by People Like Us (PLU), Singapore's first LGBT rights organization. The newsletter was photocopied and distributed among LGBT Singaporeans and for the years that it was published served as a significant form of communication within these communities. In the second, I explore censorship surrounding *Manazine*, a men's lifestyle print magazine. Both the PLU newsletter and *Manazine* are examples of "alternative" media that target an LGBT audience and stand in stark contrast to mainstream Singaporean media.

I then call attention to several examples that demonstrate the almost uniformly negative treatment of LGBT Singaporeans in print, on television, and through online media, all cases that illustrate the influence of mainstream, state-supervised media. In addition to outlining censorship and criminal cases against gay men brought to the attention of the public via newspaper, I examine media coverage of members of the LGBT communities and the state-supervised media's coverage of stage plays, television programs, and films with LGBT themes. I argue that this news coverage was significant because, in many respects, it was the only exposure that a large majority of non-LGBT Singaporeans had regarding LGBT individuals and their communities. Through outlining these cases, I argue that these oscillating negative and positive media portrayals came to create a "spectral homosexual" who, while included in the national narrative, was nonetheless portrayed (with very few exceptions) in a negative light. At the same time, this disregard for Singapore's LGBT citizens eventually produced a resistance that has fostered the emergence of the LGBT movement active within Singapore today.

During my period of research, it became clear that Singaporean authorities were attempting to influence public perception of its LGBT citizens through all forms of media. This manipulation occurred for numerous reasons, many of which are explored in detail in later chapters, but here I suggest that much of this need for control was related to the fact that, as a nation, Singapore is relatively young, only attaining full nationhood in 1965. As such, a firmly shared "national identity," which involved the creation of a sense of shared values among all Singaporeans, has been difficult to construct. Without a solid foundation on which to rest, the new nation is constantly in danger of destabilization. I suggest that the figure of the "homosexual," described above, puts this foundation at risk. Singapore is a nation composed of various groups of immigrants who come from drastically different cultures. Malay Singaporeans, most of whom are Sunni Muslims, are indigenous to the region, yet they make up only 15 per cent of the nation's population. The other notable minority, Indian Singaporeans, began arriving in the early nineteenth century – some of these predominantly adult men came to serve prison sentences or to work as indentured servants, while others were wealthy merchants who came to expand their already substantial fortunes. Most of these men were Hindu, while a small number were Muslim. Chinese Singaporeans, who hail from divergent geographic, religious, and social backgrounds from within China, came to Singapore as traders or to work in the large entrepôt that emerged in the mid-nineteenth century. This ethnically diverse population is at once multireligious, multilingual, and multicultural. Accordingly, since the founding of the nation in 1965, Singapore's government has consistently worked to inculcate one homogeneous national identity. Leaders set about to take several discordant populations with differing belief and value systems and instil a single set of patriotic ideals in attempts to define the nation. Social, political, and economic life has been arranged around the ideology of "pragmatism" since Singapore's founding. Pragmatism wasn't just about national identity; as Chua (1995, 48) points out, it was about national survival.

At the same time, however, governmental regulations continued to reinforce differences *between* communities. For instance, 78.7 per cent of Singaporeans live in public housing[4] and the Ethnic Integration Policy,[5] enacted in 1989, required that each public housing block reflect the racial breakdown of the nation (Chih 2002). Part of the purpose was to promote "racial integration and harmony" by preventing the formation of Indian and Malay racial enclaves. In the simplest terms, when a Chinese Singaporean owner sells their apartment, they must sell it to another Chinese Singaporean to maintain the racial balance of the block. This is not a problem for most Chinese Singaporeans as they form an overwhelming majority of the population, yet it does create potential problems for Indian and Malay Singaporeans, who often must wait months to find another Indian or Malay seller or buyer. Policies such as these, developed within the framework of illiberal pragmatics, constantly keep ideas of racial and ethnic *difference* at the forefront of public discourse, making integration difficult while contradicting the government's attempts at creating a truly unified nation. At the same time, by preventing the development of racial enclaves, the state also inhibits the formation of minority voting blocs, effectively ensuring that the Chinese majority in each of the nation's voting districts are the citizens who determine the results of elections. Significantly, Murray's "spectral homosexual" also serves as an example of how the Singaporean state has emphasized notions of difference in order to discourage the full integration of LGBT citizens into the nation.

"Singaporean" Values

Much has been written in recent years about how new media conflate the boundaries between the local, global, and transnational (Beliso-De Jesus 2013; Hegde 2011; Pullen 2012) and how in the process of using these media, users have been interpellated as "ideal subjects" through their exposure to these transnational communications (Kocer 2013). These notions are in accord with what I suggest has happened in Singapore – but there is a difference. Rather than simply creating "ideal subjects," the state is at the same time creating "national subjects" through interpellative online encounters with Internet media. Singapore is, by definition, a developmental state in which technocrats postulate that "state-led macroeconomic planning and industrialization can engender economic growth" (Liow 2011, 246). Developmental states also tend to exhibit widespread use of Althusser's (2001) ideological state apparatus (ISA) and repressive state apparatus (RSA) to teach the population how to act and think in accordance with the goals of the state (Liow 2011, 246). The example of the prime minister and Minister Mentor suing the *Far Eastern Economic Review* illustrates a repressive state apparatus in that the lawsuit was part of a set of specialized legal practices utilized by the government and the courts.

In Singapore, attempts at interpellation of citizens into dominant and hegemonic ideologies of the nation exemplify the mechanisms of ideological state apparatus. These include, among others, discourses of "Chineseness," "Asian values,"[6] and "family values," which, though not unique to Singapore, are present nonetheless. These ideologies normalize the ethnic Chinese male, who is both heterosexual and Mandarin speaking, as the prototypical Singaporean citizen, increasing the alienation that many non-heterosexual, non-Mandarin-speaking Singaporeans feel. More noteworthy, however, is the "national ideology" introduced in the form of the *White Paper on Shared Values* (Singapore Parliament 1991), which includes 1) nation before community and society before self; 2) family as the basic unit of society; 3) community support and respect for the individual; 4) consensus not conflict; and 5) racial and religious harmony. These values, inculcated primarily via parents in the home and civics and moral education lessons in the public schools, were intended to help individuals develop a "Singaporean" identity.

Returning now to Althusser – perhaps interpellation (or some variation thereof) is a good way of describing the instillation of shared values, but this framework misses the idea of *competing* ideologies. In a tightly controlled society such as Singapore, interpellation is certainly useful in describing the mediated relations between the state and individuals. On a pragmatic level, the state does control newspapers and radio and television stations that distribute information within the country. At the same time, however, one must ask if it is unrealistic to think that with the advent of the Internet the dominant ruling ideology will always be upheld, especially given the fact that Singaporeans are exposed to discourses that are embedded within an intertextual field of transnational media. Further, Althusser's conceptualization of interpellation could seem rather simplistic to be applied to a globally connected state such as Singapore. Recall that for Althusser, ideologies operate much like a public announcement system that "hails" the subject, who then enters a relationship with the "real." However, if all subjects (individuals) are interpellated, how do we account for various social movements within Singapore? What of individual agency? How would Althusser view the Singaporean social movements described in subsequent chapters? I suggest that he would view the subjects who participate in these social movements as being "interpellated" in that they are working within the existing socio-cultural-political framework including the ideological frames of neoliberal homonormativity in conjunction with illiberal pragmatics. Further, because I am dealing here predominantly with media, it also becomes important to think about how this communal identity is created. While acknowledging the impact of the teaching of shared values, it is also critical to think more deeply about how the state attempts to construct a homogeneous Singaporean identity via the narratives contained within online media. These attempts resulted in distinctive notions of who does and does not constitute a "Singaporean," thereby writing LGBT subjectivities out of the national narrative. In later chapters, I explore how LGBT groups changed the tone and tenor of this dialogue via the use of the Internet in their own attempts at rewriting and subsequently resituating themselves within the nation.

1993: The PLU Newsletter

> We had a *samizdat* – an underground newspaper. So, every month at a meeting we would have generated an eight-page underground newsletter and there was always going to be someone responsible for editing and selecting the articles, editing it, having it photocopied in a shop and we'd have free copies and collect donations to pay for the next issue ... and so for a few years we were quite happy with it.
>
> Singaporean activist Alex Au (2006 interview)

Issue #1 of the *People Like Us* newsletter is dated "sometime late March 1993." The creators of the newsletter described it as a "Very, Very Underground one page flyer, which will try to keep the Singapore Lesbian and Gay population up to date with the latest happenings in and around town" (*People Like Us* 1993). The editors requested that anyone who had a copy "zap it and pass it on to other People Like Us ... (selectively, please)."[7] In the opening paragraphs of the newsletter, editors spoke to its significance: "This is our very first issue. We hope that there will be more. It is important because it will go some way towards making gays and lesbians feel less isolated, as we can be, in this society. We are not sure if it is going to be regular, monthly, or bi, so to speak." The inaugural issue listed no names for contact persons but noted that in the future, "there are plans to rent a PO Box so that people can contribute." The primary topics of subsequent newsletters were censorship, the precarious position of the Singaporean LGBT community, and news from other Asian LGBT communities. In the second issue, from May 1993, editors published a small story at the bottom of the page entitled "Media Blackout" about the March on Washington for Lesbian, Gay, and Bi Equal Rights and Liberation that had occurred the previous month. It noted: "By all accounts (the march was on the front-page news at most American papers) except the Singapore media's that is. Only a tiny snippet of info appeared in the *Straits Times* the day before the

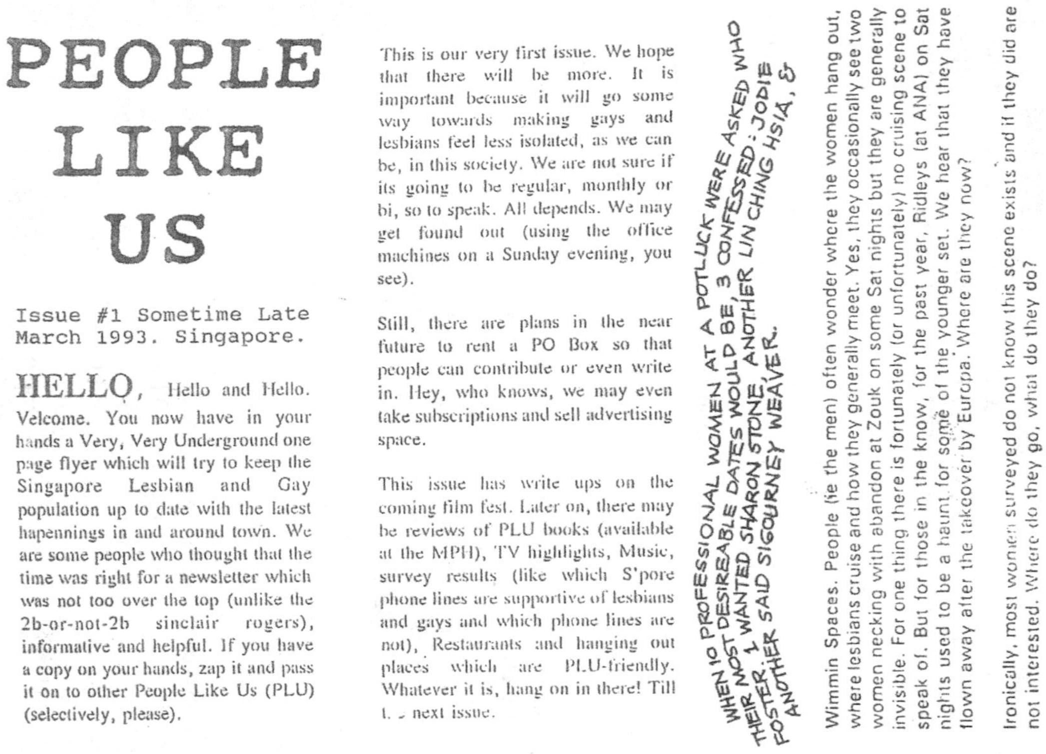

PEOPLE LIKE US

Issue #1 Sometime Late March 1993. Singapore.

HELLO, Hello and Hello. Welcome. You now have in your hands a Very, Very Underground one page flyer which will try to keep the Singapore Lesbian and Gay population up to date with the latest happenings in and around town. We are some people who thought that the time was right for a newsletter which was not too over the top (unlike the 2b-or-not-2b sinclair rogers), informative and helpful. If you have a copy on your hands, zap it and pass it on to other People Like Us (PLU) (selectively, please).

This is our very first issue. We hope that there will be more. It is important because it will go some way towards making gays and lesbians feel less isolated, as we can be, in this society. We are not sure if its going to be regular, monthly or bi, so to speak. All depends. We may get found out (using the office machines on a Sunday evening, you see).

Still, there are plans in the near future to rent a PO Box so that people can contribute or even write in. Hey, who knows, we may even take subscriptions and sell advertising space.

This issue has write ups on the coming film fest. Later on, there may be reviews of PLU books (available at the MPH), TV highlights, Music, survey results (like which S'pore phone lines are supportive of lesbians and gays and which phone lines are not), Restaurants and hanging out places which are PLU-friendly. Whatever it is, hang on in there! Till t . - next issue.

WHEN 10 PROFESSIONAL WOMEN AT A POTLUCK WERE ASKED WHO THEIR MOST DESIRABLE DATES WOULD BE, 3 CONFESSED: JODIE FOSTER. 1 WANTED SHARON STONE. ANOTHER LIN CHING HSIA, & ANOTHER SAID SIGOURNEY WEAVER.

Wimmin Spaces. People (ie the men) often wonder where the women hang out, where lesbians cruise and how they generally meet. Yes, they occasionally see two women necking with abandon at Zouk on some Sat nights but they are generally invisible. For one thing there is (unfortunately (or unfortunately) no cruising scene to speak of. But for those in the know, for the past year, Ridleys (at ANA) on Sat nights used to be a haunt for some of the younger set. We hear that they have flown away after the takeover by Europa. Where are they now?

Ironically, most women surveyed do not know this scene exists and if they did are not interested. Where do they go, what do they do?

Figure 2. Issue #1, *People Like Us* (PLU) Newsletter, March 1993
Source: *People Like Us.* Used with permission.

march, next to a picture of a quilt ... Where was our story this time?"[8] In August 1993, issue #3, editors noted the perilous situation that faced Singapore's LGBT communities, framing it within the context of media,

> Meanwhile it appears that the government is tacitly keeping up with the times (four years ago, *Mergers and Acquisitions*[9] would never have been played or *The Wedding Banquet*[10] screened), they have also made pronouncements that homosexuality will not be condoned in Singapore, which all means that they could clamp down on us at anytime. The situation is delicate.

Some subsequent issues dealt explicitly with censorship. In Issue #4 (undated) editors noted that "10 crucial minutes were snipped off *Wedding [Banquet]* – in which Simon and Wei-tung made love, which Dad espied. What's going on censors?" In Issue #5, a story appeared titled, "No Sex Please, We Are Singaporeans!" The article referred to the BBC Series *Prime Suspect* that was running on SBC (Singapore Broadcasting Corporation, the precursor to MediaCorp), in which the editor, seemingly speaking directly to the government censors asked, "We wonder why SBC is not showing the final part of this trilogy. Could it be because *Prime Suspect* #3 is about rent boys, homophobia, and police corruption? Now, we do not want to have anything to do with those issues, do we?" (*People Like Us* 1994).

Other issues of the newsletter from 1994 noted that while all the wire services were carrying stories regarding the twenty-fifth anniversary of the Stonewall riots in New York City,[11] SBC chose not to pick it up. In issue #10, three stories were reprinted: "Taiwan's Homosexuals – An Account," and "Brothers-Sisters in Japan" both reprinted from Reuters, and the other, "Kuala Lumpur Gov't Bans Gays from Appearing on Television" from the *Straits Times*. About this article, editors commented, "This article appeared in the *Straits Times* on the 18th of August 1994. Considering the size of the article, which really is quite invisible, you can imagine just how scared the *Straits Times* is in making gays more visible."

The creation of the newsletter demonstrates the impact and effectiveness of state strategies on Singapore's LGBT communities. Consistently negative representations of LGBT Singaporeans in state-controlled media encouraged the first attempts by members of Singapore's LGBT communities to respond to government interference. By documenting specific instances of censorship, the editors were laying the groundwork for later challenges to governmental authority that would take place over a decade later. At the same time, I suggest that these newsletters prompted LGBT Singaporeans to begin to write positive portrayals of themselves back into a national narrative in which they were noticeably absent. The PLU newsletter was only published for a few years and was replaced in March 1997 by the Internet site SiGNeL (Singapore Gay News List). Nonetheless, this simply constructed newsletter served as the foundation in the fight for LGBT recognition within the Singaporean public sphere.

2004: *Manazine*

In Singapore, official guidance for every aspect of life is provided to citizens through numerous laws, rules, regulations, and codes. For instance, the *Guidelines for Imported Adult-Interest Lifestyle Magazines*, issued by the Media Development Authority (MDA), are meant to reflect the "general community standards." In 2004, the guidelines read, in part, as follows:

> "Alternative Lifestyle / Deviant Sexual Activity":
> 15.1 Lifestyle magazines and articles should not encourage or promote alternative lifestyles (e.g. homosexuality) and deviant sexual activities (e.g. child pornography, bestiality, necrophilia).
> 15.2 Depictions, including stylised illustrations and photographs, of alternative lifestyles and deviant sexual activity must not be featured.[12]

An example of how this section of the code was applied occurred in early March 2004, when *Manazine,* a glossy monthly publication aimed at gay Singaporean men, became the subject of ongoing scrutiny by the MDA. Acting on the complaints from concerned parents over content issues and the fact that the publication was easily available in outlets patronized by the public, the MDA sent a letter to the publisher and chief editor, Arjan Twilhaar, objecting to 1) a male model positioned too closely to the buttocks of another male model and 2) a statement by British singer Will Young in which he told the interviewer that he "wants a boyfriend." The MDA strongly objected; "We have warned the publisher that the current state of the magazine, which features nudity and homosexual content, is unacceptable" (Fridae.com 2004a). Yet, as Twilhaar was quick to point out, these images and topics of interviews were no more sexually explicit than the content found in mainstream women's magazines such as the Singapore versions of *Cosmopolitan*, *FHM*, or *Vogue* (Twilhaar 2004). In late March 2004, the magazine was given an extension of its original print licence on the condition that it tone down its "pro-gay" content. The publisher subsequently changed the name to *RA – Restricted Access*, and while the magazine remained focused on a gay lifestyle, the content had changed; noticeably absent were the pictorials featuring young men modelling underwear or in various stages of undress. The introduction of *RA* was somewhat successful, but short-lived. According to the deal worked out with the MDA, the magazine could no longer be distributed for free in LGBT outlets. Instead, it was available only for a subscription price of S$25 per year and the reader had to produce a subscription card at the news outlet before picking up the magazine. In June 2005, seven months after its relaunch, publication of *RA* ceased.

The fact that a gay-lifestyle magazine could be published in a nation in which gay sex is criminalized is worthy of attention. On the surface, it seems nonsensical. Why promote a lifestyle that is essentially against the law? But, when looked at within a framework of illiberal pragmatics, it doesn't seem so odd. Interviews with Singaporean academics indicate that the MDA initially allowed such a magazine to be published to nurture the creative knowledge-based economy created by the introduction of the Internet in the late 1990s (see also Tan 2009). According to Richard Florida, members of the creative industries tend to want to live in cities that are "diverse, tolerant, and open to new ideas" (Florida 2009, 249). By allowing the publication of periodicals such as *Manazine*, Singapore could promote itself in this manner. However, when the Singaporean public began to complain about content, the MDA acted. In this case, the government used what is known in Singapore as the "light touch" (Pakiam 2007, 5) in which the MDA and other regulatory agencies "suggested" ways in which the publisher of *Manazine* could come to be sensitive to the greater society's concerns about LGBT issues. At the same time, by making the magazine available only by paid subscription, censors were "suggesting" to Twilhaar that many Singaporeans embrace "mainstream" values. This calibrated approach on the part of the government ensured that he would not be challenging those values or pushing for societal acceptance of LGBT Singaporeans too quickly.[13]

2005: Omissions and Fines

Mainstream publications also contributed to public perceptions of Singapore's LGBT communities. In 2005, articles appeared in the *Straits Times* and the *New Paper* that were early attempts by writers sympathetic to LGBT Singaporeans to bring attention to the lives of this population. That is not to say that before 2005 there were no articles dealing with Singapore's LGBT communities – quite the contrary. But prior to

2005, coverage was routinely negative and did little to provide recognition to these minority communities. For instance, on 31 July 2005, Ignatius Low, a regular columnist for the *Straits Times*, wrote an article titled "New Singles Rule a Cause for Celebration" (Straits Times 2005a). The column, which appeared in the "Think" section of the *Sunday Times*, outlined how new housing policies adopted by the Ministry for National Development allow unrelated singles to jointly purchase property. The article stated that several members of Parliament objected to the law in that it could possibly encourage homosexual couples to purchase property together, thereby undermining the government's ongoing campaign to build strong heterosexual families. This aside, the article neither encouraged nor glorified homosexual couples; it simply analysed the financial repercussions of the new law, for all couples – gay or straight. In fact, the government decision to allow pairs or small groups of single persons to buy property together serves to further my assertion about the significance of illiberal pragmatics as policy. This housing policy has supported what Yue refers to as "new domestic non-heteronormative sexual partnerships" (2012, 6). While ostensibly intended to correct for an oversupply of public housing stock, the policy instead encourages same-sex couples to buy homes together.

One week later, on 7 August, the *Sunday Times* ran a full-page interview, in the "Read" section, with one of Singapore's best-known and outspoken poets, Cyril Wong (Straits Times 2005b). In the interview, Wong stated that he wrote because he missed his family, "My father stopped talking to me 15 years ago when I brought home a certain friend who was very gay, and he disapproved. When he met my friend, he realized what direction I was taking. We started fighting and he said, 'Don't see your friend anymore.' I said, 'No.'" All told, the interview was objective and gave only an oblique indication of Wong's sexual orientation. Yet, neither the news story regarding changes to housing law nor the interview with Wong explicitly stated anything relating directly to the sexual orientation of the authors or subjects.

In October 2005, Singapore's MDA acted against two popular gay websites citing complaints that they contained provocative content (Straits Times 2005c). One of the websites, which was not directly named by the MDA,[14] was supposedly recruiting underage boys for nude photographs and was placed on a list of 100 banned websites. This list, the contents of which the MDA will not publicly disclose, contains ninety-eight "pornographic" sites and two that feature content related to "religious extremism." The MDA considers all of the websites on the list to be "mass impact" because they "contain content that the community regards as offensive or harmful to Singaporeans' racial and religious harmony or against the national interest" (Media Development Authority 2019).

The other site was identified in the press as "Meet Gay Singapore Friends." This was simply the tagline for Sg.boy, a popular gay social networking website. The website featured a "personals" section in which some members posted nude or semi-nude pictures of themselves. Site owners were warned to remove all objectionable content and subsequently fined S$5000 (approximately US$3,000 in October 2005) for violating Part 4 of the Internet code of practice, which governs Internet content.[15] The complainant in this case was a thirty-three-year old freelance software programmer who had "stumbled" upon the site. In his complaint, he noted that the site's registered members grew from 60,000 in 2004 – when he first noticed the site – to more than 330,000 in 2005 (The Age 2005). His main concern was that since the site was based in Singapore, most of the members must also be local. After the incident, Sg.boy was taken down and replaced by Trevvy.com, a site that turned out to be far more successful than its predecessor. The ideological work that this type of censorship accomplished should not be underestimated. As with the censorship described in the case of *Manazine*, the banning and censoring of these sites also served to exclude non-normative subjectivities from the national narrative.

2006: Tabloids and *SQ21*

In 2006, homosexuality received a great deal of attention in Singapore's national newspaper the *Straits Times* as well as the daily tabloids, the *New Paper* and *Today*. For the first time, the coverage provided by these government-owned publications was not entirely negative, and, in fact, relatively positive portrayals of LGBT Singaporeans began to sporadically appear in these daily newspapers.

Among the articles published during this period are those describing the disbanding of a gay drug syndicate (Pink News 2006) and reports of a gay teacher molesting his students (Straits Times 2005d). Most provocative, though, was news coverage of two stories by the government-owned *New Paper* in May 2006. In the first, the paper devoted the cover, "They Bathe, Then Get Dirty. I got HIV from S'pore bathhouse orgy, says man" (New Paper 2006a), and four full pages of the newspaper to two sensational (and unsubstantiated) stories of HIV spread at gay bathhouses. The first, "Health Clubs Deadly HIV Hubs," (New Paper 2006b) detailed how one intoxicated young man engaged in unprotected sex at a Singapore sauna. He claimed that because there were no private rooms available (and condoms were apparently available only inside private rooms) he decided to forgo the condom and have unprotected anal sex with two different men. The second story, "Once Inside, We Drop Our Towels," was a sordid account of activities taking place in another sauna. The article ended with the young man who contracted HIV imploring the government to "step in and do something" (New Paper 2006c). These news stories are particularly pertinent in that they remind us, once again, of the contradictory nature of illiberal pragmatics. By allowing gay bathhouses to operate legally, which they did, the government was once again promoting, or at the very least turning a blind eye to, the illegal sexual practices taking place inside.

The other New Paper article told the stories of two young men, one a medical doctor and the other a former teacher who, in separate instances, were arrested after arranging online sexual encounters involving the drug ecstasy. The men they planned to meet were undercover police officers. On 23 August 2006 the New Paper ran the headline, "Drug Sting in Hotel: First, Gay Doctor. Now ... Gay Ex-teacher Trapped with Drugs" (2006d).

These cases caused a great sensation among many mainstream Singaporeans in that they involved two behaviours long associated with Singapore's gay communities – casual sex and illicit drugs. This type of coverage reinforced the prevailing tendency of the public to equate ideas of promiscuity and decadence with gay men. In some respects, stories that appeared in the mainstream press were the only exposure most Singaporeans had to this population. By focusing media coverage on the negative aspects of LGBT communities, the government of Singapore was, knowingly or not, presenting them in an unfavourable light. The subjects of these stories were presented as social deviants, thus putting into question their place (and the place of every other sexually non-normative Singaporean) within the larger society. Yet, they were also presented as young men who had very promising futures until they "threw it all away when [they] fell to temptation" – much like Murray's "spectral homosexual." The article went on to state: "His [the teacher's] life spiraled downwards after he started engaging in homosexual sex with strangers he met over the Internet, and taking drugs." Underlying this statement is the idea that somehow these young men with very bright futures gave in to something that could have been avoided. The teacher claimed that he had only engaged in such behaviour because he suffered from untreated depression, again implying that the homosexual sex that he engaged in with strangers was an anomaly and, possibly, something over which he had no control.

During the same week the New Paper printed the sensationalized stories regarding sex and drugs, the Straits Times published a positive review for the recently released collection compiled by Singaporean poet Ng Yi-Sheng entitled *SQ21: Singapore Queers in the 21st Century* (Ng 2006). The review was titled "Coming Out in Singapore: A Collection of Personal Accounts Strives to Reach out to Family and Friends of Gay People Here" (Straits Times 2006a). The article featured photographs of Ng and Dr. Khoo Hoon Eng, a biochemistry professor at the National University of Singapore and the mother of two gay sons. Later in the year, the book was named the number one non-fiction book of 2006 by the *Straits Times*, which described the book as follows: "Brave and bittersweet, this collection of 15 stories about coming out in Singapore is unprecedented. Gay Singaporeans and their families spoke frankly to poet Ng and provided full names and photographs. Written in the first person, it is a celebration of people determined to live their lives to the fullest." Significantly, traces of illiberal pragmatics can be found in a book that highlights the lives of LGBT Singaporeans, many of whose sexual practices are illegal and punishable by up to two years in prison.

SQ21 featured headshots of all the participants, giving a human touch to LGBT Singaporeans. The book was so successful that after its initial launch at the upscale Mox Bar, subsequent well-attended book launches were held in large mainstream bookstores such as Borders and Kinokuniya. Its initial print run of two thousand copies sold out quickly. The book was also, in many respects, groundbreaking for Singapore's LGBT communities, who, for the first time, were not being portrayed as drug-addicted, perverted threats to the nation. Rather, as Alphonsus Lee, one of the participants in *SQ21* noted, "The media has made gay life out to be full of debauchery – you sleep around, you go out, you drink, you party ... – but not everyone is like that. [My partner] and I are not like that ... We're a very sedate couple; for us, washing the car is a family activity" (Ng 2006, 29).

Why would a book that celebrates the lives of sexually non-normative citizens, some of whom knowingly break the law, be named the number one non-fiction book of 2006 by a state-run newspaper? I suggest that because the book was conceptualized and published within a framework of neoliberal homonormativity, it was more acceptable to government censors as well as everyday Singaporeans. The volume featured nine men and five women of various ethnicities who spoke candidly about their lives. However, the overwhelming theme of the book, as noted in the Foreword, is "love" (2–3). Like the "sedate" couple noted above, all the interviews are framed within the context of neoliberal homonormativity and contain references to family and speak often of monogamous relationships, same-sex weddings, and organized religion. More significantly, it serves as a good example of illiberal pragmatics

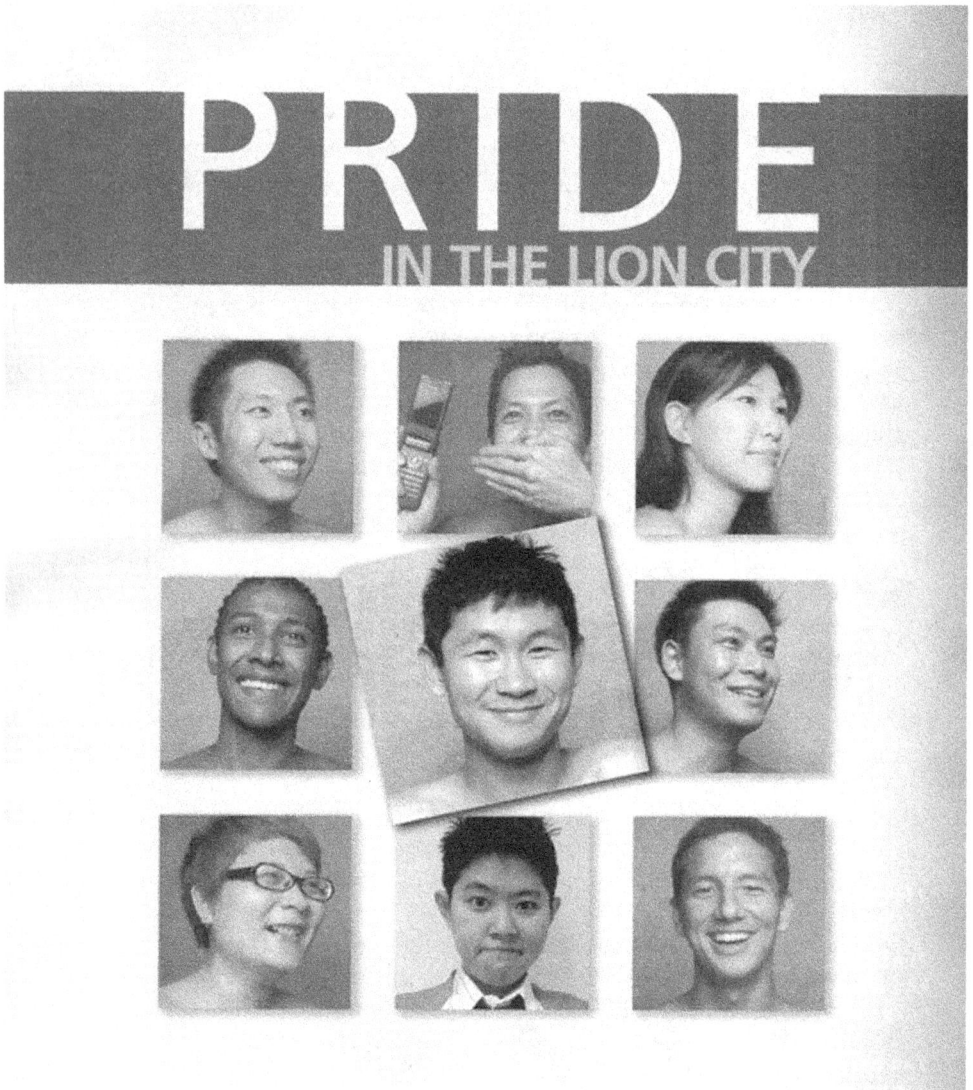

Figure 3. Promotional material for *SQ21*
Source: *SQ21.* Used with permission.

in practice. The *Straits Times* is a publication owned by Singapore Press Holdings, which has close ties to the Singaporean government and controls much of the city-state's print media. While sex between consenting adult men is illegal, and the legal code proscribes "no promotion" of homosexuality, a state-run newspaper nonetheless named a book detailing the lives of LGBT individuals as the number one non-fiction book of 2006.

A few months later, in October 2006, the *New Paper* published a cover story with the headline "11 Gay S'poreans Granted Asylum in US" (New Paper 2006e). Despite the headline, the story centred on Christopher Yeoh, a 31-year-old Singaporean who had originally travelled to the United States on a student visa. After completing his two-year course of study in Orlando, Florida, he allowed his student visa to expire. Rather than returning to Singapore, Yeoh moved to San Francisco, where he remained for the next four years. It was only after he was in the process of being deported that he claimed he might be persecuted should he return to Singapore. Yeoh was eventually denied asylum in the United States. Several things stand out regarding this case. Of prime interest is the fact that the mainstream government-controlled media presented to the public a case dealing with homosexuality in an arguably impartial manner. It neither denigrated nor glamorized homosexuality; it simply told the story. The article quoted a statement made to the *Straits Times* from the Singapore Ministry of Home Affairs in which a spokesperson said, "The police do not seek out persons to prosecute on the grounds of their homosexual identity." Whether this statement is accurate or not, the article is quite neutral; there is no condemnation, no ignoring the fact that there are LGBT individuals residing in Singapore; most importantly, these articles featured the word "gay." As one interlocutor commented, "it's kind of nice ... it is as if they are finally acknowledging that we exist. When they called us 'homosexuals,' it sounded so sterile, like we were diseased or something. I'm not sure that I'm crazy about the word 'gay' but it's definitely better than homosexual."

2008: Television

These mixed messages from the government also applied to television. In April 2008, the MDA fined MediaCorp TV Channel 5 S$15,000 (US$11,000 in 2008) for airing an episode of the home and décor series *Find and Design* (Fridae.com 2008). The episode revolved around a gay couple in America who wanted to convert a game room in their home into a nursery for their newly adopted baby. The MDA objected to the fact that the host of the program congratulated the gay couple on the adoption of their baby and explicitly acknowledged these two men and their baby as a family. Yet, only four months previously, the MDA allowed the broadcast of *The Morning After*, which normalized homosexuality and unconventional family structures. The *Find and Design* decision thus highlights the inconsistency on the part of the MDA in the enforcement of its guidelines – another example of the ambivalent bureaucracy created in an environment of illiberal pragmatism.

The MDA has strict guidelines that prohibit the positive portrayal of what they classify as "alternative lifestyles." For instance, the code dealing with broadcast television states the following:

> 11d. Sex
>   Films likely to encourage deviant sexual activities such as pedophilia, bestiality and necrophilia are not allowed for all ratings.
>   Films that depict a homosexual lifestyle should be sensitive to community values. They should not promote or justify a homosexual lifestyle.[16]

It is significant that the Media Development Authority chooses to group homosexuality under the same rubric as paedophilia, bestiality, and necrophilia. This grouping is problematic in that homosexuality is a non-normative sexual subjectivity. Yet, bestiality and necrophilia are considered mental disorders and, in many cases, involve heterosexual men and women, and paedophilia is a mental disorder that involves sexual attraction to prepubescent children. None of these have a tangible connection to LGBT subjectivity, in Singapore or elsewhere. Yet by grouping LGBT individuals with individuals suffering from a psychiatric disorder, the MDA is contributing to the misgivings of the public when it comes to non-normative sexualities.

Conclusion

These cases highlight the inconsistencies and indeterminacies in the application of regulations; the MDA was allowing the public consumption of certain television programs and magazines, while disallowing others. They allowed *The Morning After* yet disallowed *Find and Design*. They allowed *Cosmopolitan* but disallowed *Manazine*. I suggest that the reason that *The Morning After* and *Cosmopolitan* were allowed has to do with the fact that, on some level, they positively reinforce the nation-building mandate of the Singaporean government. In *The Morning After*, when the young man "comes out" to his family the knowledge of his sexual orientation, as far as the viewer knew, stayed within the family. There were no public pronouncements or dramatic speeches containing anti-government rhetoric. Even though *Cosmopolitan* featured pictorials more sexual than those found in *Manazine*, *Cosmopolitan* could maintain a print licence because it reinforced heterosexual ideals. *Find and Design* and *Manazine*, on the other hand, went directly against the national narrative of heterosexuality and, more broadly, the "shared values" introduced in the *White Paper* of 1991. More significantly, they represented the failed hetero-masculinity seen by many as a threat to the nation.

I have given examples of censorship and media coverage of issues of concern to Singapore's LGBT communities. In doing so, I have suggested that, through selective inclusion and exclusion from the government-run media, positive portrayals of LGBT Singaporeans were not being included in the construction of a national narrative. I have also included an example of generally positive media coverage to show how LGBT Singaporeans were slowly gaining recognition within the larger public sphere.

I remember being surprised when I opened the *New Paper* one afternoon in July 2007 and saw a short write-up for the film *The Blossoming of Maximo Oliveros* under the section entitled "Movies in Town." The description, accompanied by a colour photograph taken from the movie, read: "Nathan Lopez (far left) turns in a spectacular performance as a ghetto kid who develops a crush on an older man" (New Paper 2007a). Lily, a young lesbian woman, told me that she was happy to see such an endorsement but was shocked by the fact that a government-owned newspaper would highlight such a film. I suggest that such matter-of-fact editorializing on the part of the government-controlled press was, in some respects, another example of the incremental and carefully calibrated change in the government's stance towards its LGBT citizens. The press was opening slowly but within the guidelines set, very clearly, by the government.

Chapter Three

Reimagining the Nation, Online

In 1996, we already had the *samizdat* that would pass from friend to friend. But we thought this is too labour intensive and we should have a proper newsletter inspired by gay groups in America. But in Singapore then you need permission to publish a newsletter. So, I applied for a license under my personal name, because our organization was not even a registered organization. But since I applied under my personal name, it was rejected.

They probably had been monitoring me for three or four years. And they knew it was an extension of my participation in [LGBT organization] *People Like Us*. So, they turned down that application and we were denied a license to publish a newsletter. Then, someone on the editorial committee suggested the Internet. The law had not caught up with the Internet. The law was silent on electronic newsletters.

Singaporean activist Alex Au (2006 interview)

Au's brief account touches on two key themes of this chapter – the ongoing difficulties in gaining recognition within the public sphere and the subsequent newfound ability to interact online, both of which led to calls from some LGBT Singaporeans for a reconfiguration of the relationship between themselves and the nation. This often-conflicted relationship has been characterized by a long-standing desire to integrate into a nation that, in many respects, made no room for minorities, sexual or otherwise. Yet, as I demonstrate, the Internet allowed LGBT Singaporeans to reimagine themselves as part of the national narrative, one that is itself "imagined."

Lian (1999, 42) suggests that there are four cultural world orders existing simultaneously within Singapore – Confucian Chinese, Islamic Malay, Hindu Indian, and Christian Anglo Saxon, out of which the founders of Singapore constructed their nation and by extension,

Singaporean national identity. The result was a multi-ethnic, multiracial, multireligious city-state in which an all-inclusive, unified national identity was stressed. Yet, as Hall (1992, 299) contends, national identities do not incorporate all other forms of difference and, as with other forms of identity, include "play[s] of power, internal divisions and contradictions, cross-cutting allegiances and differences." Further, Anderson (1983) explains that what we conceptualize as the nation is neither a natural nor a real entity and is, rather, an "imagined community." This sense of the "imagined" is especially prevalent in post-colonial states like Singapore in which there is often a reliance on fabricated discourse that highlights a supposed deep historical past and common cultural tradition. John Kelly (1997, 257), building on Anderson, suggests that we consider the "nation" as a narrative "constituted dialogically." I suggest that national identity, at least in the case of Singapore, is highly constructed, and, as mentioned in the previous chapter, the benchmark for Singaporeanness has come to revolve around being a heterosexual, ethnic Chinese male whose mother tongue is Mandarin, an identity that excludes a vast number of Singaporeans including those who identify as LGBT. I thus find this image of the nation as "narrative" to be especially compelling when thinking about the situation faced by many LGBT Singaporeans, the positive portrayal of whom has been left out of or intentionally removed from the narrative assembled by the nation's founders – a narrative that today is as strong as ever.

When LGBT Singaporeans turned to the Internet to help organize their communities, it created new opportunities – especially in terms of writing positive portrayals of themselves into the nation's narrative. As an example, in August 2004, police announced that they were withholding permits for the Nation Party, a public celebration of LGBT life[1] scheduled for the following year. In response, activists created a series of LGBT-themed events titled IndigNation, which began in August 2005. The cancellation of the party happened to coincide with the announcement from Prime Minister Lee Hsien Loong that permission from the police would no longer be required to hold indoor talks. Organizers of IndigNation planned a series of events that countered the prevailing media narrative that framed LGBT life in Singapore around sex and illicit drugs. The first IndigNation featured art exhibits, academic lectures, and poetry readings and in the following years became Singapore's de facto gay pride celebration.

The image in figure 4 was taken from online promotional materials for the 2007 IndigNation. I suggest that it illustrates the possibilities that the Internet brought to those who were at the margins of society. The digitally enhanced image of the national flag carried in front of the Singapore

Figure 4. Logo from IndigNation 2007 online promotional materials
Source: IndigNation. Used with permission.

Parliament building by military helicopters is a powerful one. There is a lack of any symbolic reference to Western gay pride such as rainbow flags or pink triangles. By co-opting distinctly Singaporean images that had nothing to do with LGBT rights and combining them with the patriotic image of the military helicopters, the organizers of IndigNation localized the role of LGBT Singaporeans within the greater nation, proclaiming that LGBT Singaporeans were, as the promotional materials for IndigNation claimed, "as much a part of Singapore as anyone else."

By using the Internet to organize and publicize events such as Indig-Nation, LGBT Singaporeans were able to reach a much larger audience. More significantly, through participation in public events as well as online activism, they were able to stake a primary claim as *citizens* within the greater nation, rather than solely as "trans or bi men" or "lesbians." Anonymous participation on mainstream message boards and the online comment sections that followed news stories, for example, allowed LGBT Singaporeans to debate issues of import to the nation without the "interference" of their sexual orientation. Many Singaporeans, whether LGBT identified or not, defended the positions of their fellow citizens on the grounds of their "Singaporeanness," regardless of sexual subjectivity or other identity markers. In doing so, they began to create an iteration of Singaporean national identity that many hoped would mark the beginning of the realignment of the nation with non-normative notions of gender, race, ethnicity, and class.

Equating national identity with ideas of technology and modernity is a recurring theme throughout much of the literature. Whether thinking through the effects of mass media and commodities on ethnic groups in Sabah, Malaysia (Barlocco 2013), the emergence into the public sphere of Jews and homosexuals in late twentieth-century Vienna (Bunzl 2004), or the role of technology in imagining a modern future for the still-unformed nation of Indonesia (Mrázek 2002), the connections between modernity, technology, and the nation are clear. Barker (2005) wrote that technology was the driving force behind movements such as the Indonesian "New Order developmental nationalism" in which Indonesia became the first nation in the developing world to build its own satellite system. This is reminiscent of the aspirations of the Singaporean government as they attempted to make their nation the first completely "wired" nation in the world. In fact, during the primary period of research (2005–7), household access to the Internet increased from 61 to 85 per cent.[2] Further, in 2015 Singapore was ranked number one in the world in terms of networked readiness and the capacity to leverage information and communication technologies for increased competitiveness and well-being (World Economic Forum 2015).

I begin the remainder of this chapter with a vignette that illustrates the significant impact that interactions on the Internet have had on the lives of LGBT Singaporeans. I then briefly re-examine some of the difficulties present in Singapore that make the Internet so crucial to the lives of its LGBT citizens. I conclude with a detailed examination of three websites to demonstrate how online interactions contributed to a discursive production of LGBT identities in Singapore. I suggest that these online interactions led to an increased desire on the part of many LGBT Singaporeans to shift their quest for recognition from cyberspace to that of the physical world to more fully engage with the nation.

In the Pink

Edward and I met on Fridae, the online social network, in the summer of 2005. He was a gay Chinese Singaporean man in his late twenties and we connected for many reasons, among them the fact that he had lived in the United States for several years. We chatted online a few times and made plans to meet up, but those plans never came to fruition. When I returned to Singapore in the summer of 2006, we connected again online and that October ran into each other at the gym and struck up what would turn out to be a long-lasting friendship. We usually spent afternoons at Planet Fitness, a gym located at Raffles Place, the financial centre of Singapore. We would always begin with a one-hour body pump class followed by an intense hour-long spin class. On the afternoon of 9 August 2007, Edward and I finished our classes, showered, and then self-consciously changed into pink t-shirts. We left the gym, and after a lazy lunch and a stop at the market, flagged down a taxi and instructed the driver to take us to the Singapore Botanical Gardens. We were on our way to meet a large group of friends to attend In the Pink, a picnic that had been scheduled as part of IndigNation, Singapore's newly inaugurated gay pride month. The event had been planned to coincide with the celebration of Singapore's National Day holiday, yet we had read on Fridae that the gathering had been expressly forbidden by the National Parks Board out of concern that attendees would use public space to protest current legal policies applicable to gay men (Fridae. com 2007). Gatherings of this nature were strictly prohibited. As the taxi approached the entrance to the Gardens, Edward turned to me and said with a nervous laugh, "Gosh, Rob, I hope this turns out okay – I really don't want to get arrested." I shared his feeling of anxiety, but instead just rolled my eyes and said, "Relax, it's going to be fun."

But Edward's fears were, in fact, legitimate. Just a few days earlier, organizers of the picnic received a strongly worded letter from the director of the Singapore Botanic Gardens stating that the picnic and a 5k run sponsored by IndigNation, scheduled a few days later, were "organized gatherings" and, as such, permission would be needed from the National Parks Board. A spokesperson for the Board stated, "The Singapore Botanic Gardens is a premier botanical institution. We do not want it to be used as a venue for interest groups to politicize their cause ... Let's keep our green space as areas for relaxation and recreation." Miak Siew, one of the organizers of the picnic, immediately cancelled the event. But as situations like this often go, the publicity surrounding the cancellation, in this case an article that appeared on Fridae, served to increase interest in and attendance at the event. As such, the picnic became a "private" affair in which groups of people dressed in pink just happened to be picnicking at the same spot by the lake at the same time.

We arrived at the Botanical Gardens earlier than the rest of our group and made ourselves comfortable by finding a shady spot by a large stone fountain near the east entrance. Edward and I made our usual small talk; he complained of the myriad stressful situations that arose from his job as a webmaster for a popular Singaporean website and I complained about my ever-failing love life. All the while, we kept an eye out for others who might be attending the picnic. We had planned to meet at 4:00 p.m., but nonetheless Edward and I ended up waiting an hour for the rest of our group to arrive. We were a group of eight men, four of whom were expatriates. We were all dressed in pink shirts or shorts and could not help but to notice as families enjoying a day at the gardens spotted our matching clothing and commented in hushed tones, stared, or simply giggled at the sight.

While crossing the rolling, palm-lined paths of the Gardens to the lake where the picnic was taking place, we broke into smaller groups. I ended up walking with Sven, a financial analyst from Denmark, and his boyfriend, Stephan, an Indonesian software programmer. As had happened earlier with Edward, tension crept into our conversation as we speculated about what might await us. We were certainly excited about the possibility of a pleasant afternoon with friends, old and new, yet Sven and Stephan were both concerned that no one would be there or, worse, that the police would be waiting to escort us to jail for breaking the ban. When we reached the crest of the final hill, I ran ahead of the group to get a look at what lay ahead. Down below, in the small valley that surrounded the lake, were around 150 men, women, and children, many in pink clothing.

Our small group came well prepared, with blankets and the requisite wine, cheese, and fruit; much of it was pink, going with the theme of the picnic. After finding a suitable spot on the sloping lawn, someone in our group pulled out a small battery-operated boom box and, soon, the air was filled with the music of Madonna and Rihanna. As I lounged on our blanket, I looked around and saw clusters of Singaporeans and their foreign friends enjoying sunshine and camaraderie – an expatriate lesbian couple playing with their two small children, men throwing a Frisbee back and forth across the perfectly manicured lawn, dogs chasing tennis balls, and a collection of well-built men in tight pink tank tops crowding to fit onto a blanket that was way too small to fit their large group. A young lesbian couple moved from group to group offering pink cupcakes to fellow attendees as a way of introduction, and several heterosexual families joined the picnic to show their solidarity with their LGBT friends and family members. "Undercover" police officers were also present, documenting the event with digital cameras.

Without warning, the action stopped as three huge camouflage-clad Marine helicopters came into view. The music and laughter of the picnic were overpowered by the intense noise of the whirring rotors of the helicopters. As they flew overhead, one could not help but notice that one was towing an enormous Singaporean flag. Most of the Singaporeans on the crowded lawns stopped their activities and stood staring respectfully at their national flag soaring through the cloudy afternoon sky en route to the National Day Parade being held at Marina Square several kilometres away.

Why do I introduce a discussion of the Internet with a vignette that on the surface has little to do with cyberspace or emerging technology? After all, what could the Internet have to do with an event such as this that took place in a decidedly physical-world venue? I suggest that this picnic, part social protest and part celebration of the nation by Singaporeans, demonstrates how, in a little over a decade, the Internet had become integrated within everyday Singaporean life. Three aspects of this technology as they apply to Singapore's LGBT communities are worthy of attention.

First, as noted in chapter 2, Singapore is a nation in which all forms of mainstream media are tightly controlled by the government and strict codes ensure that no print publications reach out to gay communities. The Internet thus served as a vital source of information. As in many other contexts worldwide (Kaldor et al. 2012; Khondker 2011), in Singapore the Internet had become the new "underground" press. In the Pink was advertised online and notification of its eventual banning by the government was posted on dozens of blogs, websites, and forums. Because many of these forms of Internet-based communication are instantaneous, they allowed for a quick response from the event's organizers and were the sites where many individuals and activists issued calls urging people to attend regardless of the consequences.

Figure 5. National Day 2007, Singapore Botanical Gardens
Source: Photo by Kelvin Wong. Used with permission.

Second, the Internet allowed many LGBT Singaporeans to move beyond the simple exchange of information to create a virtual public sphere to discuss issues concerning their communities. "Singapore" had become an online place, not just a physical island in the Straits of Malacca. This is an important transformation because LGBT Singaporeans found it difficult to organize in public without fear of government surveillance and interference. By shifting discussions from the physical world to online, sexual minorities could debate issues safely and eventually, as the case of In the Pink, move to the physical world to make a public statement. Interactions on these discursive sites allowed LGBT Singaporeans to interact with one another as well as with those outside of their home communities. This includes Singaporeans abroad and non-Singaporeans, some of whom at one time lived or worked in the city-state. The transnational nature of these multi-sited interactions also sparked a renewed interest in participation in the public sphere.

This leads to my third and most significant point; the Internet in general, as well as specific websites described later in the chapter, empowered many LGBT Singaporeans to shift interactions from the private (or semi-private) areas of cyberspace and into the larger physical and public sphere, as happened with the picnic. As I illustrate in the sections that follow, many of the conversations that took place online contributed to greater participation in the public sphere, thus increasing public visibility of LGBT Singaporeans. In fact, one of the men in our small group at the picnic quietly mentioned that an intense private chat on the gay site Trevvy, with another gay Singaporean man, was what pushed him to "go public" with his sexual subjectivity and attend the picnic.

The image described in the previous vignette, of a hundred or so Singaporeans solemnly watching as their national flag floated across the sky, was the most vivid memory from my time in the field. In many respects, it symbolized the intense and often conflicted relationship that LGBT citizens had with their nation. Many of the LGBT Singaporeans whom I interviewed had strong feelings regarding the fact that they felt excluded from the nation while, at the same time, holding a profound desire to be a part of the nation and to assist in the nation-building process. This sentiment was especially pronounced among gay men who, even though they devoted several years to compulsory military service, still felt rejected by much of the nation. Maybe that is why I was so moved when I saw the reaction of LGBT Singaporeans when the helicopters flew overhead that afternoon. After spending so much time interacting with and interviewing these men and women, in that moment I felt I had finally witnessed a concrete manifestation of their feelings towards their nation, a nation about which many had talked so passionately.

Ongoing Frustrations

The continued inability to congregate in public was frustrating for many LGBT Singaporeans; this aggravation was compounded by the largely unenforced laws that made homosexual acts a punishable crime. The fact that the laws were on the books, but rarely enforced – the perfect archetype of illiberal pragmatics – had led many of my respondents to characterize current government policies towards gay men as "irrational" and "paranoid." In such an environment, LGBT Singaporeans had little opportunity to come to any understanding of exactly what the government had in store for them. As an example, in August 2007, I had planned to meet a friend in the late afternoon to see the gay-themed Indian film *My Brother Nikhil*,[3] as part of IndigNation. Before I left my home that morning, I checked the theatre's website to make sure that the film was still playing as scheduled, and it was. I met a respondent for a lunch interview and told her of my plans to see the film. Since she knew the owner of Pitch Black, the venue for the film, she offered to call to confirm that the film was indeed playing that afternoon. When she called, the owner of the theatre told her that the film had been banned by the Media Development Authority and would not be screened; as such I did not travel across town to the theatre. As it turns out, the film *was* screened that afternoon. These actions on the part of the government, inconsistent and often unforeseen, further alienated many LGBT Singaporeans from the nation. As one interviewee put it, the government's policy towards its LGBT citizens seemed to be "keep 'em guessing."

Another frustration involved the perception that the government had been attempting to oversee LGBT Singaporeans by segregating their bars, discos, saunas, and community centres within the confines of the Chinatown and Tanjong Pagar sections of the city.[4] These attempts at physical containment and restriction, in combination with an inconsistent legal policy targeting sexual minorities, led to a shift in LGBT public life in Singapore. This shift involved LGBT Singaporeans, both individuals and groups, using physical spaces other than those officially sanctioned by the government (as with In the Pink). The concomitant reactionary behaviour of some segments of the public and the police is worthy of further attention. While there were any number of specifically "LGBT" physical spaces recognized by the government, these had all been constructed around the idea that members of these communities were interested solely in having places to drink alcohol, dance, and have anonymous sexual encounters (i.e., bars and saunas). By and large, the government of Singapore was defining LGBT individuals (especially gay men), and the public and semi-public spaces allocated them, based largely upon the illegal sexual acts outlined in Section 377A of the penal code. In other words, they were defining a community and assigning them an identity based on *perceived* behaviours. My research showed that many LGBT Singaporeans were trying to move beyond such stereotypes and were greatly interested in participating in the nation-building process. One interlocutor, a well-known activist, stated, "you are allowed to be here, but you have no rights, you may have a voice, but you want to speak out, you can't ... that's it ... stay in your corner, don't move and don't say anything." An Indian Singaporean activist told of an indirect type of discrimination perpetuated by his government:

It's a psychological kind of oppression and that is the way the Singapore government works. I would say that there is some kind of persecution and non-acceptance or non-tolerance and that has its own psychological effect. It makes it very difficult for people to appeal to the UN or other international bodies to change things because things are going on at a level that is not so easily detectable. If you want to hold down a community, you don't go out and kill them all. But if you do it in such a way that was so subtle that gays wanted to stay at home and hide and there were no physical scars, that would be a mind fuck, the mind fuck that the Singaporean government is pulling on gays and lesbians.

When I asked a Chinese Singaporean how he felt that the government treated him as an openly gay man, he answered:

I feel like the government has certain people that they treat specially and everyone else is treated more or less the same. I don't feel as though I'm being ostracized or picked on just because I'm gay, but I can relate to the way a Malay person feels. I have lots of Malay, Indian, and *Ang Mo*[5] friends and so I feel the way they do. It's the fact that we are a minority, they are not picking on us particularly but at the same time, we are not their target audience.

The attempts at censorship, such as those described in chapter 2, led many to use the Internet as a means of refocusing, a way not only to change how LGBT Singaporeans thought about themselves and their life worlds, but to rethink their role as citizens and to attempt to effectively destabilize the power of the nation itself. Using the Internet, a communication medium that is both fluid and flexible, allowed for a similar muddling of space, a shifting of the centre, a move that at once decentred dominant notions of national identity as well as what it meant to be a LGBT Singaporean.

For instance, on 25 April 2008 "happyamsguy," an anonymous blogger from Berlin who had lived and worked in Singapore for several years, posted the item "Who says Singapore doesn't enforce anti-gay laws" on his blog *Adventures and Random Brain Waves*. In the post, he commented on the recent fining of a Singaporean television station by the Media Development Authority for airing a program that "normalizes [the] gay lifestyle and unconventional family setup," referring to the episode of *Find and Design* discussed in chapter 2. In the comments section of the posting, "Aidil Omar" countered by stating that "they [the government] don't raid multiple gay spas or clubs, they don't ban transvestites like Liang Po Po[6] on national TV, they don't shut down local gay websites that promote an alternative lifestyle." Less than twenty-four hours later, "happyamsguy" responded by reprinting an email[7] he had just received from the owners of Club One Seven, a well-known gay sauna in Singapore. The email detailed the events of 25 April in which plainclothes officers from Singapore's CID (Criminal Investigation Department) turned off the water to the sauna to perform a "spot-check." While this type of harassment from the police had not happened in several years, what was most noteworthy about the incident was the fact that the seventy-four-year old expatriate owner of the sauna confronted the police. A scuffle ensued; he was injured by the police and subsequently hospitalized.

On Saturday, 26 April an anonymous Singaporean blogger known as "Man Singapore," wrote at the end of a longer posting, "We heard that Club One Seven was raided today, anyone heard anything about it?" Hours later "Man Singapore," who is a close friend of "happyamsguy," reposted the letter from Club One Seven on his own blog. Within a day, the letter had been shared with physical-world organizations such as the counselling agency Oogachaga and had been reposted on Singaporean and international blogs and forums. The mainstream press made no mention of the incident, and in fact, "Man Singapore" reported that on the same day as the incident at Club One Seven, police had gone to Raw, another gay sauna, and did a spot check without incident.

This event is revealing on several levels. As with other examples discussed, it speaks to the speed of the transnational movement of information and the diverse networks that are formed within cyberspace. It also illustrates the engagement that Singaporeans and non-Singaporeans had with issues such as mass media, notions of public/private, and the legal ramifications of being a gay man in Singapore. The online letter written by the owner of Club One Seven and distributed to his mailing list serves as a good example of how the Internet was used to expose and subsequently resist perceived abuses by authorities in a physical culture in which resistance is next to impossible. Finally, we have another example of illiberal pragmatics in practice. Here, the Singaporean police ostensibly "check in" on saunas used by gay men for sexual purposes; they are ignoring the fact that the activities taking place inside are illegal and subsequently fail to enforce the law. This also illustrates the police forces' implementation of the "light touch" that lets the owners of such establishments know that the authorities are watching. Most importantly, many of the men with whom I interacted told me that incidents such as this – reported and discussed primarily online – encouraged them to participate in public LGBT events. In the weeks that followed this incident, I participated in a number of email exchanges with Singaporean respondents that indicated that the anger and frustration they felt over this particular incident was the "last straw." Walter, a resident physician, explained that he was tired of the constant and petty harassment and that he refused to accept being treated as a "second-class citizen." In later conversations, he let me know that he was now attending as many LGBT events as his schedule would allow.

As with many social movements that challenge the status quo, push-back from the government is inevitable. The movement of which these sites are a part is no different. As discussed in chapter 2, the Media Development Authority was aware of websites that catered to the LGBT communities. Based on content, the MDA could have censored, fined, or banned the sites outright. Yet, they didn't; they allowed them to operate without interference. Simply letting webmasters know that their sites could be shut down at any time for any reason was enough to keep them in line – another key example of illiberal pragmatics in practice.

Three major local sites are discussed in this section: SiGNeL, Fridae, and RedQuEEn. The sites differ in their content as well as the degree of interaction, but all gave LGBT Singaporeans the opportunity to discuss issues relevant to their users. SiGNeL is mainly political in nature and allows for a lively and interactive debate. Fridae is considered a "lifestyle" site, and serves as a discursive area as well, though differing in the level of interactivity. RedQuEEn, which caters to "queer women," serves as a type of online support group. There were numerous smaller, more specialized sites, including the newsgroups utilized by niche groups such as gay Buddhists (Heartland) and gay athletes (ADLUS, an acronym for Adventurers Like Us), that also fostered discussions of interest to their respective members, although the exchanges that took place on these sites were usually less about sexual identity and more about religion or sport. I suggest that all the sites discussed below served as discursive areas in which LGBT Singaporeans could in some sense redefine their relationship with the nation. More importantly, during interviews conducted with users of these sites, I was told time and again how these online interactions precipitated a shift in activism from cyberspace to the physical world.

(Web)Sites of Resistance

The websites discussed in the remainder of this section, all of which in some manner attempted to counteract the anti-LGBT rhetoric put forth by their fellow citizens and government, acted as spaces of transgression and resistance. The forum postings, blog entries, and news and special-interest stories are examples of how cyberspace served as a discursive site where various tensions came into play to create a type of productive friction, a process that opened new possibilities in terms of LGBT relations with the nation. I suggest that these websites can be considered counterpublics in that they all served as sites "for developing oppositional interpretations of its members' identities, interests, and needs" (Warner 2002, 86). While I discuss counterpublics again in the next chapter, I want to emphasize the "oppositional" nature of these websites. There were few available outlets through which citizens could challenge the prevailing anti-LGBT discourse in the physical environment of Singapore. This applied to Singaporeans of all persuasions, but this was especially significant for those in the LGBT communities, who had a particularly difficult time having their voices heard within the public sphere. The Internet thus served as an alternative public sphere (Ho, Baber, and Khondker 2002).

SiGNeL

People Like Us (PLU) is a Singapore LGBT group that works on issues of advocacy and public education. Since 1997, the Singapore Registrar of Societies has twice refused to grant the group formal registration (Offord 1999), a step necessary for the organization to hold public meetings. The last attempt at registration was refused in April 2004 because "the society is likely to be used for unlawful purposes or for purposes prejudicial to public peace, welfare or good order in Singapore; and it would be contrary to the national interest for the society to be registered."[8] From 1993 to early 1997, members of PLU met clandestinely in the physical world, but in March of 1997, due to constant government surveillance of its regularly scheduled Sunday forums, as well as the refusal of the government to provide official recognition, the organization's meetings shifted to the relative safety of cyberspace. Significantly, this move coincided with the exponential increase in the use of the Internet in Singapore. The email listserv of PLU was renamed SiGNeL (Singapore Gay News List) and served as a bulletin board where members could discuss various issues of interest to the LGBT communities. The news list proved to be a far better platform for discussing social and political issues than the Sunday forums. The shift to cyberspace allowed Singaporeans abroad as well as others who might have found it too intimidating to attend public meetings to participate in an increasingly significant online activism. These virtual interactions, as discussed in the next chapter, had the potential to move beyond cyberspace and carry over into the physical realm.

SiGNeL became a Yahoo group and email forum in July 1999. By 2007, this newsgroup had 2,443 registered members. According to the PLU website, "SiGNeL is not a 'gay' group in the sense of being restricted to gay people. SiGNeL is open to everyone regardless of sexual orientation, to serve members who are interested in, and who confine discussions to gay issues pertaining to Singapore."[9] Postings ranged from LGBT-themed articles taken from the *Straits Times* and other local newspapers to inquiries regarding legal rights in specific situations to movie reviews and announcements of public events of interest to the community. In most instances, a member posted an article or observation and the other members commented in an interactive and engaging manner. While the postings were moderated, interference was quite limited and the moderator generally disallowed only posts that were deemed defamatory to religious or ethnic groups (postings of this nature are prohibited by Singaporean law) or that do not pertain to gay, lesbian, bisexual, or transgender issues.[10] The site is completely text based, though many of the postings contain links to more interactive sites. The layout is simple and searchable. I subscribed to the list in 2006 and received daily digests containing the postings for a given day. Below is a sample listing of the contents of the digest for 1 June 2008:

1a. Re: Fr Garcia's talk at CANA From: Yawning Bread
1b. Re: Fr Garcia's talk at CANA From: Chris Hansen
2a. Re: Review: Session 3 of Catholic forum on homosexuality From: xiaoyao
3a. TODAY: 40% of Swaziland's adults HIV positive From: Roy Tan
3b. Re: TODAY: 40% of Swaziland's adults HIV positive From: Chris Tan
4a. Homosexuality in Singapore – Wikipedia From: hitchcube
4b. Re: Homosexuality in Singapore – Wikipedia From: Roy Tan
4c. Re: Homosexuality in Singapore – Wikipedia From: andrew ki
5a. TODAY: Walter Woon says gay marriage not human rights issue From: Roy Tan
   6. Calif supreme court weighs if doctors can not treat lesbian From: Yawning Bread
   7. Turkish gay group will fight ban From: Yawning Bread
   8. Memorials for Jews but not for gays. From: Bob
   9. Gay & Muslim in South Africa From: Bob.

Topics covered in this digest were typical of any given day. The postings were wide ranging and referred to local and global events. The people posting included Singaporeans residing in Singapore, Singaporeans abroad, and non-Singaporeans. Postings included commentary on and reviews of a talk by Singaporean Catholic priest and moral theologian David Garcia (part of a larger series of talks on homosexuality held at a Catholic centre), a link to a story in a local newspaper in which Singapore's attorney general refused to frame LGBT rights as human rights, and a story about gay Muslims in South Africa. Postings usually garnered some sort of response or commentary and, in many instances, generated a good deal of debate. During fieldwork, I interviewed several of the contributors to the list. I did not contribute to the discussions at hand; instead I chose to observe the tone and direction of the discussions to gain a better understanding of the way the list operated. In the following section, I examine a sample posting in which participants debated real-world issues of importance to the larger LGBT community in Singapore. It is of interest because this single posting touched on many issues faced by LGBT Singaporeans, including those of race, public space, censorship, media, and education.

On 25 April 2007, Bai Rong, a frequent contributor to the list, posted his response to Minister Mentor Lee Kuan Yue's then-recent comments to the youth branch of the ruling People's Action Party regarding what he concluded was the biological basis for homosexuality. Many in the LGBT communities and within civil society saw hope for change within Lee's comments, especially since, at the time, Parliament was considering repealing Section 377A of the penal code, the section that criminalizes consensual sexual acts between men. After all, if the founder of the nation was open to the idea that homosexual tendencies were "genetic," then the rest of society was sure to follow.[11] Bai, in keeping with his reputation for being contrary, titled his posting, "Opening Up a Gay Pandora's Box" (26 April 2007, 7:28 a.m.). He began by stating, "One must not be so naïve as to think that decriminalization of gay sex is an end in itself. Instead, it is the beginning of an end. Decriminalization of gay sex will be like opening the Pandora's Box, and many other critical issues will ensue." He then went on to list ten things that he predicted would happen if Section 377A was repealed. Most subscribers to the SiGNeL list knew that while Bai is a sexually active, openly gay Singaporean, he was at the same time a vocal and conservative Christian. In fact, his ten scenarios read like a similar list regarding "the homosexual agenda" that had been distributed worldwide by fundamentalist Christian churches based in the southern United States. Among the consequences that he outlined were such things as "gay couples allowed to adopt children," "schools, colleges, and uni [universities] will have gay societies," "gay pride march," and "less censorship of gay films." His last scenario is most telling when he speculates, "Gays may have a public space to congregate just like the Filipinos hang out at Lucky Plaza, male My-anmar men hang out at Peninsula Plaza and Thais hang out at Golden Mile Shopping Complex." He ended with the admonition that "It seems like we cannot just stop at decriminalizing gay sex; a greater force will be at work to speed us on our way to moral decay. The damage to the moral fabric of our nation will [be] irreparable." Many regular readers of SiGNeL saw Bai as an Internet "troll," someone who habitually posts controversial comments to get a reaction from the other members of a given Internet community. Yet in many respects, at least in the case of SiGNeL, the "trolls" were the ones who appeared to stir up the most interesting and revealing discussions. By taking on the role of "devil's advocate," Bai was acting as the voice of conservative Singapore, as well as that of the powerful and vocal minority Christian denominations.

The following day, "Raymond Ford" posted a point-by-point rebuttal to Bai's scenario. Ford is an American who had lived in Singapore for a number of years. While not Singaporean, he was well informed on Sin-gaporean affairs and was respected by the other members of this online community. His response centred on the American experience and was laced with comparisons between the US and Singapore. It is telling, how-ever, in that by relying on the Western model of gay rights and the evo-lutionary progress typically expected in rights movements, he replicated the expectations of many of the SiGNeL community. In response to Bai's assertion that there would be "public space" in which gays could con-gregate, Ford (slipping in a bit of Singlish) pointed out that, "377 still on the books, erm, already have places for gays dear – got saunas, clubs and bars that cater to gay clients. What you think Singapore going to have a gay village?" He concluded by reminding Bai that "the Gay rights move-ment in the USA has been going on for almost 40 years ... what you are suggesting, with the demise of Section 377A will take a long time. In the US, it has been almost 2 generations to get this far. I don't see Singapore changing like a finger being snapped" (27 April 2007, 10:46 p.m.). "Ron-ald Sim" responded to Bai by agreeing with him yet twisted his words by suggesting that moral decay will indeed fall upon Singapore, but not in the way that Bai suggested. He argued that "decriminalizing gay sex may well compel [those who espouse hatred towards homosexuals] to further extremes of wilful ignorance and hate" but went on to say that while "a flurry of national debate would surely erupt and may threaten our social fabric, beneath the chaos would lie a bastion of hope for our future gener-ations" (28 April 2007, 5:35 p.m.). The final posting in this thread is from Bobby, a Singaporean living in Australia. In commenting on Bai's fear of a gay parade in Singapore, Bobby responded by reminding readers that [in Sydney] "gay people no longer feel the need to ... support this parade, probably because they've moved on and got a life apart from the saunas of Ockie [Oxford] street. The size of the stamp duty on that new apartment they are buying with their boyfriend is more important than the last vestiges of discrimination" (29 April 2007, 6:10 p.m.).

At this point, I wish to briefly linger on this exchange and relate it to several key analytical themes that permeate this work. As mentioned earlier, this sample posting touches on several issues faced by LGBT Singaporeans. At the same time, it can serve as a lens through which to get a better understanding of how issues of rights were being framed. The posting centred on a comment made by Minister Mentor Lee Kuan Yew suggesting that there is a possible genetic basis for homosexual behaviour, leading some to believe that decriminalization was forthcoming. Bai Rong, taking a cue from American Christian discourse, listed all the possible pitfalls of decriminalizing gay sex. In making his list, I suggest that Bai was localizing the transnational by taking Western concerns, such as gay adoption or gay groups in schools, and putting a local spin on them. Apart from gay adoption, all the other scenarios proposed, gay groups in schools, gay pride marches, and a decrease in the censorship of gay media all appeared to be on the horizon in Singapore. Also of interest is Bai's comment on public space. By speculating that "gays might have a space to congregate," he was referencing the fact that many Singaporeans were not pleased that groups such as Filipino and Thai maids and Myanmar construction workers took over various shopping centres on Sunday, their only day off. In an indirect manner, Bai was equating gay men with these other, undesirable foreigners. Finally, Bobby, the Singaporean living in Sydney, spoke of the concern that gay men in Sydney have regarding "the stamp duty on that new apartment they are buying with their boyfriend." Bobby, like many gay men in nations that are more accepting of homosexuality, was thinking beyond issues of basic societal and legal acceptance, a luxury that LGBT Singaporeans do not have.

Fridae

Fridae was founded in 2001 by Stuart Koe, a Singaporean scientist and entrepreneur who earned a doctorate in pharmacy in the United States. The purpose of the site was to "build Asia's largest gay & lesbian community – united in diversity, and transcending geographical borders. Fridae empowers gay Asia to: come together, stay connected, be informed, overcome discrimination, nurture personal growth, and foster healthy relationships."[12] Koe is no longer associated with the website; in 2015, after a conflict with management, he resigned, and the site was redirected to the domain Fridae.asia.[13]

There are several versions of the site available. During the period of research, the main site (www.fridae.com) opened with an option for viewing the page in either English, traditional or simplified Mandarin, or Cantonese. All versions of the site were highly interactive, content rich, and heavy on graphics. While Fridae was clearly a commercial site, many of the features were free. Once the site was accessed, the user was given an array of choices. On the left side of the homepage was a bar that allowed the user to select from nine different options. These were News/Features, Lifestyle, Personals, Agenda, Fotos@Fridae, Shop, City Guide, Perks, and Promotions. Many of the options were self-explanatory. Others such as Perks (giving the user the ability to join the site for a nominal fee) and Agenda (a listing of events of interest to LGBT communities) were not. Until at least 2006, Fridae also had a highly trafficked Forum section where members could debate current events. While no reason was given for discontinuing the Forum section, users subsequently made use of the "comments" option provided with each article. While not as interactive as a traditional online forum, the comments section at the end of major articles was often the site of long-running debates among users.

The items posted under Latest Articles were mainly political in nature and many dealt with issues of LGBT rights. Headlines at the time included, "India Court Sets Deadline for Ministries to Reconcile Stand on Gay Sex Law," "20,000 Expected at Taipei Gay Pride," and "What the Recent Polls Mean for Hong Kong's LGBT Community." While some of the articles dealt with Singaporean issues, most them dealt with international topics. The Agenda section was also quite international, listing events in Sydney, Singapore, Kuala Lumpur, and Jakarta. Another feature of the homepage was the search function for personal ads. In addition to being able to do a quick search of over 258,000 ads for such identifiers as gender, age, and location, users were also able to "sort" profiles based on, among others, HIV status, languages spoken, occupation, and Western or Chinese horoscope. If one was willing to join the site, which cost as little as S$4 per month (approximately US$2.50 in 2006) they could then execute advanced searches that included ethnicity, religion, and languages spoken. Also of interest was the section titled City Guides. In this section the type of person that Fridae was catering to became most apparent, speaking to the idea of the "globalized" or "international" gay male (Altman 1997; Massad 2002; Provencher 2012). The cities covered in this section ranged from Singapore and Koh Samui in Southeast Asia to Shanghai and Tokyo to New Delhi, Amsterdam, and Barcelona. While the guides provided information of importance to gay tourists such as "Places to Eat," "Places to Shop," "Bars," and "Arts/Culture," what I found most telling was the section titled "Where to Stay." In smaller destinations such as Koh Samui, the lodging options revolved around LGBT-owned guesthouses. Yet, in larger, more cosmopolitan cities such as Tokyo and Manila, it was interesting to note that the majority of hotels recommended were of the four- and five-star variety. In most cases, if a two- or three-star hotel is recommended, it is because it is located within the city's gay district. The selection of this type of hotels speaks directly to Fridae's demographics. According to a 2007 survey, 81 per cent of Fridae users had completed education beyond high school and almost 50 per cent had completed a bachelor's degree or beyond. Sixty-two per cent of Fridae users reported earning greater than the 2007 Singaporean annual average income of S$30,516[14] and 21 per cent of users reported an income of greater than S$75,000 (personal communication with Stuart Koe, April 2007). Koe knew his target demographic well in that much of the content on the website appealed directly to a group of LGBT individuals who were educated and relatively affluent and many of whom had large amounts of disposable income.

I witnessed this first-hand in 2006 when I attended Nation VI, the last of the large circuit parties organized by Fridae. In 2005, after the government's refusal of permits in 2004, the party moved to Phuket, Thailand. In 2006, it was held at the secluded five-star Hilton Phuket Arcadia Resort and Spa at Karon Beach, where rooms cost approximately US$150 per night. Tickets for the three-day party averaged US$180; most attendees were not from Phuket and had to pay at least several hundred, if not thousand, dollars for airfare. In addition to the parties, organizers distributed flyers offering "day tours, dive trips, spa treatments, island hops and much more" to keep partygoers satisfied. This contrasts sharply with the Nation parties that had taken place in Singapore in past years. When the parties were hosted in Singapore, admission was much less expensive and Singaporean attendees could take public transport to the parties, which were held either at the centrally located Suntec City Convention Centre or on nearby Sentosa Island.

In recalling my experiences during the three-day (and three-night) party, I suggest that Fridae had come to contribute, to some extent, to the formation of a transnational or "global gay" identity among gay Singaporean men. Most of the men at Nation VI were perfectly muscled, impeccably groomed, tanned, well-travelled, and cosmopolitan in their outlook. When men asked me where I was from, I told them Los Angeles; almost without exception they commented on how much they either loved or hated the city. Many even mentioned specific bars or clothing shops when we were discussing Los Angeles – a clear indication that they were well travelled. It was this group of men, more than any other, that had the least interest in fighting for gay recognition within Singapore. While I attempted to conduct interviews at the party, I did not have much success. Of course, this was not the best place for such an endeavour – people were there to relax and enjoy – yet I tried nonetheless. I interviewed four Singaporean men at Nation VI and not one of them had heard of the IndigNation events that had occurred a few months previously. When I discussed my findings with one of my friends back in Singapore, a well-known gay rights activist, he just shrugged his shoulders and said, "returning to that question you asked me a few months ago, to what extent has access to the Internet shaped a certain idea of being gay ... it has – it has certainly narrowed it."

While I agree with my friend's point that the Internet can limit the idea of what it means to be gay, at the same time, I see sites such as Fridae also expanding this idea. For many gay Singaporeans, especially those from modest backgrounds, sites such as Fridae were their first exposure to a world that went beyond furtive sex in public restrooms. Fridae catered to an upscale customer. It nonetheless also helped to educate LGBT Singaporeans from all backgrounds on issues, both local and global, that directly affected their everyday lives. Fridae provided insightful, in-depth coverage and analysis of the 2007 parliamentary debates regarding Section 377A, they were a major sponsor of IndigNation, and they teamed up with local NGO Action for AIDS in the creation of physical-world awareness campaigns regarding HIV/AIDS. Fridae, more than any other site under consideration in this work, encouraged its users to make the leap from online interaction to physical-world participation. For many of the gay men with whom I interacted, Fridae had become a highly trusted source of news and information. Thus, when Fridae began their sponsorship of and online advertising for physical-world LGBT events, the response was overwhelming. I suggest that part of the reason for the unprecedented success of such physical world events was the involvement of Fridae, allowing Koe's site to live up to its tagline – "empowering gay Asia."

RedQuEEn

September 2008 marked the tenth anniversary of RedQuEEn, an Internet site for queer[15] Singaporean women, founded in 1998 by Eileena Lee. In honour of this milestone the moderator asked members to write short entries describing what the site has meant to them. One member wrote the following,

> At the risk of sounding overly emo and dramatic ... RedQuEEn saved my life.
>
> I found this little mailing list at the time when I went through a serious bout of depression. Interestingly, at the time I was out, dating, I had a job, money, friends, etc. On the outside I seemed so okay, but on the inside, it was hell ... I'm not so sure why I felt so on edge and morose as I did.

Anyway, RedQuEEn gave me lots of stuff to think about, sent me some kind friends, and provided a means for me to rant, and share news I found interesting.

So yeah, thank you RedQuEEn, Teresa

I was fortunate to be able to interview RedQuEEn's founder Eileena Lee on several occasions during fieldwork. In one such meeting, she relayed the history of RedQuEEn. In 1998, she had just come out of a relationship and needed some support. While she initially turned to SiGNeL, she soon realized that it was not a very nurturing place for her as a woman. In fact, many of the women whom I interviewed said that they regularly read SiGNeL, yet rarely contributed to the discussions at hand. Lee continued, "so I thought it may be interesting to start a space for women, dedicated to women, for women to be empowered, as women or as dykes, lesbians, queer women and eventually the integration with the general queer community. I started by thinking that I would probably find a few friends, but I guess there was a need and it grew."

SiGNeL served the LGBT community, Fridae catered to a predominantly gay male audience, but RedQuEEn was created as an online, moderated mailing list to specifically address the needs of "QuEEr women living in Singapore." A note on the site's homepage requests, "No males, please!"[16] SiGNeL has a distinctly political outlook and much of the discussion revolves around issues of recognition and rights, and as just noted, Fridae created a space of "empowerment" for a largely male community. RedQuEEn is different in that it served as a space where women could find online support, friendship, and networking opportunities. Below is a listing from the RedQuEEn digest for 17 September 2008:

1. Women's Nite 27th September 2008: Don't Shy, Just Ask! From: Women's Nite
2a. Useless me From: Good Thong
2b. Re: Useless me From: Anzen
2c. Re: Useless me From: ISOLA UluKa
2d. Re: Useless me From: Linda Mary
2e. Re: Useless me From: teddytee
2f. Re: Useless me From: Bola
2g. Re: Useless me From: Angel's Song
3a. Room for rent – Tanjong Pagar From: kwilcock
3b. Room to rent for short term stay From: Jamie Lim
4a. Room for Rent @ Hougang (REPOST) From: Louis
4b. Trishaw Operators in SIngapore- Wedding Planner From: ISOLA UluKa

Many of the postings solicited advice on dating relationships (2a–2g). Others are from women looking to rent a room (3a–4a) or, in this case, a member who was a wedding planner trying to locate fifty trishaws for a December ceremony. Posting 1 is a reminder for an event sponsored by Women's Nite, a physical-world group for lesbian and bisexual women in Singapore to gather and discuss issues relevant to their lives. Events included potluck dinners with topics such as "How do you see yourself?" ("Butch? Femme? Active? Passive? Top? Bottom?") and "Who wears the skirt?" ("Does being gay let you defy traditional gender roles? Or is the one who wears the skirt still stuck with the cooking and cleaning? This Women's Nite, let's talk about our expectations around being with another woman").

Based on interviews with several members of RedQuEEn, it appears that the main purpose was that of support. In fact, RedQuEEn eventually formed an online counselling service, Looking Glass, to deal with issues in the physical world. Lee described how the formation of this service came about,

> In 2001 two women killed themselves and we asked ourselves why did it happen and could we have done more for these women.[17] We had an Internet chat room at the time and the room was filled with lesbians who were so afraid that their parents were going to come and ask them probing questions because every day the Chinese papers would have some photo of these women. They would take photos of the bedroom and ask questions like why is there a queen size bed and take photos of the clothes – a set of feminine clothes and a set of masculine clothes. And the younger woman had a history of suicidal tendencies. We started this Internet counseling service called Looking Glass because of what happened.

Looking Glass[18] was, for several years, a successful online counselling service supported by trained volunteers from within the RedQuEEn community. In 2000, Oogachaga, a physical-world counselling agency, opened. By 2003, it was well established and served the counselling needs of Singapore's sexual minorities. Afterwards, Looking Glass closed.

One interviewee, a woman who was associated with Sayoni, another site for Singaporean queer women, dismissed the discourse on RedQuEEn as "fluff." She was referring to the fact that, while she felt that Sayoni was political in nature, RedQuEEn, for the most part, eschewed politics and instead focused more on personal issues. Yet, I argue that, on the contrary, RedQuEEn was in fact quite political. What I find so compelling about RedQuEEn is that in many respects it spoke to the invisibility of queer women within Singapore's non-normative communities as well as within the larger Singaporean society. Many of my interlocutors from RedQuEEn stressed that public visibility was a major issue for queer Singaporean women. It is forbidden to portray gay men and lesbians in a positive light within Singapore's highly censored media outlets. For queer women, this is compounded by the fact that they are not recognized at all within Singapore's penal code. Further, as one interlocutor put it, "many parents know about the same-sex relationships amongst young girls that take place in Convent schools. They are never concerned, because they think it is just a phase. So, when lesbians do 'come out' to their families, they are rarely taken seriously." I suggest that on some level, this erasure of subjectivity could be more marginalizing than that experienced by non-gender-conforming males in Singapore. Leong (1995, 14) writes of this phenomenon, "Silence, or the absence of discourse on lesbianism is not better than the legal oppression of male homosexuality: it is representative in itself by way of denying the existence of another form of human sexuality, thought, and behaviour." Sites such as RedQuEEn thus allowed queer women to become visible. The visibility began with on-line interactions and grew when those interactions moved into the public sphere in the form of events such as those sponsored by Women's Nite.

Conclusion

The three sites discussed here, SiGNeL, Fridae, and RedQuEEn, all speak to the discursive production of LGBT identities via cyberspace. Sites such as SiGNeL allowed LGBT Singaporeans to debate among themselves important issues both inside and outside of their nation. Fridae, through its innovative, interactive site, exposed LGBT Singaporeans to an international LGBT discourse while at the same time catering to local needs. RedQuEEn allowed queer women to come together for support and friendship both online and off.

Yet, as significant as these sites are in terms of bringing together and organizing LGBT Singaporeans, they are nonetheless not a substitute for the physical world. The communities formed on these sites were not isolated; rather they served as complimentary sites that allowed members to first interact in cyberspace and then to take those relationships further into the physical world. Reginald, a Singaporean trans activist and practising architect who spent a considerable amount of time living and working in London, spoke to the importance of taking Internet interaction into the physical world:

> If you look at people who use the Internet to form offline communities, things like that, when people come offline, they are able to make firmer

relationships. I'm sure that the Internet forms communities, communities that are transient. You have their username, but not any information like where they live, so for me it is a means to an end. And the end is to find yourself in the physical world, finding people who are not going to be just digital or missing bodies, because you can come on and you can come off and still be out there. But when you are able to translate that into the offline there is comfort in the physical presence amongst other people.

Shifong, a bisexual-identified insurance agent, also spoke to this dynamic:

Online communities have an influence on how I think on certain things, but whether it makes me the person I am now ... I think that the real offline immediate surrounding that I'm in now has a much more ... sort of impact as well ... you can't live online 24/7 but it does shape or influence the way you think about things when you talk to people from other countries about certain issues.

All the sites discussed here made the move from cyberspace to the physical world. SiGNeL members have been instrumental in organizing physical-world events such as IndigNation. The management of Fridae organized the Nation Party and other parties in Singapore, Thailand, and Taiwan. They are also major sponsors of such events as IndigNation as well as theatre productions with LGBT themes. Fridae was also instrumental in organizing physical world events that urged the repeal of the sodomy law contained within Section 377A of the penal code. RedQuEEn members are actively involved in planning events that are a part of Women's Nite. Online groups such as ADLUS utilize the Internet to organize running groups, tennis tournaments, and diving expeditions. Heartland, the online gay Buddhist group, plans tours of local temples or excursions to volunteer at animal sanctuaries.

Many of my interlocutors also spoke to the idea that as useful as the Internet has been, much of the information found there was not particularly useful in the Asian context:

For me when I came out, I automatically reached for the Internet for information. I found a reference to a book, but it was aimed at Westerners. I felt affirmed that there were people who had gone through the journey that I was going through, but at the same time, these people are not Asian like me and to some extent I don't feel the similarity. So, for me the whole coming out thing came about when I just decided to seek more in terms of spirituality. I read up on Buddhism and the whole honesty thing the whole coming out thing; I couldn't do it in a selfish way.

RedQuEEn is the most local in its orientation, and much of the discourse contained within the site is framed within a Singaporean context. The other sites, SiGNeL and Fridae, are much more transnational, drawing on discourse that is at once global and local. Yet, whatever their orientation, these sites sought to transform homo- and transphobic and heteronormative social, physical, and virtual space in an Asiacentric manner. For instance, in October 2006, all three sites were involved in the online promotion of Short Circuit, the first LGBT film festival in Singapore that featured the work of queer-identified Singaporean filmmakers. Significantly, the organizers used the Internet in order to circumvent governmental regulations and censorship. First, they conceived of the event as a "private" screening in order to evade censors. The one-night event was then advertised online and interested persons were directed to join a Yahoo group. Once they joined the groups, organizers were able to print out a list of email addresses, and when attendees arrived, they simply gave their email address in order to be admitted to the "by invitation only" event. I attended the festival at the Guinness Theatre and the venue was filled to capacity. Short films by well-known Singaporean filmmakers including Boo Junfeng and Sun Koh were screened to an appreciative audience. This type of tactic demonstrates the type of physical-world activism that the Internet encourages and allows – in this case, one that was focused on films by Asian directors. While the event was successful and Short Circuit 2 was held the following year, it was still a type of activism carried out within the limits proscribed under illiberal pragmatics.

In this chapter, I have illustrated the tensions between LGBT Singaporeans and the nation and how this has led to the integration of the Internet into the everyday lives of these minority citizens. I re-examined the difficulties present in the physical environment of Singapore that make the Internet so crucial to the lives of LGBT individuals. This was followed by a discussion surrounding the Internet in Singapore. I continued with an examination of three websites to demonstrate the discursive production of LGBT identities and activism via the Internet. I ended with an example of how these sites allowed LGBT Singaporeans, using various modes of Internet-mediated communication, to successfully form online communities that quietly moved into the physical world. As will be discussed in the next chapter, this movement from cyberspace to the physical world has also allowed LGBT Singaporeans to critically engage with their fellow citizens and national leaders in larger debates affecting the future direction of the nation.

Chapter Four

The Internet and a New Public Sphere

On 8 September 2007, a 38-year-old science teacher at Raffles Institution, a prestigious all-boys secondary school in Singapore, posted the following at the end of a longer entry on his personal blog: "So here it is: I, Otto Fong, have always been and always will be a gay man ... I am not going back in the closet." He continued, "When you ask me who I am, I will answer: I am a son, a brother, a long-time companion, an uncle, a teacher, a classmate, a colleague, a part of your community, a HDB dweller,[1] a Singaporean. And I am also gay" (Fong 2007). Immediately after it was posted the entry was picked up by other Singaporean bloggers who then reposted it on their own sites. Socio-political blogs with large readerships, including Singabloodypore and The Online Citizen also republished the entry. Within hours, mainstream media outlets became aware of the story and in a matter of days the Ministry of Education requested that Fong remove the entry.

Under normal circumstances, a posting such as this would have gone mostly unnoticed. Despite the illegality of male homosexual practices and the cultural stigmatization of non-normative sexualities in the city-state (Heng 2001; Leong 1995 and 1997), many Singaporeans who identify as LGBT are "out" in the sense that the word is used in Singapore and in the West. There are local television and radio personalities, poets and playwrights, and several academics and entrepreneurs who have been forthcoming regarding their sexual orientation.[2] Yet, in this case, the person publicly declaring his sexual orientation was a locally raised high school science teacher at one of the nation's most-respected secondary schools, one that had produced two of the three prime ministers who have led the nation since its formation in 1965. Further, because Fong was not perceived as the stereotypical gay man portrayed so consistently in Singapore's state-owned media as a drug-taking, hard-drinking sexual deviant (AsiaOne 2013; Straits Times 2010), the public pronouncement of his sexual orientation became more meaningful, and more threatening, for the average Singaporean. Fong was, by all accounts, a respected educator, well liked by students, parents, and administrators. He was not stereotypical nor was he a Western expatriate; he was as "Singaporean" as any of his fellow citizens.

The entry also took on greater meaning because it appeared at the height of public debate surrounding Parliament's decision to consider the repeal of Section 377A of the penal code, the section that criminalizes sex between consenting adult men. Recall that this law, part of the penal code established while Singapore was a British colony, makes acts of "gross indecency" between men a crime punishable by up to two years in prison. The 2007 review was the first in over twenty years and generated considerable public debate; according to the Ministry of Home Affairs, the feedback from the public was "emotional, divided and strongly expressed" (Straits Times 2007a).

The above vignette speaks directly to the often contentious and well-documented relationship between LGBT identity and national identity in general (Boellstorff 2004, 2005; Bunzl 2004; Parker 2009), as well as to specifically non-Western LGBT politics of identity and difference (Boellstorff 2003; Dave 2010, 2012; Gaudio 2009, 2014; Lorway 2008; Mitchell 2015; Reid 2013), like that detailed by many of the LGBT Singaporeans with whom I interacted during my time in the city-state. Fong's entry and the subsequent attention from the state-controlled mainstream media and the Ministry of Education also signalled the increasingly important role of social media in attempts by LGBT Singaporeans to reconfigure this relationship.

In this chapter, I use Fong's blog entry as a starting point to explore how and why the use of the Internet has been so crucial in the process of opening discussions on topics that had not been spoken of in the public sphere. Here, I argue that using blogs, forums, and other interactive online sites, Singaporeans of all persuasions could express opinions on controversial issues online that in turn led to productive debates in the physical world regarding such topics as citizenship rights, sexualities, and uses of public space. While Internet use by the LGBT communities discussed in chapter 3 dealt with use *within* these communities on sites dedicated specifically to LGBT issues, here I examine how all Singaporeans were able to use technology to participate in larger discussions relating to the future direction of the nation. In this instance, I suggest that public debate surrounding the case of Otto Fong represents a pivotal moment in recent Singaporean history in that it led directly to open and, more importantly, public discussions regarding such related issues as inclusion and difference, immigration, family, Asian values, and race and ethnicity.

Otto Fong in RI

A letter to all my friends and colleagues. 8th September 2007.

Monday, August 4, 2008

A Letter – Sept 2007

I am Otto Fong. I have been teaching Science in Raffles Institution for the last eight years.

Being a teacher has been the most rewarding part of my professional life thus far. My students continue to amaze me daily with their wit, maturity, independent thinking and leadership. It is very fulfilling that I am a part of an institution that moulds the future generation of Singapore's leaders.

Leaders are people who can rise above the tide of popular opinion, people who are guided by the conviction of rightness and justice and in being so guided, lead others towards that right path.

Recent events leading to my action

Recent events have made me decide to write this open letter. In April this year, Minister Mentor Mr Lee Kuan Yew – one of the school's greatest alumni – called homosexuality a "genetic variation", questioning the validity of criminalising gay sex. In July, MP Baey Yam Keng expressed support for the repeal of Section 377A of the penal code (which criminalises gay sex acts). In August, Malaysian columnist and ordained pastor Oyoung Wenfeng released his inspiring new Mandarin book 'Tong Gen Sheng', encouraging gay men and women to come out of the closet.

Hello!

A letter to all by Otto Fong.

Author

Tracker

Blog Archive

Figure 6. Otto Fong in RI, September 2007
Source: Otto Fong. Used with permission.

I explore these propositions by examining two parallel yet contradic-tory sets of events that, according to Fong, were part of a larger set of occurrences that laid the groundwork for his public coming out. These events can also be seen as paving the way for the opening of the public sphere. In August 2008, Fong gave a talk titled "From Classroom to Comics" as part of IndigNation (YouTube 2008). During the talk, he spoke of seven reasons for his public coming out; I focus on two. The first revolved around Singapore's prime ministers and statements they made between 2003 and 2007 regarding the place of sexual minorities within Singaporean society. The second was Fridae's coverage of the cancellation of the gay parties SnowBall and Squirt in 2004 and the sub-sequent denial of permits for Nation Party V in 2005. I argue that the online discourse generated in reaction to the public statements and the cancellation of the parties were the first steps in opening the door for subsequent and much larger debates. To demonstrate this transforma-tion of the public sphere, I conclude by examining some of the online debates surrounding Section 377A, with an emphasis on how these debates and the subtle discourses contained within them exemplified the movement of LGBT Singaporeans from cyberspace to the physical world.

I first necessarily situate these events by briefly examining some of the reasons that Fong felt compelled to write this entry, focusing on how it speaks to the discourse of illiberal pragmatics. This is followed by a discussion of the Singaporean public sphere with an emphasis on contextualizing public discourse regarding non-normative sexualities and how it slowly progressed from a taboo subject to one that continues to have a significant place within public discussion in Singapore.

"I don't want to be a bonsai tree"

In the weeks that followed Fong's posting, hundreds of Singaporeans responded to his coming out. His story was reposted on many widely read socio-political blogs, and many of his current and former students posted supportive comments. Friends, acquaintances, and strangers commended him on his honesty and offered words of encouragement. In the weeks following the publication of his entry hundreds of letters poured into the *Straits Times* and the *Electric New Paper*, many of which spoke to the invisibility of LGBT individuals within the Singaporean public sphere. One self-identified heterosexual wrote:

> What is so obviously missing is the subject of the debate itself – the gay
> people. For fear of societal rejection and discrimination, most gays in

Singapore remain in the closet. While Mr. Fong does not represent every gay person in Singapore, his identity and life humanizes the gay issue in a way no amount of well-constructed arguments can ever achieve. (Straits Times 2007b)

Others, including concerned parents were not so forthcoming with praise:

Students are very impressionable and prone to hero-worshipping teachers that they like. By admitting that he is gay, Mr. Otto Fong has issued an open invitation to students to find out about his lifestyle and perhaps some of them might want to follow in his footsteps. (Straits Times 2007c)

In this case, the teacher is in contact with boys who are still young and impressionable. Their sexual preferences still may be somewhat unclear and in flux, so it's probably best that the teacher doesn't reveal too much too soon. (New Paper 2007b)

He should keep such things private – I don't think it's our business to know about his personal life. It [sexual orientation] doesn't really matter if he is a good teacher – but parents will likely become wary because they don't know enough about the gay community. (New Paper 2007b)

In fact, many parents called for Fong's resignation because they feared that his sexual orientation might have an influence on their impressionable sons.

The Ministry of Education reprimanded Fong for his post and asked that he take it down, which he did. However, he was not fired from his position at Raffles Institution though he did later resign. In many respects, Fong was not prepared to deal with the almost instantaneous public attention that accompanied his posting. He had been blogging for about two months when this entry was published, and he has stated that he had intended that the blog only be read by his colleagues and friends (New Paper 2007b). He also admitted that it was "naïve" on his part to think that his tech-savvy students would not discover his blog. While Fong has not, to my knowledge, spoken to the idea that there would be consequences to his posting, surely he must have realized that there may have been repercussions, including being fired from a job that he loved. In fact, Alfian Sa'at, a prominent and award-winning Singaporean poet and playwright had been fired as a substitute teacher the previous June. The Ministry of Education sent Sa'at, some of whose writings centre on issues of homosexuality and critique of the government, a three-sentence email denying his application to continue in his position as a substitute teacher. It stated that his application had been rejected on that grounds that "only those that best meet the organisation's requirements will be considered for appointment"[3] (Yawning Bread 2007a). With this in mind, one might ask why he felt so compelled to come out? Fong himself gives a short answer on his blog: "Due to societal pressures, gay men and women learn to keep their orientation hidden for years and decades. I carried that burden with me for almost three decades, but at some point, I decided it is not a cross I wish to carry for the rest of my life" (Fong 2007).

The language that Fong used in his arguments and the way he framed his coming out resonate strongly with discourses related to the mainstreaming and normalization of homosexuality (Onwuachi-Willig 2015; Warner 1999). Fong explains:

> When I became a teacher in 1999, I looked back on the good guidance my own teachers gave me as a template, and tried to be a better teacher to my students. Besides teaching them Science, I spent considerable effort in imparting good social values: give up your seats to the needy, save the handicapped parking lot for those in wheelchairs and their caretakers, respect people regardless of profession or social status.
>
> Yet, in the eight years I have taught, I have done little for that small group of students who are gay. When the religious group Focus on the Family masqueraded as sex guidance counselors and gave a talk full of misinformation about homosexuality to our students, I was furious but kept my mouth shut. (Fong 2007)

He continued:

> When my niece returned from school saying, "Gays are disgusting!" I knew she learnt that hatred from a classmate, who had in turn absorbed that hatred from a parent. I knew that this hatred has been perpetrated for generations. But hatred grew out of fear, and hatred, as a line in a movie goes, "leads to the Dark Side." This is the same environment of hatred I grew up in, as a gay teenager and student.

Fong's main arguments for coming out revolved around family and students. He was not, as some in the blogosphere had suggested, flaunting his sexuality or persuading his students to experiment with their sexuality. Rather, he was dismayed that young persons, including his niece, were learning intolerance from classmates and that his LGBT students had no role models or counsellors with whom to speak.

By declaring that he was "a part of your community, a HDB dweller, a Singaporean," he situated himself as part of the national and local culture. In addition, he asked:

> Do you know what a bonsai tree is? A bonsai tree is an imitation of a real tree. It is kept in a small pot with limited nutrients, trimmed constantly to fit someone else's whim. It looks like a real tree, except it can't do many things a real tree can. It cannot provide shelter, it cannot find food on its own; its life and death are totally reliant on its owner. It is the plant version of the 3-inch Chinese bound foot for women: useless and painful.

His analogies of the bonsai tree and women with bound feet – motifs that are particular to Asian cultures – to describe how he felt about being in the closet, further situated his experiences squarely within the local and regional. In making a list of his various identities (a son, a brother, a long-time companion etc.) he placed emphasis on familial relationships, indicating that he saw himself as an integral part of a family structure, rather than simply as an individual. He ended the list of subjectivities with, "And I am also gay." It was not his primary subject position, but one of many. By making it a statement apart from the other subjectivities, it became almost an afterthought, as if to make clear that he understood that it is *part* of who he is, rather than *who* he is. He also stressed that he knew the demands of living in a society such as Singapore's, in which it is expected that people put the common good first and respect authority:

> Until Section 377A is repealed, there will be precious little the Ministry of Education can do to help these students. As a teacher, I am bound by my professional duty to follow the directives of my superiors.

He ended his entry with the following request,

> I hope, dear friends and colleagues, that you look back and remember what I am, and see that I am not someone you fear. I am essentially the same person – flawed, imperfect, but brought up properly by two loving parents to lead a productive, beneficial, and meaningful life. My friends and family love me for who I am, and I hope you can too. I come out to you with as much hope and trepidation as when I first came out to my mother and father. Your support and understanding are very important to me at this moment.

Fong's focus throughout the posting was on family, parents, friends, and students. Notice that he wrote, "I come out to you with as much hope and trepidation as when I first came out to my mother and father." He was speaking to his readers as if they were members of his own family. The tone of the entry was gentle, and while it did focus on Fong as an individual, it made no demands. Apart from the "coming out" theme of the entry, there was little hint of Western discourses of LGBT subjectivity that prioritize the individual. He was not asking for overt social acceptance, but understanding. He was not demanding special rights here, but asked "to enjoy the respect that all other Singaporeans enjoy." Yet, despite the familial tone of the posting I suggest that Fong was, consciously or not, enacting what George (2006, 3) calls "contentious journalism" in which media activists on the margins set their sights on "challenging the consensus that powerful interests try to shape and sustain through mainstream media." Even though Fong's posting was aimed at family and friends, it gained traction via its distribution to thousands of others over the Internet. The shift from a semi-private blog posting to one that many Singaporeans read and subsequently commented on publicly in mainstream newspapers demonstrates the effect of this type of media activism on the public sphere.

The Public and the Private

Besides the fact that Fong's story exemplifies "contentious journalism," I use it for several additional reasons. On one level, it is representative of the power and speed of the Internet. This technology allowed for an almost instantaneous dissemination of information. Fong posted his blog entry on 8 September 2007 and it was removed on 10 September 2007. In the two days preceding removal, the document had circulated internationally and was read by thousands of people. This same technology also allowed authorities at Raffles Institution and the Ministry of Education to become aware of the blog entry, to quickly communicate with one another as well as concerned parents, and to subsequently request that Fong remove the posting. Fong's story also speaks directly to the politics of "coming out" in a society such as Singapore. Many responses to the blog entry questioned his motives for coming out as well as its timing since it was published at the height of public discussion regarding the repeal of Section 377A.

Perhaps the most compelling reason to use this story is that it represents a conflation of the public and the private. It exemplifies a key moment in Singapore's recent history in which citizens began talking *publicly* about and debating controversial issues such as the role of LGBT individuals within Singaporean society that had previously been relegated to the private. The one-sided presentation of information via state-related media outlets outlined in chapter 2, was coming to be replaced by the presence of multiple perspectives, debates, and dialogues. LGBT Singaporeans had been granted public and semi-public spaces in which to interact. These included bars, saunas, and other entertainment spaces – but no spaces dedicated to political debates regarding the place of LGBT within Singaporean society. As such, the members of these communities had taken upon themselves to create semi-private areas, in cyberspace, in which to discuss issues of relevance to their communities. The discourse generated by Otto Fong's coming out serves to exemplify the constantly shifting boundaries of private and public encountered on the Internet. It also demonstrates how Singaporeans in general utilized the Internet to renegotiate claims on public space. Because LGBT Singaporeans inhabited both the physical and the virtual, they were making claims on the public sphere that demonstrate shifting constructions of the public and how people and discourse move between these boundaries. The claims that LGBT Singaporeans were making, especially those discussed, here confound public and private and create a set of overlapping publics.

Recall the history of the LGBT rights organization People Like Us (PLU). For a time, members of PLU held regularly scheduled meetings in coffee shops, where they discussed issues and disseminated information of relevance to their communities; this is reminiscent of the salons and coffeehouses Habermas (1989) wrote about. During this period such public discussions were taboo. Eventually the meetings were discovered by government authorities, who then assigned undercover officers to attend the meetings to keep track of what was being discussed. When members of PLU discovered this, they took the decision to move these meetings from the physical realm of Singapore to the virtual realm, in the form of the online group SiGNeL. Because of this move to cyberspace the LGBT communities of Singapore could draw in even more participants to ongoing discussions, including Singaporeans who did not want to (or could not) be publicly associated with such a group. The websites utilized by LGBT Singaporeans became the new coffeehouses and served as new spaces in which these citizens could critique long-standing political and social ideologies and put forth alternatives to received opinions and ideas.

This shift to cyberspace serves as an example of how terms such as public and private become ambiguous in a public arena such as the one that existed in Singapore. A lack of safe space in the public sphere led to a withdrawal and subsequent move to the private sphere. While the discussions were taking place online and therefore lacked visibility, they nonetheless inspired many to leave the relative safety of the virtual and take their activism into the physical world.

"Homosexuals are people like you and me"

Between 2003 and 2007, Minister Mentor Lee Kuan Yew, current Prime Minister Lee Hsien Loong, and former prime minister Goh Chok Tong made statements to the press regarding the place of gay men[4] within Singaporean society in the context of Section 377A. These statements were generally positive and served as the beginning of the normalization of homosexuality within the Singaporean public sphere. In July 2003, *Time* magazine published an interview with then Prime Minister Goh Chok Tong in which he stated the following regarding the place of gay men within Singapore's civil service: "So let it evolve and in time to come, the population will understand that some people are born that way. We are born this way and they are born that way but they are like you and me" (Elegant 2003). A few days later, he clarified his comments in an article in the *Straits Times*:

> We would employ you so long as you declare yourself, I mean, in certain positions in government. In the past, if we know you're gay, we would not employ you but we just changed this quietly. We know you are. We'll employ you.
>
> In certain sensitive positions, you have to tell so that if you tell, you are open about this, you cannot be blackmailed ... If you are working in a sensitive position and you're trying to hide your sexual preferences and instinct, I mean, you are born that way and of course, if you're discovered by somebody else, then he can blackmail you. You have to openly declare and people know you're gay. Then, you can't be blackmailed. (Straits Times 2003)

Lee Hsien Loong, Goh's successor, endorsed his position on 6 October 2005 at a meeting with the Foreign Correspondents Association. A reporter from *Time* asked, "Could you discuss at some greater length your attitude towards homosexuals and the gay community? I remember that your predecessor described them in an interview as 'people like you and me.' Is that how you feel?" He continued, "The reason for asking is that sometimes your administration manages to give every impression of being somewhat homophobic." Lee answered, "No, I don't think we are homophobic. I agree with Mr. Goh Chok Tong that homosexuals are people like you and me" (Yawning Bread 2005).

On 21 April 2007 Minister Mentor Lee Kuan Yew attended a public dialogue session at the popular nightspot Saint James Power Station sponsored by the Young PAP (the youth branch of the ruling People's

Action Party). He stated the following in response to a question regarding the paradigms for censorship in the next two decades:

> You take this business of homosexuality. It raises tempers all over the world, and even in America. If in fact it is true – and I have asked doctors this – that you are genetically born a homosexual because that's the nature of the genetic random transmission of genes, you can't help it. So why should we criminalise it? But there's such a strong inhibition in all societies – Christianity, Islam, even the Hindu, Chinese societies, and we are now confronted with a persisting aberration. But is it an aberration? It's a genetic variation. So what do we do? I think we pragmatically adjust, carry our people. Don't upset them and suddenly upset their sense of propriety and right and wrong. But at the same time let's not go around like this moral police do in Malaysia, barging into people's rooms and say "khalwat."[5] That's not our business. So, you have to take a practical, pragmatic approach to what I see is an inevitable force of time and circumstance. (PLURAL 2007)

All three of these statements were embraced by some members of the LGBT communities in Singapore as a sign that the government was continuing to loosen its anti-LGBT stance. Many postings on *SiGNeL* responded with guarded optimism to these public proclamations. About the statement by Goh, one member stated, "Prime Minister Goh is saying that the bottom line is that we are all equal ... though full recognition is still a while away, words like those from the foremost man in our country should be seen as a great milestone, a great promise of things to come." Another responded to Minister Mentor Lee Kuan Yew's statement, "one thing is clear – we are getting there. Slowly and quite surely. On this issue, this country cannot be rushed or we may go into catharsis. Perhaps there is much wisdom in doing it more patiently and one step at a time. That at least is not going two steps backwards." Like these SiGNeL members, Fong was impressed with Minister Mentor Lee's statement and he credited it, in part, in influencing his decision to come out on his blog. While these statements do, in some manner, indicate that Singapore's government was willing to accommodate or tolerate its LGBT citizens, they do not go so far as to imply acceptance. Instead, the statements spoke directly to the discourse of illiberal pragmatism in that, on the one hand, Lee was sympathizing with an LGBT subjectivity based on a "genetics" argument, yet reiterating the idea that the country is not yet ready for change. Hence, the status quo would continue.

While the stance of these government officials on the treatment of LGBT individuals may have signalled tolerance, the fact remained that the Ministry of Education saw things differently, as was indicated by their request that Fong remove his posting. This is a good example of how statements given by governmental spokespersons do not always map onto lived reality. The nation's past and present prime ministers, over a period of years, each made public statements that in many respects normalized homosexuality. Yet, when a situation such as Fong's posting arose, all the government parties involved changed positions. To understand the stark contrast between what Singapore's government said and what it did, it is necessary to contextualize these statements as part of a complex Singaporean position that is heterogeneous, uneven, and shifting. I was not surprised that in interview after interview, respondents repeated the same phrases that had come to characterize this disconnect: "inconsistent," "bipolar," and "schizophrenic." LGBT Singaporeans had been hearing contradictory statements as to their status within society for so long that they began to ignore them, and despite the positive nature of some of these statements, it was clear that actions such as the request that Fong remove his blog posting seemed contradictory.

Yet, ultimately, I suggest that these statements, as tenuous and contradictory as they were, gave LGBT Singaporeans more visibility. Further, these public statements were the first crack in the opening of the public sphere. In some way, these public proclamations, small but significant, gave LGBT Singaporeans reason to believe that change was indeed possible. These statements also represented subtle shifts in government policy and speak to the pragmatic nature of Singapore's ruling party. LGBT Singaporean voices were beginning to be heard and authorities were listening.

"Contrary to public interest"

A second set of occurrences also helped to further LGBT claims on public space. As with the speeches detailed above, they were initiated and subsequently brought to public attention via the Internet. In contrast to the positive nature of the public speeches, the actions by the Singaporean government regarding the cancellation of several public LGBT circuit parties were distinctly negative. Circuit parties are enormous dance events usually held in large venues such as convention centres or hotel ballrooms. These multi-day parties are characterized by significant numbers of attendees, celebrity disc jockeys invited from clubs around the globe, and dancing by scantily clad participants. They are known as circuit parties because they move from city to city, often occur year after year, and many attendees go from one party to the next, in a circuit. While most major metropolitan areas in the United States and Europe had been hosting these parties for decades, it was a relatively new phenomenon in Southeast Asia in 2000.

Since 2001, the owners of Fridae had been organizing a series of such parties in Singapore including the winter-themed SnowBall and the water-themed Squirt. The largest and best-known of these parties, Nation, was held annually in conjunction with the National Day holiday that commemorates Singapore's independence from Britain in 1965. The third party, Nation.03, attracted over eight thousand partygoers and, according to organizers, generated revenues over the three-day event of S$6 million (approximately US$3.5 million in 2004). These parties drew a great deal of media attention over the years due to the fact that the normally conservative government was so lenient as to allow the parties to happen, as well as the fact that organizers had secured commercial sponsorship by such international corporations as Motorola, Cathay Pacific Airlines, Heineken, Pepsi, and Subaru. Additionally, the party was written up in *Time* magazine (Price 2003) and nominated for "best event experience" at the 2005 Singapore Tourism Board Awards. The international press was even writing of the potential of Singapore to become the new capital of "gay" Asia (Agence France-Press 2003).

This party received a great deal of attention and brought Singapore into the worldwide spotlight; this in turn attracted a larger and more diverse crowd of partygoers from around the globe. Because of this international media attention as well as former Prime Minister Goh's statement regarding the hiring of gay civil servants, many in Singapore's LGBT communities were beginning to feel more comfortable about their sexuality as well as their place within Singaporean society. The optimism generated by the positive media coverage of these events came to a halt in early December 2004. Without comment, Singapore's Police Entertainment Licensing Unit (PELU) refused a permit for the SnowBall party scheduled for later that month. Party organizers and members of the LGBT community at large were at a loss as to why the government would, after two successful years, deny the permit for this party. After all, the PELU had approved permits for several such events including SnowBall (2002–3), Nation Parties (2001–4), Squirt (2004), Boys of Summer (2003), and Paradise (2003).

Eventually, local media reported on the government's perception that the parties promoted a "homosexual" lifestyle, and an official government press release stated that they were "contrary to public interest." On 9 December 2004, the Public Affairs Department of the Singapore Police Force issued a statement denying permission for the *Snowball* party based on events that had occurred at the 2004 *Nation* party, including the following justification:

a) The promotional materials were widely advertised on Fridae.com, a known gay portal;

b) Observations during the indoor Opening [party] showed that patrons of the same gender were seen openly kissing and intimately touching each other. Some of the revellers were cross-dressed, for example, males wearing skirts. Patrons were also seen using the toilets of the opposite sex. The behaviour of these patrons suggested that most of them were probably gays/lesbians and this was thus an event almost exclusively for gays/lesbians;

c) A number of couples of the same sex were seen hugging and kissing in public after the event while waiting for taxis and checking into the nearby hotels after the party;

d) Several letters of complaint were received from some patrons about the openly gay acts at the Ball.

The statement also said:

The Police recognise that there are some Singaporeans with gay tendencies. While Police do not discriminate against them on this basis, the Police also recognise that Singapore is still, by and large, a conservative and traditional society. Hence, the Police cannot approve any application for an event which goes against the moral values of a large majority of Singaporeans. Future applications for events of similar nature will be closely scrutinized. (Fridae.com 2004b)

The release went on to state that, "the event [SnowBall.04] is likely to be organised as a gay party which is contrary to public interest in general." Interestingly, the press statement used "contrary to public interest," a catch-all phrase that can include anything from LGBT parties such as Nation to the importation of pornography to acts of terrorism.

In March 2005, Senior Minister of the State for Health, Balaji Sadasivan, gave a second reason for cancelling the parties. During a speech before Parliament, Sadasivan cited the work of an unnamed epidemiologist who suggested that Nation.04 encouraged "gays from high prevalence societies to interact with local gay men, seeding the infection in the local community" (Sadasivan 2005; see also Goh 2008; Yeo 2009). The Ministry of Health claimed that this was the reason why Singapore had seen a 28 per cent increase in the number of new HIV infections.[6] That April, Fridae announced that it had received faxed notification that the PELU had rejected its permit for Nation V. The organizers of the party decided not to fight the Police Entertainment Licensing Unit and instead rescheduled the party for Phuket, Thailand. The party was held in Phuket in 2005 and 2006. The 2006 Nation Party was the last. Stuart Koe, founder and CEO of Fridae stated: "When we first started throwing parties, the concept of a multi-day gay party with international DJ's and punters flying in from around the world was fairly novel in Asia. Now there are a number of impressive party organizers in the region – it is time for *Fridae* to focus on empowering the Asian gay community through other means" (Phuket Gazette 2006).

The reaction to the cancellation of these parties from Singapore's LGBT communities was swift. Take for instance two representative postings that appeared on a Fridae forum in the days following news that authorities had refused to grant the permit for Nation V:

> 1) Let's just wait another few years, I'm sure that sooner or later, the old guy [referring to Minister Mentor Lee Kuan Yew] and the rest of the old gang previously in power, will die off ... Then we will see, how we, as citizens of Singapore, can finally feel we ARE citizens of Singapore by having a real SAY over the governance of OUR country.
>
>   2) We are the minorities in the picture of a nation, but we paid our taxes and are a peace-loving group of people. We may be small, but we are entitled to our right as human beings with needs and passions. To take away our basic needs is to deny us the privilege of being a citizen and a human being. The rights to be heard and freedom of speech is non-existent in Singapore's gay community. Therefore, I propose we be heard! And it's about time we be recognised for who we are!

While these are just two comments from among hundreds, they are typical of those posted on the forums. The topic of this forum was the cancellation of Nation Party, but the comments did not so much address the party as they did the exclusion of LGBT individuals from society and their subsequent claims on public space and citizenship. Note that in the second comment, there is a hint at a call for action that goes beyond online discussion and activism. The commenter suggests that "we be heard," an intimation that it is time to leave comparatively safe online spaces and relocate the discussion to the physical world. A third comment from the same forum went so far as to suggest a physical-world protest on the scale of Stonewall:

> 3) We need a louder voice to voice our discontent! We can complain in this forum until the cows come home but it wouldn't make a diff[erence]!

> We have been too passive, and it's about time that the gay community in Singapore has a face, and a loud voice to be heard! Anybody organizing something similar to Stonewall? I volunteer to be the front guy holding the huge banner!

Significantly, this comment acknowledges the limitations of online organizing by pointing out that voicing discontent in an online "echo chamber" has a very limited effect, if any at all, on the physical world. The poster is suggesting that the only way to bring about change is through visibility – by showing faces and using voices in the public sphere.

Much of the discourse generated by the events discussed thus far has centred on issues of visibility within the public sphere. Otto Fong's coming out, the speeches made by Singapore's current and past prime ministers, and the cancellation of the circuit parties all touched directly on this issue. Visibility became especially important in Singapore, where historically LGBT citizens had been invisible within the public sphere. Otto Fong touched on this idea in his blog entry when he lamented the lack of support LGBT Singaporeans receive from society:

> So, I know gay friends who are not out to anyone. They have no advice about relationships and they have to find their own way. So that is how people say that gay people cannot have long lasting committed relationships, we have no guidance from anyone whatsoever. We have no support. The people that we trust, our own parents, our schools, our places of worship tell us we are sick and cannot have happy lives. (Fong 2007)

In an interview with a Thai newspaper, Stuart Koe spoke of the convoluted relationship between LGBT Singaporeans and the nation. He said, "We've found that there are limits as to how much public space the government is willing to allow us to have. [The government] has not clamped down on the community – so long as we are not too visible about it." He continued, "Nation has been very visible, Fridae has been very vocal and I think the government was uncomfortable with that. The [LGBT] bars and clubs are still in existence, still operational ... So long as the gay community doesn't have a voice in the public arena, then the government is fine with that" (Phuket Gazette 2006).

This lack of visibility within the public sphere, as Koe suggests, was the impetus for much of the backlash that occurred with Otto Fong's coming out as well as with the Nation Party. Until these events became public, and thus visible, the government was satisfied that they had the LGBT communities under control. Yet in both instances, the stories leaked into the realm of the public and thus created a problem. The government-controlled Singaporean press made no mention of Nation.04 even though the event attracted over eight thousand partygoers. But, when the party began garnering international media coverage and the composition of the partygoers shifted from the local to the global, the government took notice and acted. There was also a distinct demonizing of the international at play here. Recall Sadasivan's speculation that "gays from high prevalence societies ... interact with local gay men, seeding the infection in the local community" (Sadasivan 2005). The idea here was that these transnational interactions were having a detrimental effect on local health.

Finally, in 2006, Singaporean authorities refused permits for a Fridae-sponsored party, Feelin' Good. The party was to feature well-known Australian disc jockey Kate Monroe and was to be thrown at the Ministry of Sound, a mainstream nightclub located in Clarke Quay, a heavily advertised tourist destination. Two days before the party was to be held, Singaporean police called the management of the Ministry of Sound and demanded that they not allow the event to take place. If the management refused, police threatened to come to the venue and shut the party down. The reason the police gave for the cancellation was that the party would "promote gay activities" (Fridae.com 2006). Ironically, the party was organized at a mainstream club and advertised on state-owned radio stations as well as local publications such as *IS* (*In Singapore*) to comply with Prime Minister Lee's suggestion that such parties not be organized solely for "gays and lesbians." Again, as with the above examples, I suggest that behaviour that had previously only been imagined as taking place behind closed doors, was now out in the open. The virtual was slowly seeping into the public sphere and the effects were becoming noticeable.

Counterpublics

Because of these actions on the part of the Singaporean government, individuals such as Fong began to act. At the same time, other individuals and groups, also feeling exclusion from the dominant public discourse, created their own alternative discursive spaces online, including blogs. As Eckert and Chadha (2013) point out, these online activities do not point to the creation a monolithic virtual public sphere, but rather to the formation of what Fraser (1990) referred to as "counterpublics." In doing so, these marginalized groups were able interact with their fellow LGBT Singaporeans to rethink their own national identities. More significantly, they also gained the ability to contest, challenge, and

correct the dominant public discourse surrounding LGBT Singaporeans through debates with their fellow citizens on "mainstream" news
sites such as the *Straits Times* and *Today*. For these reasons, I situate
the Internet communities, such as those found on sites such as SiGNeL
and RedQuEEn, as very clear examples of counterpublics or perhaps as
Ong might describe them, "cyberpublics" (Ong 2006) that challenge authoritarian rule. Members of such groups are very aware of their subor-
dinate status within society and the concomitant lack of a proper public
forum in which to participate in debates regarding issues that affect
their communities and their nation. They are also aware that they are,
by and large, seen as the Other and, as such, misunderstood by many of
their fellow citizens. This engagement went beyond websites and blogs
created by and for members of the LGBT communities; events such as
Fong's blog posting prompted LGBT Singaporeans to engage with their
fellow citizens on mainstream sites as well.

I suggest that the online discussions surrounding the Otto Fong blog
posting, the public speeches by past and current prime ministers, and
the cancellation of the circuit parties served as clear cases of counterpublics overlapping with publics. This is because discussions and debates were taking place not exclusively on LGBT websites, but in the
comment sections of major state-run newspapers including the *Straits
Times* and the *New Paper*. What is interesting about this phenomenon
is that LGBT Singaporeans have historically been excluded from the
larger public sphere. When they could use digital interventions, such
as those available on sites within their own Internet communities, they
formed counterpublics, and as Fraser contends, these counterpublics
served as "parallel discursive arenas" (Fraser 1990, 67) where members of inferior groups devise and subsequently disseminate counter-
discourses, which allow them to reinterpret various aspects of their
subjectivities. This is certainly the case with the groups under consideration in Singapore. Yet, LGBT Singaporeans have taken this one step
further. These counterpublics, by the content of their conversations as
well as their overlap with publics, were themselves transformed from
counterpublics into publics. Interactions on mainstream websites facili-
tated this overlapping of publics and counterpublics and have in many
respects blurred the distinction between them.

Further, because of its distributive nature, the Internet allowed for
a democratization of the public sphere; it became "a public of publics" (Bohman 2004, 140) rather than a monolith. In many respects, the
Internet increased both the scope and scale of the public sphere and
enabled people who would not or could not interact in the physical
world to participate in discussions. These interactions were also able

to "de-gender" and "de-racialize" the public sphere, allowing populations that were marginalized *within* the LGBT communities to actively
participate. Unregulated access to emerging technologies such as the
Internet was a major reason why LGBT individuals in Singapore had
been able to make claims regarding public space and citizenship rights.
The Internet is a radically decentralized as well as interactive communication system; this makes for a medium that is difficult for a state
to control. It is precisely these conditions that allowed for the production, in cyberspace, of electronically mediated discourse, thus making
possible the questioning of and subsequent attempt to reconfigure the
public sphere. The Internet thus served as a site of productive tension,
transgression, or "resistance" (Ho, Baber, and Khondker 2002) that fa-
cilitated the move from the online to the physical.

Conclusion

On 15 July 2007, I attended what was the first public meeting of politicians, activists, and religious figures who came together to discuss
the proposed repeal of Section 377A of Singapore's penal code. The
standing-room-only forum, entitled Peculiar Legislation: 377(A) –
Symbol or Statute?[7] took place in a conference room at the National Library. It was organized by the theatre company W!ld Rice and was held
in conjunction with the final performance of Alfian Sa'at's play *Asian
Boys Volume III*.[8] The audience, which numbered over two hundred,
consisted mainly of supporters of the law's repeal, though there were
detractors present as well. At the front of the room was a panel that consisted of MP (Member of Parliament) Baey Yam Keng, Nominated MP
Siew Kum Hong, gay and civil rights activist Alex Au, Fridae founder
and CEO Stuart Koe, and the Reverend Dr. Yap Kim Hao, the first Asian
Bishop of the Methodist Church in Singapore who also served on Singapore's Inter-Religious Organisation (IRO) council. The panellists were
"preaching to the choir" regarding the repeal of the law; in fact, dissenting opinions during the two-hour event were rare. The forum itself was
productive in that it presented various reasons for repealing the law
including those dealing with economic factors, religious prohibitions,
and issues of constitutional law. More importantly, the event was covered by all mainstream media. In the political climate of the time, there
was little doubt in anyone's mind that eventually, after much debate in
Parliament, the law would remain intact. Yet, as I spoke with attendees
after the forum had ended, I was told the same thing repeatedly, namely
that such a public forum would not have been possible even one year
previously. Without exception, everyone I spoke with, both at the event

and afterwards, attributed the success of this event to two things. First, online advertising for the event. Much more importantly, I was told time and again that individuals attended the event as the result of what they had read on the Internet as well as online discussions in which they had participated regarding the debate over 377A.

Three months later, on 23 October 2007 Prime Minister Lee Hsien Loong gave the final speech to Singapore's Parliament regarding the debate over Section 377A of the penal code. In it, he spoke of Otto Fong and the consequences of his "coming out":

> So, for example, the recent case of Mr. Otto Fong who is a teacher in Raffles Institution. He's gay, he's a good teacher by all accounts. He put up a blog which outed, described his own sexual inclinations and said, explained how he was gay. And he circulated it to his colleagues and it became public. So, Ministry of Education looked at this, the school spoke to the teacher, the teacher understood that this was beyond the limit because what you live is your own thing but what you disseminate comes very close to promoting a lifestyle, so spoke to him, he took down his blog, he posted an explanation, he apologised for what he had done and he continues teaching in today. So, there is space, there are limits. De facto gays have a lot of space in Singapore. They hold, gay groups hold public discussions, they publish websites, I've visited some of them. (Lee 2007)

In the same speech, Lee said, "We should recognise that homosexuals are part of our society. They are our kith and kin. This is not just in Singapore, this is so in every society, in every period of history, back to prehistoric times, or at least as long as there have been records, biblical times and probably before." While likely not conscious of it, I nonetheless suggest that by referring to LGBT Singaporeans as "kith and kin" Lee was situating them within the family unit and thus utilizing the same normalizing discourse that Fong himself used. The speech serves as another example of illiberal pragmatics in which the then–prime minister speaks kindly of LGBT people while simultaneously reminding listeners that "there are limits."

This speech was, for many, a welcome and public acknowledgment of LGBT Singaporeans. Numerous individuals with whom I spoke felt that it was a great step forward for the prime minister to come out and speak publicly, in generally positive terms, regarding such a stigmatized segment of society. Further, Lee did so in front of Parliament and a national television audience. By acknowledging Otto Fong and his blog entry, he was helping to bring a once-taboo topic of discussion into Singapore's public sphere. He was completing the cycle that I have outlined in this chapter in which citizens initially discussed issues in cyberspace and eventually moved that conversation into the public sphere. Habermas claimed that an emerging public was "gradually replaced by a public sphere in which the ruler's power was merely represented before the people with a sphere in which state authority was publicly monitored through informed and critical discourse by the people" (Habermas 1989, xi). This is what happened in Singapore. LGBT Singaporeans began by countering, online, marginalizing discourses, and, as discussed in the next chapter, took the fight for recognition into the public sphere.

In this chapter, I have outlined several sets of events that straddled the line between the virtual and the physical. These events brought about significant changes in how Singaporeans of all persuasions approached the public sphere. I have argued that a blog entry by Otto Fong was pivotal in that it prompted many Singaporeans, of all sexual orientations, to think about larger issues of non-normative sexualities and to discuss them openly within the forums of online blogs and websites, including those within their communities and those contained within such mainstream media outlets as the *Straits Times*. I have also demonstrated how it has encouraged many to engage in meaningful debates in public forums in the *physical* world, far removed from the relative anonymity provided by cyberspace. This blog entry, in which a gay man felt compelled to publicly acknowledge his homosexuality, became, in part, the motivation that encouraged LGBT Singaporeans to begin writing positive and encouraging portrayals of themselves back into the narrative of the nation.

Chapter Five

Pushing the Boundaries in the Physical World

Lakshmi and I usually met once a week for lunch, followed by a visit to any number of local Hindu temples – spaces where we could escape the noise of the city, relax a bit, and get caught up with the goings-on in each other's lives. We had met at the book launch for *SQ21* in August 2006. I introduced myself to her after I was told by a mutual friend that she had lived in California for several years and had managed a small temple honouring the Hindu goddess Kali in Laguna Beach, a temple that I had frequented several times over the years. While it turned out that this information was incorrect (she had managed a goddess temple in Texas), we nonetheless quickly bonded over our common interest in the divine feminine. On a hot afternoon in February 2007, we met for long south Indian lunch at a small restaurant in the Little India section of the city. Later, we took a taxi to the Sri Mariamman Temple in nearby China-town. After paying our respects to the goddess, we found our way to the courtyard, found a shady spot of ground on which to sit, and began sorting through her latest relationship issues. Sensing that she didn't want to talk about her relationship anymore, I changed the topic by mentioning an article that I had been rereading earlier in the day. It had appeared in the *New Paper* (2006e) and dealt with LGBT Singaporeans abroad who were claiming asylum due to perceived threats of political persecution should they return to Singapore. In the article, a spokesperson for the Ministry of Home Affairs stated, "The police do not seek out persons to prosecute on the grounds of their homosexual identity." At the time of my conversation with Lakshmi, the last prosecution of two men for consensual sexual acts under Section 377A had been in 1993; the men had been arrested for gross acts of indecency at a public swimming pool.

As both of us had been involved in various online LGBT forums in Singapore, she as a participant and I as an observer, we were struck by the fact that contributors to these forums had not picked up on this statement. In fact, Lakshmi expressed surprise that activist bloggers had not embraced the statement as another sign that times were changing. Lakshmi, who had a long involvement with the LGBT movement in Singapore, reminded me that she was growing weary of the inability of activists to embrace the incremental changes in Singapore's social and political climate and finally understand that the government was slowly but surely changing policy for the better. In fact, she was so disillusioned by the state of LGBT activism in Singapore that she had recently made the decision to stop contributing to a growing online lesbian support group she had founded several years previously. She had also ceased attending public LGBT events such as IndigNation. When I asked her about what she would like to see happen in terms of LGBT rights in Singapore she answered, "I think we already have gay rights, Robert. We have the right to own a house after a certain age,[1] I think it's okay to be thirty-five and responsible, you can nominate your next of kin for your CPF[2] and it could be your partner ... I think the government has come to a point where [they] say, 'You are who you are.'" She continued, "How much is enough, Robert? Really, I mean, what do these guys want?" As I was walking home from our outing, I could not help but think about Lakshmi's question. In hindsight, I frame her acceptance of minimal government recognition within illiberal pragmatics; Singaporean authorities were trying to keep everyone happy and some, including Lakshmi, were. She could live with the idea that her government granted some rights to LGBT Singaporeans but not others. Yet there were other LGBT Singaporeans who wanted more.

In this chapter, the focus shifts from limited online engagement by LGBT activists to physical-world engagement. I argue that many of the events described in previous chapters – namely marginalization by the government, formation of online communities, and the subsequent move from cyberspace into the public sphere – ultimately enabled some LGBT Singaporeans to create a local iteration of a LGBT movement, albeit one necessarily informed by illiberal pragmatics and homonormativity. Despite these constraints, organizers chose to use the framework of international human rights discourse, one that includes neoliberal ideals, as a main component. These claims did not come without resistance. The primary opposition came from the Singaporean government. In the period from 2004 to 2008, authorities banned or refused permits for numerous events associated with the furthering of the Singaporean LGBT movement. But local Christian and Muslim groups and international organizations, including the Singapore division of the US-based Focus on the Family, joined together in pushing back as well, framing this quest within a complicated nexus that included ideas of morality and choice. Finally, there were also those from within the LGBT communities who believed that these claims were being made in a manner that was counterproductive.

Recall that in 2007, Section 377A of Singapore's penal code, which criminalizes homosexual acts between consenting adult men, was being considered for modification or repeal in what was the first review of the penal code in nearly twenty years. Members of Singapore's Parliament debated this and other issues – including whether to continue granting men immunity in cases of marital rape and whether to maintain the death penalty for the importation of narcotics. The debates were highly publicized, and portions were rebroadcast on state-owned television stations each evening. Just a few months earlier, numerous events that were scheduled as part of IndigNation, Singapore's de facto gay pride month, were denied permits. Both the cancellation of the events and the televised debates generated intense public debate, much of it online. It was here that LGBT Singaporeans defended their events to their fellow citizens and deliberated among themselves the pros and cons of the way that IndigNation was being structured and then modified in response to actions by authorities. IndigNation organizers also answered unsympathetic critics from within the LGBT communities who thought that the content of some events was pushing the fight for recognition and rights in the wrong direction. Singaporeans of all persuasions weighed in on the issues online, but also increasingly within the mainstream press, and as described in the previous chapter, with forays into the physical world. As such, I use these two episodes – the parliamentary debates surrounding changes to the penal code and the cancellation of IndigNation events – as lenses through which to examine in greater detail the complex issues surrounding LGBT rights in Singapore.

To achieve this goal, I begin by examining who is allowed to frame rights within Singapore; I accomplish this by exploring two examples of perceived attempts at foreign influence in Singaporean affairs. The first involves the censorship of individuals, particularly foreigners, who wished to contribute to the discussion of LGBT issues through their participation in IndigNation. This pride month, which began in 2005 as a celebration of LGBT contributions to Singaporean culture, had, by 2007, transformed into a budding social movement that was vocally protesting discrimination. The second involves a letter written by the International Gay and Lesbian Human Rights Campaign (IGLHRC) to Singapore's Prime Minister Lee Hsien Loong regarding the repeal of Section 377A. I use this letter to demonstrate how outside organizations were framing rights claims within Singapore and how Singaporean authorities subsequently dismissed such claims.

I then look at a speech given by Member of Parliament Thio Li-ann during the Singapore parliamentary debates of 2007 to demonstrate how issues of LGBT rights, particularly those that apply to gay men, were being framed by opponents. In examining IndigNation and the speeches, I highlight the specific discourses put forward by LGBT rights and civil society organizations who favoured repeal of the law as well as those being employed by conservative Christian churches, a driving force behind the campaign to keep this law in place. I then examine who was claiming rights from within Singapore and ask whom they were claiming rights for, paying attention to how rights were being framed on the local level.

I end the chapter by looking at the speech by Prime Minister Lee Hsien Loong, who supported keeping Section 377A in place, that brought a close to the parliamentary debates. The prime minister, while acknowledging the contributions of LGBT individuals to Singaporean society, nonetheless outlined – point by point – why he believed Parliament should keep Section 377A intact. I suggest here that by preserving the law, Lee was perpetuating the policies of illiberal pragmatism that have come to frame Singaporean policy. I further argue that he was also attempting to maintain the fine balance that existed between several antipodes that frame Singaporean culture and inform most policy decisions: cosmopolitans versus the middle class, Singapore versus the West, Christians versus others, and tradition versus modernity. Lastly, I suggest that, consciously or not, all parties discussed in this chapter were pushing the boundaries of acceptable political discourse, thus further widening the opening of the public sphere that was discussed in the previous chapter.

Contextualizing "Rights"

When asked about LGBT rights in Singapore, many interviewees echoed the sentiments of Shaffiq, a 34-year-old Malay Singaporean archivist: "I am out to my family, I am out to my company, no problems. I have a wonderful partner and my family loves him like another son. We spend a few nights a week at my family's home and the remainder at his. We have a great circle of friends ... our lives are good." While not everyone had as comfortable a situation as Shaffiq, it is easy to see his point, especially in a society such as Singapore, where many LGBT live their lives "in the closet" for fear of upsetting family and gaining disapproval from society. In Shaffiq's case, as with others, acceptance by family and employer was a blessing.

As detailed in previous chapters, in addition to online resources, LGBT Singaporeans had access to any number of outlets that catered to their communities, ranging from bars and saunas to support centres and social organizations. Many were fortunate enough to be able to leave Singapore for extended time abroad, whether for work or play, where they could experience LGBT life in other, more open cities. As Lakshmi mentioned, people could designate that their government-mandated savings (CPF) be assigned to their same-sex partner upon death. LGBT Singaporeans were also able to form virtual communities online that had come to serve as the catalyst for events in the physical world. For many, acceptance by family and employer, availability of social outlets in the online and physical worlds, travel opportunities, and minimal governmental recognition were enough. I suggest that this lack of interest in seeking fundamental change was a product of illiberal pragmatics in that there appears to be a resentment of the fact that even if they had wanted to protest, things simply wouldn't change. Like Lakshmi and Shaffiq many of the LGBT Singaporeans with whom I interacted were satisfied with their lives and as such were hesitant to seek more rights than had been allotted them; they were not necessarily interested in fighting for approval from the state. However, an equal number of LGBT Singaporeans were prepared to claim acknowledgment from the government and the rights that come with such recognition.

Towards the end of his article dealing with a history of laws regarding homosexual acts in the Asian context, Douglas Sanders discusses the lack of rights in Singapore. To make his point, he presents a list of issues affecting LGBT Singaporeans including:

(1) being charged with a crime for having sex, (2) getting fired from your job, (3) being denied benefits available to heterosexual couples (pensions, health insurance, rent-controlled apartments), (4) equal rights in relation to children (custody, access, adoption, fertility treatment), (5) equal rights in immigration law to sponsor a partner, (6) social recognition and support (registered partnership or marriage), (7) open inclusion in public institutions (teachers, professors, the judiciary, the cabinet, human rights commissions). (Sanders 2009)

While Sanders's list was, by all accounts, accurate, he failed to take into consideration that apart from a very few Western states no nation on earth, especially within Asia, granted all these rights. Many of my respondents spoke about issues from the above list; from the perspective of international human rights, these are rights that should be available to all persons, regardless of sexual orientation or geographic location. But what struck me was that many activists and laypeople with whom I spoke, exposed to international discourses of rights on the Internet, were not satisfied with acceptance from family and employer or limited recognition from the state. They felt that the only suitable course of action was to push for immediate and full inclusion. In interview after interview, respondents told me that the only place to start would be with the decriminalization of gay sex via the repeal of Section 377A.

Who Can Speak?

In June 2006, Chris Tan, a Singaporean PhD student who was also re-searching the LGBT communities of Singapore, sent me an email requesting that I participate in an academic panel, Signs of Our Times, as part of that August's IndigNation celebration. Organizers had proposed that Tan would speak on the gay geography of Singapore's Chinatown and I would present previous research findings on emerging gay communities in urban Hyderabad and Mumbai, India. I readily agreed and was looking forward to sharing my findings with a receptive and engaging audience. A few days later, I received an email from one of the organizers of IndigNation. While he was enthusiastic about my participation on the panel, he was concerned that as a foreigner, there were certain rules and regulations that would govern my appearance. In fact, Singapore has a very strict code in this regard.[3] For me, as a foreigner, to speak at a public forum was no easy task, as evidenced by the following scenarios proposed by the organizer in his email:

1. We apply for the speaking permit, and it is approved. Everything will be fine then.
2. We apply for the speaking permit, and it is not approved. It will have no effect on IndigNation – but on you – I don't know, a bit of a wild card.
3. We don't apply for a speaking permit, someone reads your paper for you, and you participate in the Q&A (Plan B). There is a small risk that the authorities may then make a fuss about us deliberately "circumventing" the rules. Small risk, but a risk that cannot be eliminated. IndigNation organisers have no fear, we are used to riding out such storms in teacups, and anyway we will point to the rules and say it's perfectly legit. We in fact won't be circumventing any rules. But you as a newbie to Singapore may be stressed out by things. I don't think there'll be any further consequences on you though, because as I said, it's within the rules.
4. We don't apply for a speaking permit, someone reads your paper for you, and you participate in the Q&A. Nobody notices or cares. (Personal correspondence 18 July 2006)

Because I was just beginning my research and staying in Singapore on a visitor's pass that could be revoked at any time and for any reason, I did not want to have any more involvement with the Immigration and Checkpoints Authority than was necessary. We ultimately settled on Plan B, in which I sat in the audience while a friend read my paper. At the end of the reading, I joined the other panellists at the front of the room and participated in the question and answer. No mention was made by the panel discussant as to why I did not read my own paper, but one person did ask me afterwards if I had a cold or a sore throat that necessitated someone else presenting my work. When I explained the situation, he just laughed and said, "Welcome to Singapore, sweetie!" The evening proceeded without incident; however, as I was sitting in the front of the room during the question and answer, one of the other panellists called my attention to a man and woman sitting in the back of the room who looked rather out of place – as if they were *trying* to look like they belonged at an LGBT event. I was later told that they were likely undercover police officers sent to keep an eye on the evening's proceedings – illustrating once again illiberal pragmatics in practice.

I use this anecdote to introduce questions surrounding foreign influence on Singapore's affairs. While we could skirt the rules in my case, during the 2007 IndigNation things did not work out so well. Douglas Sanders, a retired law professor from the University of British Columbia, then living and working in Thailand, was scheduled to give a talk titled "Sexual Orientation in International Law: The Case of Asia." He had also been invited to give a similar talk at Singapore's Institute for Southeast Asian Studies (ISEAS). While he had been granted a professional visit pass for the IndigNation talk, controversy among staff at ISEAS over his proposed topic prompted the Immigration and Checkpoints Authority to cancel his pass. I had registered online for the talk at ISEAS, and a few days before the event I received an email stating that Professor Sanders's talk had been cancelled; no reason for the cancellation was given.[4] The Reverend Troy Perry, an American, was also denied a pass to give his IndigNation talk that was sponsored by the Singaporean LGBT Christian group Safehaven. He chose to enter Singapore on a visitor's pass, and he did attend the event. Yet, as I did the previous year, he sat in the audience while members of the group took turns reading excerpts from one of his books. It was only after the readings were completed that he took the stage and participated in the question and answer session.

Singaporean authorities were quite content to reserve public comment on issues surrounding governmental policy for Singaporeans. Regarding the situation with Doug Sanders and the Reverend Troy Perry,

Senior Minister of State for Law and Home Affairs Associate Professor Ho Peng Kee stated:

> The context is important. It's not that foreigners cannot make their comments or views known on Singapore policies. No, in fact they all do! But it's quite different if local activists, in the context of a situation in Singapore where we know that there's an ongoing debate for some time already on a topic which is divisive, a topic which has caused two sides in particular to expound different points of views, whether we want to invite a foreigner to come here to speak to a Singapore audience. And from what we know, Professor Sanders is a known activist for the human rights of gays and lesbians. We can hear his views or read it online. But it's quite different to invite him here to speak to a Singapore audience at this time. (Channel NewsAsia 2007)

It is worth mentioning that during the 2006 IMF gathering in Singapore, the *Straits Times* reported that the authorities would "[stand] by their decision to deny entry to foreign activists deemed 'undesirable' for the upcoming International Monetary Fund (IMF) and World Bank meetings" (Straits Times 2006b). It was somehow acceptable, then, for outsiders to comment on Singaporean society in print or online, but once that discourse took place on Singaporean soil, things changed.

On 22 October 2007, the International Gay and Lesbian Human Rights Campaign (IGLHRC) sent a letter to Prime Minister Lee urging the repeal of Section 377A. This letter serves as an interesting example of how international rights organizations attempted to influence local policy decisions. In contrast to the interventions discussed in the next section, which, for the most part, privileged the local, the methods of organizations such as IGLHRC were clearly global in scale. In the letter IGLHRC outlined four distinct points that it wished Prime Minister Lee to consider. Among these points were such issues as privacy, equality of all citizens before the law, free speech, and global trends. Yet, none of these concepts held much influence in the context of Singapore civil society. Take for example the suggestion from IGLHRC that "only by repealing both Art. 377[5] and Art. 377A will Singapore comply with the principle that all citizens should be equal before the law, as stipulated in both national and international law ... only the repeal of both articles will uphold the right of individuals to a private life" (IGLHRC 2007a). During the debates of 2007, Member of Parliament Siew Kum Hong echoed this idea when he argued, "The amendment of Section 377 without also repealing Section 377A is therefore unconstitutional under Article 12(1) of the Constitution, which provides that 'All persons are equal under the law and entitled to the equal protection of the law'" (Siew 2007). This was clearly in agreement with the letter from IGLHRC. Yet, Member of Parliament Indranee Rajah countered the idea that "all citizens be equal before the law" in her speech before Parliament. She claimed that homosexuals were treated equally under the law: "We don't look at your sexual orientation in determining whether you should be prosecuted or you should be charged" (Rajah 2007). In other words, if someone is charged with theft, the government will not say "We will prosecute you if you are homosexual but will not if you are heterosexual." What she was getting at here was that there are only certain instances in which persons should be treated equally under the law. She used the example of a person who is under the age of consent who engages in sexual intercourse with an adult. While the minor may claim "consent," Singaporean law required that in this instance, minors should not be treated equally under the law because "they are a special interest group and have to be treated differently and they require certain protections." "Homosexuals," according to Rajah, are not a special interest group and therefore do not require protection under the law.

IGLHRC claimed that by maintaining Section 377A, "free expression and speech are curtailed, as those who wish to engage in same sex relationships as well as those who wish to support them fear public discussion" (IGLHRC 2007a). This is certainly true, especially from the standpoint of public health. If persons who engage in same-sex relationships cannot honestly and openly discuss and obtain information relating to their sexual health, complications can arise. Regardless, there is no guarantee of free expression in Singapore. There are several laws that restrict freedom of speech currently in place; they are intended to prohibit speech that could potentially cause disharmony within Singapore's multireligious, multiracial society. As such, any speech critical of race or religion is strictly prohibited. This is not limited to the physical world. There have been several high-profile cases in which bloggers have been charged with sedition for posting inflammatory remarks on their sites, including a 16-year-old boy who was charged in March 2015 and subsequently convicted of "wounding religious feelings" and of obscenity for postings related to Minister Mentor Lee (CNN.com 2015). In such an environment, I suggest that any argument regarding free speech likely fell on deaf ears.

Lastly, the letter suggested that "maintaining Section 377A puts Singapore at odds with global trends in the last decade to protect people from discrimination" (IGLHRC 2007a). They cited examples of decriminalization from within the region – Hong Kong, China, Japan, South Korea, and Taiwan – as well as internationally – South Africa,

Sweden, Ecuador, and the United States. Many local politicians resisted the global framing of rights by claiming that such interpretations of LGBT rights were a Western import not suited to Singaporean society. By framing rights in this manner, leaders were rejecting the idea of the universality of rights and shifting the focus to that of the relative or local. Yet, the "local" can be highly problematic in the case of Singapore, especially when it is juxtaposed with other terms such as "global." Singapore's spatial and historical construction lies at the very heart of a nexus in which the global and local converge. Geographically and spatially, Singapore is at once a city and a state. Its historical formation has been highly influenced by transnational late-capitalist flows of ideas, commodities, and peoples. The "local," in the case of Singapore, is in many respects inseparable from the "global."

IndigNation

On 4 August 2005, I attended the first ContraDiction prose and poetry reading at Utterly Art, a small gallery located above a Chinese medical shop on South Bridge Road in the Chinatown section of the city. ContraDiction was the first event of many that took place that August at IndigNation, Singapore's newly created pride month. The Contra-Diction reading that night, as well as the event of the subsequent year, which took place at the upscale gay bar and lounge Mox, took on a decidedly grassroots feel. Organized by poet Dominic Chua and writer Ng Yi-Sheng, the events of 2005 and 2006 featured local LGBT writers reading their work; in between, young musicians took to the stage with guitars and showcased their talents. In 2005, audience members began the evening by perusing local artist Martin Loh's *Cerita Budak-Budak*, an exhibit of Peranakan[6] paintings recently commissioned to illustrate a children's book. At a little before 8 p.m., people began to fill the folding plastic chairs neatly arranged in semicircular rows framing the small stage at the front of the gallery space; because of the large number in attendance, those who could not find chairs sat on the floor below the single microphone stand. Just prior to the reading, bottles of wine, plastic cups, and plates of cheese and crackers were passed from one person to the next creating a sense of camaraderie among those of us in attendance. In 2006, audience members at Mox sipped on wine and cocktails while reclining on comfortable, overstuffed furniture and large daybeds arranged in the dimly lit attic space on the third floor of a pre-war shop house. In both instances, writers took the stage and read their work, much to the enjoyment of the audience.

It is too simplistic to claim that the events of 2005 and 2006 were only about prose, poetry, music, and community for, in fact, IndigNation, of which ContraDiction was the inaugural event, was organized in response to the banning of the annual gay Nation Party earlier in 2005. When asked about the origins of the events, Alex Au, well-known LGBT activist and blogger and one of the organizers of the first IndigNation, replied, "the gay community is indignant and extremely unhappy. All the talk about society opening up is just empty words" (Au 2005). When asked what he was hoping to achieve with the first ContraDiction, organizer Dominic Chua responded, "Gay and lesbian people need to begin to see themselves and their lives reflected in words, and to begin to shed some of the homophobia that they pick up and internalize from the culture around them." The first ContraDiction event was simply subtitled "A Night with Gay Poets," whereas the second was dubbed "Queer Words Spoken in IndigNation," indicating a change in tone. The works, given a rating of RA-18 (restricting the audience to those over the age of eighteen) by the Media Development Authority (MDA), spanned a variety of topics including erotic trysts, the myriad difficulties involved in having same-sex relationships, circumcision, and the sex lives of Filipina maids. The ContraDiction events of 2005 and 2006 were certainly political in nature; the very fact that these events had been staged suggests a claim on public space. Yet, at the same time, their implementation was very respectful and restrained.

In 2007, however, the mood at the third annual ContraDiction was different. It was held at 72–13, a new arts venue located in a converted rice warehouse on the banks of the Singapore River. Instead of the intimate venues of years past, the 2007 reading took place in a vast gallery space, accommodating a much larger crowd; long rows of plastic chairs filled the cavernous gallery, which was illuminated by glaring incandescent lights. Rather than a relaxed feel, this year's event took on a decidedly edgy and overtly political tone. At the beginning of the evening, writer Ng Yi-Sheng, wearing only a pair of shorts and draped in a rainbow flag, a universal symbol of LGBT pride, went to the front of the room and announced that yet another in this year's lineup of IndigNation events had been cancelled due to the inability of organizers to obtain the required permits from authorities. He then had the audience count with him the number of events that had been banned that year. "One ... the film *My Brother Nikhil* ... they counted, two ... the talk by Doug Sanders ... three ... the talk by the Reverend Troy Perry." The events were counted, and the crowd chanted along until they had reached the end of the list that numbered ten in total.[7] Next, Alex Au took the stage to show slides of five sets of photographs whose public exhibition had not been approved by the MDA. The images, part of a larger exhibition entitled *Kissing*, was deemed inappropriate by authorities because it promoted "a homosexual lifestyle."

Indeed, many of the events that were part of the 2007 IndigNation were cancelled due to the withholding of permits by the Police Entertainment Licensing Unit or the MDA. Some were refused permits because the governmental entities felt that they were "against public interest," while others because organizers had not filed the necessary paperwork or made proper safety arrangements. LGBT rights activists had a field day with these cancellations, charging censorship and discrimination, creating a buzz within the Singaporean press, both online and off, and generating dozens of reports and interviews in international media outlets. Yet, it was not just governmental regulators who took exception to the IndigNation events of 2007. Many within the LGBT communities in Singapore felt that the organizers of this year's events had gone too far; rather than sticking with the original intent of IndigNation, that of celebrating and embracing diversity, of showcasing to the rest of Singaporean society the "other side" of LGBT life, they had turned, in the words of one interlocutor, "aggressively political." Many of my acquaintances, who had actively participated in previous celebrations, would have nothing to do with the events of 2007. One young Indian Singaporean woman with a history of involvement with the community said of IndigNation:

> It's giving us some visibility but I'm not sure if fighting is the way to go ... I made a conscious decision to not be a part of it because I feel we don't need the cancellation of a party [meaning the 2005 Nation Party] to be proud of who we are. I think if you want to do pride it should not be prompted by something negative; there should be a positive reason. So, for me it is a radical step to not be part of IndigNation.

For many LGBT Singaporeans, like the woman quoted above, situating LGBT subjectivity as an imagined dividing line where cultural and social mores were created and positioned in terms of difference was not an effective manner in which to conduct activism. They were simply not comfortable with this confrontational "us versus them" framework within which IndigNation was being enacted.

Alex Au's *Kissing* exhibit was not given approval by the MDA because it promoted "a homosexual lifestyle" (Yawning Bread 2007b). Lakshmi later suggested that "Alex never actually thought that it would be approved. He simply wanted to be able to say that his photo exhibit was 'banned by the MDA,'" further strengthening his arguments for LGBT rights in Singapore, especially within the international arena. Before ContraDiction began, Au showed five sets of photographs. Some of the photographs were as innocuous as two fully clothed women or men kissing in a loving embrace. Yet, two photographs, had they been allowed public exhibition, could have sent a different type of message to the larger population. In the first, an older overweight Caucasian male is kissing a very young Chinese man. In the accompanying photo, the same older man is kissing a different young Chinese man while the first man watches from behind a curtain. I do not have direct knowledge of the artistic motivation behind such photographs. Yet, one of my informants, the head of a prominent gay website noted that "if you are trying to convince Singaporeans that gays are just like everyone else ... exhibiting such sensational photographs as representative of the community seems counterproductive." He suggested that by reinforcing the stereotype of older foreign Caucasians entering the nation to seduce young Singaporean men, Au could have been perceived as simply perpetuating myths, especially those dealing with the idea that one can be "converted" or "recruited" into being homosexual. Another respondent proposed that these photographs could also have been seen as illustrating Minister Sadasivan's claims regarding foreign men entering Singapore and "seeding the infection of HIV."

Activists also made much of the fact that a "fictional, metatexutal farce" penned by writer Ng Yi-Sheng, titled *Lee Low Tar*, was not given approval as part of an evening of prose readings entitled *Tall Tales and Short Stories*. The story was cleverly written as a letter from the MAD, the Media Authority for Development (a play on the MDA) rejecting Ng's application to read a fictional story. It provided a scathing critique of the "old men" running the country and drew attention to the hypocrisy contained within Singaporean sexual, social, and political policies. The fictional story, outlined in the letter, told the tale of a young man and his sexual exploits. First, as a child, the main character seduces a wheelchair-bound nursing home patient and proceeds to have sex with him in a handicapped toilet stall. As a young man, he has relations with his commanding officer in the army, and finally as an adult, he has a sexual tryst with "the founder of the country." The MDA sent Jean Chong, one of the organizers of IndigNation, a very short letter stating that, "Your application for a story reading session, entitled *Tall Tales and Short Stories*, has been approved on condition that the reading of *Lee Low Tar* is taken out." The email continued, "The content of *Lee Low Tar* has been disallowed as it had gone beyond good taste and decency in taking a disparaging and disrespectful view of public officers"

(Ng 2007). Because this one piece had not been approved, organizers decided to cancel the event outright in protest. The MDA was concerned that the piece in question was not suitable for public presentation. Many of my respondents were disturbed at how activists such as Au and Ng were framing issues of rights. Were they claiming that being able to publicly exhibit controversial materials was somehow a step towards full societal inclusion of LGBT Singaporeans? I suggest that the photo exhibit and proposed performance were but two examples of how activists were attempting to push the limits of acceptable public discussion.

Pushing Back: Localizing Transnational Discourse

One such organization that was localizing the transnational was the Pelangi Pride Centre (PPC), a community organization that was founded to "promote positive self-esteem of sexual minorities and in turn, promote sexual health to fight the spread of STI (Sexually Transmitted Infections), especially HIV infection, which causes AIDS" (Pelangi Pride Centre 2008). During my time in Singapore, many of the public events staged by PPC dealt with issues of "coming out," the importance of familial support for LGBT youth, and spirituality. What stood out most was that the organizers at PPC tended to stage events that worked within the current system. I observed that the way in which rights were framed, while not as confrontational as those of IndigNation 2007, was more successful in the Singaporean context in that they sought to slowly acclimate the general population to notions of LGBT equality. Eileena Lee, one of the founding members of PPC, commented on how this organization approached rights:

> How you go about organizing is crucial. When you organize things that you know are going be banned that's taking an antagonistic approach. Part of the process of IndigNation is to test the waters with the government. Pelangi Pride Centre has different goals ... A few years ago we organized a coming out event with a local NGO. Someone asked what is this about and we said it's about a mother's love for her child. So, our approach is not to be antagonistic or on the offensive. (IGLHRC 2007b)

She continued by describing the events held at Pelangi Pride Centre:

> We run monthly events about coming out. We expose gay people to positive information about themselves. We also have events for straight people to come to, so they can understand LGBTQ issues and we put our

information in libraries. We run activities for parents of gay people. We talk about ourselves as Singaporeans who are part of a family unit.

When reading through these statements I was reminded of interviews that I conducted with several Chinese-acculturated lesbian Singaporeans who were practising Buddhists. Unlike so many of their counterparts who were aggressively advocating for rights, this group of women were convinced that a gradual, family-centred, non-violent path was the only way for LGBT Singaporeans to obtain full social and legal recognition. Many of these women were directly involved with PPC, and their influence in the planning and presentation of events was evident.

Between April and August of 2007, I attended numerous events sponsored by Pelangi Pride Centre. We Are Family: Conversations with Family and Friends featured parents of LGBT youth telling their stories. A father sat with his teenaged daughter and told the crowd about the difficulties and joys of having a lesbian child. One mother, who spoke only Hokkien, used a translator to tell a moving story of shame, anger, and eventual acceptance regarding her lesbian daughter.[8] Two events were centred on religion: Love, Sex, and Happiness – A Buddhist Perspective, and A Gay Perspective on Being Christian. During these events a Buddhist nun and a Methodist minister, respectively, spoke of the spiritual responsibilities that come with being LGBT. A gay medical doctor who specializes in sports medicine led a seminar entitled GLBTQ Fitness and Injury Prevention. The Centre also hosted the première of the lesbian documentary Women Who Love Women: Conversations in Singapore. These events were advertised and presented in such a way that they attracted large crowds and fostered dialogue among attendees. Rather than focusing on an overt agenda of gaining rights, they instead called for understanding and patience. All the events, except for the sports medicine seminar, centred on ideas of family and on a subtle and gradual approach to LGBT rights that began with self-honesty and a "coming-out" process that placed great importance on the family. Also of interest here is the way in which organizers aided that coming-out process. While organizers saw the Internet as a great tool for bringing people together, it was also recognized that it could serve as a "closet" (see Gorkemli 2012). Eileena Lee stated:

Each time we send out invitations for PPC events we ask for people to give us their full name and their telephone numbers. I think that people are still really scared to do that and so we feel that that is important just sending the email with their name and telephone number is just like that first step to coming out, something simple because we saw the fear, people would try "oh can I just give my first name" and we always insist on both names and the email handle because how do you encourage people to have honest and meaningful friendships when you don't even use your name[?]

Again, notice that PPC is using a gentle, non-confrontational approach, even when insisting that people use their full names when registering for events. This resonates strongly with the culturally sensitive *tongzhi* approach to sexuality outlined in chapter 1. In a 2007 interview with the International Gay and Lesbian Human Rights Commission (IGLHRC), Lee commented on her approach to LGBT rights:

> In the same week of the banned activities [referring to IndigNation] we organized a talk by Rev. Oyoung WenFang [the first openly gay Malaysian Chinese pastor ordained by Metropolitan Community Church]. Over 80 people attended and the event wasn't banned. We reached out to our own communities and we publicized it in the mainstream press. The point of the publicity was about the book he wrote. (IGLHRC 2007b)

In addition to gently exposing their fellow citizens to LGBT Singaporeans, PPC addressed issues relating to class. During an interview, Audrey, a young Chinese bartender who had never attended an IndigNation event, asked, "What is IndigNation doing to educate the heartlanders? Everything IndigNation is doing is very highbrow and none of the heartlanders are aware of what is going on." Audrey was referring to the fact that most of the participants at IndigNation were individuals who fit a conventional CMEL (Chinese, middle-class, English-educated/speaking, liberal) profile. The term heartlanders was popularized in 1999 by then–prime minister Goh Chok Tong when he used it to characterize much of Singapore's population, a demographic who are generally less educated, members of the working class, inhabitants of government-controlled Housing Development Board estates, and distinctly local in their perspective on most issues. In many respects, it is a term that stands in direct opposition to ideas of the "cosmopolitan" and represents a large proportion of the population. Singapore's government consistently uses the image of heartlanders as uneducated and traditional when arguing against change. In terms of the debate over LGBT rights, many religious leaders claimed that "the heartlanders can't handle it" as if they were somehow out of touch with the world around them. Yet, I think that Audrey had a point.

There was a very real disconnect between those claiming rights for the LGBT communities of Singapore and those they were claiming rights *for*. A large majority of those directly involved with the movement were rather affluent, foreign-educated Singaporeans who lived for long periods of time outside of their nation. They were bringing back with them Western notions of what it meant to be LGBT, which often made little sense within the Singaporean context, especially to those who come from heartland backgrounds. These cosmopolitan activists, in many cases, had nothing to lose. One well-known activist had recently graduated from an Ivy League university in the United States and another came from a family that owns several successful businesses in Singapore and abroad. Others attended university in Australia or the United Kingdom, where they had been active participants in local LGBT rights organizations.

The events staged by PPC were more sensitive to the needs of non-cosmopolitan Singaporeans through a recognition and privileging of the local. Many of the events featured IndigNation revolved around foreign speakers, which were not of great interest to many heartlanders with whom I spoke. Some events at IndigNation were aimed specifically at those whose main language was Mandarin, specifically "sing-alongs" in both English and Mandarin in 2006 and 2007. However, most events nonetheless excluded those who were not comfortable communicating in English. This included not only those who were Chinese-acculturated but Indian- and Malay-acculturated LGBT Singaporeans. On the issue of language, a Chinese-acculturated artist noted that Chinese-speaking Singaporeans

> partly because of language cannot integrate as easily, but partly because they are more in tune with how things work, they are more apt to compromise and find the middle way. I think that Chinese-acculturated Singaporeans even if they are English speaking may have an entirely different way of negotiating their space and their lives and a very different way of seeing their future.

Western Discourses

In 1993, Wong Kan Seng, Minister of Foreign Affairs for the Republic of Singapore attended the UN World Conference on Human Rights in Vienna. In his statement to the conference, he noted that most rights were still a contested notion:

> There may be a general consensus. But this is coupled with continuing and, at least for the present, no less important conflicts of interpretation. Singaporeans, and people in many other parts of the world do not agree, for instance, that pornography is an acceptable manifestation of free

expression or that homosexual relationships are just a matter of lifestyle choice. Most of us will also maintain that the right to marry is confined to those of the opposite sex. (Wong 1995)

Fourteen years later, in September 2007, MP Sin Boon Ann, head of the Government Parliamentary Committee for Community Development, Youth and Sports spoke to the *Straits Times* regarding granting more rights to homosexuals: "We are a conservative society and will not be trailblazers in this regard." He added that Singapore's public stand on the issue was a "statement of values" rather than a "statement of rights and obligations" (Straits Times 2007d). These statements both serve as further examples of the localization of the transnational. If Singaporean authorities insisted on a local interpretation of rights, the question then became, "how are they framing the discussion?" I suggest that considering Singapore's history as a nation that embraces all things technological, much of the debate regarding LGBT rights was framed within the matrix of "science." Science as an analytic also meshes well with the nation's historical reliance on ideas of pragmatism, grounded in what the government would term "objectivity." At the same time, framing the discussion exclusively in terms of science left little room for discourses of human rights. In April 2007, Minister Mentor Lee Kuan Yew commented on homosexuality at a forum sponsored by the Young PAP:

> You take this business of homosexuality. It raises tempers all over the world and even in America! If in fact it is true – and I've asked doctors this – that you are genetically born a homosexual, because that's the nature of the genetic random transmission of genes, you can't help it. So why should we criminalise it? But there's such a strong inhibition in all societies – Christianity, Islam, Hindu, Chinese societies and we are now confronted with a persisting aberration. But is it an aberration? *It is a genetic variation*. So, what do we do? I think we pragmatically adjust. (PLURAL 2007; my emphasis)

This statement set off a deluge of letters to the editor and generated thousands of postings to online forums; the debate raged for months. I suggest that by shifting questions of sexual orientation from the realm of free choice (as suggested above by Minister Wong) to those of science (a genetic mutation), Lee Kuan Yew was, in a somewhat backwards manner, trying to argue for a greater socio-legal leniency towards LGBT people.

Yet, while much of Singaporean society welcomes the benefits of science, there was great debate as to whether homosexuality was caused by a genetic variation or was simply a "lifestyle choice," one made as the result of one's upbringing and immediate environment. Many conservative writers in Singapore, including prominent academics, argued that in the case of homosexuality, science could not be the answer, that surely there was agency involved in "deciding" one's sexual orientation. Thio Li-ann, a vocal opponent of LGBT rights and a professor of law at National University of Singapore, argued that "while difficult, change is possible and a compassionate society would help those wanting to fulfil their heterosexual potential. There is hope" (Thio 2007).

Janet Halley elucidated in detail arguments involving both sides of the broader issue, which she termed "essentialism" and "constructivism" (Halley 1994, 506). She outlined why she believed that, considering what were then recent discoveries regarding a potential genetic link that predisposed some people to homosexuality, it was a mistake for activists to lean too heavily on these findings and that "pro-gay legal arguments should not focus on positive claims of biological causation, or on pure constructivist claims that homosexuality is a historically contingent artefact, but should repair to a common middle ground." Halley included in her article the now-infamous study by Simon LeVay (1991) in which he found that certain portions of the anterior hypothalamus were larger in heterosexual males than in homosexual males. This study generated much press and breathed new life into efforts by activists in the West to gain LGBT rights. If they could claim that there was a biological basis for their behaviour, then surely lawmakers would put them in the same category as racial minorities and grant them equal protections. It is nonetheless problematic in that LeVay was conflating homosexual *conduct* and homosexual *identity*. Halley also noted that LeVay failed to take into consideration those who identify as bisexual. But even if we include bisexuality within LeVay's dichotomous framework of homosexuality/heterosexuality, where do others fit in? There exists an entire spectrum of sexualities that do not fit into this neatly delineated scale. I interviewed several married men who had sex with other men on a regular basis, yet not one of them self-identified as "gay" or even "bisexual." They were simply heterosexual men who enjoyed sexual contact with other men. What about those whom one interlocutor referred to as "inactive" gays – those who, for whatever reason, had never had a sexual encounter with another man yet still considered themselves "gay"? It is interesting in this respect to think about how gay men are defined within Singaporean society by the crimes they are purported to commit. A large portion of the argument put forth by activists in Singapore regarding Section 377A revolved around the idea that by criminalizing homosexual sex, you are criminalizing gay men; or as Halley put it, "because the characteristic that differentiates them, and that constitutes the basis for discrimination against them, is immutable"

(Halley 1994, 504). But how can one be discriminated against if one does not engage in the illegal behaviour? And what about the many, especially those who identify as "queer," who reject the idea of a stable, fixed identity? Lastly, what about the Internet "gay-for-pay" phenomenon involving self-identified heterosexual men who have sex on camera with other self-identified heterosexual men in exchange for monetary compensation (Escoffier 2003; Ward 2015)? You are left with men who are sexually active with other men who do not self-identify as "gay" and self-identified "gay" men who have never had sex with another man. Clearly, conduct and identity are not equivalent. So, is the question of the transmission of a gene even relevant? Perhaps it is. But so is the environmental question – especially in the Singaporean atmosphere in which the ever-quickening pace of everyday life is complicated by, among other factors, the Internet and frequent transnational encounters.

I should note here that in the Singaporean context, there are certain traits that are considered inborn and therefore protected by law. These include race and religion. In many of the debates that took place in the face of the 2007 parliamentary debates over 377A, Singaporeans opposed to the repeal of the law pointed out that unlike race or religion – characteristics that "one cannot change" – sexual orientation is a "lifestyle choice" and therefore not afforded the same protections. Time and again, people posted comments on forums echoing the words of Thio Li-ann during her speech before Parliament in which she asserted that "race is a fixed trait. It remains controversial whether homosexual orientation is genetic or environmental, perhaps both. There are no ex-Blacks but there are ex-gays" (Thio 2007). Because such traits as race and religion are seen my many as being inborn, they are intrinsically tied to ideas of blood, and blood is what ties one to the nation; sexual orientation is relegated to a "choice."

Talking Cock

On 8 November 2007, the website TalkingCock published a humorous letter (TalkingCock.com 2007) titled, *Dear Ah Beng: Gay People Keep Wanting to Hantam Me. How?* The original letter, written in Singlish,[9] is reproduced below. Following that is my translation.

Dear Ah Beng,
I made a speech recently calling chao ah quahs and pondans abnormal, and saying that if they have sex, they should be convicted as criminals. Now they're sending me nasty emails and letters threatening to hantam me. How?
(Ms) Thio Hoot Leow

Dear Hoot Leow,

Aiyah, you go and say people for what? Ha?

I know theoretically, cannot go and hantam people just for what they say, lah, even if what they say is si beh stupid.

But this is Singapore, mah!

Stare at people oreddy consider kiam pak, you lagi go and say people, confirm tio hoot liao!

And dun think ah quah are all soft-soft, lembek-lembek type, can only give you girly slap, that kind.

I heard from someone (donno who) that they can do really hiong things to you – like stuffing a straw up your nose and making you drink from it!

Even worse, they can call their macho friends. You think they got no macho friends, ah? Eh, why you think Changi Village there got so many ladyboys? Because Hendon Camp is nearby and got a lot of demand straight from the commandos there! (OK, maybe "straight" is not the best word.) If you think ah quah mm si lang, commando lagi mm si lang!

So how like that? I think you better take cover, and hide from all the ah quahs hunting you.

How to hide? Well, from my esperien, ah quahs really only look out for hamsum men, and stay far, far away from argly women.

I just saw your photo, so I think you're quite safe lah.

Relac,
Ah Beng

Dear Ah Beng,

I made a speech recently calling dirty effeminate men and transvestites abnormal and saying that if they have sex, they should be convicted as criminals. Now they're sending me nasty emails and letters threatening to beat me. How is this possible?

(Ms) Thio Hoot Leow

Dear Hoot Leow,

Why do you say these things about people?

I know theoretically that you cannot go and beat people just for what they say, even if what they say is extremely stupid.

But this is Singapore!

Staring at people is considered grounds for a beating, then you again go and say things, which call for worse than a beating!

And don't think effeminate men are all soft and weak and can only give you a girly slap.

I heard from someone (I don't know who) that they can do really fierce things to you – like stuffing a straw up your nose and making you drink from it!

Even worse, they can call their macho friends. You think they have no macho friends? Why do you think that Changi Village has so many ladyboys? Because Hendon Camp[10] is nearby and got a lot of demand straight from the commandos there! (OK, maybe "straight" is not the best word.) If you think effeminate men are like old ladies, the commandos are even more like old ladies!

How do you like that? I think you better take cover, and hide from all the effeminate men hunting you.

How should you hide? Well, from my experience, effeminate men really only look out for handsome men, and stay far, far away from ugly women.

I just saw your photo, so I think you're quite safe.

Relax,
Ah Beng

This satirical letter, created by the editors of the website TalkingCock, is a good example of how transnational rights issues affecting Singapore's LGBT communities are incorporated into larger discussions of local Singaporean civil society. The letter refers to an incident that occurred in October 2007 in which Nominated Member of Parliament Thio Li-ann gave a speech to Parliament urging them to preserve Section 377A of Singapore's Penal Code. During the speech, titled "Two Tribes Go to (Culture) War," she claimed, among other things, that "anal penetrative sex is inherently damaging to the body and a misuse of organs, like shoving a straw up your nose to drink" (Thio 2007). This phrase, "like shoving a straw up your nose to drink," grabbed attention more than any other part of her speech. It caused a great stir in the Singaporean blogosphere and in the years since, has been used as a jumping-off point by academics writing about Singapore (Lim 2013; Ong 2015; Radics 2015). Singaporean bloggers characterized her speech in interesting ways, ranging from calling her Herr Thio (Choo 2007) to link her with Adolph Hitler to commenting on her unique brand of "Thiology" (George 2007b). Her sensational proclamations prompted outrage among many Singaporeans in that Thio is a professor of law at National University of Singapore. Countless Singaporean bloggers, and many of my interviewees, felt that she used her position as a professor at the National University as a bully pulpit from which to put forth her own conservative religious views under the guise of speaking as an academic. Rather than crafting an argument based on issues of rights or constitutional law (her academic specialty), many respondents pointed out that she based her argument almost entirely on issues of morality and fear of the social consequences of a "homosexual agenda."

The editors of TalkingCock were using the character of "Ah Beng," a common Singlish term that refers to "an unsophisticated Chinese boy, usually Hokkien. Stereotypically, he speaks gutter Hokkien and likes neon-coloured clothes, spiky, moussed hair, and accessories such as handphones or pagers, all of which are conspicuously displayed. He also likes to squat, even when a seat is available."[11] The editors had him speak Singlish in a very loutish and uncouth manner. At the same time, they had Thio Li-ann write her letter in Singlish, thus bringing her down to his level and simultaneously letting the reader know exactly how they felt about her. They changed her name from Thio Li-ann to Thio Hoot Leow, which is a play on the Singlish phrase Tio Hoot Liao, meaning "took a beating." They also incorporated local derogatory terms *ah quah* (Singlish for "faggot") and *pondan* (Malay for transvestite). Finally, the letter poked fun at stereotypes of gay men, especially those that portray all gay men as effeminate; in fact, they are even portrayed as aggressive. Things are turned around when Ah Beng suggests to Thio that gay men may even resort to violence such as "stuffing a straw up (her) nose and making (her) drink from it!" This satirical letter also recontextualized these issues by including them within a larger commentary on such concerns as the importance of public debate, freedom of speech, and the separation of church and state. All the while, the writers of this letter did not let the reader forget that embedded within and around these concerns were larger local issues of race, class, language, and sexual orientation.

Conclusion

On 23 October 2007, towards the end of my fieldwork, Singapore's parliamentary debates regarding proposed changes to the penal code came to an end. The last speech delivered that day was by Prime Minister Lee Hsien Loong regarding Section 377A. The speech was well received by Singaporeans on both sides of the debate. In the speech, Prime Minister Lee outlined point by point why he was in favour of keeping the law in place. He ended the speech by stating, "So I suggest, Mr. Speaker, and I suggest to the members of the House, we keep this balance, leave Section 377A alone. I think that there is space in Singapore and room for us to live harmoniously and practically all as Singapore citizens together" (Lee 2007).

What I find so compelling about this speech is that Prime Minister Lee talked publicly about Singapore's LGBT citizens. Towards the beginning of the speech he reiterated the idea that Singapore is basically a conservative society with the family as the basic building block. He then clarified his statement by adding, "And by family in Singapore we mean one man, one woman marrying, having children and bringing up children within that framework of a stable family unit ... It's not so in other countries, particularly in the West anymore but it is here." He continued, "I acknowledge that not everybody fits into this mould. Some are single, some have more colourful lifestyles, some are gay, but a heterosexual, stable family is a social norm. And I think the clear majority of Singaporeans want to keep it this way, want to keep our society like this." He also situated LGBT Singaporeans within the context of the family:

> They [homosexuals] include people who are responsible, invaluable, highly respected contributing members of society. And I would add that among them are some of our friends, our relatives, our colleagues, our brothers and sisters or some of our children. They too must have a place in this society and they too are entitled to their private lives. We shouldn't make it harder than it already is for them to grow up and to live in a society where they are different from most Singaporeans.

Lastly, he acknowledged the public presence of LGBT Singaporeans within the larger culture:

> De facto gays have a lot of space in Singapore. They hold, gay groups hold public discussions, they publish websites, I've visited some of them. There are films, plays on gay themes. In fact, sometimes people ask "Why are there so many? Aren't there other subjects in the world?" But since we have allowed it the last few years, maybe this is a letting off pressure. Eventually, we will find a better balance ... There are gay bars and clubs. They exist, we know where they are. Everybody knows where they are. They don't have to go underground.

In publicly speaking of a segment of Singaporean society that has for so long been relegated to the margins, Lee, consciously or not, was expanding the scope and scale of acceptable public discourse. In other words, he was pushing the limits of the distinctly Singaporean conceptualization of OB markers.

An OB marker, (Lyons and Gomez 2005) short for "out of bounds marker," is a Singaporean term used to designate those topics that are permitted to be discussed within the public sphere. The term is taken from the sport of golf, yet there is a major difference between how it is used in golf and how it is used in the Singaporean context. In the case of golf, OB markers are clearly defined physical boundaries that enclose the area in which golfers can play. In the case of Singapore, these boundaries are fluid and can change from one moment to the next. Recall the inconsistent and unforeseen changes in government policy that occurred regarding the denial of permits for the SnowBall and Nation parties. This serves as a perfect example of how OB markers shifted, depending on several factors including Singapore's current political climate. In the case of the parties, events that were previously permissible were suddenly banned. This inconsistency works in reverse as well; a long-running blanket ban on mentioning gay rights activists Stuart Koe and Alex Au in the Singaporean press was inexplicably lifted in mid-2007.

According to Tan (2000, 103), OB markers are invoked to "limit political engagement, civic action, and participation, and anything else remotely linked to politics." Traditionally, the government of Singapore has sole discretion regarding the positioning of the boundaries for acceptable public discourse. To expand the boundaries, Singaporeans needed permission of the government. One prominent LGBT rights activist compared this model with others:

> Singapore is a society where things don't happen without permission and the way to get things done is to get permission. You need to find a way to get permission or approval, whereas the Western model is quite the reverse. In spite of disapproval, people say "this is my right," it's that kind of rhetoric, but when you are using that type of rhetoric in a society like Singapore that believes things have to be pre-approved before they happen, it's like banging your head against the wall.

This has certainly been the case. Yet, I argue that Singapore's LGBT communities, through their innovative use of the Internet, have successfully, and without explicit permission, challenged the boundaries put in place by their government and moved from the online to the physical environment of Singapore. Organizations such as Pelangi Pride Centre have utilized a homonormative approach to LGBT rights. As such, they have framed their events in a manner that is non-confrontational and takes into consideration the needs and concerns of the greater society. By not framing their public events within an international LGBT rights nexus they have been able to circumvent and quietly challenge government authority. The story *Lee Low Tar* that was to be presented by Ng Yi-Sheng at IndigNation 2007 serves as another compelling example. The very fact that Ng wrote the story in the form of a response to the rejection of a fictitious story is telling. After reading the story, it should be clear that Ng knew well in advance that his story would not be approved for public presentation, ending his submission with the following note to the MDA:

> Note: The author is aware that there is a high chance this text may not be permitted for public reading during IndigNation, and thus has supplied a backup text (an extract from his university memoir, *Diary of a Stone Monkey*). He nonetheless wishes to make it clear that *Lee Low Tar* was written specifically for this reading, and is his preferred text for the night. MDA will of course be aware that the denial of a license to read this story will generate negative publicity for itself while increasing public interest in the story, allowing for its greater distribution. (Ng 2007)

As it turns out, Ng's prediction was correct. The story was not permitted to be read in public, many within Singapore's civil society and LGBT rights organizations wrote of the denial of the permit, and many more Singaporeans read the story online than could have ever attended the IndigNation reading. The same type of situation occurred with Alex Au's *Kissing* exhibit. Au was not granted permission to publicly display his photographs. But the local and international publicity generated by the actions of the government encouraged a noticeable increase in attendance at other IndigNation events.

Chapter Six

The Illiberal Pragmatics of Activism

In August 2008, Singapore's government took the decision to allow groups to stage public demonstrations at the Speakers' Corner within Hong Lim Park without having to obtain a police permit. The only prerequisite was that the events had to be organized by Singaporean citizens and that participants be citizens or legal permanent residents.

The Speakers' Corner originated in 2000 in response to critics' claims of government censorship and was created as a space in which *individuals* could publicly articulate their opinions. It was used often when it first opened; in 2000, over four hundred people signed up to speak but this number dwindled to twenty-six in 2005 – a decrease that can be attributed to the availability of the Internet as a means of expressing opinion and dissent. Yet, with the decision to allow groups to hold demonstrations, and the absence of the requirement to obtain a permit from the police department, interest in using the Corner increased noticeably (Channel NewsAsia 2008). Beginning on 1 September 2008, groups could meet and protest if they had pre-registered with the National Parks Board, the organization designated to take over management of the Speakers' Corner from the Singapore Police Department. In one of the first events staged at the Speakers' Corner, in October 2008, over five hundred people gathered to protest the mishandling of their financial accounts by Lehman Brothers. The space has been widely used since.

On 18 October 2008, concerned members of Singapore's LGBT communities began organizing their first official public pride celebration at local night spot DYMK (Does Your Mother Know). There was much debate, both online and off, regarding just how to go about presenting a positive face of Singapore's LGBT communities to a public that, by and large, still misunderstood them. Initially, some participants had suggested a Western-style LGBT pride celebration complete with the formulaic elements – disco music, drag queens, rainbow banners, and speeches calling for the granting of rights. Eventually, others within the community questioned this tactic. They felt that it would give the suggestion that the celebration was based clearly on "Western" notions of what it meant to be LGBT rather than one that was situated in the local. As such, organizers found a different tactic. On 16 May 2009, over two thousand LGBT Singaporeans along with their family members and supporters publicly gathered to celebrate their nation's diversity at an event dubbed Pink Dot[1] (see Chua 2012, 2014; Oswin 2014; Tan 2015b). Rather than staging the event as a protest, the organizers framed it as one that promoted the freedom of all Singaporeans, including LGBT Singaporeans, to choose whom to love – reminiscent of the successful deployment of "love" in *SQ21* discussed in chapter 2. The website promoting the event made sure that participants understood:

> It is NOT a protest [emphasis in the original] – absolutely not. It is a congregation of people who believe that everyone deserves a right to love, regardless of their sexual orientation. Fear and bigotry can get in the way of love – between friends, family and other loved ones – so this is an event for everyone who believes that LGBT individuals are equally deserving of strong relationships with our family and friends. (pinkdot.sg 2019a)

Events such as Pink Dot represented a shift in that LGBT, rather than simply gay and lesbian, subjectivities were being represented. That is not to say that events such as IndigNation or websites such as SiGNeL were never concerned with sexual minorities beyond gay men and lesbians – they certainly were. But the emphasis was on specific minority subjectivities. By opening the umbrella, Pink Dot became that much more inclusive and by extension, more mainstream. In addition to advertising the event on the group's website, a YouTube channel was established so that videos of the event could be shared (https://www.youtube.com/user/pinkdotsg) and a Facebook page was created, where users were encouraged to pledge their attendance (https://www.facebook.com/pinkdotsg/). The online advertising that relied on the Internet combined with the physical space of the Speakers' Corner brought forth Pink Dot, which demonstrates the interplay of the online and the physical. The event culminated with the formation of a dot composed of participants clad in pink clothing. Photographs were then taken and shared extensively over social media. The event was covered internationally but received minimal coverage from Singapore's government-controlled media (BBC.com 2009; US State Department 2010).

Figure 7. Inaugural Pink Dot, 2009
Source: Pink Dot SG. Used with permission.

In May 2010, Pink Dot was staged again and attracted over four thousand participants. Organizers extended the 2009 theme of "Freedom to Love" to "Love within Families" to emphasize the diversity of Singaporean families and the importance of kinship. The 2010 version of the Pink Dot website featured several LGBT Singaporeans and their families in a series of online videos – "Pink Dot 2010: Focusing on our Families" – that told of the initial difficulties faced by parents of LGBT children and their eventual acceptance back into the family unit.[2] These videos accomplished two things; first, they put a human face to LGBTs in Singapore by showing parents and children discussing the process of maintaining the cohesiveness of the family in what is often a difficult situation. I suggest that the very public aspect to these stories speaks to the influence of Western thought and the grand "coming out" narrative in which one publicly declares their sexual orientation. Second, and equally important, the videos utilized language that emphasized "traditional" Singaporean familial relations in which being a son or daughter of one's parents takes precedence over publicly declaring oneself as LGBT – a way of thinking very in line with *tongzhi*. There were four videos in the series,[3] which according to the Pink Dot website, are about "celebrating the bonds of LGBT people and their families" (pinkdot.sg 2019b). These videos serve as an example of the selective appropriation and combination of the Western notion of "coming out" and the *tongzhi* notion of *hui jia* (回家 homeward or return home) in that while the children do publicly acknowledge their sexual identity to family and friends, causing initial difficulties, in the end all the children "return home" to the love and acceptance of their parents, gesturing once again to the significance of illiberal pragmatics.

"Focusing on Our Families" (Part 1)

The first video of the series is titled *When One Door Closes, a Closet Door Opens: A Singaporean Mother's Appeal to Parents of LGBT Sons and Daughters*. It features Eileena Lee, a 38-year-old sports therapist and her 67-year-old mother, Mdm Yiap Geok Khuan. The video begins with Mdm Yiap, dressed in a pink blouse, speaking about her daughter while photographs of mother and child together in the 1970s flash on the screen. Mdm Yiap speaks Mandarin throughout the video and the transcript below is taken from the English subtitles.

MADAME YIAP: My daughter was very pretty when she was a little girl. Her hair was long like a Japanese doll's. My customers adored her. When she was in secondary school, she didn't like wearing skirts. I started to worry. At that time, I had no concept of homosexuality. I just didn't want her to be a "tomboy."

(Eileena appears wearing a pink polo shirt.)

EILEENA: There was a lot of passive-aggressiveness in our relationship. I would know that she is unhappy about me but then she will pick on an incident which is totally not what she is unhappy about, but she will use that to be unhappy about me.

(Mdm Yiap and Eileena appear together on the screen.)

MADAME YIAP: I was prejudiced. All my gestures told her that I didn't care about her, and I was very cold towards her. We stopped communicating and we drifted apart. I didn't know what being gay was about so I thought she could change. I tried reading up, but there was no answer. I started to look at it differently (long, dramatic pause). I must accept it. This was a gift from God. I had to accept it.

(More old pictures of mother and daughter.) (Eileena appears on screen alone and addresses the camera.)

EILEENA: It's a relief that I can finally be authentic. Now she wouldn't expect me to find a man to marry ... she will probably expect me to bring home a girlfriend if eventually I find a life partner.

(Madame Yiap appears on screen alone and addresses the camera.)

MADAME YIAP: As parents, shouldn't we love them even more? We should not (long pause) reject them. We must support them even more so that they can do even more for society.

(The screen reads: Not every LGBT person has the love and understanding of his or her family.)

(Cut to Madame Yiap and Eileena laughing and trying on a pair of pink rabbit ears).

(The screen reads: That's why we have to come together to show them they have our support.)

(The screen reads: Hong Lim Park 15.05.2010 Pink Dot.)

This is the most viewed of the four videos that comprise this series. Part of the reason for this is the sincerity that both Madame Yiap and her daughter Eileena display throughout. The video itself runs for little more than two and a half minutes, yet it contains a great deal of information. It not only tells of the sometimes-difficult relationship between mother and daughter, it also helps to explain how Eileena's sexual orientation is being framed – potentially for the benefit of other parents who are in the same situation as Madame Yiap. Specifically, when Madame Yiap states, "This was a gift from God. I had to accept it." I suggest here that her statement implies that Eileena was "born this way" and that there is no point in trying to change her. It also speaks on some level to the Singaporean discourse surrounding trans individuals, who are seen to have a congenital medical condition that can be "corrected" with pharmaceuticals and surgery. By emphasizing the notion that her child was "born this way" and that it was "a gift from God," Madame Yiap calls attention to the immutability of Eileena's orientation. As such, Madame Yiap is situating it squarely within the prevailing Singaporean world view thereby potentially lessening the sense of conflict that non-normative sexualities often bring to family dynamics.

"Focusing on Our Families" (Part 2)

The second video, titled *From Son to Daughter: A Singaporean Family's Transformation*, features trans woman Jamie Yee, a 36-year-old nurse, and her parents, Mdm Yee Yoke Lan, 58, and Yee Chang Kim, 70. The set-up of this video is quite like the first and begins with the parents, both dressed in pink shirts, against a white background. As they speak, old photos of Jamie and her family flash on the screen. Like Mdm Yiap, Mr Yee speaks Mandarin throughout the video.

MDM YEE: When I gave birth to Jamie, on the very first day that she was out, she had to go for a complete blood change because she had severe jaundice. So, actually, from that time, I already knew that she was a very special baby.

JAMIE: When I was about 5, when I was in kindergarten, I was always gravitating towards the girls' toys, cooking, and dolls, and stuff like that. (Jamie appears alone on the screen, wearing a plaid shirt with pink highlights.)

JAMIE: After National Service is when I actually started my transition. I was working in a restaurant as a girl and I'd saved up some money and I was thinking about going for the surgery but, I remembered that mom actually told me, cause my dad is very conservative, and she was saying, she was warning me not to do anything drastic until after my dad has passed on, so that he doesn't have to deal with it. But it kept going on in my head that it's not fair that I keep wishing that my dad passes on so that I can do what I want to do ... So, I sat down (she is sobbing – "you'd think that after all of these years that it would be easy") I actually sat down with mum and spoke to her and said that I could actually go ahead without letting anybody know but I needed their blessings. (Jamie's parents appear on screen.)

MR YEE: When I heard that Jamie was going for the operation, my heart ached. It still does. I asked myself, "Why did my child turn out like this?" I could not accept it then. I spent some time thinking about it. Since Jamie had decided to undergo the surgery, if I were to stop her, something bad may happen. After considering it carefully, I thought that she should make her own decision. If she wants to undergo the surgery, she should go ahead with it. It was her wish.

MDM YEE: We used Medisave[4] and our savings to help her, to help pay for the operation costs so we decided to let her go ahead and do it in Singapore where we feel that with us around giving her the support, it would be much safer. We would feel better.

MR YEE: As parents, no matter what our child turns out to be, we still need to care for them. We cannot possibly take care of them for life. When we get old or leave this world who will take care of them? We can only hope that they can take care of themselves.

(Jamie and her parents appear on screen smiling and holding a Pink Dot placard.)

JAMIE: Home is supposed to be a safe place where you can go to for warmth and love and I guess that's important because at the end of the day you know that there's somebody that you can go home to who doesn't judge you, who loves you for who you are.

(The screen reads: Pinkdot [sic] celebrates the family. Hong Lim Park 15.05.2010)

As with the previous video, this one relies on the sincerity displayed by the participants to get the message across. The difficulties that Jamie experienced as a woman going through her transition become clear as she is visibly upset and speaking through tears while recounting her story. Further, her mother reiterates the gravity of Jamie's situation when referring to the fact that she and her husband used their retirement savings to help their daughter pay for her surgery. As with Mdm Yiap, the Yees show a deep concern for their daughter's well-being and emphasize the overarching theme of Pink Dot – "Love within Families." The way Jamie's journey is presented informs the viewer that they will be experiencing a story that begins with familial and personal strife and ends with the individual and family healthy, content, and intact.

Both stories relate a "coming-out" narrative that is very familiar to many LGBT individuals, both in Singapore and the West, in which an individual publicly and deliberately declares their sexual orientation. At the same time, however, these stories are framed in a way that rejects large portions of the master Western "coming-out" narrative that involves a linear series of stages (Savin-Williams & Diamond 2000) that culminate in public disclosure, revolve around the individual, and often lead to a separation from the family. To the contrary, the videos are centred on family and a desire on the part of both the children and parents to maintain harmony within the household. There is neither desire for separation nor overemphasis on the individual. Much like the narratives of LGBT South Asians that Gopinath (2005) considers in her work, the narratives of the LGBT Singaporeans related here "run counter to the standard 'lesbian' and 'gay' narratives of the closet and coming out that are organized exclusively around a logic of recognition and visibility" (16). These Singaporean narratives further reject the assumption that "to be public and visible implies acceptance" (Boellstorff 2003, 232) in that all the participants understand they are still unacknowledged and stigmatized by a large proportion of the general population. This group of activists have selectively taken elements of the regional *tongzhi* discourse and the transnational "LGBT" discourse and converted them in such a way as to frame the "coming-out" narrative in a manner that is easily comprehended on the local level.

It is not easy to determine the exact impact of these videos, but judging from the comments on YouTube, they were effective in getting the intended message across. For instance, the video featuring Jamie Yee garnered numerous comments that suggest a positive impact:

> hey jamie, u make me cry when u cried. I love your courage, your strength and that u are truly my hero and my inspiration. Now i know that i don't need to be afraid of my sexuality!
>
> im a straight woman ... thank you SO MUCH for sharing your story like this. i have since decided to share this video with other people i know.

The video featuring Eileena Lee and her mother received comments that demonstrated an effect beyond the physical borders of Singapore, such as:

> Australia is going through a marriage equality plebiscite and I'd like to use parts of this video for the Chinese community.

Finally, Eileena Lee shared the following message she received regarding her video:

> Hey Eileena!
>
> You may not know me, but I know you from the [Pink Dot] video. You two were inspirational! Seriously, your mum is really great! ♥
>
> Help me say thank you to your mum for giving such inspirational speech in the video.
>
> Because your mum speaks in Chinese, it gives a special touch to the video. This enables Chinese-speaking mums to understand how it's like not to discriminate and accept who we are. It just reaches out to them and it's great to see that at least some families do not discriminate us for who we are.
>
> To me, the video really makes a big difference because at least my mum understands what your mum said because both their daughters are some-one special. =). (Lee 2010)

I suggest that the key to the appeal of these videos lies in the language and I believe the brief comments above attest to this appeal. In many respects, these narratives speak for themselves, and it should be clear why Pink Dot has become so successful. I will, however, briefly note some salient features. First, Eileena's mother (Mdm Yiap) and Jamie's father (Mr Yee) speak only Mandarin in the videos. This invokes a connection with the heartlanders and sends the clear message that the people involved with Pink Dot are not all CMEL (Chinese, middle class, English-educated/speaking, liberal). Second, the language used by all the parents and their children is characterized by discursive practices that index their mutual concern – there is little hint of concern for the self. I suggest that this points to a hint of *tongzhi* thought within these families. Mdm Yiap speaks of her "worry" that her daughter will turn out to be a "tomboy." Mr Yee wonders, "Who will take care of them?" Jamie wants to delay her surgery until her father dies to spare his feelings. The concern for the well-being of their children is especially prominent when Mdm Yiap asks, "shouldn't we love them even more?" and Mr Yee states that "no matter what our child turns out to be, we still need to care for them." The language used by all participants is very non-threatening, and there are no demands for "rights." On the contrary, the discourse focuses on the family. Unlike the IndigNation events, there is nothing overtly sexual about Pink Dot. In fact, Pink Dot comes off as a large picnic – with groups of families and friends relaxing on blankets, a sing-along (the 2011 song was "I Want to Hold Your Hand" by the Beatles), and children playing ball. It could be argued that the desexualization of the Pink Dot celebrations as well as a lack of a distinct activist agenda led the Singaporean LGBT movement into the trap of being "respectably queer" (Ward 2008), but I maintain here that what Pink Dot represents is the "mainstreaming of gay and lesbian liberation" (Duggan, 2002; Vaid, 1995; Warner, 1999) under the sign of the neoliberal project – a very specific form of soft, complicit activism that demonstrates the illiberal pragmatics of governance and the ongoing effects of neoliberalism paired with homonormativity.

Since then, Pink Dot has continued successfully, growing each year. In 2013, for instance, the theme was "home." Twenty-one thousand Singaporeans participated (an increase of six thousand since the 2012 event) in the event in which attendees held pink flashlights creating a sea of pink that lit up the night sky. In 2016, the number of attendees was a record breaking 28,000. In 2017, the most recent iteration of the event for which data are available, attendance was down to around 20,000. Considering the growing success of Pink Dot, one might wonder why attendance is down. One significant reason revolves around government interference in the planning and implementation of Pink Dot. Recall the prohibition against foreign involvement in Singaporean affairs discussed in chapter 5. In June 2016, the Ministry of Home Affairs issued a press release regarding the foreign sponsorship of Pink Dot (Ministry of Home Affairs 2016). It framed Pink Dot as an LGBT event and stated, "The Government's general position has always been that foreign entities should not interfere in our domestic issues, especially political issues or controversial social issues with political overtones. These are political, social or moral choices for Singaporeans to decide for ourselves. LGBT issues are one such example." Of the eighteen sponsors listed for 2016, a majority were foreign corporations such as Google, Apple, Microsoft, Facebook, Goldman Sachs, and Bloomberg.

Further, in recent years, the Public Order Act, which states that only Singaporean citizens and permanent residents can participate in public assemblies or processions, was not aggressively enforced, especially with Pink Dot. Foreigners could be present within Hong Lim Park but were not permitted to take part in the rally. In 2017, after the act was renegotiated, entry points surrounding Hong Lim Park were lined with barricades staffed by security officers whose task it was to check the National Registration Identity Card (NRIC) of attendees. Bag checks were also instituted due to recent high-profile terror attacks in the region as well as internationally (Straits Times 2017). Individuals convicted of illegally joining in events at the Speakers' Corner faced up to a S$3,000 fine for the first offence (Today Online 2017a).

More importantly, however, Pink Dot is a key example of illiberal pragmatics in practice. On the one hand, sex between men, whether they identify as straight, gay, bi, trans, or any number of subjectivities, is illegal, yet the government allows (and some might say encourages) events such as Pink Dot. It is also a rare expression of dissent in highly regulated Singapore. For instance, at the tenth Pink Dot, held in July 2018, the theme was "We Are Ready." Event "ambassadors" led the crowd in making ten declarations on the changes that the LGBT communities were looking for. Many of these were related to issues described in this and previous chapters, including the ability for LGBT organizations to formally register under the Societies Act, positive portrayals of LGBTs in mainstream media and without censorship, and the need for LGBT Singaporeans to be seen as equal citizens in the eyes of the law (pinkdot.sg 2018).

As LGBT recognition has grown over the years, non-governmental opponents have become more vocal, especially those from illiberal segments of the population. Take for example the case of the women's group AWARE (the Association of Women for Action and Research), Singapore's oldest secular women's organization. In March 2009, several women, who were members of the prominent conservative Church of Our Saviour, launched a "covert plot" (Loh 2011, 100) to wrest control of AWARE from the then-standing secular executive committee. Beginning in early 2009, membership in the organization started to grow without any identifiable reason. When AWARE held its annual general meeting in late March of that year, organizers expected the same thirty to forty core members to attend and vote the preordained slate of candidates into office. In what has been described as a "bloodless coup" (Economist 2009), more than one hundred women showed up, many of whom had only joined AWARE in recent weeks. Armed with their own slate of candidates and overwhelming numbers, they easily won nine out of twelve executive committee seats. The newly elected executive committee defended their actions by stating that AWARE had lost sight of its original objectives and had become radically "pro-lesbian" and "pro-homosexual" after the instructor's guide for an AWARE-developed Comprehensive Sexuality Programme used in Singapore schools stated that "homosexuality is perfectly normal" and that "anal sex can be healthy." In a follow-up conversation with an AWARE board member, I was informed that the instructors were never told to promote homosexuality or anal sex; they were simply being made aware that to demonize homosexuality in the schools could cause gender non-conforming students to become insecure or to withdraw and that anal sex was a pertinent topic because statistics showed that many teens were engaging in the practice. In April 2009, the old executive committee announced that they were requesting an Extraordinary General Meeting to call for a no-confidence vote in the new executive committee. The meeting was held on 2 May 2009, with over three thousand individuals showing up to vote, and the old executive committee managed to regain its leadership of AWARE.

Pushback from other organizations opposed to LGBT recognition and rights has arisen directly in response to Pink Dot as well. Beginning in 2014, Noor Deros, a Muslim religious teacher in Singapore, began the Wear White Facebook group (https://www.facebook.com/wearwhitesg/). The profile picture consists of a white teardrop against a black background and the cover photo features the words "Return to Fitrah" (return to the natural) written in white against a pink background. The idea behind the group is to encourage "traditional" family values and to protest the normalization of non-heterosexual relationships as promoted by Pink Dot. The page has not been substantially updated since the 2016 Pink Dot event, Noor stating that his movement has shifted focus away from LGBT issues to other educational programs (Today Online 2016). The campaign against Pink Dot has continued with a new group, LoveSingapore (http://www.lovesingapore.org.sg) and a new name, We.Wear.White under the guidance of Christian pastor Lawrence Khong of the First Community Baptist Church of Singapore. Mr. Khong has spoken out publicly against homosexuality in Singapore and has stated that his campaign "is a message to LGBT activists that there is a conservative majority in Singapore who will push back and will not allow them to promote their homosexual lifestyle and liberal ideologies that openly and outrightly contradict our laws ... and the conservative majority's views on public morality, marriage and family."

Lastly, openly gay American singer Adam Lambert and Taiwanese singer A-Mei both came under fire from Singaporean anti-LGBT forces in recent years. Lambert was scheduled to perform at a New Year countdown concert in 2015. Online petitions were circulated protesting his appearance in Singapore because "It is never 'just entertainment,' especially when the national stage is used. Unfortunately, our concerns to address the probability of lewd acts on a public platform have been downplayed and turned into yet another political LGBT rights issue" (Channel NewsAsia 2015). A separate pro-Lambert petition was also drafted online, accusing the organizers of the original petition of "obvious sexual orientation discrimination." It garnered 24,000 signatures before being closed. Further, during her 2013 performance in Singapore, Taiwanese pop star A-Mei showed support for LGBT by waving a small rainbow flag while singing the songs *Cai Hong* (rainbow) and *Tian Mi Mi* (sweet like honey). The large screens at the concert also featured opposite and same-sex couples in the audience kissing (Fridae.com 2013).

Chapter Seven

Epilogue

In this book, I have provided ethnographic data and analysis that capture how a social movement was created at the nexus of illiberal pragmatics and an ever-present discourse of neoliberal homonormativity in contemporary Singapore. In providing a short history of how LGBT Singaporeans have strategically used the Internet in the pursuit of acknowledgment from their fellow citizens and recognition from their government, I have demonstrated how the use of Internet-based media has allowed these marginalized individuals and collectives to stake claims of membership in the nation. Yet, the story of an Internet-based social movement in an authoritarian state is certainly not new. As mentioned in the chapter 1, marginalized groups worldwide have been employing available Internet-based media for over two decades, sometimes affecting change, sometimes not. So, what makes the materials presented in this book different?

This ethnography suggests that use of the Internet to bypass government regulations or to organize movements is not always as straightforward as it might appear. When this project was first conceptualized as a doctoral dissertation in 2003, the use of the Internet for organizing social movements was still relatively exceptional. Thus, the project and the subsequent dissertation focused on the unique outcomes of Internet-based social movements, with an emphasis on notions of the transnational circulation of an international LGBT rhetoric and its effects on LGBT subjectivity in Singapore. Yet, as might be expected upon revisiting materials collected over a fourteen-year period, I began to wonder if something was missing, if there was some other, more compelling, theoretical framework that might change the nature of the project.

When I first began the project, Audrey Yue had not yet elaborated the idea of illiberal pragmatics, at least not in its present form. In early 2007, during fieldwork in Singapore, I travelled to Sydney to give a paper at the Queer Asian Sites Conference in which I outlined some preliminary thoughts on how LGBT Singaporeans were using the Internet to affect change in their nation. Yue was in the audience and during the discussion challenged some of my rather naive notions regarding "heartland" economics and the motivations of the Singaporean government. After my talk, I thanked her for her comments; we chatted for a bit and then went our separate ways. On the return flight to Singapore a few days later, I made a note in my journal to follow up on Yue's work. That never happened. Once back in Singapore, I jumped right back into fieldwork and the writing of the dissertation, and did not give Yue any more thought.

It was not until 2009, when I was a postdoctoral writing fellow at the University of Wollongong, that a senior colleague in media studies recommended that I look at Yue's work – especially that dealing with illiberal pragmatics. Her theorization immediately felt appropriate in that it captured the essence of what I perceived was happening in Singapore. Illiberal pragmatics is a theoretical frame that points out the inconsistency of where homosexual sex is illegal and subject to state criticism (illiberalism) while simultaneously tolerated, and in some cases encouraged, as a means of attaining status as a creative, modern city-state (pragmatics). In looking at a Singaporean LGBT rights movement within the framework of illiberal pragmatics, I hope to have given the reader the means to better understand an ongoing social movement taking place within a nation whose leaders have traditionally frowned upon dissent.

I have also drawn attention to the virtual aspects of activism enacted in the shadow of illiberal pragmatics. I have used the term "virtual" in various contexts throughout this work, but two in particular are key. The first frames the virtual as "not quite." In this sense, one could view the efforts of LGBT Singaporeans as a failure of sorts; over twenty years of effort with little to show – after all, as I write this Epilogue in mid-2019, Section 377A is still on the books and sex between consenting adult men is still illegal. Yes, Singapore's government has in the past few decades acknowledged that its LGBT citizens experience discrimination not faced by other citizens. The government has sanctioned events such as Pink Dot and to a lesser degree IndigNation. From a Western standpoint, one might ask, "What is the point of a 'protest' if it is approved by the government?" Perhaps more significantly, Singapore's government has pledged to keep, but not enforce, Section 377A, which many, both within Singapore and elsewhere, see as no change at all. But the question must be raised – What is our frame of reference for this social change? What are we comparing the Singaporean situation to? It seems that if we take a Western perspective on this change, nothing of great import has happened. However, in order to understand non-Western social movements, we must approach them on their own terms, rather than on those of the West (see Offord 2016). In doing so, we dispense with Western timelines and constant comparisons to the West. By demonstrating the pitfalls of a global neoliberal homonormativity in chapter 1 and to a lesser extent in chapters 3 and 5, we gain insight into the problems that arise when Eurocentric models are applied to non-Western cultures. Clearly LGBT activists in Singapore have been exposed to and influenced by transnational rights discourse from the West and elsewhere, but as I have demonstrated in chapter 6, some activists have gone to great lengths to localize this rhetoric, allowing it to make sense in the Singaporean context. The change produced via this localized rhetoric may seem inconsequential on the surface, but for the Singaporeans with whom I lived and interacted, these changes were significant.

The second way I have framed the virtual is as "possibility." Throughout this work, I have demonstrated how illiberal pragmatics unintentionally creates a very productive liminal space within which to affect change. Beginning with the newsletters of the early 1990s to the de facto LGBT pride celebration IndigNation in 2005 to the Pink Dot events that began in 2009, LGBT Singaporeans have embraced the "almost there" aspects of the virtual. This air of possibility is demonstrated by the many LGBT Singaporeans who have been "making do" by using the Internet "in a different register" (de Certeau, 1984, 32) than was originally intended and have moved beyond the simple exchange of information to create a virtual public sphere (chapter 4) in which to discuss issues of concern to their communities and to employ various democratic tactics in response to the strategies of the powerful. Many LGBT rights and civil society organizations have thus been able to debate issues safely and develop a cohesion that could be threatened if their activities and discussions took place exclusively in the physical world. Through an ongoing process of reassessment and correction, as noted in chapters 2, 4, and 6, activists are able to adjust to the ever-changing demands of their government. Significantly, the 2017 theme for IndigNation was "Unafraid to Assemble," indicating a willingness to keep fighting in light of recent government regulations restricting the right of assembly, as witnessed at the 2017 Pink Dot. This possibility is bolstered by "virtual" memories of other struggles, such as the Stonewall riots that took place on the other side of the world a half-century ago. These memories are made possible, in part, by the presence of the Internet and the policies created by the Singaporean government that unintentionally allowed LGBT Singaporeans access to international discourse and sub-sequently to organize physical-world events online in order to avoid detection as well as to create their own "sites" of resistance, as outlined in chapter 3.

The situation of LGBT Singaporeans has certainly changed since the spring of 1993, when PLU published their initial photocopied newsletter described in chapter 2. During the intervening years, Sin-gapore's LGBT communities have witnessed a great deal of positive change implemented, encouraged, or tolerated by their government. Pro-LGBT statements by past and present prime ministers, the ability of non-heterosexual couples to jointly purchase property, the prolif-eration of businesses that cater to an LGBT clientele, and the ongo-ing IndigNation and Pink Dot events are but a few examples. These changes have certainly led to easier and more secure lives for many, but not all, of Singapore's LGBT citizens. Singapore's first prime minister (later Minister Mentor), Lee Kuan Yew, died in March 2015. Many of my interlocutors speculated that upon his passing, outdated ways of think-ing and corresponding difficulties would pass with him. Eventually, they claimed, a new guard would usher in an era of freedom and equal-ity under the law for LGBT Singaporeans – beginning with the repeal of Section 377A. My respondents are patiently waiting – confident that change will come.

I feel compelled to end with a return to the quote from Suchen Chris-tine Lim's telefilm that I used in the Introduction: "There had been a seismic shift in Singapore that night. No one noticed anything. Nothing seemed to have changed and in fact, nothing really did." A series of profound changes happened within one Singaporean household, when a son "came out" to his mother. The personal dynamics between broth-ers as well as that of mother and son were changed forever, the dreams of a mother for her son's future permanently altered. And yet, as Lim points out, after the dust settled, the family adjusted and continued as before. This is an apt metaphor for the story that I have told in this book – one of ongoing melancholy and tension followed by an uneasy catharsis and a return to the status quo. In both cases nothing *seems* to have changed. Lim's characters find acceptance and move on. The LGBT Singaporeans of whom I write have spent almost two decades organizing successful events in order to unite their own communities, gain the respect of their fellow citizens, and ultimately to garner the attention of their elected leaders in an attempt to effect change. On the surface, perhaps, things have not changed that much, but, after all is said and done, this story is still unfolding, and the future for LGBT Sin-gaporeans is yet to be determined – the struggle continues.

Timeline of Events

1991   Singaporean Parliament publishes *White Paper on Shared Values*

1993   *People Like Us* (PLU) newsletter begins publication

1997   March: SiGNeL e-list established

1997–8 Economic crisis in the Asian region

1998   Broadband Internet introduced in Singapore

1998   RedQuEEn founded by Eileena Lee

2000   Oogachaga counselling service is founded

2001   Looking Glass counselling service founded

2003   Prime Minister Goh Chok Tong states that LGBT Singaporeans are "like you and me"

2004   *Manazine* comes under the scrutiny of the MDA. Publisher relaunches as *Restricted Access (RA)*

Nation V, scheduled for August 2005 cancelled

Prime Minister Lee Hsien Loong announces that permission from the police would no longer be required to hold indoor talks

Permission for SnowBall party denied

2005   Senior Minister of the State for Health, Balaji Sadasivan, blames parties like Nation IV for the rise in HIV infections in the country

First IndigNation event ContraDiction prose and poetry reading

Lee Hsien Loong echoes the comments of Prime Minister Goh Chok Tong when he states, "I agree with Mr. Goh Chok Tong that homosexuals are people like you and me"

2006   Nation VI held in Phuket, Thailand. Permission for Feelin' Good party denied

SQ21 by Ng Yi-Sheng published

2007   IndigNation talks by Douglas Sanders and Troy Perry
       talks are cancelled due to their visas being cancelled by
       Singaporean officials

       Works by Alex Au and Ng Yi-Sheng are not allowed to be
       exhibited or performed at IndigNation

       Minister Mentor Lee Kuan Yew states that homosexuality has
       a genetic component and questions why it is criminalized

       Peculiar Legislation: 377(A) – Symbol or Statute

       In the Pink picnic at Singapore Botanical Gardens

       Otto Fong comes "out" on his personal blog

       The International Gay and Lesbian Human Rights Campaign
       (IGLHRC) sends a letter to Prime Minister Lee urging the
       repeal of Section 377A

       Speech by Prime Minister Lee Hsien Loong on government
       decision to maintain Section 377A of the Penal Code.
       Parliament debates and votes to maintain it

       The Morning After airs

2008   MDA fines MediaCorp TV Channel 5 for airing *Find and
       Design* episode featuring a gay couple with an adopted
       child

       Singapore's government takes the decision to allow groups
       to stage public demonstrations at the Speakers' Corner
       within Hong Lim Park without having to obtain a police
       permit

2009   First Pink Dot Event

Notes

1. Little Earthquakes

1 I faithfully reproduce the terms used by my interlocutors. In most instances, individuals are identified as Singaporean but with a prefix indicating their ethnic background. Hence, throughout this book, I will utilize such terms as Chinese Singaporean, Malay Singaporean, and Indian Singaporean.

2 The *Straits Times* television section described the program as "Divorced mom finds herself at the centre of major family changes, right at the time of her son's coming out as gay."

3 Television programs may explore LGBT themes, but the Media Development Authority (MDA) program code states, "Information, themes and subplots on lifestyles such as homosexuality, lesbianism, bisexualism, transvestism [*sic*], paedophilia, and incest should be treated with utmost caution. Their treatment should not in anyway promote, justify, or glamorise such lifestyles. Explicit depictions of the above should not be broadcast." "Free-to-Air Television Code," February 2004.

4 For example, in the early 1990s the Singapore Broadcasting Corporation (SBC) ran a Mandarin soap opera "A Bright Future" (锦绣前程) that featured an embarrassingly stereotypical effete gay character in love with a masculine heterosexual character.

5 See Peletz (2007) for a brief discussion of variations on "normal" sexuality in Singapore prior to the 1960s.

6 Activist Roy Tan has been instrumental in starting and updating these types of sites. See for example the "Homosexuality in Singapore" channel on YouTube (https://www.youtube.com/user/groyn88001/) and the "LGBT History in Singapore" entry on Wikipedia (https://en.wikipedia.org/wiki/LGBT_history_in_Singapore), both accessed 16 December 2019.

7 Gibson (1993) asserts that Singapore, like the American theme park Disneyland, is considered by some to be "the happiest place on earth." Further, he suggests that like Disneyland, Singapore is sterile, conformist, and lacking in any type of substantial authenticity or originality. He notes that while Singapore is, on the surface, a clean and well-run city-state, it is in fact a technocratic, authoritarian state with a draconian legal system.

8 Of the blogs listed, only Mr. Brown and Yawning Bread are still updated regularly. The remainder have either folded or have not been updated in several years.

2. The "Spectral Homosexual" and the Singaporean Media

1 I have not been able to locate any articles in *Lianhe Wanbao* from 2006 that address gay issues. I believe that he was referring to a five-part exposé of Singapore's underground gay scene that appeared in *Lianhe Wanbao* in July 2004. Part of the series dealt with gay men reverting to the "normal path."

2 Lee Kuan Yew was the Republic of Singapore's first prime minister from 1965 to 1990. Lee was followed by Goh Chok Tong, who served from 1990 to 2004. In 2004 Lee Kuan Yew's son, Lee Hsien Loong, became the city-state's third and current prime minister. Lee created the position of minister mentor in 2004 and appointed his father, who remained in the position until it was abolished in 2011.

3 The use of lawsuits to silence critics continues. According to Human Rights Watch (2016), a Singaporean court ordered a blogger to pay S$150,000 in damages to Prime Minister Lee Hsien Loong for a 2014 blog post criticizing the Prime Minister.

4 Singapore Department of Statistics (2016) Latest Data, https://www .singstat.gov.sg/find-data/search-by-theme/households/households /latest-data, accessed 17 December 2019.

5 Ethnic Integration Policy Is Implemented, 1st Mar 1989 (2014) http://eresources.nlb.gov.sg/history/events/d8fea656-d86e-4658-9509 -974225951607, accessed 17 December 2019.

6 For more on the notion of Chineseness, see Chun (1996); for more on Asian values see Sen (1997) and Jenco (2013).

7 Under the Newspaper and Printing Presses Act (1974) the PLU Newsletter was considered a newspaper and would therefore require a permit. According to the Act, "'newspaper' means any publication containing news, intelligence, reports of occurrences, or any remarks, observations or comments, in relation to such news, intelligence, reports of occurrences, or to any other matter of public interest, printed in any language and published

for sale or free distribution at regular intervals or otherwise, but does not include any publication published by or for the Government."

8 When asked about this particular news story, several respondents noted that the AIDS quilt was a significant image in 1993 Singapore in that the quilt indexed HIV/AIDS, which in turn indexed "gay."

9 *Mergers and Acquisitions* was a stage play by Singaporean Eleanor Wong. It featured Singapore's first live lesbian kiss.

10 *The Wedding Banquet* (also known as *Xi Yan*), released in 1993, was a romantic comedy in which a partnered gay Taiwanese-American man takes part in a marriage of convenience to satisfy his parents.

11 The Stonewall demonstrations that occurred in New York in 1969, often referred to as the pioneering event that gave rise to the gay liberation movement in the United States, underpin a great deal of LGBT collective memory, including in Singapore.

12 Guidelines for Imported Adult-Interest Lifestyle Magazines, Media Development Authority, Singapore.

13 Cherian George (2007a, 142) suggests that the light touch works because of the memory of the "heavy hand," of which the *FEER* case is an example.

14 While the site was not named, many suspect that it was fluffboy.com.

15 https://www.imda.gov.sg/-/media/Imda/Files/Regulation-Licensing -and-Consultations/content-and-standards-classification/Policiesand ContentGuidelines_Internet_InterneCodeOfPractice.pdf, accessed 6 December 2019).

Prohibited Material 4.

(1) Prohibited material is material that is objectionable on the grounds of public interest, public morality, public order, public security, national harmony, or is otherwise prohibited by applicable Singapore laws.

(2) In considering what is prohibited material, the following factors should be taken into account:

 (a) whether the material depicts nudity or genitalia in a manner calculated to titillate;

 (b) whether the material promotes sexual violence or sexual activity involving coercion or non-consent of any kind;

 (c) whether the material depicts a person or persons clearly engaged in explicit sexual activity;

 (d) whether the material depicts a person who is, or appears to be, under sixteen years of age in sexual activity, in a sexually provocative manner or in any other offensive manner;

 (e) whether the material advocates homosexuality or lesbianism, or depicts or promotes incest, paedophilia, bestiality and necrophilia;

 (f) whether the material depicts detailed or relished acts of extreme violence or cruelty;

      (g)   whether the material glorifies, incites or endorses ethnic, racial or religious hatred, strife or intolerance.

16   Free-to-Air TV Programme Code, https://www.imda.gov.sg/-/media /Imda/Files/Regulation-Licensing-and-Consultations/content-and -standards-classification/Video-Games/Industry_TV_ContentGuidelines _FTATVProgCode1.pdf, accessed 6 December 2019.

3. Reimagining the Nation, Online

1   More information on The Nation Party appears in chapter 4. For a detailed description of the Nation Party, see note 17 in Lim (2005, 388).

2   See https://data.gov.sg/dataset/individual-internet-access?view_id =2a8b0d94-2118-4bc2-8913-8a1223358f05&resource_id=b50a0c64-b2d1 -42df-96c2-a5dd9ee794a6, accessed 18 December 2019.

3   *My Brother Nikhil* (2004) is a Hindi film that tells the story of a closeted gay man who contracts HIV.

4   For an in-depth discussion of gay Chinatown, see Tan (2015a).

5   *Ang Mo*, Hokkien for "red-hair," is a pejorative term used to describe Caucasians. Another variation is *Ang Mo Gao*, meaning "red-haired monkey."

6   Liang Po Po (literally Grandma Liang) was a cross-dressing role played by Singaporean actor Jack Neo.

7   For the full text of the email, see http://leejean.livejournal.com/656628 .html?mode=reply&style=mine, accessed 17 December 2019.

8   Reply by the Registrar of Societies to People Like Us, 8 April 2004.

9   SiGNeL: Introduction. https://web.archive.org/web/20110624110609 /http://plu.sg/society/?p=39, accessed 16 December 2019.

10   SiGNeL: Content Guidelines. https://web.archive.org/web/20110624111803/ http://www.plu.sg/society/?p=40, accessed 16 December 2019.

11   This manner of thinking, in which the people take direction on social issues from the government, was spoken of by many Singaporean interviewees.

12   http://www.fridae.asia/about/, accessed 17 December 2019.

13   For clarity of citations, I use Fridae.com for any work appearing prior to 2015 and Fridae.asia for that appearing after 2015.

14   Singapore Ministry of Manpower, Summary Table: Income, https://stats .mom.gov.sg/Pages/Income-Summary-Table.aspx.

15   I use the term "lesbian" throughout because that is how the vast majority of Singaporean women with whom I interacted identified; in this section I switch to "queer women" in keeping with the language utilized by the members of RedQuEEn.

16   Although male, I was given a membership on the list from Eileena Lee. Access to the RedQuEEn site proved an invaluable tool in recruiting lesbians for this project.

17 For details, see Fridae.com, 2001, "Suicide and Open Verdicts on Deaths of Lesbian Couple," http://www.fridae.asia/gay-news/2001/07/17 /166.suicide-and-open-verdicts-on-deaths-of-lesbian-couple, accessed 17 December 2019.

18 RedQuEEn and Looking Glass are both references to the works of Lewis Carroll. Interestingly, Fridae was named after the character from Daniel Defoe's *Robinson Crusoe*.

4. The Internet and a New Public Sphere

1 HDB is Singapore's Housing Development Board, a government agency responsible for the building, sale, and maintenance of units within the public housing estates that house approximately 80 per cent of Singapore's population.

2 This is a privileged group of individuals who are not representative of the overall LGBT communities in Singapore. Fong, who studied film in Beijing and is an Australian permanent resident, would be considered part of this group.

3 While not necessarily qualifying him under the MOE's guidelines, Sa'at did win the National Arts Council Young Artist's Award in 2001. His plays had been translated into several languages and performed internationally. His work had also been nominated numerous times at the local Life! Theatre Awards. He quit medical school in his final year in order to pursue his career as a writer.

4 Lesbians, bisexuals, and trans individuals are not covered under Section 377A of the penal code. While many in the LGBT communities believed that these public statements also applied to all LGBT, they nonetheless privilege gay men.

5 *Khalwat* is a term used within Singapore's Malay community that is invoked when someone is in close proximity to an unrelated person of the opposite sex. Laws relating to this act are contained in Malaysia's Syariah Criminal Provisions Act.

6 An increase of unprotected sex during and after the parties may have had some impact on the number of new HIV diagnoses in Singapore. I suggest that the presence of activists from Action for AIDS at these events encouraged men to get tested, revealing the positive HIV status of a large number of men who had not been tested previously.

7 The title of this forum is a play on the gay Singaporean novel *Peculiar Chris* by Johann Lee. It was originally published in 1992 and was the first gay novel that many of my interlocutors had encountered.

8 *Asian Boys Volume III* was the third and final instalment of Sa'at's *Asian Boys* series. The forum was held because one of the scenes in *Volume III* dealt specifically with Section 377A.

5. Pushing the Boundaries in the Physical World

1 Lakshmi was referring to the recent government ruling that allowed single persons to buy government-owned housing flats once they reach the age of thirty-five. Previously, only married couples were granted ownership of such flats. The new rules also permitted two unrelated persons over the age of thirty-five to purchase a flat together (see chapter 2).

2 CPF or Central Provident Fund is a compulsory social security savings plan.

3 Singaporean citizen Cyril Wong was not permitted to read his own poetry at the 2006 ContraDiction because organizers had forgotten to submit his name and national registration number to authorities when applying for the permit.

4 On 23 May 2008 Douglas Sanders presented his paper at the fifth annual conference of the Asian Law Institute organized by the National University of Singapore law faculty. This incident is exemplary of the inconsistency of the enforcement of statutes by Singapore's ruling party. I suggest he was allowed to present his paper because by this time, the question of Section 377A had been settled. Further, this was a regional law meeting that was not in any way framed as a "gay rights" forum.

5 Article 377 criminalized sodomy (any form of sexual intercourse which does not have the potential for procreation) between consenting heterosexual couples. It was repealed in October 2007. Article 377 has since been replaced with a new law that criminalizes sex with dead bodies.

6 *Peranakan* is a term used for the descendants of the very early Chinese immigrants to parts of Southeast Asia who have adopted Malay customs in an effort to be assimilated into the local communities. Its meaning has extended to cultural customs as well. In many respects, it "queers" cultures.

7 The complete list includes the public lecture by Douglas Sanders, the In the Pink Picnic in the Botanic Gardens, the *Kissing* photo exhibition by Alex Au, the Pink Run, four scheduled movie screenings, the talk by Reverend Troy Perry, and the public reading of the story *Lee Low Tar* by Ng Yi-sheng.

8 This mother and daughter retold their story in a video promoting Pink Dot. For more, see chapter 6 and Phillips (2013).

9 Singlish is the English-based creole involving loan words from Malay and Chinese dialects.

10 Changi Village is a beach on the eastern end of Singapore known for, among other things, male-to-female transgender individuals who work as prostitutes. Hendon Camp is a nearby military installation.

11 See http://www.talkingcock.com/html/lexec.php?op=LexLink&lexicon=lexicon&keyword=Ah%20Beng&page=1, accessed 17 December 2019.

6. The Illiberal Pragmatics of Activism

1 Pink Dot is a play on the phrase "little red dot," an arguably derogatory reference to Singapore's representation on world maps, by former president of Indonesia B.J. Habibie. Pink, often associated with sexual minorities, is also the colour that results from mixing red and white, the two colours of the Singaporean flag.

2 All four videos (including a version of video 1 with both Mandarin and English subtitles) can be found at http://pinkdot.sg/come-make-pink-dot-2010-come-make-history/, accessed 16 December 2019.

3 There are two other videos besides those examined here. The third video looks at two brothers, one of whom identifies as gay, and the fourth is a comprehensive overview of several LGBT Singaporean stories. It is hosted by the 2010 ambassadors: Adrian Pang (actor and television presenter), Tan Kheng Hua (actress), and Johnson Ong (aka DJ Big Kid – DJ and music producer).

4 Medisave is a national medical savings scheme which helps individuals put aside part of their income into an account to meet their future personal hospitalization, day surgery, and certain outpatient expenses. See https://www.moh.gov.sg/content/moh_web/home/costs_and_financing/schemes_subsidies/medisave.html, accessed 16 December 2019.

References

The Age. 2005. Singapore Bans Gay Website. https://www.theage.com.au
/national/singapore-bans-gay-website-20051028-gdmc3v.html (accessed
5 December 2019).

Agence France-Press. 2003. Singapore Is Asia's New Gay Capital. http://
window.org/sw03/030914af.htm (accessed 30 November 2017).

Althusser, Louis. 2001. *Lenin and Philosophy, and Other Essays*. New York:
Monthly Review Press.

Altman, Dennis. 1997. On Global Queering, *Australian Humanities Review* 2(2):
1–8.

Anderson, Benedict. 1983. *Imagined Communities: Reflections on the Origin and
Spread of Nationalism*. London: Verso.

AsiaOne. 2013. More Men Using Cocktail of Drugs to Get High. http://
www.asiaone.com/health/more-men-using-cocktail-drugs-get-sexual-high
(accessed 5 December 2019).

Asia Sentinel. 2013. The Exotic World of Singaporean Journalism. www
.asiasentinel.com/politics/the-exotic-world-of-singaporean-journalism/
(accessed 5 December 2019).

Au, Alex. 2005. IndigNation in the News. https://web.archive.org/web
/20160329113136/http://www.yawningbread.org/apdx_2005/imp-209
.htm (accessed 18 December 2019).

Augé, Marc. 2009. *Non-Places: Introduction to an Anthropology of Supermodernity*.
New York: Verso.

Barker, Joshua. 2005. Engineers and Political Dreams – Indonesia in the
Satellite Age. *Current Anthropology* 46(5): 703–7. https://doi.org/10.1086
/432652.

Barlocco, Fausto. 2013. Consuming Ethnic Identities: "Materializing" the
Nation and the Minority in Sabah. *Sojourn: Journal of Social Issues in Southeast
Asia* 28(3): 465–84. https://doi.org/10.1355/sj28-3c.

BBC.com. 2009. Singapore Gays in First Public Rally. http://news.bbc
.co.uk/2/hi/asia-pacific/8054402.stm (accessed 5 December 2019).

Belisio-De Jesus, Aisha. 2013. Religious Cosmopolitanisms: Media,
Transnational Santería, and Travel between the United States and Cuba.
American Ethnologist 40(4): 704–20. https://doi.org/10.1111/amet.12049.

Berry, Chris, Fran Martin, and Audrey Yue. 2003. *Mobile Cultures: New Media in
Queer Asia*. Durham: Duke University Press.

Boellstorff, Tom. 2003. Dubbing Culture: Indonesian Gay and Lesbi
Subjectivities and Ethnography in an Already Globalized World. *American
Ethnologist* 30(2): 225–42. https://doi.org/10.1525/ae.2003.30.2.225.

Boellstorff, Tom. 2004. Zines and Zones of Desire: Mass-Mediated Love,
National Romance, and Sexual Citizenship in Gay Indonesia. *Journal of
Asian Studies* 63(2): 367–402. https://doi.org/10.1017/s0021911804001019.

Boellstorff, Tom. 2005. *The Gay Archipelago: Sexuality and Nation in Indonesia*.
Princeton: Princeton University Press.

Boellstorff, Tom. 2008. Queer Techne: Two Theses on Methodology and Queer
Studies. In *Queer Methods and Methodologies: Intersecting Queer Theories and
Social Science Research*, 215–30, ed. Kath Browne and Catherine J. Nash.
Farnham: Ashgate.

Bohman, James. 2004. Expanding Dialogue: The Internet, the Public Sphere
and Prospects for Transnational Democracy. In *After Habermas: New
Perspectives on the Public Sphere*, 131–55, ed. Nick Crossley et al. Oxford:
Blackwell.

Brown, Gavin. 2012. Homonormativity: A Metropolitan Concept that
Denigrates "Ordinary" Gay Lives. *Journal of Homosexuality* 59(7): 1065–72.
https://doi.org/10.1080/00918369.2012.699851.

Bunzl, Matti. 2004. *Symptoms of Modernity: Jews and Queers in Late-Twentieth-
Century Vienna*. Berkeley: University of California Press.

Campbell, John Edward. 2004. *Getting It on Online: Cyberspace, Gay Male
Sexuality, and Embodied Identity*. New York: Harrington Park Press.

de Certeau, Michel. 1984. *The Practice of Everyday Life*. Berkeley: University of
California Press.

Chan, Cassandra. 2003. Breaking Singapore's Regrettable Tradition of Chilling
Free Speech with Defamation Laws. *Loyola of Los Angeles International and
Comparative Law Review*. http://digitalcommons.lmu.edu/ilr/vol26
/iss2/4 (accessed 5 December 2019).

Chang, Stewart L. 2015. Gay Liberation in the Illiberal State. *Washington
International Law Journal* 24: 1–46. https://scholars.law.unlv.edu/facpub
/1107.

Chang, T.C., Shirlena Huang, and Victor R. Savage. 2004. On the Waterfront:
Globalization and Urbanization in Singapore. *Urban Geography* 25(5): 413–36.
https://doi.org/10.2747/0272-3638.25.5.413.

Channel NewsAsia. 2007. Foreigners Will Not Be Allowed to Interfere in Singapore's Domestic Affairs. http://charmthebear.blogspot.com/2007/09 /cna-foreigners-will-not-be-allowed-to.html?m=0 (accessed 16 December 2019).

Channel NewsAsia. 2008. 31 Registrations at Speakers' Corner One Month after Relaxed Rules. http://forums.vr-zone.com/chit-chatting/334255 -news-31-registrations-speakersa-corner-one-month-after-relaxed-rules.html (accessed 16 December 2019).

Channel NewsAsia. 2015. Anti-Adam Lambert Petition in Singapore Gains 20,000 Signatures. http://www.channelnewsasia.com/news/singapore /anti-adam-lambert-petition-in-singapore-gains-20-000-signatures-8253100 (accessed 28 November 2017).

Chih, Hoong Sin. 2002. The Quest for a Balanced Ethnic Mix: Singapore's Ethnic Quota Policy Examined. *Urban Studies* 39(8): 1347–74. https://doi .org/10.1080/00420980220142673.

Choo, Jon. 2007. Herr Thio Li-ann. http://jonchoo.blogspot.com/2007/10 /herr-thio-li-ann.html (accessed 18 December 2019).

Chou, Wah-shan. 2000. *Tongzhi: Politics of Same-Sex Eroticism in Chinese Societies*. New York: Haworth Press.

Chronicle.com. 2007. A Pandora's Box in Singapore. http://chronicle.com /weekly/v53/i42/42a03801.htm (accessed 18 December 2019).

Chua, Beng Huat. 1995. *Communitarian Ideology and Democracy in Singapore*. London: Routledge.

Chua, Lynette. 2012. Pragmatic Resistance, Law and Social Movements in Authoritarian States: The Case of Gay Collective Action in Singapore. *Law & Society Review* 46(4): 713–48. https://doi.org/10.1111/j.1540-5893.2012 .00515.x.

Chua, Lynette. 2014. *Mobilizing Gay Singapore: Rights and Resistance in an Authoritarian State*. Singapore: NUS Press.

Chun, Allen. 1996. Fuck Chineseness: On the Ambiguities of Ethnicity as Culture as Identity. *boundary* 2 23(2): 111–38. https://doi.org/10.2307 /303809.

CNN.com. 2015. Teenage Blogger Amos Yee Tests Limit of Singapore's Laws (and Patience). http://www.cnn.com/2015/09/14/asia/singapore -amos-yee/ (accessed 7 June 2016).

Dave, Naisargi. 2010. To Render Real the Imagined: An Ethnographic History of Lesbian Community in India. *Signs* 35(3): 595–619. https://doi.org /10.1086/648514.

Dave, Naisargi. 2012. *Queer Activism in India: A Story in the Anthropology of Ethics*. Durham: Duke University Press.

Decena, Carlos. 2011. *Tacit Subjects: Belonging and Same-Sex Desire among Dominican Immigrant Men*. Durham: Duke University Press.

Deleuze, Gilles. 2002. The Actual and the Virtual. In *Dialogues II*, 148–52. Rev. ed. Trans. Eliot Ross Albert. New York: Columbia University Press.

Dhoest, Alexander, Lukasz Szulc, and Bart Eeckhout, eds. 2016. *LGBTQs, Media and Culture in Europe*. London: Taylor & Francis.

Duggan, Lisa. 2002. The New Homonormativity: The Sexual Politics of Neoliberalism. In *Materializing Democracy: Toward a Revitalized Cultural Politics*, ed. Russ Castronovo and Dana Nelson. Durham: Duke University Press.

Eckert, Stine, and Kalyani Chadha. 2013. Muslim Bloggers in Germany: An Emerging Counterpublic. *Media, Culture & Society* 35(8): 926–42. https://doi.org/10.1177/0163443713501930.

The Economist. 2009. Taken Unawares: Liberals Rally to Take on the Christian Right. http://www.economist.com/node/13611576 (accessed 18 December 2019).

Edelman, Elijah. 2009. The Power of Stealth: (In)Visible Sites of Female-to-Male Transsexual Resistance. In *Out in Public: Reinventing Lesbian/Gay Anthropology in a Globalizing World*, 164–79, ed. Ellen Lewin and William L. Leap. Malden, MA: Wiley-Blackwell.

Elegant, Simon. 2003. The Lion in Winter. https://web.archive.org/web/20180426124535/http://www.singapore-window.org/sw03/030707ti.htm (accessed 18 December 2019).

Escoffier, Jeffrey. 2003. Gay-for-Pay: Straight Men and the Making of Gay Pornography. *Qualitative Sociology* 26(4): 531–55. https://doi.org/10.1023/b:quas.0000005056.46990.c0.

Far East Economic Review. 2006. From the Editor. https://web.archive.org/web/20130414221238/http://www.feer.com/articles1/2006/0610/free/p006.html (accessed 18 December 2019).

Florida, Richard. 2002. *The Rise of the Creative Class and How It's Transforming Work, Leisure, Community, and Everyday Life*. New York: Perseus Group.

Fong, Otto. 2007. A Letter – September 2007. http://ottofong.blogspot.com/2008/08/letter-sept-2007.html (accessed 16 December 2019).

Foucault, Michel. 2002. The Subject and Power. In *Power: Volume 3: Essential Works of Foucault 1954–1984*, 326–48, ed. James Faubion. London: Penguin.

Fraser, Nancy. 1990. Rethinking the Public Sphere: A Contribution to the Critique of Actually Existing Democracy. *Social Text* 25/26:56–80. https://doi.org/10.2307/466240.

Fridae.com. 2004a. Too Gay for Singapore. http://www.fridae.asia/gay-news/2004/03/05/15.toogay-for-singapore (accessed 18 December 2019).

Fridae.com. 2004b. S'pore Police Rejects Snowball.04 Licence Application. http://www.fridae.asia/gay-news/2004/12/09/1344.spore-police-rejects-snowball04-licence-application (accessed 16 December 2019).

Fridae.com. 2006. Press release: Feelin' Good Party at MOS Singapore Cancelled. http://www.fridae.asia/gay-news/2006/03/25/1601.press

-release-feelin-good-party-at-mos-singapore-cancelled (accessed 16 December 2019).

Fridae.com. 2007. The Pink Non-Picnic. http://www.fridae.asia/gay -news/2007/08/12/1923.the-pink-non-picnic (accessed 16 December 2019).

Fridae.com. 2008. Singapore TV Station Fined S$15,000 for Showing a "Normal" Gay Family. http://www.fridae.asia/gay-news/2008 /04/25/2047.singapore-tv-station-fined-s-15000-for-showing-a-normal-gay -family (accessed 16 December 2019).

Fridae.com. 2013. Taiwanese Pop Star A-mei Affirms Support for Gay Acceptance at Singapore Concert. http://www.fridae.asia/gay-news /2013/01/28/12211.taiwanese-pop-star-a-mei-affirms-support-for-gay -acceptance-at-singapore-concert (accessed 16 December 2019).

Gaudio, Rudolf. 2009. *Allah Made Us: Sexual Outlaws in an Islamic African City.* Malden, MA: Wiley-Blackwell.

Gaudio, Rudolf. 2014. Trans-Saharan Trade: The Routes of "African Sexuality." *Journal of African History* 55(3): 317–30. https://doi.org/10.1017 /s0021853714000619.

George, Cherian. 2006. *Contentious Journalism and the Internet: Towards Democratic Discourse in Malaysia and Singapore.* Singapore: Singapore University Press.

George, Cherian. 2007a Consolidating Authoritarian Rule: Calibrated Coercion in Singapore. *Pacific Review* 20(2): 127–45. https://doi.org/10.1080 /09512740701306782.

George, Cherian. 2007b. ST'S Janadas Devan Exposes Li-ann's Thiology. http://blog.freedomfromthepress.info/2007/10/27/sts-janadas-devan -exposes-li-anns-thiology/(accessed 16 December 2019).

George, Cherian. 2012. *Freedom from the Press: Journalism and State Power in Singapore.* Singapore: National University of Singapore Press.

Gibson, William. 1993. Disneyland with the Death Penalty. http://www. wired.com/wired/archive/1.04/gibson.html (accessed 16 December 2019).

Goh, Debbie. 2008. It's the Gays' Fault: News and HIV as Weapons against Homosexuality in Singapore. *Journal of Communication Inquiry* 32(4): 383–99. https://doi.org/10.1177/0196859908320295.

Gopinath, Gayatri. 2005. *Impossible Desires: Queer Diasporas and South Asian Public Cultures.* Durham: Duke University Press.

Gorkemli, Serkan. 2012. "Coming Out of the Internet": Lesbian and Gay Activism and the Internet as a "Digital Closet" in Turkey. *Journal of Middle East Women's Studies* 8(3): 63–88. https://doi.org/10.2979/jmiddeastwomstud.8.3.63.

Habermas, Jurgen. 1989. *The Structural Transformation of the Public Sphere: An Inquiry into a Category of Bourgeois Society.* Cambridge, MA: MIT Press.

Hall, Stuart. 1992. The Question of Cultural Identity. In *Modernity and Its Futures,* 274–31, ed. Stuart Hall, David Held, and Anthony McGrew. Cambridge: Polity Press.

Halley, Janet. 1994. Sexual Orientation and the Politics of Biology: A Critique of the Argument from Immutability. *Stanford Law Review* 46(3): 503–68. https://doi.org/10.2307/1229101.

Hegde, Radha S., ed. 2011. *Circuits of Visibility: Gender and Transnational Media Cultures*. New York: New York University Press.

Heng, Russell. 2001. Tiptoe Out of the Closet: The Before and After of the Increasingly Visible Gay Community in Singapore. *Journal of Homosexuality* 40(3/4): 81–97. https://doi.org/10.1300/J082v40n03_05.

Ho, K.C., Zaheer Baber, and Habibul Khondker. 2002. "Sites" of Resistance: Alternative Websites and State-Society Relations. *British Journal of Sociology* 53(1): 127–48. https://doi.org/10.1080/00071310120109366.

Howard, Philip, and Malcolm Parks. 2012. Social Media and Political Change: Capacity, Constraint, and Consequence. *Journal of Communication* 62(2): 359–62. https://doi.org/10.1111/j.1460-2466.2012.01626.x.

Human Rights Watch. 2016. Singapore: Bloggers, Internet Users Increasingly Targeted. https://www.hrw.org/news/2016/01/27/singapore-bloggers -internet-users-increasingly-targeted (accessed 16 December 2019).

IGLHRC. 2007a. Letter to the Prime Minister Regarding the Repeal of Article 377A. https://www.outrightinternational.org/sites/default/files/156-1.pdf (accessed 16 December 2019).

IGLHRC. 2007b. Singapore: Religious Homophobia, Gay Activism & Repealing the Sodomy Law. https://www.outrightinternational.org /content/singapore-religious-homophobia-gay-activism-repealing -sodomy-law (accessed 16 December 2019).

Jenco, Leigh. 2013. Revisiting Asian Values. *Journal of the History of Ideas* 74(2): 237–58. https://doi.org/10.1353/jhi.2013.0014.

Juris, Jeffrey. 2012. Reflections on #Occupy Everywhere: Social Media, Public Space, and Emerging Logics of Aggregation. *American Ethnologist* 39(2): 259–79. https://doi.org/10.1111/j.1548-1425.2012.01362.x.

Kaldor, Mary, Sabine Selchow, Sean Deel, and Tamsin Murray-Leach. 2012. *The "Bubbling Up" of Subterranean Politics in Europe*. Civil Society and Human Security Research Unit, London School of Economics and Political Science, London, UK.

Kelly, John. 1997. The Privileges of Citizenship: Nations, States, Markets, and Narratives. In *Nation Making: Emergent Identities in Postcolonial Melanesia*, 253–73, ed. Robert Foster. Ann Arbor: University of Michigan Press.

Khondker, Habibul. 2011. Role of the New Media in the Arab Spring. *Globalizations* 8(5): 675–9. https://doi.org/10.1080/14747731.2011.621287.

Kocer, Suncem. 2013. Making Transnational Publics: Circuits of Censorship and Technologies of Publicity in Kurdish Media Circulation. *American Ethnologist* 40(4): 721–33. https://doi.org/10.1111/amet.12050.

Leap, William. 2012. Queer Linguistics, Sexuality, and Discourse Analysis. In *The Routledge Handbook of Discourse Analysis*, 558–71, ed. James Paul Gee and Michael Handford. London: Routledge.

Lee, Eileena. 2010. Post Pink-Dot – 3. https://eileenalee.wordpress.com/category/pink-dot/ (accessed 18 September 2018).

Lee, Hsien Loong. 2007. Official Parliamentary Reports (Hansard). https://sprs.parl.gov.sg/search/topic.jsp?currentTopicID=00002031-WA&currentPubID=00004748-WA&topicKey=00004748-WA.00002031-WA_1%2B%2B (accessed 16 December 2019).

Leong, Laurence. 1995. Walking the Tightrope: The Role of Action for AIDS in the Provision of Social Services in Singapore. In *Gays and Lesbians in Asia and the Pacific: Social and Human Services*, 11–30, ed. Gerard Sullivan and Laurence Wai-Teng Leong. Binghamton: Harrington Park Press.

Leong, Laurence. 1997. Singapore. In *Sociological Control of Homosexuality: A Multi-Nation Comparison*, 127–44, ed. Donald J. West and Richard Green. New York: Plenum Press.

LeVay, Simon. 1991. A Difference in Hypothalamic Structure between Homosexual and Heterosexual Men. *Science* 253(5023): 1034–7. https://doi.org/10.1126/science.1887219.

Lian, Kwen Fee. 1999. The Nation-State and the Sociology of Singapore. In *Reading Culture: Textual Practice in Singapore*, ed. Phyllis Chew and Anneliese Kramer-Dahl. Singapore: Times Academic Press.

Lim, Christine Suchen. 2007. *The Lies That Build a Marriage: Stories of the Unsung, Unsaid and Uncelebrated in Singapore*. Singapore: Monsoon Books.

Lim, Eng-Beng. 2005. Glocalqueering in New Asia: The Politics of Performing Gay in Singapore. *Theatre Journal* 57(3): 383–405. https://doi.org/10.1353/tj.2005.0112.

Lim, Eng-Beng. 2013. Glocalqueer Pink Activism. In *Performance, Politics, and Activism*, 154–66, ed. Peter Lichtenfels and John Rouse. London: Palgrave.

Liow, Eugene Dili. 2011. The Neoliberal-Developmental State: Singapore as Case Study. *Critical Sociology* 38(2): 241–64. https://doi.org/10.1177/0896920511419900.

Loh, Chee Kong. 2011. Investigative Journalism in Singapore. In *The AWARE Saga: Civil Society and Public Morality in Singapore*, 96–105, ed. Terence Chong. Singapore: NUS Press.

Lorway, Robert. 2008. Defiant Desire in Namibia: Female Sexual-Gender Transgression and the Making of Political Being. *American Ethnologist* 35(1): 20–33. https://doi.org/10.1111/j.1548-1425.2008.00003.x.

Lyons, Lenore, and James Gomez. 2005. Moving beyond the OB Markers: Rethinking the Space of Civil Society in Singapore. *Sojourn* 20(2): 119–31. https://doi.org/10.1355/sj20-2a.

Massad, Joseph. 2002. Re-Orienting Desire: The Gay International and the Arab World. *Public Culture* 14(2): 361–85. https://doi.org/10.1215/08992363-14-2-361.

McGlotten, Shaka. 2013. *Virtual Intimacies: Media, Affect, and Queer Sociality*. Albany: State University of New York Press.

McLelland, Mark. 2003. Private Acts/Public Spaces: Cruising for Gay Sex on the Japanese Internet. In *Japanese Cybercultures*, 141–55, ed. Nanette Gottlieb and Mark McLelland. London: Routledge.

Media Development Authority. 2019. IMDA's Approach to Regulating Content on the Internet. https://www.imda.gov.sg/regulations-licensing-and-consultations/content-standards-and-classification/standards-and-classification/internet (accessed 6 December 2019).

Merry, Sally Engle. 2006. *Human Rights and Gender Violence: Translating International Law into Local Justice*. Chicago: University of Chicago Press.

Miller, Daniel, and Don Slater. 2000. *The Internet: an Ethnographic Approach*. Oxford: Berg.

Ministry of Home Affairs. 2016. MHA Statement on Foreign Sponsorships for Pink Dot 2016. https://www.mha.gov.sg/Newsroom/press-releases/Pages/MHA-Statement-on-Foreign-Sponsorships-for-Pink-Dot-2016.aspx (accessed 30 November 2017).

Mitchell, Gregory. 2015. *Tourist Attractions: Performing Race and Masculinity in Brazil's Sexual Economy*. Chicago: University of Chicago Press.

Mrázek, Rudolf. 2002. *Engineers of Happy Land: Technology and Nationalism in a Colony*. Princeton, NJ: Princeton University Press.

Murray, David A.B. 2012. *Flaming Souls: Homosexuality, Homophobia, and Social Change in Barbados*. Toronto: University of Toronto Press.

The New Paper. 2006a. They Bathe, then Get Dirty: I Got HIV from S'pore Bathhouses. 21 May.

The New Paper. 2006b. Health Clubs Deadly HIV Hubs? 21 May.

The New Paper. 2006c. Once Inside, We Drop Our Towels. 21 May.

The New Paper. 2006d. Drug Sting in Hotel: First, Gay Doctor. Now ... Gay Ex-Teacher Trapped with Drugs. 23 August, 1.

The New Paper. 2006e. We've Not Heard of It. 18 October, 4.

The New Paper. 2007a. Movies in Town. 10 July, 29.

The New Paper. 2007b. Blog Not Meant for His Students. https://web.archive.org/web/20071020235355/http://newpaper.asia1.com.sg/printfriendly/0,4139,141783,00.html (accessed 16 December 2019).

Ng, King Kang. 1999. *The Rainbow Connection: The Internet & the Singapore Gay Community*. Singapore: KangCuBine.

Ng, Yi-Sheng. 2006. *SQ21: Singapore Queers in the 21st Century*. Singapore: Oogachaga Counseling and Support.

Ng, Yi-Sheng. 2007. *Lee Low Tar*. http://www.sayoni.com/articles/entertainment/1906--lee-low-tar (accessed 16 December 2019).

Offord, Baden. 1999. The Burden of (Homo)sexual Identity in Singapore. *Social Semiotics* 9(3): 301–16. https://doi.org/10.1080/10350339909360441.

Offord, Baden. 2003. Singaporean Queering of the Internet: Toward a New Form of Cultural Transmission of Rights Discourse. In *Mobile Cultures: New Media in Queer Asia*, 133–57, ed. Chris Berry, Fran Martin, and Audrey Yue. Durham: Duke University Press.

Offord, Baden. 2016. Singapore, Indonesia, and Malaysia: Arrested Development! In *The Lesbian and Gay Movement and the State: Comparative Insights into a Transformed Relationship*, 135–52, ed. Manon Tremblay, David Paternotte, and Carol Johnson. London: Routledge.

Ong, Aihwa. 2006. *Neoliberalism as Exception: Mutations in Citizenship and Sovereignty*. Durham: Duke University Press.

Ong, Keng Sen. 2015. Evangelicalism and the Gay Movement in Singapore: Witnessing and Confessing through Masks. In *The Routledge Companion to Art and Politics*, 148–58, ed. Randy Martin. London: Routledge.

Onwuachi-Willig, Angela, and Alexander Nourafshan. 2015. From Outsider to Insider and Outsider Again: Interest Convergence and the Normalization of LGBT Identity. 42 *Florida State University Law Review* 521.

Oswin, Natalie. 2007. Producing Homonormativity in Neoliberal South Africa: Recognition, Redistribution, and the Equality Project. *Signs: Journal of Women in Culture and Society* 32(3): 649–69. https://doi.org/10.1086/510337.

Oswin, Natalie. 2014. Queer Time in Global City Singapore: Neoliberal Futures and the "Freedom to Love." *Sexualities* 17(4): 412–33. https://doi.org/10.1177/1363460714524765.

Pakiam, Geoffrey. 2007. The Internet and Civil Society in Singapore. https://www.researchgate.net/publication/327549146_The_Internet_and_Civil_Society_in_Singapore_London_Global_Partners_2007 (accessed 16 December 2019).

Parker, Richard. 2009. *Bodies, Pleasures, and Passions: Sexual Cultures in Contemporary Brazil*. Nashville: Vanderbilt University Press.

Pelangi Pride Centre. 2008. About Us. https://web.archive.org/web/20080510134740%20/http:/www.pelangipridecentre.org/about/about.htm (accessed 16 December 2019).

Peletz, Michael. 2007. *Gender, Sexuality, and Body Politics in Modern Asia*. Ann Arbor: Association for Asian Studies.

People Like Us. 1993. *PLU Newsletter*. Singapore.

People Like Us. 1994. *PLU Newsletter*. Singapore.

Peterson, David. 2011. Neoliberal Homophobic Discourse: Heteronormative Human Capital and the Exclusion of Queer Citizens. *Journal of*

Homosexuality 58(6–7): 742–57. https://doi.org/10.1080/00918369.2011
.581918.

Phelan, Shane. 1997. The Shape of Queer: Assimilation and Articulation.
Women and Politics 18(2): 55–73. https://doi.org/10.1300/J014v18n02_03.

Phillips, Robert. 2013. "We aren't really that different": Globe-Hopping
Discourse and Queer Rights in Singapore. *Journal of Language and Sexuality*
2(1): 122–44. https://doi.org/10.1075/jls.2.1.05phi.

Phuket Gazette. 2006. Going Out with a Bang. 21 October, 14–15.

pinkdot.sg. 2018. 10 Declarations for Equality. https://pinkdot.sg/2018/07
/10-declarations-for-equality/ (accessed 17 December 2019).

pinkdot.sg. 2019a. Frequently Asked Questions. https://pinkdot.sg/about-
pink-dot-sg/faq/ (accessed 17 December 2019).

pinkdot.sg. 2019b. Watch. https://pinkdot.sg/watch/ (accessed 17 December
2019).

Pink News. 2006. Officers Pose as Gay Men to Catch Drug Dealers. https://
www.pinknews.co.uk/2006/03/10/officers-pose-as-gay-men-to-catch
-drug-dealers/ (accessed 16 December 2019).

PLURAL. 2007. Homosexuality: Gov't Not Moral Police But It's Mindful of
People's Concerns. http://pluralsg.wordpress.com/2007/04/24
/government-not-moral-police-mm-lee/ (accessed 16 December 2019).

Postill, John. 2016. Freedom Technologists and the Future of Global Justice.
https://www.tni.org/en/publication/freedom-technologists-and-the-
future-of-global-justice (accessed 16 December 2019).

Price, David. 2003. Singapore: It's In to Be Out. https://web.archive
.org/web/20130827041829/http://www.time.com/time/magazine
/article/0,9171,474512,00.html (accessed 18 December 2019).

Provencher, Denis. 2012. *Queer French: Globalization, Language, and Sexual
Citizenship in France*. Hampshire: Ashgate.

Pullen, Christopher, ed. 2012. *LGBT Transnational Identity and the Media*. New
York: Palgrave.

Radics, George Baylon. 2015. Section 377A in Singapore and the (De)
Criminalization of Homosexuality. *Reconstruction* 15.2. http://profile.nus.edu.
sg/fass/socrgb/radics_reconstruction_15.2.pdf (accessed 16 December 2019).

Rajah, Indranee. 2007. Ms. Indranee Rajah's Remarks during the Debate on
Amendments to the Penal Code. https://web.archive.org/web
/20081010132039/http://www.straitstimes.com/STI/STIMEDIA
/pdf/20071023/Indranee%20Rajah.pdf (accessed 16 December 2019).

Reid, Graham. 2013. *How to Be a Real Gay: Gay Identities in Small-Town South
Africa*. Scottsville: University of KwaZulu-Natal Press.

Reuters.com. 2009. Far Eastern Economic Review to Shut after 63 Years. http://
www.reuters.com/article/dowjones-FEER-idUSHKG23852320090922
(accessed 17 December 2019).

Rodan, Garry. 1998. The Internet and Political Control in Singapore. *Political Science Quarterly* 113(1): 63–89. https://doi.org/10.2307/2657651.

Rodan, Garry. 2004. Transparency and Authoritarian Rule in Southeast Asia: Singapore and Malaysia. London: Routledge.

Sadasivan, Balaji. 2005. Ministry of Health Budget Speech (Part 3) Given in Parliament. 9 March.

Sanders, Douglas. 2009. 377 and the Unnatural Afterlife of British Colonialism in Asia. *Asian Journal of Comparative Law* 4: 1–49. https:doi.org/10.1017/S2194607800000417.

Savin-Williams, Ritch, and Lisa Diamond. 2000. Sexual Identity Trajectories among Sexual-Minority Youths: Gender Comparisons. *Archives of Sexual Behavior* 29(6): 607–27. https://doi.org/10.1023/A:1002058505138.

Sen, Amartya. 1997. *Human Rights and Asian Values.* New York: Carnegie Council on Ethnic and International Affairs.

Shields, Rob. 1999. Virtual Spaces? *Space and Culture* 2(4/5): 1–12. https://doi.org/10.1177/120633120000100401.

Shields, Rob. 2003. *The Virtual.* London: Routledge.

Siew, Kum Hong. 2007. Speech on the Penal Code (Amendment) Bill. http://siewkumhong.blogspot.com/2007/10/speech-on-penal-code-amendment-bill-22.html (accessed 18 December 2019).

Singapore Department of Statistics. 2010. Census of Population 2010 Statistical Release 1: Demographic Characteristics, Education, Language and Religion. https://www.singstat.gov.sg/publications/cop2010/census10_stat_release1 (accessed 16 December 2019).

Singapore Parliament. 1991. White Paper on Shared Values (Paper cmd. 1 of 1991). Singapore: Singapore National Printers.

Stivale, Charles. 1998. *The Two-Fold Thought of Deleuze and Guattari.* New York: Guildford Press.

The Straits Times. 2003. Government More Open to Employing Gays Now. 4 July.

The Straits Times. 2005a. New Singles Rule a Cause for Celebration. 31 July, 30.

The Straits Times. 2005b. Confessions of a Poet. 7 August, L25.

The Straits Times. 2005c. MDA Bans Gay Website and Fines Another. 28 October.

The Straits Times. 2005d. Teacher at Boys' School Charged with Molesting Students. 9 December.

The Straits Times. 2006a. Coming Out in Singapore. 20 August, 22.

The Straits Times. 2006b. Singapore Stands by Decision to Bar Some Activists. 11 September.

The Straits Times. 2007a. Big Changes to Penal Code to Reflect Crime's Changing Nature. 18 September.

The Straits Times. 2007b. Gay Teacher's Outing a Milestone in Debate.
15 September.

The Straits Times. 2007c. Gay Teacher's Outing Not Appropriate.
18 September.

The Straits Times. 2007d. People Most Likely to Be Anti-gay: The Religious
and Those Who Conform to Social Norms. 20 September.

The Straits Times. 2010. Gay Sex Romp Turned Fatal: Dead Man Had
Consumed Sex Drugs with Gay Partner. 22 June.

The Straits Times. 2017. Pink Dot Rally to Have Barricades, Security Officers,
as well as Checks of Bags and ID. 30 May.

TalkingCock.com. 2007. Dear Ah Beng: Gay People Keep Wanting to Hantam
Me. How? http://www.talkingcock.com/html/article.php?sid=2402
(accessed 18 December 2019).

Tan, Kevin Y.L. 2000. Understanding and Harnessing Ground Energies in Civil
Society. In *State-Society Relations in Singapore*, 98–105, ed. Gillian Koh and
Ooi Giok Ling. Singapore: Oxford University Press.

Tan, Chris. 2009. "But They Are Like You and Me": Gay Civil Servants and
Citizenship in a Cosmopolitanizing Singapore. *City & Society* 21(1): 133–54.
https://doi.org/10.1111/j.1548-744x.2009.01018.x.

Tan, Chris. 2011. Go Home, Gay Boy! Or, Why Do Singaporean Gay Men
Prefer to "Go Home" and Not "Come Out"? *Journal of Homosexuality*
58(6/7): 865–82. https://doi.org/10.1080/00918369.2011.581930.

Tan, Chris. 2015a. Rainbow Belt: Singapore's Gay Chinatown as a Lefebvrian
Space. *Urban Studies* 52(12): 2203–18. https://doi.org/10.1177
/0042098014544761.

Tan, Chris. 2015b. Pink Dot: Cultural and Sexual Citizenship in Gay
Singapore. *Anthropological Quarterly* 88(4): 969–96. https://doi.org/10.1353
/anq.2015.0058.

Thio, Li-ann. 2007. Two Tribes Go to (Culture) War: Speech at Singapore
Parliamentary Debates, Penal Code Revisions, 22–3 October 2007.

Today Online. 2016. "Traditional Values" Wear White Campaign Returning on
Pink Dot Weekend. http://www.todayonline.com/singapore/network
-churches-revives-campaign-wear-white-pink-dot-weekend (accessed 18
December 2019).

Today Online. 2017a. Only Singaporeans and PRs Allowed to Attend Pink
Dot 2017: Organisers. http://www.todayonline.com/singapore/only
-singaporeans-and-prs-allowed-attend-pink-dot-2017-organisers (accessed
18 December 2019).

Turner, Victor. 1967. *The Forest of Symbols: Aspects of Ndembu Ritual*. Ithaca:
Cornell University Press.

Twilhaar, Arjan. 2004. Editor's Note. *Restricted Access (1):1*. Singapore: Xung
Asia Pte. Ltd.

US State Department. 2010. 2009 Human Rights Report: Singapore. https://2009-2017.state.gov/j/drl/rls/hrrpt/2009/eap/136008.htm (accessed 18 December 2019).

Vaid, Urvashi. 1995. *Virtual Equality: The Mainstreaming of Gay and Lesbian Liberation*. New York: Anchor.

Ward, Jane. 2008. *Respectably Queer: Diversity Culture in LGBT Activist Organizations*. Nashville: Vanderbilt University Press.

Ward, Jane. 2015. *Not Gay: Sex between Straight White Men*. New York: NYU Press.

Warner, Michael. 1999. *The Trouble with Normal: Sex, Politics, and the Ethics of Queer Life*. New York: Free Press.

Warner, Michael. 2002. *Publics and Counterpublics*. New York: Zone Books.

Weeks, Jeffery. 2007. *The World We Have Won*. London: Routledge.

Wei, Wei. 2007. "Wandering Men" No Longer Wander Around: The Production and Transformation of Local Homosexual Identities in Contemporary Chengdu, China. *Inter-Asia Cultural Studies* 8(4): 572–88. https://doi.org/10.1080/14649370701568029.

Weiss, Meredith L. 2014. New Media, New Activism: Trends and Trajectories in Malaysia, Singapore, and Indonesia. *International Development Planning Review* 36(1): 91–109. https://doi.org/10.3828/idpr.2014.6.

Weiss, Margot. 2008. Gay Shame and BDSM Pride: Neoliberalism, Privacy, and Sexual Politics. *Radical History Review* 100: 87–101. https://doi.org/10.1215/01636545-2007-023.

Wong, Kan Seng. 1995. Statement by Wong Kan Seng, Minister for Foreign Affairs of the Republic of Singapore, Vienna, 16 June 1993. In *Human Rights and International Relations in the Asia-Pacific Region*, ed. J. Tang. London: Pinter.

World Economic Forum. 2015. The Global Information Technology Report. Geneva. http://www3.weforum.org/docs/WEF_GITR2015.pdf (accessed 18 December 2019).

Yawning Bread. 2005. Lee Hsien Loong's Answer to the Gay Question at the FCA. https://web.archive.org/web/20160830120601/http://yawningbread.org/apdx_2005/imp-225.htm (accessed 18 December 2019).

Yawning Bread. 2007a. Teacher Unaccountably Terminated. https://web.archive.org/web/20070613172552/http://www.yawningbread.org/arch_2007/yax-754.htm (accessed 18 December 2019).

Yawning Bread. 2007b. My Kissing Project, Part 1. https://web.archive.org/web/20160730213208/http://www.yawningbread.org/arch_2007/yax-751.htm (accessed 18 December 2019).

Yeo, T.E. Dominic. 2009. Cyber HIV/AIDS Intervention in Singapore: Collective Promises and Pitfalls. *International Journal of Communication* 3: 1025–51.

YouTube. 2008. Otto Fong – From Classroom to Comics Part 1/11. https://
   www.youtube.com/watch?hl=ja&gl=JP&v=u_dXqImO01c (accessed
   18 December 2019).

Yue, Audrey. 2007. Creative Queer Singapore: The Illiberal Pragmatics of
   Cultural Production. *Gay and Lesbian Issues and Psychology Review* 3(3):
   149–60.

Yue, Audrey. 2011. Doing Cultural Citizenship in the Global Media Hub:
   Illiberal Pragmatics and Lesbian Consumption Practices in Singapore. In
   Circuits of Visibility: Gender and Transnational Media Cultures, 250–67, ed. R.
   Hegde. New York: New York University Press.

Yue, Audrey. 2012. Introduction: Queer Singapore: A Critical Introduction. In
   Queer Singapore: Illiberal Citizenship and Mediated Cultures, 1–25, ed. Audrey
   Yue and Jun Zubillaga-Pow. Hong Kong: Hong Kong University Press.

Index

Anthropological Horizons

Editor: Michael Lambek, University of Toronto

Rural Nostalgias and Transnational Dreams: Identity and Modernity among Jat Sikhs/Nicola Mooney (2011)

Dimensions of Development: History, Community, and Change in Allpachico, Peru/ Susan Vincent (2012)

People of Substance: An Ethnography of Morality in the Colombian Amazon/Carlos David Londoño Sulkin (2012)

'We Are Still Didene': Stories of Hunting and History from Northern British Columbia/Thomas McIlwraith (2012)

Being Māori in the City: Indigenous Everyday Life in Auckland/Natacha Gagné (2013)

The Hakkas of Sarawak: Sacrificial Gifts in Cold War Era Malaysia/Kee Howe Yong (2013)

Remembering Nayeche and the Gray Bull Engiro: African Storytellers of the Karamoja Plateau and the Plains of Turkana/Mustafa Kemal Mirzeler (2014)

In Light of Africa: Globalizing Blackness in Northeast Brazil/Allan Charles Dawson (2014)

The Land of Weddings and Rain: Nation and Modernity in Post-Socialist Lithuania/ Gediminas Lankauskas (2015)

Milanese Encounters: Public Space and Vision in Contemporary Urban Italy/ Cristina Moretti (2015)

Legacies of Violence: History, Society, and the State in Sardinia/Antonio Sorge (2015)

Looking Back, Moving Forward: Transformation and Ethical Practice in the Ghanaian Church of Pentecost/Girish Daswani (2015)

Why the Porcupine Is Not a Bird: Explorations in the Folk Zoology of an Eastern Indonesian People/Gregory Forth (2016)

The Heart of Helambu: Ethnography and Entanglement in Nepal/Tom O'Neill (2016)

Tournaments of Value: Sociability and Hierarchy in a Yemeni Town, 20th Anniversary Edition/Ann Meneley (2016)

Europe Un-Imagined: Nation and Culture at a French-German Television Channel/ Damien Stankiewicz (2017)

Transforming Indigeneity: Urbanization and Language Revitalization in the Brazilian Amazon/Sarah Shulist (2018)

Wrapping Authority: Women Islamic Leaders in a Sufi Movement in Dakar, Senegal/ Joseph Hill (2018)

Island in the Stream: An Ethnographic History of Mayotte/Michael Lambek (2018)

Materializing Difference: Consumer Culture, Politics, and Ethnicity among Romanian Roma/Péter Berta (2019)

Virtual Activism: Sexuality, the Internet, and a Social Movement in Singapore/Robert Phillips (2020)